ii. Tract index: Every document affecting the relevant tract is filed under its own parcel identification number.
iii. Marketable title acts: Limits the title examiner's search by providing that chain of title need only be established within a certain range of years.

OTHER OWNERSHIP RIGHTS

WATER RIGHTS

1. Riparian Doctrine: Water belongs to the owners of land bordering the watercourse.
   a. Natural Flow: Riparian owner is entitled to water without diminution in its quantity.
   b. Reasonable Use: Riparian owner must share with other riparian owners and is entitled only to reasonable use.
2. Prior Appropriation Doctrine: An individual may divert and use water whether or not she borders the watercourse; individual rights are established by actual use.

RIGHT TO LATERAL AND SUBJACENT SUPPORT

Strict liability for owner of land whose excavations cause a neighboring parcel to subside, or which damage buildings on adjacent land.

GIFTS

IN GENERAL

1. *Definition:* A gratuitous voluntary lifetime transfer of property from a donor to donee.
2. Requirements:
   a. Present intent to make a gift;
   b. Delivery by donor; and
   c. Acceptance by donee
3. Classification:
   a. *inter vivos:* Made during donor's lifetime; irrevocable unless donor retains right to revoke.
   b. *gifts causa mortis:* Lifetime gift by donor in contemplation of impending death.
      i. Contemplation of impending death;
      ii. Automatic revocation if donor survives peril;
      iii. Ambiguity of donor's intent; and
      iv. Death from different peril.

INTEREST IN LAND: ESTATES

TYPE	
***PRESENT POSSESSORY ESTATES** – Property interest i[...]ssessior*	
FEE SIMPLE ABSOLUTE:	Right given by pre[...]
FEE SIMPLE DETERMINABLE:	Right given by a grantor
FEE SIMPLE ON CONDITION SUBSEQUENT:	Right given by a grantor
FEE TAIL (FEE SIMPLE CONDITIONAL):	Right given by a grantor
LIFE ESTATE:	Right given by a grantor
***CONCURRENT ESTATES** – Property interest in land currently possessed by several individuals at the same time*	
TENANCY IN COMMON:	Deed, will, or law of intestate succession
JOINT TENANCY:	Deed and will, but not by intestate succession; requires the followin Four Unities: **1.** Time: Co-tenants acquire at same time **2.** Title: Interests acquired under same instrument **3.** Interest: Co-tenants have exactly same interest **4.** Possession: Co-tenants each have possession of entire estate
TENANCY BY ENTIRETY:	Deed, will, or law of intestate succession
***LEASEHOLDS (LANDLORD AND TENANT)** – Interest in land according to the terms of a lease agreeme*	
PERIODIC TENANCY:	Created by lease; contractual agreement
TENANCY FOR YEARS:	Created by lease; contractual agreement
TENANCY AT WILL:	Created by lease; contractual agreement
TENANCY AT SUFFERANCE:	Created by operation of law when tenant wrongfully remains i possession after end of lawful lease term
***FUTURE INTERESTS** – An interest in property that is not presently possessory, but will come into possession*	
REVERSION (IN GRANTOR):	Automatically at end of transferred estate or by express reservation by grantor after transferring title
POSSIBILITY OF REVERTER (IN GRANTOR):	Occurrence of event terminating a fee simple determinable
RIGHT OF ENTRY (IN GRANTOR):	Occurrence of condition terminating a fee simple on condition subsequent
EXECUTORY INTEREST (IN GRANTEE):	Occurrence of condition as specified by grantor
REMAINDERS (IN GRANTEE):	Occurrence of limitation (not a condition) terminating a prior possessory estate simultaneously created

b. Interest in Property: A BFP has superior rights to others claiming an interest in the same property, including the actual owner, where the BFP takes possession in good faith and pays value.

2. Adverse Possessor (AP):
   a. *Definition*: One who takes possession contrary to the possessory rights of another. Requires that possession by the AP throughout the entire statutory period required be:
      i. Actual; open and notorious; exclusive; continuous; and hostile under Claim of Right.
   b. Interest in Property: Adverse possessor acquires superior title good against all the world.

LANDLORD AND TENANT

THE LEASE

The interest in property between a landlord and tenant is controlled by the lease.

1. For a proper lease:
   a. Formal lease requirements:
      i. Identification of landlord and tenant;
      ii. Adequate description of the premises;
      iii. Amount of rent/dates to pay rent (if no rent amount, reasonable value); and
      iv. Duration of lease.
   b. Statute of Frauds (if lease > 1 year):
      i. Must be in writing; and
      ii. Signed by the party to be charged.
2. The lease terms create the type of estate ("leasehold").
   a. Periodic Tenancy: Right to occupy tenancy for fixed period (year, month, week, or day).
   b. Tenancy for Years: Right to occupy tenancy beginning on a fixed date and ending on a fixed date.
   c. Tenancy at Will: Right to occupy tenancy "at will" as long as both landlord and tenant so desire.
   d. Tenancy at Sufferance: Holdover tenant is treated as trespasser and evicted, or new periodic tenancy is imposed.
3. The lease defines rights and duties between Landlord and Tenant.
   a. *Example*: All L's duties are done in exchange for T's payment of rent, if landlord breaches duties, tenant can withhold rent, if T breaches duties (e.g., fails to pay rent), L can evict.
   b. Lease terms/duties are independent:
      i. Failure to perform by one party does not excuse other party from performing.
      ii. Exception: if warranty of habitability is breached.
4. Other legal considerations arising from lease:
   a. Assignments/Subleases (see chart on p.1)
   b. Fixtures: Personal property or chattels that have been permanently attached to land:
      i. Common Law: Becomes property of landlord.
      ii. American courts: Look to objective intent of tenant, determined by: manner of attachment, damage from removal, fixture in context of property. *Sigrol Realty Corp. v. Valcich*, 11 N.Y.2d 668, 180 N.E.2d 904, 225 N.Y.S.2d 748 (1962).
      iii. Trade fixtures: Used to carry on a trade or business; tenant can remove but is responsible for any damage. Restatement of Property: all fixtures installed by T are trade fixtures.

LANDLORD'S RIGHTS / REMEDIES

1. Security deposit: L retains amount of posted deposit for T's costs and damages.
2. Rent acceleration clause: If T defaults on rent, all future rents become immediately due and payable.
3. Sue for unpaid rent: In the absence of an acceleration clause, L may only sue for the rental amount owed for the current lease period.
4. Eviction: If T materially breaches any lease term, including failure to pay rent timely; may evict by: ejectment, self-help (physical ouster), or summary proceedings.

DUTIES OF LANDLORD

1. Duty to Deliver Possession:
   a. Right to Possess: Breach if someone has superior right to possess at time of commencement of lease; T not required to move in
   b. Actual Possession: Under English Rule, L must deliver actual possession. *Dieffenbach v. McIntyre*, 208 Okla. 163, 254 P.2d 346 (1952); under American Rule (minority), L's not required to deliver. *Hannan v. Dusch*, 154 Va. 356, 153 S.E. 824 (1930).
2. Covenant of Quiet Enjoyment (implied): L promises that neither L nor third party will interfere with T's use and enjoyment of premises.
   a. Actual Eviction: Physical expulsion or exclusion from possession.
   b. Partial Eviction: Denial of possession for only part of the premises.
      i. Common Law: T's obligation to pay entire rent is suspended until possession of entire premises restored.
      ii. Restatement: T can abate rent or terminate lease and seek damages; cannot remain in possession and pay no rent.
   c. Constructive Eviction: L wrongfully performs or fails to perform some duty that substantially deprives T of use and enjoyment of premises.
      i. Common Law: L has no duty to repair premises unless L & T so agree; Statute/Case Law: L makes reasonable repairs. *Chambers v. N. River Line*, 179 N.C. 199, 102 S.E. 198 (1920).
3. Warranty of Fitness for Particular Purpose (implied):
   a. Common Law: In the absence of express lease provision, no warranty by L that premises would be fit for any purpose. *Anderson Drive-In Theatre Inc. v. Kirkpatrick*, 123 Ind. App. 388, 110 N.E.2d 506 (1953).
   b. Exceptions: Short-term lease of furnished residence and building under construction when rented. *Ingalls v. Hobbs*, 156 Mass. 348, 31 N.E. 286 (1892).
4. Warranty of Habitability (implied): L required to take all reasonable action to maintain premises in habitable condition, including duty to repair residential leases only; for commercial leases, implied warranty of suitability for intended commercial purpose. *Davidow v. Inwood North Professional Group*, 747 S.W.2d 373 (Tex. 1988).
5. Retaliatory eviction: L may not evict T, refuse to renew lease, terminate a periodic tenancy, or increase T's rent in retaliation for T's prior actions. *Edwards v. Habib*, 397 F.2d 687 (D.C. Cir. 1968).
   a. Not applicable to commercial leases.
   b. Tenant bears burden of demonstrating retaliatory motive of landlord.

LANDLORD'S TORT LIABILITIES

Generally, L not liable to T or third parties for injuries sustained on the premises.

1. Exceptions:
   a. Common Areas. *Johnson v. O'Brien*, 258 Minn. 502, 105 N.W.2d 244 (1960).
   b. Latent Defects: L fails to disclose.
   c. Negligent Repairs: Only if L voluntarily undertakes to make repair.

DUTIES OF TENANT

1. Duty to Pay Rent: T's obligation to pay rent is independent of L's duties; therefore T must continue to pay rent even if L fails to fulfill duties, unless warranty of habitability is breached.
2. Duty to Take Possession: No duty unless express or implied in lease.
3. Restrictions on use of leased premises:
   a. Cannot use property for illegal purpose
   b. Cannot commit waste (see "Doctrine of Waste" section under "Concurrent Estates").
4. Duty to Repair: No duty unless T expressly agrees; if premises completely destroyed, T might be obligated to rebuild.
5. Duty to Deliver Premises at End of Lease:
   a. T must give premises over timely or be treated as a holdover.
   b. Wrongful Abandonment: If T fails to pay rent and abandons the premises, L may:
      i. Accept the abandonment as a surrender and end the lease,
      ii. Leave premises vacant and sue for rent owed, or
      iii. Re-let premises to minimize T's damages.

TENANT'S RIGHTS / REMEDIES

1. Remain in possession, and
   a. Abate rent, or
   b. Suspend rent
2. Terminate lease, and
   a. Sue for damages, or
   b. Quit premises.

REAL COVENANTS & EQUITABLE SERVITUDES

EQUITABLE SERVITUDES

1. Generally, same as real covenants except that no privity is required;
2. Therefore, must be enforced in equity.
3. Creation: *Tulk v. Moxhay*, 2 Phillips 774, 41 Eng. Rep. 1143 (Ch. 1848).
   a. Express agreement.
   b. Implied:
      i. Implied Reciprocal Agreement.
      ii. Common Scheme.
      iii. Subdivision Plat.
      iv. California rule: will not be enforced unless in deed. *Werner v. Graham*, 181 Cal. 174, 183 P. 945 (Cal. 1919).

Real Covenants & Equitable Servitudes continues on page 3

REAL COVENANTS

1. Types of Real Covenants: Restrictive Covenants and Affirmative Covenants
2. Creation of Real Covenants:
   a. Intent: Promisors intend to bind their successors in interest, or covenant will only be enforced against original parties. *Moseley v. Bishop*, 470 N.E.2d 773 (Ind. App. 1984).
   b. Touch and Concern: Successor to burden will only be bound where the covenant has a connection to her use and enjoyment of the land. *Neponsit Property Owners' Assn. v. Emigrant Industrial Savings Bank*, 278 N.Y. 248, 15 N.E.2d 793 (1938).
   c. Privity of Estate:
      i. Horizontal (for burden to run): between original promisor and promisee.
      ii. Vertical (for benefit to run): between original parties and their assigns or successors.
   d. Must also comply with Statute of Frauds.
3. Scope of Real Covenants: Benefit to dominant estate and burden to servient estate.
4. Termination of Real Covenants: Not really termination, but burden or benefit will not run once horizontal/vertical privity is gone.

EASEMENTS

SCOPE OF EASEMENTS

1. Any change in use beyond the intent of the parties that created the easement is beyond the scope of the easement and not allowed.
2. Intent of parties is guiding principle.
3. Increases in frequency or intensity of use are generally permissible.
4. Scope may be determined from duration of easement, location of easement, or reasonable expectation of parties.

TRANSFER OF EASEMENTS

1. In Gross:
   a. Burden: Always transfers with land.
   b. Benefit: Generally transferable unless use as transferred creates unreasonable burden on servient estate.
2. Appurtenant:
   Note: No separate document is required to effectuate transfer, nor is notice of either required.
   a. Burden: Always transfers with land.
   b. Benefit: Always transfers with land.

TERMINATION OF EASEMENTS

Termination of easements can be made by:

- By Terms.
- Merger of Dominant and Servient Estates.
- Prescription.
- Forfeiture.
- Changed Conditions.
- Frustration of Purpose.
- Abandonment—requires intent and clear act.

CREATION OF EASEMENTS

1. Express Grant: Usually contained in a deed.
2. Deed: Owner of land may convey entire estate and reserve an easement for her own use, or to the benefit of a third party.
3. Donative Transfer: Created by gift deed or will; consideration not necessary unless intent is not clear.
4. Contract: Reciprocal easements are adequate consideration.
5. Estoppel: Easement is asserted in equity when land owner who permits certain use attempts to revoke that use at a later time. Requires foreseeable and reasonable reliance, and claimant's changed position, based on prior permission.
6. Implication: In the absence of express agreement, intent of parties to create an easement can be implied from:
   a. Prior use requires that
      i. Dominant/servient estates were originally a single estate;
      ii. Prior use is permanent or long term, and not temporary;
      iii. Prior use is apparent and not concealed [*Romanchuk v. Plotkin*, 215 Minn. 156, 9 N.W.2d 421 (1943)]; and
      iv. Prior use is reasonably necessary to enjoy the property.
   b. Necessity requires either of the following:
      i. Unity of title followed by a severance;
      ii. Strict necessity, e.g., parcel is landlocked.
7. Prescription: Like adverse possession, use must be:
   a. Adverse—inconsistent with owner's use;
   b. Open/notorious—sufficient to put owner on notice;
   c. Continuous; and
   d. Uninterrupted for duration of statutory period.

TYPES OF EASEMENTS

1. Easement in Gross: Not attached to the land, will not transfer unless the owner of the land so intends.
2. Easement Appurtenant: Attached to the land, rights transfer to any new purchaser of the land.
   a. Dominant estate: Estate benefited, appurtenant easement transfers automatically when dominant estate is transferred.
   b. Servient estate: Estate burdened, need not be adjoining to dominant estate.
3. Negative Easements: Owner of easement has right to demand that the owner of the servient estate refrain from using land in a certain way.

FUTURE INTERESTS

TYPES OF FUTURE INTERESTS

1. In Grantor:
   a. Reversion.
   b. Possibility of reverter.
   c. Right of entry.
2. In Grantee:
   a. Executory Interest:
      i. Springing interest; shifting interest.
   b. Remainders:
      i. Vested:
         1. Indefeasibly,
         2. Subject to Open/Partial Divestment—class gifts.
      ii. Contingent:
         1. Subject to Condition Precedent,
         2. Unborn or Unascertained person.

RULE IN SHELLEY'S CASE

Example: Life estate in A, and remainder in "A's heirs" or the "heirs of A's body"

Effect: If the two estates are either both legal or both equitable, remainder is deemed to be in A, not A's heirs or the heirs of A's body

Doctrine of Merger: Where A has life estate and next vested estate, they merge to form a fee simple.

DOCTRINE OF WORTHIER TITLE

Example: O gives life estate in A, remainder in O's heirs; (future interest must be limited to heirs of grantor, and not issue or devise).

Effect: A will get a life estate and O has a reversion; O's heirs get nothing unless O dies within A's lifetime, at which point they get O's reversion.

RULE AGAINST PERPETUTITIES (RAP)

No interest is good unless it must vest, if at all, no later than 21 years (plus a period of gestation) after some life in being at interest creation.

1. Affected Interests: Contingent remainders, executory interests, vested remainders limited in favor of class of persons.
2. "Life in Being": Any life in existence at the time of the creation of the interest that is in any way connected to the interest.

Examples: Parent of class members, person named in instrument of conveyance, life tenant whose death creates interest.

3. "Within 21 Years": Satisfied if it can be shown that the interest vests during the measuring "life in being" plus 21 years (plus any period of gestation for the measuring life); time of death of measuring life is therefore relevant. *Lucas v. Hamm*, 56 Cal.2d 583, 364 P.2d 685 (1961).
4. Special RAP Cases:
   a. Unborn widow:
      i. Gift to issue is invalid.

Examples: O conveys property to son for life, then to son's widow for life, then to issue. Son could remarry a woman not yet born, and pre-decease her before she gives birth to other members of the class.

   b. Fertile octogenarian: *Jee v. Audley*, 29 Eng. Rep. 1186 (Ch. 1787).
      i. Gift to children is invalid

Example: T gives property to A for life, then to A's children "who attain the age of 25."

Example: A could have a child when he is 80 years old, and then die; the youngest child will not reach age 25 within 21 years of the death of A and the gift cannot vest to the entire class of children.

   c. Charitable transfers: RAP is wholly inapplicable to charitable transfers.

LAWS AFFECTING INTERESTS

DESCRIPTION OF PROPERTY

1. Metes and bounds.
2. Government survey.
3. Reference to plat/map.
4. Resolving inconsistencies:
   a. Natural monuments.
   b. Artificial monuments.
   c. References to adjacent tracts.
   d. Courses/directions.
   e. Distances.
   f. Area or quantity.
   g. Place names.

TYPES OF DEEDS

1. General Warranty Deed (contains six covenants of title):
   a. Covenant of Seisin: Promise by grantor who owns property to be conveyed.
   b. Covenant of Right to Convey: Promise grantor has power and legal ability to convey property.
   c. Covenant of Against Encumbrances: Promise property is free from encumbrances.
   d. Covenant of Quiet Enjoyment: Promise no third party with legal claim of superior title against grantee and that grantor will compensate grantee for losses incurred as a result.
   e. Covenant of Warranty: Promise grantor will defend against superior claims and will compensate grantee for losses incurred as a result.
   f. Covenant of Further Assurances: Promise grantor will do whatever is reasonably necessary to perfect title if title is defective.
2. Special Warranty Deed: Same covenants as general warranty, but only for the period of time that the grantor owned the property.
3. Quitclaim Deed: Contains no warranties and gives whatever interest in property grantor may have.

ZONING

1. Enacted pursuant to state police power for health, welfare, and safety of community.
2. Prevents certain use of property in favor of public good.
3. May be challenged on constitutional grounds or where benefit is primarily for private, and not public, interests.

NUISANCE

Owner of land may sue for interference with the use and enjoyment of her property. At common law, applied to noise, aesthetic harms, environmental changes, etc.

1. Private nuisance: substantial and unreasonable interference with the private use and enjoyment of another's land. *Hendricks v. Stalnaker*, 181 W.Va. 31, 380 S.E.2d 198 (1989).
   a. Interference must be substantial.
   b. Defendant's conduct must be intentional and unreasonable:
      i. Gravity of the harm outweighs utility, or
      ii. Utility outweighs harm, but harm is serious. *Boomer v. Atlantic Cement Co.*, 26 N.Y. 2d 219, 309 N.Y.S.2d 312, 257 N.E. 2d 870 (N.Y. 1970).
2. Public nuisance: harm to the community's use or enjoyment of public land.
3. Defense to a Nuisance Claim:
   a. Coming to the nuisance.
   b. Contributory negligence.
   c. Assumption of the risk.
   d. Undue hardship.
4. Remedies for Nuisance:
   a. Enjoin D from acting, and
   b. Require D to pay.

THE REAL ESTATE CONTRACT

The sale of land is accompanied by a contract binding the buyer and seller to perform. Requires (must comply with Statute of Frauds):

1. Names of buyer and seller,
2. Description of realty to be sold,
3. Essential terms of the sale, and
4. Signature of party against whom enforcement is sought.

MORTGAGES

The purchase price is usually secured by the buyer from a third-party lender, which results in a lien on the property in favor of the lender.

1. Foreclosure: If the buyer defaults in repaying the lender, the property may be foreclosed upon and sold to repay the buyer's debts; the lender or one with a senior lien on the property will then be paid first out of the proceeds of the sale.
2. Equity of Redemption: Upon default, the buyer has the right to remedy the default and gain clear title to the land; some states limit the time in which the buyer may redeem after foreclosure.
3. Purchase Money Mortgage: When loan funds are used in part to purchase property, the mortgage securing the loan is a purchase money mortgage.

THE REAL ESTATE CLOSING

At closing, seller conveys marketable title in exchange for the buyer's providing the purchase price, and the rights of the parties shift from sale contract to deed.

1. Marketable Title: All defects and encumbrances must be removed by the time of closing; any defect, including those that do not appear in the chain of title, may make the title unmarketable.
2. Equitable Conversion:
   a. Once buyer and seller have signed an enforceable contract (prior to closing, they enter into the contract for the sale of land) equity converts:
      i. Buyer's interest into interest in realty
      ii. Seller's interest into interest in personalty (the purchase price)
   b. Death of party: If buyer or seller dies before closing, converted rights pass to estate of either.
   c. Risk of loss: If property is destroyed, under the general rule buyer is now the owner of the property and will bear the loss.
3. Breach:
   a. Buyer's Remedies: Upon seller's failure to provide marketable title, buyer can demand specific performance, receive damages, or rescind contract.
   b. Seller's Remedies: Upon buyer's failure to pay the purchase price, seller can demand specific performance, receive damages, or rescind contract.

THE DEED

After closing, the duties of the buyer and seller are contained ("merged") in the deed.

1. Formalities:
   a. Statute of Frauds:
      i. Must be in writing and signed by the grantor, and
      ii. Must describe property.
   b. Delivery of the Deed:
      i. Delivery is presumed where deed is in possession of grantee at time the issue arises; deed is recorded by grantor.
      ii. If grantor retains deed in his possession and dies, no legal delivery.
      iii. Deposit with third party: Delivery effective if grantor intended to vest title in grantee and surrendered control to third party; delivery with conditions (no delivery unless); condition is certain to occur and is within control of the grantee.

EMINENT DOMAIN / TAKINGS

1. *Definitions:* A taking of private property (real or personal) for public use without just compensation, can be either physical or regulatory, direct or indirect (property is merely burdened); if government pays just compensation, taking is constitutional and therefore permissible.
2. "Public Use": Must be rationally related to accomplishing a public purpose or use results in a public benefit. *Hawaii Housing Authority v. Midkiff*, 467 U.S. 229 (1984).
3. "Just Compensation": Fair market value, valued at highest and best use, special value to owner is not relevant. *United States v. Fuller*, 409 U.S. 488 (1973).
4. Sovereign may not use its eminent domain power to take property of one private party for sole purpose of transferring it to another private party, even if first party is paid just compensation [*Kelo v. City of New London, Conn.*, 545 U.S. 469 (2005)]. However, state may use its eminent domain power to transfer property from one private party to another if purpose of taking is future use by public, hence a city's exercise of eminent domain power in furtherance of economic development plan satisfied constitutional "public use" requirement [*Kelo v. City of New London, Conn.*, 545 U.S. 469 (2005)]. Many states responded to *Kelo* by limiting the power to take property for economic development purposes.

RECORDATION

Grantee who can show that she received her interest in a deed executed earlier than a competing claimant will be recognized as the true owner. Exception: if subsequent purchase is a bona fide purchase (BFP).

1. Types of Recording Statutes:
   a. Pure Race: Whoever records first.
   b. Notice: Unrecorded conveyance is invalid against a BFP who has no notice, regardless of who records first.
   c. Race-Notice: Whoever records first, unless that person has notice of a prior grant.
2. Chain of Title: A title search can give notice of prior interests in the property at issue.
   a. Title Examination:
      i. Grantor/grantee index: Title is traced back through the seller in grantor's indices, and forward to each buyer through grantee indices.

Laws Affecting Interests continues on page 5

QUICK COURSE OUTLINE

PROPERTY

CONCURRENT ESTATES

RIGHTS OF CO-TENANTS BETWEEN THEMSELVES

1. Possession: Co-tenants are equally entitled to possession of the property and cannot exclude other co-tenants.
2. Contribution for expenses: Co-tenants in rightful possession of property bear the cost of maintenance and upkeep such as taxes, insurance, and ordinary repairs. *Barrow v. Barrow*, 527 So. 2d 1373 (Fla. 1988).
3. Right to lease property: A co-tenant may lease the property without the consent of the other co-tenants, but lessee takes subject to the rights of the nonconsenting co-tenants. *Carr v. Deking*, 52 Wash. App. 880, 765 P.2d 40 (1988).
4. Accounting: Co-tenant in possession is responsible for accounting of all rents and profits from third party lessees. *Georgen v. Maar*, 2 A.D.2d 276 [3d Dept. 1956], 153 N.Y.S.2d 826 (1956).
5. Ouster/Partition: Co-tenant takes affirmative actions to take sole possession and exclusive use of the property; co-tenant may file action for partition in court to divide property into individual tenancies, unless all co-tenants voluntarily agree to divide. *Penfield v. Jarvis*, 175 Conn. 463, 399 A.2d 1280 (1978).
6. Effect of will: Since a co-tenant's interest ceases at death, the co-tenant has no interest that can pass by will. *Huff v. Metz*, 676 So. 2d 264 (Miss. 1996).

DOCTRINE OF WASTE (TENANT'S DUTY TO REPAIR)

A tenant who is not the owner of land, or possesses the same interest in property at the same time as one or more co-tenants, is responsible to her co-tenants for any decrease in the value of the property through waste. *Kimbrough v. Reed*, 943 P.2d 1232 (Idaho 1997).

1. Permissive Waste: Tenant allows land to fall into disrepair; must preserve land and structures to a reasonable degree.
2. Voluntary (Affirmative) Waste: Tenant cannot use natural resources on land; use is permissible only for repair and maintenance, where permission is expressly given, or where land is only suitable for such use.
3. Ameliorative Waste: Tenant's use substantially changes the value of property, but the use increases the value of the land; may do it where the market value of future interests is not impaired, and change in character of neighborhood deprives the property of value in its current form.

COMMUNITY PROPERTY

1. *Example:* A husband and wife form a community, which is a separate entity that owns property for the benefit of the husband and wife; all property acquired during marriage is generally characterized as community property.

Separate Property: Property acquired by gift, bequest, or devise during the marriage is characterized as separate property, belonging to the individual spouse who receives it.

2. Division of the Community:
   a. At Death: Community dissolves at death of one spouse; each spouse owns half an interest in each community asset.
   b. At Divorce: Community dissolves upon divorce and all community assets are owned by each spouse as tenants in common and may be divided according to settlement.

LICENSES & PROFITS

LICENSE

1. Bare revocable interest to use property for limited purpose and duration.
2. Irrevocable License: Cannot be revoked if consideration is given.

PROFITS

Right to come onto land solely to remove minerals or other value.

TYPES OF PROPERTY INTERESTS

INTERESTS IN THINGS

1. Wild Animals:
   a. Right to possess: Deprive them of natural liberty [*Pierson v. Post*, 3 Cai. R. 175 (N.Y. Sup. 1805).]:
      i. Actual physical possession.
      ii. Mortally wounding/continued pursuit.
      iii. Capture/netting.
2. Natural Gas and Oil:
   a. Right to possess: Whoever extracts first regardless of where.
3. Lost Property:
   a. *Definition*:
      i. Lost: Possessor can no longer find it.
      ii. Mislaid: Possessor voluntarily leaves it, but forgets where.
      iii. Abandoned: Possessor voluntarily relinquishes possession; ordinarily belongs to finder.
      iv. Treasure trove: Property hidden and found, owner unknown.
   b. General Rule: Prior possessor has superior rights to finder. *Armory v. Delamirie*, 1 Strange 525, 93 Eng. Rep. 664 (1722).
   c. Owner of Land *(Locus in Quo)*: Owner of land where lost property is found has superior rights to finder who is trespasser. *Favorite v. Miller*, 407 A.2d 974 (Conn. 1978).
4. Bailments/Borrowed Property:
   a. *Definition of Bailment*: Owner (bailor) transfers possession (but not title) to another (bailee), who is in lawful possession of the transferred property and has title against wrongdoers.
   b. Legal Relationship: Bailee is liable to bailor for negligent damage to property, or conversion.

OTHER INTERESTS IN LAND

1. Easements: A nonpossessory interest entitling holder to some type of use or enjoyment of another person's land.
2. Covenants/Equitable Servitudes: A covenant is a type of servitude created by deed or contract and whose benefits or burdens "run with the land" to bind successors in interest. When the rules regarding real covenants are not met, the agreement may be enforced in equity as an equitable servitude.
3. Licenses: Owner grants permission to another to use the land.
4. Profits: An easement entitling holder to come onto the land in order to take something off it.

MISCELLANEOUS PROPERTY INTERESTS

1. Bona Fide Purchaser (BFP):
   a. *Definition*: One who takes possession:
      i. In good faith,
      ii. For valuable consideration, and
      iii. Without notice of any wrongful possession.

Types of Property Interests continues on page 2

LEGAL CONSIDERATIONS ARISING FROM LEASE

	SUBLET		ASSIGNMENT	
	Tenant (T1) transfers less than the entire remaining estate to transferee (T2)			
	Privity of Estate	Privity of Contract	Privity of Estate	Privity of Contract
T2 to Landlord (L)	NO	NO	YES	NO
Unless	1. T2 agrees with T1 to assume all lease provisions 2. T2 enters into separate agreement with L			
T1 to L	YES	YES	NO	YES
T2 to T1	T1 can be reimbursed by T2 for any rent paid to L under sublease		T1 can be reimbursed by T2 for any rent paid to L under assignment	

INTEREST OWNED	UNIQUE FEATURES	HOW TERMINATED
Estate in perpetuity, lasts forever	Highest estate recognized by law	Never terminated; perpetual
Estate in perpetuity, lasts forever	Terminates automatically on occurrence of an event; otherwise lasts forever	Occurrence or nonoccurrence of condition sometime in future, as set out in governing instrument
Estate in perpetuity, lasts forever	Doesn't terminate automatically; unless condition occurs, lasts forever	Grantor elects to terminate due to occurrence of condition
Estate for duration of owner's life	Assures that lands stay within a family from generation to generation by passing to owner's heirs	Owner's death
Estate with duration measured by life of another	Measuring life can be either land holder or another party	Measuring life ends
present and future interests can be concurrent.		
Equal right of possession of the whole by each co-tenant, regardless of the actual share owned; may be freely conveyed	Modern Law: Any conveyance to two or more people creates a presumption of a tenancy in common	Partitioned through mutual agreement of co-tenants or judicial decree
Equal right of possession of the whole by each co-tenant, regardless of the actual share owned; however, cannot be freely conveyed (Right of Survivorship: once a co-tenant dies, remaining co-tenants take property free and clear of deceased co-tenant's interest)	**1.** Common Law: Any conveyance to two or more people creates a presumption of a joint tenancy **2.** Conveyance: If any co-tenant conveys interest, transferee takes as a tenant-in-common, while remaining co-tenants continue to hold in joint tenancy	Partitioned through mutual agreement of co-tenants or judicial decree
Equal right of possession of the whole by each co-tenant, regardless of the actual share owned; may be freely conveyed	Any conveyance to two or more people creates a presumption of a tenancy in common	Partitioned through mutual agreement of co-tenants or judicial decree
nt, in the form of duties owed between a landlord and the renter of the land.		
Right to occupy tenancy for fixed period (year, month, week, or day)	Automatically renews for a like period at the end of the preceding period	Notice must be given by either landlord or tenant a minimum of one whole period before last day of current period; death does not terminate
Right to occupy tenancy beginning on a fixed date and ending on a fixed date	Can also last for a period measured by the happening of an event or condition	Fixed end date arrives, or ending event takes place; no notice required
Right to occupy tenancy "at will" as long as both the landlord and tenant so desire	Law disfavors; some states have statutes requiring notice to terminate	May be terminated by either party without notice; death of either party can also terminate
Holdover tenant is treated as trespasser and evicted, or new periodic tenancy is imposed	Landlord has the right to elect either eviction or creation of new tenancy	If landlord chooses to evict, tenancy ends
sometime in the future.		
Balance of estate left after grantor transfers less than she has	May or may not become possessory in future; freely alienable, devisable, and descendible	Interest does not become possessory if prior estate given by grantor does not end
Balance of estate in fee simple absolute, left after grantor originally transfers less than she has	Landlord has the right to elect either eviction or creation of new tenancy	If landlord chooses to evict, prior tenancy ends
Balance of estate in fee simple absolute, left after grantor originally transfers less than she has	Does not go to grantor automatically; grantor must elect to enforce interest	If condition occurs and landlord chooses to enforce interest, prior tenancy ends
Balance of estate in fee simple absolute, left after grantor originally transfers less than she has	**1.** Springing interest: Becomes possessory upon occurrence of a condition, if no present possessory estate exists in another transferee **2.** Shifting interest: Becomes possessory after divesting a present possessory freehold	If condition occurs, prior tenancy ends unless property is currently possessed and interest is springing (and therefore cannot divest an existing possessor)
An interest limited by the existence of a currently possessory estate created at the same time	**1.** Vested Remainders: Not subject to RAP, possessory right is certain **a.** Indefeasibly Vested: Born, ascertainable person **b.** Subject to Open/Partial Divestment: Class of persons, with at least one living member; interests divest in part as new class members are born; class closes when: **i.** Person who produces class members dies; or **ii.** Rule of Convenience: When any class member is entitled to demand possession of entitled shares; no outstanding present possessory estates/conditions precedent for any class member **2.** Contingent remainders: Subject to RAP, right to take is uncertain **a.** Subject to Condition Precedent: Words condition a person's right to take **b.** Unborn, unascertained persons	Remainder interest may never become possessory if outstanding, presently possessory estate continues to exist

CASENOTE® Legal Briefs®

PROPERTY

Keyed to Courses Using

Singer, Berger, Davidson, and Peñalver's
Property Law: Rules, Policies, and Practices
Eighth Edition

Authored by: Publisher's Editorial Staff

ASPEN PUBLISHING

This publication is designed to provide accurate and authoritative information in regard to the subject matter covered. It is sold with the understanding that the publisher is not engaged in rendering legal, accounting, or other professional services. If legal advice or other expert assistance is required, the services of a competent professional person should be sought.

— From a Declaration of Principles adopted jointly by a Committee of the American Bar Association and a Committee of Publishers and Associates

To contact Customer Service, e-mail customer.service@aspenpublishing.com, call 1-800-950-5259, or mail correspondence to:

Aspen Publishing
Attn: Order Department
P.O. Box 990
Frederick, MD 21705

Printed in the United States of America.

1 2 3 4 5 6 7 8 9 0

ISBN 978-1-5438-0741-7

About Aspen Publishing

Aspen Publishing is a leading provider of educational content and digital learning solutions to law schools in the U.S. and around the world. Aspen provides best-in-class solutions for legal education through authoritative textbooks, written by renowned authors, and breakthrough products such as Connected eBooks, Connected Quizzing, and PracticePerfect.

The Aspen Casebook Series (famously known among law faculty and students as the "red and black" casebooks) encompasses hundreds of highly regarded textbooks in more than eighty disciplines, from large enrollment courses such as Torts and Contracts to emerging electives such as Sustainability and the Law of Policing. Study aids such as the *Examples & Explanations* and the *Emanuel Law Outlines* series, both highly popular collections, help law students master complex subject matter.

Major products, programs, and initiatives include:

- **Connected eBooks** are enhanced digital textbooks and study aids that come with a suite of online content and learning tools designed to maximize student success. Designed in collaboration with hundreds of faculty and students, the Connected eBook is a significant leap forward in the legal education learning tools available to students.
- **Connected Quizzing** is an easy-to-use formative assessment tool that tests law students' understanding and provides timely feedback to improve learning outcomes. Delivered through CasebookConnect.com, the learning platform already used by students to access their Aspen casebooks, Connected Quizzing is simple to implement and integrates seamlessly with law school course curricula.
- **PracticePerfect** is a visually engaging, interactive study aid to explain commonly encountered legal doctrines through easy-to-understand animated videos, illustrative examples, and numerous practice questions. Developed by a team of experts, PracticePerfect is the ideal study companion for today's law students.
- The **Aspen Learning Library** enables law schools to provide their students with access to the most popular study aids on the market across all of their courses. Available through an annual subscription, the online library consists of study aids in e-book, audio, and video formats with full text search, note-taking, and highlighting capabilities.
- Aspen's **Digital Bookshelf** is an institutional-level online education bookshelf, consolidating everything students and professors need to ensure success. This program ensures that every student has access to affordable course materials from day one.
- **Leading Edge** is a community centered on thinking differently about legal education and putting those thoughts into actionable strategies. At the core of the program is the Leading Edge Conference, an annual gathering of legal education thought leaders looking to pool ideas and identify promising directions of exploration.

Format for the Casenote® Legal Brief

Nature of Case: This section identifies the form of action (e.g., breach of contract, negligence, battery), the type of proceeding (e.g., demurrer, appeal from trial court's jury instructions) or the relief sought (e.g., damages, injunction, criminal sanctions).

Fact Summary: This is included to refresh your memory and can be used as a quick reminder of the facts.

Rule of Law: Summarizes the general principle of law that the case illustrates. It may be used for instant recall of the court's holding and for classroom discussion or home review.

Facts: This section contains all relevant facts of the case, including the contentions of the parties and the lower court holdings. It is written in a logical order to give you a clear understanding of the case. The plaintiff and defendant are identified by their proper names throughout and are always labeled with a (P) or (D).

Issue: The issue is a concise question that brings out the essence of the opinion as it relates to the section of the casebook in which the case appears. Both substantive and procedural issues are included if relevant to the decision.

Party ID: Quick identification of the relationship between the parties.

Concurrence/Dissent: All concurrences and dissents are briefed whenever they are included by the casebook author.

Analysis: This last paragraph gives you a broad understanding of where the case "fits in" with other cases in the section of the book and with the entire course. It is a hornbook-style discussion indicating whether the case is a majority or minority opinion and comparing the principal case with other cases in the casebook. It may also provide analysis from restatements, uniform codes, and law review articles.

Holding and Decision: This section offers a clear and in-depth discussion of the rule of the case and the court's rationale. It is written in easy-to-understand language and answers the issue presented by applying the law to the facts of the case. When relevant, it includes a thorough discussion of the exceptions to the case as listed by the court, any major cites to the other cases on point, and the names of the judges who wrote the decisions.

Quicknotes: Conveniently defines legal terms found in the case.

Palsgraf v. Long Island R.R. Co.

Injured bystander (P) v. Railroad company (D)

N.Y. Ct. App., 248 N.Y. 339, 162 N.E. 99 (1928).

NATURE OF CASE: Appeal from judgment affirming verdict for plaintiff seeking damages for personal injury.

FACT SUMMARY: Helen Palsgraf (P) was injured on R.R.'s (D) train platform when R.R.'s (D) guard helped a passenger aboard a moving train, causing his package to fall on the tracks. The package contained fireworks which exploded, creating a shock that tipped a scale onto Palsgraf (P).

RULE OF LAW

The risk reasonably to be perceived defines the duty to be obeyed.

FACTS: Helen Palsgraf (P) purchased a ticket to Rockaway Beach from R.R. (D) and was waiting on the train platform. As she waited, two men ran to catch a train that was pulling out from the platform. The first man jumped aboard, but the second man, who appeared as if he might fall, was helped aboard by the guard on the train who had kept the door open so they could jump aboard. A guard on the platform also helped by pushing him onto the train. The man was carrying a package wrapped in newspaper. In the process, the man dropped his package, which fell on the tracks. The package contained fireworks and exploded. The shock of the explosion was apparently of great enough strength to tip over some scales at the other end of the platform, which fell on Palsgraf (P) and injured her. A jury awarded her damages, and R.R. (D) appealed.

ISSUE: Does the risk reasonably to be perceived define the duty to be obeyed?

HOLDING AND DECISION: (Cardozo, C.J.) Yes. The risk reasonably to be perceived defines the duty to be obeyed. If there is no foreseeable hazard to the injured party as the result of a seemingly innocent act, the act does not become a tort because it happened to be a wrong as to another. If the wrong was not willful, the plaintiff must show that the act as to her had such great and apparent possibilities of danger as to entitle her to protection. Negligence in the abstract is not enough upon which to base liability. Negligence is a relative concept, evolving out of the common law doctrine of trespass on the case. To establish liability, the defendant must owe a legal duty of reasonable care to the injured party. A cause of action in tort will lie where harm, though unintended, could have been averted or avoided by observance of such a duty. The scope of the duty is limited by the range of danger that a reasonable person could foresee. In this case, there was nothing to suggest from the appearance of the parcel or otherwise that the parcel contained fireworks. The guard could not reasonably have had any warning of a threat to Palsgraf (P), and R.R. (D) therefore cannot be held liable. Judgment is reversed in favor of R.R. (D).

DISSENT: (Andrews, J.) The concept that there is no negligence unless R.R. (D) owes a legal duty to take care as to Palsgraf (P) herself is too narrow. Everyone owes to the world at large the duty of refraining from those acts that may unreasonably threaten the safety of others. If the guard's action was negligent as to those nearby, it was also negligent as to those outside what might be termed the "danger zone." For Palsgraf (P) to recover, R.R.'s (D) negligence must have been the proximate cause of her injury, a question of fact for the jury.

ANALYSIS

The majority defined the limit of the defendant's liability in terms of the danger that a reasonable person in defendant's situation would have perceived. The dissent argued that the limitation should not be placed on liability, but rather on damages. Judge Andrews suggested that only injuries that would not have happened but for R.R.'s (D) negligence should be compensable. Both the majority and dissent recognized the policy-driven need to limit liability for negligent acts, seeking, in the words of Judge Andrews, to define a framework "that will be practical and in keeping with the general understanding of mankind." The Restatement (Second) of Torts has accepted Judge Cardozo's view.

Quicknotes

FORESEEABILITY A reasonable expectation that change is the probable result of certain acts or omissions.

NEGLIGENCE Conduct falling below the standard of care that a reasonable person would demonstrate under similar conditions.

PROXIMATE CAUSE The natural sequence of events without which an injury would not have been sustained.

Note to Students

Aspen Publishing is proud to offer *Casenote® Legal Briefs*—continuing thirty years of publishing America's best-selling legal briefs.

Casenote® Legal Briefs are designed to help you save time when briefing assigned cases. Organized under convenient headings, they show you how to abstract the basic facts and holdings from the text of the actual opinions handed down by the courts. Used as part of a rigorous study regimen, they can help you spend more time analyzing and critiquing points of law than on copying bits and pieces of judicial opinions into your notebook or outline.

Casenote® Legal Briefs should never be used as a substitute for assigned casebook readings. They work best when read as a follow-up to reviewing the underlying opinions themselves. Students who try to avoid reading and digesting the judicial opinions in their casebooks or online sources will end up shortchanging themselves in the long run. The ability to absorb, critique, and restate the dynamic and complex elements of case law decisions is crucial to your success in law school and beyond. It cannot be developed vicariously.

In addition to *Casenote® Legal Briefs*, Aspen Publishing offers the following study aids:

- *Casenote® Legal Briefs*
- *Emanuel® Law Outlines*
- Emanuel® *Law in a Flash* Flash Cards
- Emanuel® *CrunchTime®* Series

Each of these series is designed to provide you with easy-to-understand explanations of complex points of law. Each volume offers guidance on the principles of legal analysis and, consulted regularly, will hone your ability to spot relevant issues. We have titles that will help you prepare for class, prepare for your exams, and enhance your general comprehension of the law along the way.

To find out more about our law school tools for success, visit us at *www.AspenPublishing.com* or email us at *customer.service@aspenpublishing.com*. We'll be happy to assist you.

How to Brief a Case

A. Decide on a Format and Stick to It

Structure is essential to a good brief. It enables you to arrange systematically the related parts that are scattered throughout most cases, thus making manageable and understandable what might otherwise seem to be an endless and unfathomable sea of information. There are, of course, an unlimited number of formats that can be utilized. However, it is best to find one that suits your needs and stick to it. Consistency breeds both efficiency and the security that when called upon you will know where to look in your brief for the information you are asked to give.

Any format, as long as it presents the essential elements of a case in an organized fashion, can be used. Experience, however, has led *Casenote® Legal Briefs* to develop and utilize the following format because of its logical flow and universal applicability.

NATURE OF CASE: This is a brief statement of the legal character and procedural status of the case (e.g., "Appeal of a burglary conviction").

There are many different alternatives open to a litigant dissatisfied with a court ruling. The key to determining which one has been used is to discover *who is asking this court for what.*

This first entry in the brief should be kept as *short as possible.* Use the court's terminology if you understand it. But since jurisdictions vary as to the titles of pleadings, the best entry is the one that addresses who wants what in this proceeding, not the one that sounds most like the court's language.

RULE OF LAW: A statement of the general principle of law that the case illustrates (e.g., "An acceptance that varies any term of the offer is considered a rejection and counteroffer").

Determining the rule of law of a case is a procedure similar to determining the issue of the case. Avoid being fooled by red herrings; there may be a few rules of law mentioned in the case excerpt, but usually only one is *the* rule with which the casebook editor is concerned. The techniques used to locate the issue, described below, may also be utilized to find the rule of law. Generally, your best guide is simply the chapter heading. It is a clue to the point the casebook editor seeks to make and should be kept in mind when reading every case in the respective section.

FACTS: A synopsis of only the essential facts of the case, i.e., those bearing upon or leading up to the issue.

The facts entry should be a short statement of the events and transactions that led one party to initiate legal proceedings against another in the first place. While some cases conveniently state the salient facts at the beginning of the decision, in other instances they will have to be culled from hiding places throughout the text, even from concurring and dissenting opinions. Some of the "facts" will often be in dispute and should be so noted. Conflicting evidence may be briefly pointed up. "Hard" facts must be included. Both must be *relevant* in order to be listed in the facts entry. It is impossible to tell what is relevant until the entire case is read, as the ultimate determination of the rights and liabilities of the parties may turn on something buried deep in the opinion.

Generally, the facts entry should not be longer than three to five *short* sentences.

It is often helpful to identify the role played by a party in a given context. For example, in a construction contract case the identification of a party as the "contractor" or "builder" alleviates the need to tell that that party was the one who was supposed to have built the house.

It is always helpful, and a good general practice, to identify the "plaintiff" and the "defendant." This may seem elementary and uncomplicated, but, especially in view of the creative editing practiced by some casebook editors, it is sometimes a difficult or even impossible task. Bear in mind that the *party presently* seeking something from this court may not be the plaintiff, and that sometimes only the cross-claim of a defendant is treated in the excerpt. Confusing or misaligning the parties can ruin your analysis and understanding of the case.

ISSUE: A statement of the general legal question answered by or illustrated in the case. For clarity, the issue is best put in the form of a question capable of a "yes" or "no" answer. In reality, the issue is simply the Rule of Law put in the form of a question (e.g., "May an offer be accepted by performance?").

The major problem presented in discerning what is *the* issue in the case is that an opinion usually purports to raise and answer several questions. However, except for rare cases, only one such question is really the issue in the case. Collateral issues not necessary to the resolution of the matter in controversy are handled by the court by language known as *"obiter dictum"* or merely *"dictum."* While dicta may be included later in the brief, they have no place under the issue heading.

To find the issue, ask *who wants what* and then go on to ask *why did that party succeed or fail in getting it.* Once this is determined, the "why" should be turned into a question.

The complexity of the issues in the cases will vary, but in all cases a single-sentence question should sum up the issue. *In a few cases,* there will be two, or even more rarely, three issues of equal importance to the resolution of the case. Each should be expressed in a single-sentence question.

Since many issues are resolved by a court in coming to a final disposition of a case, the casebook editor will reproduce the portion of the opinion containing the issue or issues most relevant to the area of law under scrutiny. A noted law professor gave this advice: "Close the book; look at the title on the cover." Chances are, if it is Property, you need not concern yourself with whether, for example, the federal government's treatment of the plaintiff's land really raises a federal question sufficient to support jurisdiction on this ground in federal court.

The same rule applies to chapter headings designating sub-areas within the subjects. They tip you off as to what the text is designed to teach. The cases are arranged in a casebook to show a progression or development of the law, so that the preceding cases may also help.

It is also most important to remember to *read the notes and questions* at the end of a case to determine what the editors wanted you to have gleaned from it.

HOLDING AND DECISION: This section should succinctly explain the rationale of the court in arriving at its decision. In capsulizing the "reasoning" of the court, it should always include an application of the general rule or rules of law to the specific facts of the case. Hidden justifications come to light in this entry: the reasons for the state of the law, the public policies, the biases and prejudices, those considerations that influence the justices' thinking and, ultimately, the outcome of the case. At the end, there should be a short indication of thedisposition or procedural resolution of the case (e.g., "Decision of the trial court for Mr. Smith (P) reversed").

The foregoing format is designed to help you "digest" the reams of case material with which you will be faced in your law school career. Once mastered by practice, it will place at your fingertips the information the authors of your casebooks have sought to impart to you in case-by-case illustration and analysis.

B. Be as Economical as Possible in Briefing Cases

Once armed with a format that encourages succinctness, it is as important to be economical with regard to the time spent on the actual reading of the case as it is to be economical in the writing of the brief itself. This does not mean "skimming" a case. Rather, it means reading the case with an "eye" trained to recognize into which "section" of your brief a particular passage or line fits and having a system for quickly and precisely marking the case so that the passages fitting any one particular part of the brief can be easily identified and brought together in a concise and accurate manner when the brief is actually written.

It is of no use to simply repeat everything in the opinion of the court; record only enough information to trigger your recollection of what the court said. Nevertheless, an accurate statement of the "law of the case," i.e., the legal principle applied to the facts, is absolutely essential to class preparation and to learning the law under the case method.

To that end, it is important to develop a "shorthand" that you can use to make marginal notations. These notations will tell you at a glance in which section of the brief you will be placing that particular passage or portion of the opinion.

Some students prefer to underline all the salient portions of the opinion (with a pencil or colored underliner marker), making marginal notations as they go along. Others prefer the color-coded method of underlining, utilizing different colors of markers to underline the salient portions of the case, each separate color being used to represent a different section of the brief. For example, blue underlining could be used for passages relating to the rule of law, yellow for those relating to the issue, and green for those relating to the holding and decision, etc. While it has its advocates, thecolor-coded method can be confusing and time-consuming (all that time spent on changing colored markers). Furthermore, it can interfere with the continuity and concentration many students deem essential to the reading of a case for maximum comprehension. In the end, however, it is a matter of personal preference and style. Just remember, whatever method you use, underlining must be used sparingly or its value is lost.

If you take the marginal notation route, an efficient and easy method is to go along underlining the key portions of the case and placing in the margin alongside them the following "markers" to indicate where a particular passage or line "belongs" in the brief you will write:

N	(NATURE OF CASE)
RL	(RULE OF LAW)
I	(ISSUE)
HL	(HOLDING AND DECISION, relates to the RULE OF LAW behind the decision)
HR	(HOLDING AND DECISION, gives the RATIONALE or reasoning behind the decision)
HA	(HOLDING AND DECISION, applies the general principle(s) of law to the facts of the case to arrive at the decision)

Remember that a particular passage may well contain information necessary to more than one part of your brief, in which case you simply note that in the margin. If you are using the color-coded underlining method instead of marginal notation, simply make asterisks or checks in the margin next to the passage in question in the colors that indicate the additional sections of the brief where it might be utilized.

The economy of utilizing "shorthand" in marking cases for briefing can be maintained in the actual brief writing process itself by utilizing "law student shorthand" within the brief. There are many commonly used words and phrases for which abbreviations can be substituted in your briefs (and in your class notes also). You can develop abbreviations that are personal to you and which will save you a lot of time. A reference list of briefing abbreviations can be found on page x of this book.

C. Use Both the Briefing Process and the Brief as a Learning Tool

Now that you have a format and the tools for briefing cases efficiently, the most important thing is to make the time spent in briefing profitable to you and to make the most advantageous use of the briefs you create. Of course, the briefs are invaluable for classroom reference when you are called upon to explain or analyze a particular case. However, they are also useful in reviewing for exams. A quick glance at the fact summary should bring the case to mind, and a rereading of the rule of law should enable you to go over the underlying legal concept in your mind, how it was applied in that particular case, and how it might apply in other factual settings.

As to the value to be derived from engaging in the briefing process itself, there is an immediate benefit that arises from being forced to sift through the essential facts and reasoning from the court's opinion and to succinctly express them in your own words in your brief. The process ensures that you understand the case and the point that it illustrates, and that means you will be ready to absorb further analysis and information brought forth in class. It also ensures you will have something to say when called upon in class. The briefing process helps develop a mental agility for getting to the *gist* of a case and for identifying, expounding on, and applying the legal concepts and issues found there. The briefing process is the mental process on which you must rely in taking law school examinations; it is also the mental process upon which lawyers rely in serving their clients and in making a living.

Abbreviations for Briefs

acceptance	acp
affirmed	aff
answer	ans
assumption of risk	a/r
attorney	atty
beyond a reasonable doubt	b/r/d
bona fide purchaser	BFP
breach of contract	br/k
cause of action	c/a
common law	c/l
Constitution	Con
constitutional	con
contract	K
contributory negligence	c/n
cross	x
cross-complaint	x/c
cross-examination	x/ex
cruel and unusual punishment	c/u/p
defendant	D
dismissed	dis
double jeopardy	d/j
due process	d/p
equal protection	e/p
equity	eq
evidence	ev
exclude	exc
exclusionary rule	exc/r
felony	f/n
freedom of speech	f/s
good faith	g/f
habeas corpus	h/c
hearsay	hr
husband	H
injunction	inj
in loco parentis	ILP
inter vivos	I/v
joint tenancy	j/t
judgment	judgt
jurisdiction	jur
last clear chance	LCC
long-arm statute	LAS
majority view	maj
meeting of minds	MOM
minority view	min
Miranda rule	Mir/r
Miranda warnings	Mir/w
negligence	neg
notice	ntc
nuisance	nus
obligation	ob
obscene	obs
offer	O
offeree	OE
offeror	OR
ordinance	ord
pain and suffering	p/s
parol evidence	p/e
plaintiff	P
prima facie	p/f
probable cause	p/c
proximate cause	px/c
real property	r/p
reasonable doubt	r/d
reasonable man	r/m
rebuttable presumption	rb/p
remanded	rem
res ipsa loquitur	RIL
respondeat superior	r/s
Restatement	RS
reversed	rev
Rule Against Perpetuities	RAP
search and seizure	s/s
search warrant	s/w
self-defense	s/d
specific performance	s/p
statute	S
statute of frauds	S/F
statute of limitations	S/L
summary judgment	s/j
tenancy at will	t/w
tenancy in common	t/c
tenant	t
third party	TP
third party beneficiary	TPB
transferred intent	TI
unconscionable	uncon
unconstitutional	unconst
undue influence	u/e
Uniform Commercial Code	UCC
unilateral	uni
vendee	VE
vendor	VR
versus	v
void for vagueness	VFV
weight of authority	w/a
weight of the evidence	w/e
wife	W
with	w/
within	w/i
without	w/o
without prejudice	w/o/p
wrongful death	wr/d

Table of Cases

CHAPTER 1

Trespass: The Right to Exclude and Rights of Access

Quick Reference Rules of Law

State v. Shack

State (P) v. Attorney for migrant farmworkers (D)

N.J. Sup. Ct., 277 A.2d 369 (1971)

NATURE OF CASE: Appeal from a conviction of trespassing.

FACT SUMMARY: Tejeras (D) and Shack (D) entered upon private property, against the orders of the owner of that property, to aid migrant farmworkers employed and housed there.

RULE OF LAW

Real property rights are not absolute; and "necessity, private or public, may justify entry upon the lands of another."

FACTS: Tejeras (D) and Shack (D) worked with migrant farmworkers. Tejeras (D) was a field worker for the Farm Workers Division of the Southwest Citizens Organization for Poverty Elimination (SCOPE), a non-profit corporation funded by the Office of Economic Opportunity that provided for the "health services of the migrant farm worker." Shack (D) was a staff attorney with the Farm Workers Division of Camden Regional Legal Services, Inc. (CRLS), also a nonprofit corporation funded by the Office of Economic Opportunity that provided (along with other services) legal advice for, and representation of, migrant farmworkers. Tejeras (D) and Shack (D), pursuant to their roles in SCOPE and CRLS, entered upon private property to aid migrant workers employed and housed there. When both Tejeras (D) and Shack (D) refused to leave the property at the owner's request, they were charged with trespassing under a New Jersey statute which provides that "any person who trespasses on any lands . . . after being forbidden so to trespass by the owner . . . is a disorderly person and shall be punished by a fine of not more than $50." After conviction for trespassing, Tejeras (D) and Shack (D) brought this appeal.

ISSUE: Does an owner of real property have the absolute right to exclude all others from that property?

HOLDING AND DECISION: (Weintraub, C.J.) No. Real property rights are not absolute; and "necessity, private or public, may justify entry upon the lands of another." This rule is based upon the basic rationale that "property rights serve human values. They are recognized to that end and are limited by it." Here, a central concern is the welfare of the migrant farmworkers—a highly disadvantaged segment of society. Migrant farmworkers, in general, are "outside of the mainstream of the communities in which they are housed and are unaware of their rights and opportunities, and of the services available to them." As such, here, the "necessity" of effective communication of legal rights and of providing medical services for the migrant farmworkers justifies entry upon the private property. Of course, the owner of such property has the right to pursue his farming activities without interference, but, here, there is no legitimate need for the owner to exclude those attempting to assist the migrant farmworkers. Furthermore, the migrant farmworker must be allowed to receive visitors of his choice, so long as there is no behavior harmful to others, and members of the press may not be denied access to any farmworker who wishes to see them. In any of these situations, since no possessory right of the farmer-employer-landowner has been invaded (i.e., since he has no right to exclude such persons), there can be no trespassing. Reversed and remanded.

ANALYSIS

Generally, the right to exclusive possession is considered the oldest, most widely recognized right of private property in land. This case, though, illustrates the central limitation on the right to possession or use of private property, i.e., it may not be used to harm others. Here, the exclusion of Tejeras (D) and Shack (D) was, therefore, invalid because it would harm a very disadvantaged segment of society (the farmworkers). Note, that under this principle, an owner of property, also, has no right to maintain a nuisance, to violate a building code, or to violate any "police power" laws (i.e., laws for the general public welfare).

Quicknotes

TRESPASS Unlawful interference with, or damage to, the real or personal property of another.

Commonwealth v. Magadini

State (P) v. Convicted trespasser (D)

Mass. Sup. Jud. Ct., 52 N.E.3d 1041 (2016)

NATURE OF CASE: Appeal from trespass conviction on the grounds that the trial court failed to properly instruct the jury on the necessity defense.

FACT SUMMARY: Magadini (D), who was convicted on several counts of trespassing, contended that he presented sufficient evidence to support the foundational conditions of a necessity defense and that, therefore, the trial court erroneously refused to instruct the jury on the elements of that defense.

RULE OF LAW

A trial court errs in refusing to provide jury instructions on the necessity defense to the crime of trespass where the defendant has presented some evidence on each of the defense's foundational conditions.

FACTS: Magadini (D), a 67-year-old, lifelong resident of Great Barrington, violated several no trespass orders by sleeping in the lobbies or hallways of three commercial establishments. Apparently, he did so on cold, or very cold, days so he could keep warm, because on those days his garments were insufficient to keep him warm. One trespass incident, however, involved him using the bathroom of one of the establishments, despite requests to leave the premises, during the summer. Magadini (D) had become homeless after leaving his parents' home. He generally lived outside year-round, but during the winter months, he tried to find a more sheltered area, and although he used blankets, gloves, and scarves to try to stay warm during cold weather, when the weather was severe, he would seek shelter in private buildings. Although at one point he had stayed at a local homeless shelter for a few months, apparently he had been asked to leave, so he had no place to stay except the outdoors, and he took up residence in a gazebo behind the town's city hall. He considered the gazebo to be his home, and he was registered to vote from that address. He had been employed in the past but was currently unemployed, and he had tried to find an apartment, but could not afford the upfront fees involved. He knew of a homeless shelter in another town that was around 20 miles away, but he wanted to stay in Great Barrington, which was his hometown, and he did not have a driver's license. At trial for his trespass crimes, Magadini (D) requested that the judge instruct the jury on the necessity defense, but the judge refused to do so, finding that Magadini (D) had had other available legal alternatives, such as "motels, and hotels, the police station," and that the evidence was lacking on Magadini's (D) inability to "rent a hotel room on these isolated evenings." The judge also allegedly excluded evidence relevant to the defense. Magadini (D) was convicted on the trespass charges, and appealed, contending that the judge had erred in refusing Magadini's (D) requested jury instructions on the necessity defense. The state's highest court granted review.

ISSUE: Does a trial court err in refusing to provide jury instructions on the necessity defense to the crime of trespass where the defendant has presented some evidence on each of the defense's foundational conditions?

HOLDING AND DECISION: (Hines, J.) Yes. A trial court errs in refusing to provide jury instructions on the necessity defense to the crime of trespass where the defendant has presented some evidence on each of the defense's foundational conditions. The common-law defense of necessity exonerates one who commits a crime under the pressure of circumstances if the harm that would have resulted from compliance with the law exceeds the harm actually resulting from the defendant's violation of the law. There are four underlying foundational conditions of the defense: (1) a clear and imminent danger, not one that is debatable or speculative; (2) a reasonable expectation that the defendant's action will be effective as the direct cause of abating the danger; (3) there is no legal alternative that will be effective in abating the danger; and (4) the legislature has not acted to preclude the defense by a clear and deliberate choice regarding the values at issue. To be entitled to a necessity defense instruction, a defendant must present some evidence on each of these conditions. As to the first, "clear and imminent danger" condition, this condition was present except during the incident in which Magadini (D) had to use the bathroom during the summer. It is clear that the weather conditions on the dates of the remaining offenses presented a "clear and imminent danger" to a homeless person. Moreover, the timing of each of those incidents, in the early morning or late evening hours when Magadini (D) was either sleeping or lying down, suggests the dangerousness of the circumstances where sleeping may place one in the same position for an extended period and, thus, increases the potential harm from the weather. To satisfy the third condition, the absence of legal alternatives, a defendant must demonstrate that he made himself aware of any available lawful alternatives, or showed them to be futile in the circumstances. In other words, the defendant must present enough evidence to demonstrate at least a reasonable doubt that there were no effective legal alternatives

Continued on next page.

available before being entitled to an instruction on the necessity defense. This does not require a showing that the defendant has exhausted or shown to be futile all conceivable alternatives, only that a jury could reasonably find that no alternatives were available. Here, the evidence was sufficient to meet Magadini's (D) burden. In determining whether there has been sufficient evidence of the foundational conditions to the necessity defense, all reasonable inferences should be resolved in favor of the defendant, and, no matter how incredible his testimony, that testimony must be treated as true. Taken in this light, there is at least "some evidence" that Magadini (D) lacked effective legal alternatives to trespass during cold days and nights. Here, Magadini (D) testified that he essentially lived outdoors year-round; that he had been asked to leave the town's homeless shelter and could not return there; and that he had attempted to rent apartments. Some of this evidence was corroborated by police officers and others. The Commonwealth (P) argues that Magadini (D) failed to meet his burden because he presented no evidence that he was unable to rent an apartment outside of Great Barrington, that he was unable to gain entry to the shelter in the nearby town, and that he would still be excluded from the local homeless shelter. The Commonwealth's (P) argument is unavailing, since an actor facing a "clear and imminent danger" is not required to conceptualize all possible alternatives. So long as the defendant's evidence, taken as true, creates a reasonable doubt as to the availability of such lawful alternatives, the defendant satisfies the third element, and, therefore, Magadini (D) has done so here. Moreover, the alternatives proposed by the Commonwealth (P) do not appear to be effective alternatives: where the only local homeless shelter had previously denied the defendant entry at 3:00 a.m. following a blizzard and had later told him he had to leave, the law does not require the defendant to continue to seek shelter there in order to demonstrate that doing so is futile. The defendant's conduct is viewed at the time of the danger, and actions that the defendant could have taken to find shelter before the dangerous condition arose do not negate the conclusion that there were no lawful alternatives available at the time of his unlawful conduct. A defendant does not have to rebut every alternative that is conceivable; rather, a defendant is required to rebut alternatives that likely would have been considered by a reasonable person in a similar situation. Also, it cannot be said that as a matter of law a homeless defendant must seek shelter outside of his or her home town in order to demonstrate a lack of lawful alternatives, and the law does not permit punishment of the homeless simply for being homeless. Once the foundational requirements are met, the necessity defense allows a jury to consider the plight of a homeless person against any harm caused by a trespass before determining criminal responsibility. Because Magadini (D) satisfied the foundational conditions entitling him to the defense, the judge's failure to instruct the jury about the defense requires a new trial. The convictions, other than the one for trespass that occurred during the summer, therefore are vacated and remanded. The conviction for the summer trespass is affirmed.

ANALYSIS

The doctrine of necessity has its roots in the notion that the law deems the lives of all persons far more valuable than any property. As the level of harm that could arise from the unlawful conduct increases, so does the requirement for considering lawful alternatives. Here, although Magadini's (D) conduct may not have been appreciated by owners, managers, and residents of the private buildings in which he sought cover, there was no evidence that his presence did, or had the potential to, cause physical harm to any persons. Accordingly, the requirement to consider alternatives could be viewed more leniently where the potential harm was only property-related than it would be viewed where the unlawful conduct had the potential to harm both persons and property.

Quicknotes

NECESSITY DEFENSE A defense to liability for unlawful activity where the conduct is unavoidable and is justified by preventing the occurrence of a more serious harm.

Uston v. Resorts International Hotel, Inc.

Card counter (P) v. Hotel (D)

N.J. Sup. Ct., 445 A.2d 370 (1982)

NATURE OF CASE: Appeal from lower court decision in favor of plaintiff.

FACT SUMMARY: Uston (P) was well known for his ability to count cards. Resorts International Hotel, Inc. (D) excluded Uston (P) from its casino because his ability increased his chances of winning.

RULE OF LAW

Owners of property open to the public do not have the right to unreasonably exclude particular members of the public.

FACTS: Uston (P) developed a system of counting cards that allowed him to win at blackjack. Uston (P) was well known for this practice and for teaching the system to others. Because of his ability to increase the chances of his winning, under the Gambling Commission's rules, Resorts International Hotel, Inc. (Resorts) (D) excluded Uston (P) from its casino. Uston (P) brought suit for access. A lower court ruled for Uston (P) and Resorts (D) appealed.

ISSUE: Do owners of property open to the public have the right to unreasonably exclude particular members of the public?

HOLDING AND DECISION: (Pashman, J.) No. Owners of property open to the public do not have the right to unreasonably exclude particular members of the public. The old common law rule gave owners of private property the absolute right to exclude members of the public from the property regardless of the nature of their use of the property. The civil rights amendments and statutes subsequently prevented owners of public facilities from excluding others based on race. To the extent that a property caters to the public, it must also take into account the rights of that public. Uston (P) did not come to the casino to disrupt the activities going on there, nor was he a security risk. Resorts (D) had no legitimate interest in excluding Uston (P) from a place to which the public was invited. Affirmed.

ANALYSIS

The current majority American rule disregards the right of reasonable access applied in the above case. Instead it grants to proprietors of amusement places an absolute right to arbitrarily eject or exclude any person consistent with state and federal civil rights laws. The majority rule may have originated in response to anti-segregation measures taken by the federal government.

Quicknotes

COMMON LAW A body of law developed through the judicial decisions of the courts as opposed to the legislative process.

STATUTE A law enacted pursuant to the legislature's power and consistent with specified procedure so that it regulates a particular activity.

Glavin v. Eckman

Neighbor (P) v. Neighbor (D)

Mass. App. Ct., 881 N.E.2d 820 (2008)

NATURE OF CASE: Appeal from jury's verdict in favor of plaintiff.

FACT SUMMARY: Eckman (D) cut down ten large oak trees on Glavin's (P) property without Glavin's (P) permission.

RULE OF LAW

Restoration costs are an appropriate measure of damages for loss of trees when the typical measures such as diminution in value of property or value of the cut timber fail to provide a fair and adequate measure of the plaintiff's damages.

FACTS: Glavin (P) and Eckman (D) owned property near each other on Martha's Vineyard, Massachusetts. In order to improve his view of the ocean, Eckman (D) sought to cut down a number of trees on adjoining property as well as trees on Glavin's (P) property. Eckman (D) asked Glavin's (P) permission to cut down ten oak trees on Glavin's (P) property. Glavin (P) denied the request. Eckman (D) subsequently hired an independent contractor to cut down the trees. The contractor cut down trees on the adjoining land owner's property, with permission, but also cut down the ten oak trees on Glavin's (P) property without any permission. Glavin (P) brought suit under G.L. c. 242 § 7 for wrongful cutting of trees on his property. A jury found for Glavin (P), and awarded him $30,000 in restoration costs based on evidence presented at trial. The trial judge then, pursuant to the statute, trebled the damages due to Eckman's (D) intentional cutting down of the trees. Eckman (D) appealed on the grounds the restoration costs are impermissible under the statute. Eckman (D) also argues that he is not liable for the actions of the independent contractor who actually cut down the trees.

ISSUE: Are restoration costs an appropriate measure of damages for loss of trees when the typical measures such as diminution in value of property or value of the cut timber fail to provide a fair and adequate measure of the plaintiff's damages?

HOLDING AND DECISION: (Grasso, J.) Yes. Restoration costs are an appropriate measure of damages for loss of trees when the typical measures such as diminution in value of property or value of the cut timber fail to provide a fair and adequate measure of the plaintiff's damages. First, it is true that normally, diminution in value of property or cut timber is used as measures of damages. Nothing in the statute, however, limits the measure of damages to those two methods. The trial judge has the discretion to allow any fair and adequate measure of damages. For restoration costs, a test of reasonableness is employed. Here, the cutting down of ten trees was significant, and was carried out willfully. The jury heard expert evidence regarding the restoration of the costs, and their award cannot be said to be unreasonable. Regarding Eckman's (D) argument that he is not liable for the actions of the independent contractor, we disagree. While the contractor had control over the means of the tree removal, Eckman (D) retained control over the scope of the project. Lastly, the judge's trebling of the damages was allowed by statute, and we are not inclined to disagree with a legislative determination that such trebling is appropriate. Affirmed.

ANALYSIS

The significant portion of this decision is its allowance of the restoration damages for tree cutting. As noted in the decision, more traditional measures of damages are most often employed for wrongful cutting of trees. Here, plaintiffs gained a valuable new tool to recover damages for similar factual scenarios.

Quicknotes

DAMAGES Monetary compensation that may be awarded by the court to a party who has sustained injury or loss to his person, property, or rights due to another party's unlawful act, omission, or negligence.

INDEPENDENT CONTRACTOR A party undertaking a particular assignment for another who retains control over the manner in which it is executed.

TREBLE DAMAGES An award of damages triple of the amount awarded by the jury, provided for by statute for violation of certain offenses.

Jacque v. Steenberg Homes, Inc.

Property owner (P) v. Company (D)

Wis. Sup. Ct., 563 N.W.2d 154 (1997)

NATURE OF CASE: Appeal from decision that vacated jury's punitive damages award.

FACT SUMMARY: The Jacques (P) brought suit against Steenberg Homes, Inc. (Steenberg) (D) claiming intentional trespass to their land when Steenberg (D) plowed a path across their field, over their protests, in order to deliver a mobile home.

RULE OF LAW

When nominal damages are awarded for an intentional trespass to land, punitive damages may also be awarded at the jury's discretion.

FACTS: Steenberg Homes, Inc. (Steenberg) (D) was delivering a mobile home. It found the easiest route of delivery was through the Jacques' (P) land. Despite the Jacques' (P) protests, Steenberg (D) plowed a path through the Jacques' (P) field. The Jacques (P) sued Steenberg (D) for intentional trespass. At trial, Steenberg (D) conceded intentional trespass but argued that punitive damages could not be awarded since no compensatory damages had been awarded. Though the jury awarded $1 in nominal damages and $100,000 in punitive damages, the circuit court set aside the punitive damages award. The court of appeals affirmed and the Jacques (P) appealed.

ISSUE: When nominal damages are awarded for an intentional trespass to land, may punitive damages also be awarded at the jury's discretion?

HOLDING AND DECISION: (Bablitch, J.) Yes. When nominal damages are awarded for an intentional trespass to land, punitive damages may also be awarded at the jury's discretion. Steenberg (D) argued that punitive damages could not be awarded by the jury without an award of compensatory damages as a matter of law. The Jacques (P) argued that the rationale supporting the compensatory damage award requirement is not applicable when the wrongful act is an intentional trespass to land. This court agrees. The rationale for the requirement is that if the individual cannot show actual harm, society has little interest in having the unlawful, but harmless, conduct deterred and punitive damages are inappropriate. The issue of whether nominal damages can support a punitive damage award in intentional trespass to land cases is one of first impression. This court has recognized that in certain circumstances of trespass, the actual harm is not the damage to the land, but the loss of the individual's right to exclude others from his property, and has implied that the loss of this right may be punished by a large damage award despite the lack of measurable harm. Thus, the compensatory damages requirement should not apply when the tort supporting the award is intentional trespass to land. Next, we consider whether the $100,000 damage award was excessive. The court must consider three factors in determining whether a punitive damage award violates the Due Process Clause: (1) the degree of reprehensibility of the conduct; (2) the disparity between the harm suffered and the award; and (3) the difference between this remedy and the penalties authorized or imposed in comparable cases. Here the $100,000 award was not excessive. Steenberg's (D) intentional trespass demonstrated an indifference and reckless disregard for the law and for the rights of others. Moreover, such an award is necessary to deter similar conduct in the future. Reversed and remanded.

ANALYSIS

The Supreme Court has recognized the interest of a landowner in the right to exclude others from his land as one of the essential property rights. The law recognizes that harm occurs in every trespass to land by the nominal damage award, whether or not actual damages are sustained. The potential harm resulting from intentional trespass to land, which if repeated might ripen into prescription or adverse possession, may result in the owner's loss of property rights. Moreover, society's interest in deterring wrongdoing supports the conclusion in this case as well.

Quicknotes

COMPENSATORY DAMAGES Measure of damages necessary to compensate victim for actual injuries suffered.

DUE PROCESS CLAUSE Language in the Fifth and Fourteenth Amendments to the United States Constitution providing that no person shall be deprived of "life, liberty, or property without due process of law."

PUNITIVE DAMAGES Damages exceeding the actual injury suffered for the purposes of punishment of the defendant, deterrence of the wrongful behavior, or comfort to the plaintiff.

TRESPASS TO LAND Physical invasion of the plaintiff's property intended and caused by the defendant's conduct.

McClure Management, LLC v. Taylor

Hotel (D) v. African American (P)

W. Va. Sup. Ct., 849 S.E.2d 604 (2020)

NATURE OF CASE: Appeal from order denying a motion for judgment as a matter of law or, alternatively, for a new trial in an action brought under a state statute prohibiting discrimination in public accommodations on the basis of race.

FACT SUMMARY: Hotel guests Taylor (P) and Turner (P), both African Americans, brought an action against the hotel operator, McClure Management, LLC (McClure Hotel *or* hotel) (D), and a hotel employee, Adams (D), alleging discrimination in violation of the West Virginia Human Rights Act (WVHRA) arising out of the denial of long-term apartment rooms based on Taylor (P) and Turner's (P) race. The jury found in favor of Taylor (P) and Turner (P), and awarded each of them $475,000.00.

RULE OF LAW

(1) A trial court does not err in denying a motion for judgment as a matter of law or, alternatively, for a new trial, in a public accommodation discrimination action where the evidence presented, viewed in the light most favorable to the nonmoving party, establishes a prima facie case of discrimination in a place of public accommodation, notwithstanding that the denial of public accommodation was only partial.

(2) A trial court does not abuse its discretion by rejecting a defendant's assertion that a jury verdict in a racial discrimination case is excessive where the jury was properly instructed on the damages it could award without objection by the defendant, the award is not monstrous, outrageous, or the product of bias or corruption, and, based on the evidence presented, the verdict seems to be fair and appropriate.

FACTS: Taylor (P) and Turner (P), both African Americans who were performing work for Price Gregory Int'l Inc. (Price Gregory) in the natural gas business, had to go to West Virginia for work. Coming from different states, they each needed a place to stay, and contacted McClure Management, LLC (McClure Hotel *or* hotel) (D) for long-term apartments. Taylor (P) called the hotel (D) and asked if they had long-term apartment rooms available. Adams (D), a hotel (D) employee who answered this call told him that long-term apartment rooms were available. However, after arriving at the McClure Hotel (D) in person and speaking with Adams (D), Taylor (P) stated that Adams (D) told him that there was a "waiting list" for the long-term apartment rooms, but he could stay in a "nightly room," which the hotel (D) referred to as a "sleeper room." The "sleeper rooms" were more expensive on a nightly basis than the long-term apartment rooms. Taylor (D) claimed that he observed White coworkers who were hired after him and who arrived at the hotel (D) after him being provided with long-term apartment rooms while he remained in a "sleeper room." He explained that he knew who was "hired in what order pretty much from who's on site at the safety meetings and who's not there." Taylor (P) asked Adams (D) why these coworkers who were hired after him and arrived at the hotel (D) after him were being provided with long-term apartment rooms when she had informed him that none were available. According to Taylor (P), Adams (D) told him that these coworkers were ahead of him on the "waiting list." Taylor (P) asserted that this could not have been the case because the coworkers had not yet been hired by Price Gregory when he arrived at the hotel (D). Turner (P) had a similar experience. Taylor (P) and Turner (P) brought their complaint to the hotel's (D) general manager, who told them that the hotel did not have a "waiting list," and referred them back to Adams (D). Shortly thereafter they were provided with long-term apartment rooms. After that, Adams (D) made disparaging remarks to Taylor (P), and also called Taylor's (P) work manager at Price Gregory to complain about Taylor (P), relating to a late payment, after which Taylor (P) did not receive more work from Price Gregory. Apparently, Adams (D) had also made disparaging remarks about Taylor (P) to the Price Gregory manager. Adams (D) also complained to Price Gregory about Turner (P), even though Turner (P) did not have any late payments. Although some of the men's White coworkers also had late payments, Adams (D) did not call Price Gregory about them. Taylor (P) and Turner (P) brought suit under the West Virginia Human Rights Act (WVHRA) against McClure Hotel (D) and Adams (D), alleging discrimination on the basis of race in a place of public accommodation. The WVHRA makes it unlawful for any person who is the owner, lessee, proprietor, manager, superintendent, agent, or employee of any place of public accommodations to refuse, withhold from or deny to any individual because of his or her race, religion, color, national origin, ancestry, sex, age, blindness or disability, either directly or indirectly, any of the accommodations, advantages, facilities, privileges, or services of the place of public accommodations. A jury returned a

Continued on next page.

verdict for Taylor (P) and Turner (P), awarding each of them $475,000.00. The hotel (D) and Adams (D) moved for judgment as a matter of law or, alternatively, for a new trial. The trial court denied the motion. On appeal to the state's highest court, the hotel (D) and Adams (D) asserted that the trial court had erroneously denied their motion on the grounds that Taylor (P) and Turner (P) failed to establish a prima facie case of discrimination under the WVHRA, and that the jury verdict was excessive. The state's highest court granted review.

ISSUE:

(1) Does a trial court err in denying a motion for judgment as a matter of law or, alternatively, for a new trial, in a public accommodation discrimination action where the evidence presented, viewed in the light most favorable to the nonmoving party, establishes a prima facie case of discrimination in a place of public accommodation, notwithstanding that the denial of public accommodation was only partial?

(2) Does a trial court abuse its discretion by rejecting a defendant's assertion that a jury verdict in a racial discrimination case is excessive where the jury was properly instructed on the damages it could award without objection by the defendant, the award is not monstrous, outrageous, or the product of bias or corruption, and, based on the evidence presented, the verdict seems to be fair and appropriate?

HOLDING AND DECISION: (Armstead, C.J.)

(1) No. A trial court does not err in denying a motion for judgment as a matter of law or, alternatively, for a new trial, in a public accommodation discrimination action where the evidence presented, viewed in the light most favorable to the nonmoving party, establishes a prima facie case of discrimination in a place of public accommodation, notwithstanding that the denial of public accommodation was only partial. To make a prima facie case of discrimination in a place of public accommodation under the West Virginia Human Rights Act (WVHRA), the complainant must prove the following elements: (a) that the complainant is a member of a protected class, (b) that the complainant attempted to avail himself or herself of the accommodations, advantages, privileges or services of a place of public accommodation, and (c) that the accommodations, advantages, privileges or services were withheld, denied, or refused to the complainant. The hotel (D) and Adams (D) do not dispute that the first two elements are satisfied, but contend that Taylor (P) and Turner (P) did not establish that the accommodations, advantages, privileges, or services of the McClure Hotel (D) were withheld, denied, or refused, since the hotel (D) provided them with "sleeper rooms" upon arrival, and long-term apartment rooms once they became available. Viewing the evidence adduced at trial in a light most favorable to Taylor (P) and Turner (P), they offered considerable evidence of the denial, refusal, and withholding of the long-term apartment rooms through the following: (1) Taylor's (P) testimony that he called the hotel, asked about long-term apartment rooms and was told these rooms were available; (2) upon appearing in person at the hotel, Taylor (P) was told that the long-term apartment rooms were not available and that he would be placed on a "waiting list"; (3) the hotel did not have a "waiting list"; (4) Taylor (P) and Turner (P) testified that they both observed White coworkers—later-hired and later-arriving—being provided with long-term apartment rooms ahead of them; (5) after observing these coworkers being provided with long-term apartment rooms ahead of them, Taylor (P) and Turner (P) testified that they asked Adams (D) why this occurred, and she again referred them to the non-existent "waiting list"; (6) Taylor (P) and Turner (P) brought their complaint to the hotel's (D) general manager who told them that the hotel did not have a "waiting list," and referred them back to Adams (D); and (7) Taylor (P) and Turner (P) testified that they were provided with long-term apartment rooms shortly after complaining to the hotel's general manager. Based on the foregoing, it is clear that Taylor (P) and Turner (P) presented ample evidence from which a jury could have concluded that they were denied long-term apartment rooms for a period of their stay on the basis of their race. Moreover, contrary to the hotel's (D) and Adam's (D) argument, Taylor (P) and Turner (P) established a prima facie claim under the WVHRA notwithstanding that there was not a total withholding of accommodations, i.e., the men were provided with "sleeper rooms" upon arrival, and subsequently were provided with long-term apartments. Such a narrow, restrictive interpretation of the WVHRA is not supported by the statute's plain language, purpose, or caselaw. The WVHRA's language does not restrict unlawful discriminatory practices to only those situations in which there has been a complete withholding of accommodations. The WVHRA is written broadly, applies to indirect denials of public accommodations, and is intended to "eliminate all discrimination in ... places of public accommodations by virtue of race." Further, although the numerous disparaging remarks Adams (D) made to Taylor (P) and Turner (P) by themselves cannot establish a claim under the WVHRA, such comments (which the hotel (D) and Adams (D) characterize as mere rudeness) may be considered when examining whether a prima facie case of discrimination was established. Taken together

Continued on next page.

with all the other evidence presented, these disparaging comments support a finding that Taylor (P) and Turner (P) established a prima facie case of public accommodation discrimination. Accordingly, the hotel's (D) and Adams's (D) assignment of error as to this issue is rejected. Affirmed as to this issue.

(2) No. A trial court does not abuse its discretion by rejecting a defendant's assertion that a jury verdict in a racial discrimination case is excessive where the jury was properly instructed on the damages it could award without objection by the defendant, the award is not monstrous, outrageous, or the product of bias or corruption, and, based on the evidence presented, the verdict seems to be fair and appropriate. First, the trial court properly instructed the jury on the damages it could award, including damages for "emotional distress, upset, humiliation, and embarrassment, and impairment to reputation." As noted in the trial court's order denying the hotel's (D) and Adams's (D) motion for judgment as a matter of law, or, alternatively, a new trial, "[w]hen it came to assessing the damages in this case, the jury was appropriately instructed, without objection by the [defendants] as to the specific language used[.]" Second, the argument that the jury verdict was excessive downplays and minimizes the evidence of racial discrimination adduced at trial. The jury heard evidence that Taylor (P) and Turner (P) were denied the long-term apartment rooms through the guise of a non-existent "waiting list"; that similarly situated White coworkers were given long-term apartment rooms immediately; that Adams (D) did not call Price Gregory to complain about a White coworker who was similarly situated to Taylor (P) regarding the late payment of rent; and testimony from both Taylor (P) and Turner (P) about the distress that this treatment caused them. Third, there was no support for the hotel's (D) and Adams's (D) speculative assertion that the jury must have entertained a mistaken view of the case. The hotel (D) and Adams (D) failed to establish that the jury's verdict was based "on its own distaste for how Adams treated, interacted with, or allegedly thought about" Taylor (P) and Turner (P). Finally, the law of the state is that courts must not set aside jury verdicts as excessive unless they are monstrous, enormous, at first blush beyond all measure, unreasonable, outrageous, and manifestly show jury passion, partiality, prejudice or corruption, or the jury's mistaken view of the case. Here, the jury verdict did not meet any of these criteria; instead, there was no reason to believe that the jury did anything other than listen to the evidence and calculate an award, based upon the instructions given to them, that they felt was just, fair, and appropriate. For all these reasons, the trial court did not abuse its discretion in denying the motion for a new trial based on the excessiveness of the verdict. Affirmed as to this issue. Affirmed.

ANALYSIS

As this case illustrates, damages for discrimination in a place of public accommodation may be awarded on the basis of such factors as emotional distress, upset, humiliation, and embarrassment, and impairment to reputation, even in the absence of a showing of out-of-pocket losses or other quantifiable damages. Here, the evidence of emotional distress, upset, humiliation, and embarrassment was the testimony of Taylor (P) and Turner (P). For example, Taylor (P) testified that he felt, among other things, "[e]mbarrassment, humiliation." Turner (P) testified that "You know, it took years for us to get to this position, you know, on our job, you know, and then for someone to call your job to destroy your livelihood, which is me taking care of my family, my kids, that hurts, that hurts me. I was embarrassed, you know, I was ashamed, you know." Apparently, the jury in this case believed the men, and awarded damages accordingly.

Quicknotes

DISCRIMINATION Unequal treatment of a class of persons.

MOTION FOR JUDGMENT AS A MATTER OF LAW One party's motion submitted any time before the case is submitted to the jury, or after a contrary verdict by the jury, requesting the court enter a judgment in its favor because no legally sufficient evidence has been brought on which a jury could find for the other party.

PRIMA FACIE CASE An action where the plaintiff introduces sufficient evidence to submit the issue to the judge or jury for determination.

Lloyd Corporation Ltd. v. Tanner

Property owner (D) v. Protestors (P)

407 U.S. 551 (1972)

NATURE OF CASE: Appeal from federal Circuit Court of Appeals decision holding that protestors (P) had a first amendment right to pass out handbills protesting the Vietnam War within a private shopping mall.

FACT SUMMARY: Tanner (P) and others passed out handbills protesting the Vietnam War within a shopping center owned privately by Lloyd Corporation, Ltd. (D). Security guards from Lloyd (D) removed them from the premises.

RULE OF LAW

An invited member of the public does not have general rights of free speech on privately owned property.

FACTS: Lloyd Corporation, Ltd. (D) owns and operates a large shopping center in Portland, Oregon. All of the stores are located in a large, multi-level building complex. The stores are accessed via the interior of the mall. There are no public streets or sidewalks within the mall. Lloyd (D) has a strict policy banning the distribution of handbills by any person or entity within the mall. Lloyd (D) does allow charitable groups such as the Boy Scouts and the American Legion to use an auditorium within the mall. Lloyd (D) also allows the Salvation Army and similar entities to solicit funds from patrons in the mall. Presidential candidates have also used the auditorium to give campaign speeches. Tanner (P) and others passed out handbills on one occasion protesting the Vietnam War. One customer of the mall complained. Lloyd's (D) security guards removed the protestors from the mall. Tanner (P) brought this suit for a declaratory judgment on the grounds his right to free speech was violated. The lower U.S. District Court (D. Oregon) and the Ninth Circuit Court of Appeals found in favor of Tanner (P). Both courts essentially held the mall was the functional equivalent of a public business district within a municipality. Accordingly, first amendment rights existed within the mall. The United States Supreme Court granted Lloyd's (D) petition for further review.

ISSUE: Does an invited member of the public have general rights of free speech on privately owned property?

HOLDING AND DECISION: (Powell, J.) No. An invited member of the public does not have general rights of free speech on privately owned property. The First and Fourteenth Amendment protect the rights of free speech and assembly against state action, not against of the owner of private property. In a prior case, this Court held that when a corporation owns an entire town and hires the local police to protect the residents, free speech rights do exist in such an entity. In that situation, the private corporation assumed all of the attributes of a municipality. That is not the case here. The mall is completely privately owned and does not provide any municipal services. The public's use of the mall is for private purposes, from shopping to dentist appointments. The sheer size of the mall also is not dispositive. One could not reasonably argue that a small retail store, open to the public, must allow handbilling on or in its premises. The same theory applies to the mall. Reversed and remanded.

DISSENT: (Marshall, J.) Lloyd's (D) mall constitutes a public business district where First Amendment rights should be protected. Lloyd (D) invites charitable organizations and presidential candidates to speak at the auditorium within the mall. Lloyd (D) also allows the Salvation Army and similar entities to solicit funds from patrons in the mall. The mall allows the public to shop, to see a dentist, and even lawyers. For many Portland residents, they will be able to receive all of their required services within the mall. If free speech is going to reach these residents, it must do so within the confines of the mall. Although some patrons may be annoyed by protestors passing out handbills, that one factor pales in comparison to the significance of First Amendment rights. As more municipalities allow these types of malls, restricting free speech rights within them will make it harder for citizens to communicate their issues with members of their community.

ANALYSIS

The essential holding of this case remains good law. The First and Fourteenth Amendments protect against only state action, not private action. However, various state supreme courts and legislatures have expanded their state constitutional rights to free speech to include large, quasi-public land, such as shopping malls.

Quicknotes

DECLARATORY JUDGMENT A judgment of the court establishing the rights of the parties.

FIRST AMENDMENT Prohibits Congress from enacting any law respecting an establishment of religion, prohibiting the free exercise of religion, abridging freedom of speech or the press, the right of peaceful assembly and the right to petition for a redress of grievances.

Matthews v. Bay Head Improvement Association

Private citizen (P) v. Homeowner's association (D)

N.J. Sup. Ct., 471 A.2d 355 (1984)

NATURE OF CASE: Action under the public trust doctrine.

FACT SUMMARY: Bay Head Improvement Association (D) permitted only members to use its beach area between 10:00 a.m. and 5:30 p.m. in the summer.

RULE OF LAW

The public's right to enjoy tidal lands includes a right of access over privately held dry sand lands.

FACTS: Bay Head Improvement Association (the Association) (D) was incorporated as a nonprofit organization to regulate and protect the privately held beaches of the Borough of Bay Head. The Association (D) owned title to 6 of the 26 beachfront lots of land and leased other properties from residents. It operated these lots as a private beach for the benefit of the community, providing lifeguards, beach cleaners, and membership police. The Association (D) limited public access to the dry sand area during certain hours of the day and times of the year. The public could access the foreshore area during low tide from the adjacent boroughs. Matthews (P) brought suit claiming that the public had the right to gain access to the tidal land across the property owned by the Association (D).

ISSUE: Does the public's right to enjoy tidal lands include a right of access over privately held dry sand lands?

HOLDING AND DECISION: (Schreiber, J.) Yes. The public's right to enjoy tidal lands includes a right of access over privately held dry sand lands. Tidal areas and the foreshore are held in the public trust to insure the public's right to use and enjoy such areas. The right to enjoy such areas is meaningless without proper access. The doctrine of public trust also requires that the public have use of the dry sand area so they may fully enjoy their right in the tidal area. Because the Association (D) is a quasi-public institution, it cannot deny the public membership to its beaches. Furthermore, the public right to enjoyment is severely limited by the fact that there are no public beaches in the borough. The public must be given access to the Association's (D) land.

ANALYSIS

The court refrained from stating that the public's interest amounted to a prescriptive easement over privately held beach land. Public use does not readily lend itself to prescription due to the difficulties involved in proving continuous use and taking. In the alternatives, courts have relied on custom and implied dedication to confer access rights.

Quicknotes

PRESCRIPTION The acquisition of an easement in or on another's property as a result of continuous use for the statutory period.

PUBLIC TRUST DOCTRINE The government holds lands that are submerged beneath the water, or that are capable of being submerged, in trust for the public's benefit.

STATE ACTION Actions brought pursuant to the Fourteenth Amendment claiming that the government violated the plaintiff's civil rights.

Martin v. City of Boise

Homeless residents (P) v. Municipality (D)

920 F.3d 584 (9th Cir. 2019)

NATURE OF CASE: Appeal from summary judgment for defendant municipality in action challenging the constitutionality of ordinances criminalizing the use by homeless individuals of public property as camping places to sit, lie, or sleep.

FACT SUMMARY: Homeless individuals (P) who had been cited for violating City of Boise (Boise) (D) ordinances criminalizing the use of public property as camping places to sit, lie, or sleep challenged the retrospective and prospective application of those ordinances as violative of the Eighth Amendment's prohibition on cruel and unusual punishment.

RULE OF LAW

The Eighth Amendment's prohibition on cruel and unusual punishment bars a municipality from prosecuting people criminally for sitting, lying, or sleeping outside on public property when those people have no home or other shelter to go to.

FACTS: The City of Boise (Boise) (D) had more homeless residents than shelters or beds that could accommodate those residents. It also had two ordinances that attempted to control its increasing homeless population. One ordinance, the "Camping Ordinance," made it a misdemeanor to use "any of the streets, sidewalks, parks, or public places as a camping place at any time." The Camping Ordinance defined "camping" as "the use of public property as a temporary or permanent place of dwelling, lodging, or residence." This Camping Ordinance was sufficiently broad that it was enforced against homeless individuals who lay bare on the ground, or covered by only a blanket. The second ordinance, the "Disorderly Conduct Ordinance," banned "[o]ccupying, lodging, or sleeping in any building, structure, or public place, whether public or private ... without the permission of the owner or person entitled to possession or in control thereof." Several former or current Boise residents (P)—some of whom were formerly or currently homeless, and who had been cited for violations of the ordinances, and most of whom had been fined and/or sentenced to time served, with some receiving additional jail time—challenged the ordinances in federal district court, both retrospectively and prospectively, contending that the ordinances violated the Eighth Amendment's prohibition on cruel and unusual punishment. The district court granted summary judgment to Boise (D). A three-judge panel of the Ninth Circuit Court of Appeals reversed and remanded. Boise (D) petitioned for rehearing and en banc review, which the Ninth Circuit denied. The Ninth Circuit then reviewed the district court's decision on remand [which again granted summary judgment to Boise (D) on the substantive issue presented].

ISSUE: Does the Eighth Amendment's prohibition on cruel and unusual punishment bar a municipality from prosecuting people criminally for sitting, lying, or sleeping outside on public property when those people have no home or other shelter to go to?

HOLDING AND DECISION: (Berzon, J.) Yes. The Eighth Amendment's prohibition on cruel and unusual punishment bars a municipality from prosecuting people criminally for sitting, lying, or sleeping outside on public property when those people have no home or other shelter to go to. The Eighth Amendment limits the criminal system in three ways. First, it limits the type of punishment the government may impose; second, it proscribes punishment "grossly disproportionate" to the severity of the crime; and third, it places substantive limits on what the government may criminalize. It is the third limitation that is pertinent here. Precedent from the U.S. Supreme Court has sought to delineate the limits on what government may criminalize. In *Robinson v. California*, 370 U.S. 660 (1962), the Court held that a statute that made the "status" of narcotic addiction a criminal offense was invalid. Six years later, in *Powell v. Texas*, 392 U.S. 514 (1968), the Court in a plurality decision upheld a law making public drunkenness a criminal offense. In doing so, the Court distinguished *Robinson* on the ground that the statute in *Robinson* criminalized "status," whereas the statute in *Powell* criminalized conduct, albeit involuntary conduct. In other words, the *Powell* court explained that *Robinson* did not deal with the question of whether certain conduct cannot constitutionally be punished because it is, in some sense, "involuntary." The four dissenting justices in *Powell*, along with one justice who concurred in the result only, however, took the position that the Eighth Amendment prohibits government from punishing an involuntary act or condition if it is the unavoidable consequence of one's status or being. This principle compels the conclusion that the Eighth Amendment prohibits the imposition of criminal penalties for sitting, sleeping, or lying outside on public property for homeless individuals who cannot obtain shelter. Whether sitting, lying, and sleeping are defined as acts or conditions, they are universal and unavoidable consequences of being human. Moreover, any conduct at issue here is involuntary and inseparable from status—they are one and the same,

Continued on next page.

given that human beings are biologically compelled to rest, whether by sitting, lying, or sleeping. Thus, just as the state may not criminalize the state of being "homeless in public places," the state may not criminalize conduct that is an unavoidable consequence of being homeless—namely sitting, lying, or sleeping on the streets. This holding is narrow: It in no way dictates to government that it must provide shelter to the homeless, or that it must permit anyone who wishes to sit, lie, or sleep on the streets at any time and at any place. It only prohibits government from criminalizing indigent, homeless people for sleeping outdoors, on public property, on the false premise they have a choice in the matter when there are more homeless in a jurisdiction than there are beds for them in shelters.

DISSENT: (Smith, J.) The majority panel's decision shackles the hands of public officials trying to redress the serious societal problem of homelessness, which in large part is the result of legislative policy decisions. However, neither the criminal justice system nor the judiciary is equipped to resolve such a problem. Notwithstanding these limitations of government, criminalizing conduct that results from these governmental shortcomings is not unconstitutional. The well-meaning majority panel instead creates new constitutional rights out of whole cloth, and, thereby impermissibly makes public policy. First, determining the precise number of homeless in a given jurisdiction on any given day or night can be a monumental task. In some large cities, such a task is impossible, and, for some jurisdictions, not financially feasible. This will require such municipalities to stop enforcing laws that prohibit public sleeping and camping, and effectively permits homeless individuals to sleep and live wherever they wish on most public property. The ramifications of the panel's opinion could extend to the striking down of laws that prohibit public defecation and urination, since such bodily functions are life-sustaining activities that no one can resist. Although the suffering of the homeless is undeniable, the Eighth Amendment is not a vehicle through which to critique public policy choices or to hamstring a local government's enforcement of its criminal code. The case should have been reconsidered en banc.

ANALYSIS

The court's holding does not cover individuals who do have access to adequate temporary shelter, whether because they have the means to pay for it or because it is realistically available to them for free but they choose not to use it. Nor does the decision mean that a jurisdiction with insufficient shelter can never criminalize the act of sleeping outside. Even where shelter is unavailable, an ordinance prohibiting sitting, lying, or sleeping outside at particular times or in particular locations might well be constitutionally permissible. So, too, might an ordinance barring the obstruction of public rights of way or the erection of certain structures. Whether some other ordinance is consistent with the Eighth Amendment will depend, as here, on whether it punishes a person for lacking the means to live out the universal and unavoidable consequences of being human in the way the ordinance prescribes.

Quicknotes

CRUEL AND UNUSUAL PUNISHMENT Punishment that is excessive or disproportionate to the offense committed; it is prohibited by the Eighth Amendment to the United States Constitution.

EN BANC The hearing of a matter by all the judges of the court, rather than only the necessary quorum.

SUMMARY JUDGMENT Judgment rendered by a court in response to a motion made by one of the parties, claiming that the lack of a question of material fact in respect to an issue warrants disposition of the issue without consideration by the jury.

CHAPTER 2

Competing Justifications for Property

Quick Reference Rules of Law

Johnson v. M'Intosh

Landowner (P) v. Landowner (D)

21 U.S. 543 (1823)

NATURE OF CASE: Appeal from action of ejectment.

FACT SUMMARY: Johnson (P) claimed title to a parcel of land through a grant from Native Americans, while M'Intosh (D) claimed the land based on a grant from the newly formed United States government.

RULE OF LAW

The act of discovery gives the discovering sovereign the power to extinguish the native title of occupancy.

FACTS: In 1763 the King of Britain proclaimed that no British subject could purchase or acquire the land reserved to Native Americans. In 1775, the Tabac Indians conveyed a tract of land in Virginia to Louis Vivant. Thomas Jefferson succeeded to a portion of the lands acquired by Louis Vivant and willed it to his heir Johnson (P) upon his death. In 1776, the colony of Virginia declared its independence from British rule and subsequently acceded to the United States. Fourteen years later, the United States government sold the land in question to M'Intosh (D), who then took possession of the land. Johnson (P) brought an action for ejectment against M'Intosh (D) based on his prior claim. The trial court ruled against Johnson (P), and he appealed.

ISSUE: Does the act of discovery give the discovering sovereign the power to extinguish the native title of occupancy?

HOLDING AND DECISION: (Marshall, C.J.) Yes. The act of discovery gives the discovering sovereign the power to extinguish the native title of occupancy. Although the British government acknowledged Indian possession of the land by the act of discovery, they retained the right to terminate that possession at any time. The Tabac Indians, at most, had the right to convey possession. The discovering country held title to the land. The United States took over Great Britain's claim to title by treaty and, thus, was the party with the authority to transfer the title. Therefore, Johnson (P) was not granted valid title. Affirmed.

ANALYSIS

The Court claims to be applying a kinder rule than that of conquest because it is admitting the existence of a Native American right to occupy the land. However, the Court then states that right to possession is only valid so long as the Native Americans were peaceful inhabitants, thereby immediately negating their rights. Moreover, since absolute title cannot exist at the same time in different governments over the same land, the Court reasons that it would be inconsistent to vest absolute title to the Native Americans as a distinct nation and country.

Quicknotes

DEED A signed writing transferring title to real property from one person to another.

EJECTMENT An action to oust someone in possession of real property unlawfully and to restore possession to the party lawfully entitled to it.

TENANTS-IN-COMMON Two or more people holding an interest in property, each with equal right to its use and possession; interests may be partitioned, sold, conveyed, or devised.

The Antelope

[Seized foreign vessel containing a cargo of Africans]

23 U.S. 66 (1825)

NATURE OF CASE: Appeal from judgment awarding ownership of individuals alleged to be slaves.

FACT SUMMARY: The United States seized the *Antelope,* a ship owned by Spanish subjects that had been engaged in the slave trade and that had been captured off the coast of Africa by pirates on a ship flying the flag of the Oriental Republic. When seized, the *Antelope* (renamed the *General Ramirez* by the pirates, who were mostly U.S. citizens) contained a cargo of 281 Africans, some of whom had been captured by the pirates from different American and Portuguese ships. Spain and Portugal claimed that many of the Africans aboard the *Antelope* belonged to those nations' subjects.

RULE OF LAW

The mere presence on board a ship engaged in the slave trade of individuals alleged to be slaves is not sufficient proof of ownership of those individuals.

FACTS: The ship *Arraganta* was a privateer ship—a warship with a governmental commission to prey on an enemy's commerce—manned by a officers and crew who were U.S. citizens. The ship flew the flag of the Oriental Republic, a Latin American revolutionary government seeking independence from Spain and Portugal. Off the coast of Africa, the *Arraganta* captured an American vessel, from which were taken 25 Africans. The *Arraganta* also captured several Portuguese vessels, from which Africans also were taken, and a Spanish vessel, the *Antelope,* from which a considerable number of Africans were taken. The *Arraganta* and the *Antelope* then sailed together to the coast of Brazil, where the *Arraganta* was wrecked, and its master and a great part of its crew were made prisoners. The rest of the crew, with the armament of the *Arraganta,* were transferred to the *Antelope,* which, thus armed, assumed the name the *General Ramirez,* under the command of John Smith, a citizen of the United States; and on board this vessel were all the Africans who had been captured by the *Arraganta* in the course of its voyage. The *Antelope* (now called the *General Ramirez*), thus freighted, was found hovering near the coast of the United States by a revenue cutter. The ship was seized because it was suspected of being used either for piracy or for smuggling slaves (which was outlawed in the United States) and brought into a Georgia port for adjudication as to whom, if anyone, the Africans belonged. There were 281 Africans on the ship when it was seized. The Portuguese and Spanish governments, respectively, claimed ownership of a great number of the Africans on behalf of their subjects, with the Portuguese government asserting that at least 130 Africans were the property of its subjects. Spain presented evidence that 93 of the Africans had been enslaved by Spanish subjects. However, no proof was presented as to ownership by Portuguese subjects. The United States opposed Spain's and Portugal's claims. The Circuit Court for Georgia granted freedom to the Africans taken from the American vessel and divided the remainder between Spain and Portugal. The United States appealed, claiming the Africans were entitled to their freedom, and the United States Supreme Court granted review.

ISSUE: Is the mere presence on board a ship engaged in the slave trade of individuals alleged to be slaves sufficient proof of ownership of those individuals?

HOLDING AND DECISION: (Marshall, C.J.) No. The mere presence on board a ship engaged in the slave trade of individuals alleged to be slaves is not sufficient proof of ownership of those individuals. Although civilized nations have increasingly come to believe that slavery is unlawful, and although it can hardly be denied that slavery is contrary to the law of nature, the law of nations, which places nations on equal footing with each other, still has not outlawed slavery, since it is still legal in many nations, including the United States. Therefore, as a matter of international law, slavery is legal in those nations that have not outlawed it, and ownership of slaves as property in such countries must be honored by other nations. However, when a claim is made that individuals aboard a ship that has been seized, as here regarding the *Antelope,* are slaves, sufficient proof to support such a claim must be presented. Here, Spain was able to provide such proof regarding 93 of the Africans. Although proof was offered that several Africans were taken from ships that flew Portuguese flags, this alone is insufficient to prove that those individuals were rightfully acquired as slaves, especially since no Portuguese claimant has come forward with proof of ownership. Accordingly, except for those individuals proved to have rightfully been acquired as slaves by Spanish subjects, the remainder of the African individuals must be released to the United States, to be disposed of according to law. Affirmed in part and reversed in part.

ANALYSIS

In support of the Spanish claim, evidence was produced that showed (1) the documents under which the

Continued on next page.

Antelope sailed from Havana, Cuba, on the voyage on which the ship was captured, (2) the ship was owned by a Spanish house of trade in Havana, (3) the ship was employed in the business of purchasing slaves, and (4) the ship had purchased and taken on board a considerable number when the ship was seized as prize by the *Arraganta*. The United States Supreme Court was divided as to whether such proof was sufficient to prove title to the Africans in the Spanish claimants, and, therefore, the issue was left undecided by the Court. Accordingly, much of the Circuit Court's decree, which directed restitution to the Spanish claimants for the Africans found on board the *Antelope* when it was captured by the *Arraganta*, was effectively affirmed.

Quicknotes

RESTITUTION The return or restoration to rightful owner to prevent unjust enrichment.

International News Service v. Associated Press

Wire service (D) v. Wire service (P)

248 U.S. 215 (1918)

NATURE OF CASE: Appeal from granting of injunctive relief.

FACT SUMMARY: Associated Press (AP) (P) sued to enjoin International News Service (D) from publishing as its own, news stories obtained from early editions of AP (P) publications.

RULE OF LAW

Publication for profit of news obtained from other news-gathering enterprises is a misappropriation of a property right.

FACTS: Associated Press (AP) (P) sued International News Service (INS) (D) for the latter's admitted use of AP (P) news stories in INS (D) publications. INS (D) would obtain advance publication of AP (P) news and would then use such in its newspapers. AP (P) contended it had a proprietary right to all news it gathered through the efforts of its contributors. INS (D) contended any such right terminated upon its first publication. The court of appeals issued AP (P) an injunction, and the United States Supreme Court granted a hearing.

ISSUE: Is the publication for profit of news obtained from other news-gathering enterprises a misappropriation of a property right?

HOLDING AND DECISION: (Pitney, J.) Yes. Publication for profit of news obtained from other news-gathering enterprises is a misappropriation of a property right. News itself is a collection of observable facts that obviously cannot be owned vis-à-vis the public at large. The nonprofit communication of news, regardless of source, is endemic in a free society and involves no property right. However, when two competing news organizations are involved, each gaining its livelihood from beating the other's deadline, the use of such news, for profit, is a misappropriation of the other's product. As a result, injunctive relief is properly issued. Affirmed.

DISSENT: (Holmes, J.) There is no general property right held in the combination of words or the thoughts and facts expressed by those words. Even if it took some labor and genius to produce that combination another person is not excluded from using those same words. However, another ground supporting AP (P) in this instance is that of unfair trade. If its words are repeated in such a way by any competitor, including INS (D), that produces a misrepresentation that materially injures it, then that type of appropriation is actionable. If a competing news service capitalizes upon its competitor's enterprise and expense and releases a contemporaneous story implying that it is the original source, then that amounts to being a fraud. It is a question of how strong an infusion of fraud is necessary to turn a flavor into a poison. The dose seems strong enough here to need a remedy from the law. Having not given proper attribution to the true source of the news reported, INS (D) should be enjoined from publishing news obtained from AP (P) for a number of hours following its publication unless it gives the proper attribution to the true sources of the reporting.

DISSENT: (Brandeis, J.) The issue is whether INS (D) was enjoined in this case because AP (P) gathered the news first or because INS (D) did not reveal the source of the stories it had taken from AP (P) editions. AP (P) contends its news stories are the product of its time and labor, and therefore constitute property deserving of legal protection. However, the law protects only certain creations of the mind, such as literary efforts, the arts, and inventions. These are all properly protected by copyright statutes. The knowledge and property AP (P) seeks to protect has never been held to deserve protection in the past. Also, INS's (D) manner of using the stories does not constitute unfair commercial practice. There is no breach of contract or fraud involved in INS's (D) manner of purchasing AP (P) newspapers on the open market. Lastly, INS's (D) failure to cite AP (P) as its source does not run afoul of any current copyright laws. Courts are not the proper place for a determination of whether AP (P) has a claim here. The legislature could review such matters and determine that AP's (P) arguments here deserve some measure of protection.

ANALYSIS

Some commentators suggest this case as a prime example of the "first in time–first in right" principle of ownership. Some go so far as to argue it provides authority for the proposition that all things created, either tangible or intangible, belong to the creator. This expands the reach of this case beyond news gathering and into any area wherein exclusivity of design or idea is important. This would include everything from clothing design to computer programming.

Continued on next page.

Quicknotes

COPYRIGHT Refers to the exclusive rights granted to an artist pursuant to Article I, section 8, clause 8 of the United States Constitution over the reproduction, display, performance, distribution, and adaptation of his work for a period prescribed by statute.

INJUNCTION A court order requiring a person to do or prohibiting that person from doing a specific act.

MISAPPROPRIATION The unlawful use of another's property or funds.

Bayliss v. Bayliss

Ex-wife (P) v. Ex-husband (D)

Ala. Sup. Ct., 550 So. 2d 986 (1989)

NATURE OF CASE: Appeal from decision regarding payment of college expenses.

FACT SUMMARY: Cherry Bayliss (P) sought to have her ex-husband (D) contribute to their son's college costs.

RULE OF LAW

Alabama trial courts may order divorcing parents to provide for the college educations of their children.

FACTS: Cherry Bayliss (P) and John Bayliss (D) were divorced when their son Patrick was 12 years old. Six years later, Cherry (P) filed a petition to modify the divorce judgment to require that John (D) help pay for Patrick's college costs. Cherry (P) asserted that John (D) had refused to pay although he had ample financial resources. [The lower court ruled that John Bayliss need not contribute to the college expenses. Cherry Bayliss appealed.]

ISSUE: May Alabama trial courts order divorcing parents to provide for the college educations of their children?

HOLDING AND DECISION: (Houston, J.) Yes. Alabama trial courts may order divorcing parents to provide for the college educations of their children. Alabama law provides that the courts may give custody and education to either parent upon granting a divorce. Since 1926, state courts have increasingly determined that college education is a legally necessary expense. Since 1983, Alabama courts have acknowledged that certain necessary support may be required for children who have reached 18 years of age, the age of majority. It is a reasonable interpretation of "children" to include offspring over the age of majority. In the present case, the trial court may order John Bayliss (D) to pay Patrick's college costs if it appears that he probably would assist if there had been no divorce. Therefore, the case is remanded to make this determination. Reversed.

ANALYSIS

States are split on this issue. Numerous states agree with Alabama's position. On the other hand, some courts have ruled that when children reach the age of majority, all support duties are ended. See, e.g., *Dowling v. Dowling*, 679 P.2d 480 (Alaska 1984).

Quicknotes

NONCUSTODIAL PARENT A parent who is not awarded the primary care and control of a child by the court in a dissolution or separation proceeding.

STARE DECISIS Doctrine whereby courts follow legal precedent unless there is good cause for departure.

Ex parte Christopher

[Parties are not identified.]

Ala. Sup. Ct., 145 So. 3d 60 (2013)

NATURE OF CASE: Appeal from order requiring a divorced parent to pay post-minority educational support. [The complete procedural posture of the case is not presented in the casebook extract.]

FACT SUMMARY: Carolyn, the divorced mother of C.C., a 19-year-old, argued that she could not be ordered to pay a portion of C.C.'s college expenses, contending that a trial court was not authorized to award post-minority educational support when such application was made before the child attained the age of majority.

RULE OF LAW

A child-custody statute, which provides that upon divorce a court may "give the custody and education of the children of the marriage to either father or mother," does not authorize a court to award post-minority educational support for a child when application is made before the child attains the age of majority.

FACTS: Carolyn and Phillip divorced in 2010. In 2011, four days before one of their children, C.C., turned 19, Phillip petitioned the trial court to order Carolyn to pay a portion of C.C.'s college expenses. Carolyn answered that she was financially unable to contribute to C.C.'s college education and that precedent from the state's highest court, in *Ex parte Bayliss*, 550 So. 2d 986 (Ala.1989), authorizing awards of post-minority educational support, had to be reversed. On the basis of *Bayliss*, the trial court ordered Carolyn to pay 25 percent of C.C.'s college expenses of $9,435 per semester under the state's child-custody statute, which provided that: "Upon granting a divorce, the court may give the custody and education of the children of the marriage to either father or mother, as may seem right and proper. . . ." Carolyn appealed, and the state's highest court granted review to determine if it had correctly decided *Bayliss*.

ISSUE: Does a child-custody statute, which provides that upon divorce a court may "give the custody and education of the children of the marriage to either father or mother," authorize a court to award post-minority educational support for a child when application is made before the child attains the age of majority?

HOLDING AND DECISION: (Moore, C.J.) No. A child-custody statute, which provides that upon divorce a court may "give the custody and education of the children of the marriage to either father or mother," does not authorize a court to award post-minority educational support for a child when application is made before the child attains the age of majority. The statute neither defines "children" nor designates when a child becomes an adult and thus ineligible for parental support. Thus, the issue in interpreting the statute is to determine the legislature's intent. The definition of the term "child" is made in the context of the "parent-child relationship," which a leading legal dictionary defines in such a way as to make clear that "child" refers to a minor child that is supported by the parent, and whose educational needs are met by the parent. Accordingly, the term "children" in the statute unambiguously refers to minors. This is supported by the common law, which defined "child" in the divorce context as a minor, and under which the parental-support obligation ceased at the age of majority. In 1983, this Court recognized an exception to the ordinary and common-law definition of "child" as a minor in favor of a majority trend in other jurisdictions to require a noncustodial parent to support a disabled child past the age of majority. From that recognition, the Court in *Bayliss*, viewing "children" as "dependents," further expanded the obligations of noncustodial parents to encompass college payments for children who had passed the age of majority—an obligation never recognized at common law. *Bayliss*, therefore, was incorrectly decided. When the legislature reduced the age of majority in 1975 from 21 to 19, the Court did not gain the authority to raise the age back to 21 or higher to serve any kind of public policy purposes. By reweighing and altering that balance as it pertains to college education, the *Bayliss* Court improperly overrode the statutory designation of the age of majority. The *Bayliss* Court openly departed from the principle of stare decisis. By reversing *Bayliss* and returning to the legislature the power to decide if post-minority educational support should be authorized in a divorce case, this Court does not make new law but, instead, corrects the prior misinterpretation of the law as it is. Thus, this decision is remedial, returning the stream of judicial power to its proper channel. Reversed and remanded.

DISSENT: (Shaw, J.) The focus of the Court's interpretation of the child-custody statute at issue should have been on the phrase "children of the marriage," not just "children." The plain language of this phrase refers to the offspring of the divorcing parents' marriage, so that both adult children of married parents and minor children of married parents are "the children of the marriage." By the ordinary and plain usage of the phrase "children of the

Continued on next page.

marriage," C.C. is the mother's and the father's child and one of the "children of the marriage" even though he is not a minor. This phrase is sufficiently clear to apply to this case, and the majority erred in focusing its interpretive inquiry on just "children."

ANALYSIS

A minority of states permit judges to order noncustodial parents to pay for post-minority education expenses if they find that the parent would have paid for such expenses if not for the divorce, and a majority of jurisdictions do not permit involuntary orders of support for post-secondary education. This may be because, as the majority points out in rebuttal to Justice Shaw's dissent, reading the phrase "children of the marriage" in a child-custody statute as not limited to minor children would produce the absurd and unjust result that a court could assign custody of the adult children of a marriage to one of the divorcing parties, thus stripping the children of their adult status and reducing them to the status of minors subject by law to the direction and control of their parents.

Quicknotes

STARE DECISIS Doctrine whereby courts follow legal precedent unless there is good cause for departure.

Pierson v. Post

Hunter (D) v. Hunter (P)

N.Y. Sup. Ct. of Judicature, 2 Am. Dec. 264 (1805)

NATURE OF CASE: Action of trespass on the case.

FACT SUMMARY: Post (P) was hunting a fox. Pierson (D), knowing this, killed the fox and carried it off.

RULE OF LAW

Property in wild animals is acquired only by occupancy, and pursuit alone does not constitute occupancy or vest any right in the pursuer.

FACTS: Post (P) found a fox upon certain wild, uninhabited, unpossessed wasteland. He and his dogs began hunting and pursuing the fox. Knowing that the fox was being hunted by Post (P) and within Post's (P) view, Pierson (D) killed the fox and carried it off. The trial court rendered judgment for Post (P).

ISSUE: Where property in wild animals is acquired only by occupancy, does pursuit alone constitute occupancy or vest a right in the pursuer?

HOLDING AND DECISION: (Tompkins, J.) No. Property in wild animals is acquired only by occupancy, and pursuit alone does not constitute occupancy or vest any right in the pursuer. One authority holds that actual bodily seizure is not always necessary to constitute possession of wild animals. The mortal wounding of an animal or the trapping or intercepting of animals so as to deprive them of their natural liberty will constitute occupancy. However, here, Post (P) only showed pursuit. Hence, there was no occupancy or legal right vested in Post (P), and the fox became Pierson's (D) property when he killed and carried it off. The purpose of this rule is that if the pursuit of animals without wounding them or restricting their liberty were held to constitute a basis for an action against others for intercepting and killing the animals, "it would prove a fertile source of quarrels and litigation." Reversed.

DISSENT: (Livingston, J.) A new rule should be adopted—that property in wild animals may be acquired without bodily touch, provided the pursuer be in reach or have a reasonable prospect of taking the animals.

ANALYSIS

The ownership of wild animals is in the state for the benefit of all her people. A private person cannot acquire exclusive rights to a wild animal except by taking and reducing it to actual possession in a lawful manner or by a grant from the government. After the animal has been lawfully subjected to control, the ownership becomes absolute as long as the restraint lasts. Mere ownership of the land that an animal happens to be on does not constitute such a reduction of possession as to give the landowner a property right in the animal, except as against a mere trespasser who goes on such land for the purpose of taking the animal.

Quicknotes

OCCUPANCY Period of time during which a party possesses and uses real property.

TRESPASS Unlawful interference with, or damage to, the real or personal property of another.

Popov v. Hayashi

Baseball fan (P) v. Baseball fan (D)

Cal. Super. Ct., 2002 WL 31833731 (2002)

NATURE OF CASE: Action for conversion, trespass to chattels, injunctive relief, and constructive trust.

FACT SUMMARY: Both Popov (P) and Hayashi (D) intended to establish and maintain control over a baseball that gave Barry Bonds his 73rd home run in 2001, but just as Popov (P) was getting it in his glove, a crowd engulfed him, and brought him to the ground. Hayashi (D), who was near Popov (P) and who also was brought to the ground by the crowd, found the ball and pocketed it. Popov (P) claimed he had established sufficient possession of the ball to gain title to it and brought suit to compel Hayashi (D) to return the ball to him.

RULE OF LAW

Where an actor undertakes significant but incomplete steps to achieve possession of a piece of abandoned personal property and the effort is interrupted by the unlawful acts of others, the actor has a legally cognizable pre-possessory interest in the property sufficient to support a claim of conversion.

FACTS: Barry Bonds, a professional baseball player, hit a record-setting 73rd home run on October 7, 2001. On that day, Popov (P) and Hayashi (D) and many others had positioned themselves in an area of the stadium where Bonds hit the greatest number of home runs in the hopes of catching a record-setting ball (so they brought their baseball gloves with them). The ball hit by Bonds initially landed in Popov's (P) glove, but it was not clear whether the ball was secure there, as Popov (P) may have lost his balance while reaching for the ball. However, even as the ball was going into his glove, a crowd engulfed him and he was tackled and brought to the ground, with people hitting and grabbing him. Hayashi (D), who had been near Popov (P), was also forced by the crowd to the ground, where he saw the ball. He pocketed it and revealed it only when a camera was trained on him, presumably because he wanted proof that he was the owner of the ball. Popov (P), seeing the ball, grabbed for it, believing it to be his, but Hayashi (D) refused to give it to him. Popov (P) then brought suit for conversion, trespass to chattels, injunctive relief, and constructive trust.

ISSUE: Where an actor undertakes significant but incomplete steps to achieve possession of a piece of abandoned personal property and the effort is interrupted by the unlawful acts of others, does the actor have a legally cognizable pre-possessory interest in the property sufficient to support a claim of conversion?

HOLDING AND DECISION: (McCarthy, J.) Yes. Where an actor undertakes significant but incomplete steps to achieve possession of a piece of abandoned personal property and the effort is interrupted by the unlawful acts of others, the actor has a legally cognizable pre-possessory interest in the property sufficient to support a claim of conversion. As an initial matter, there was no trespass to chattels—which requires injury to the chattel—because the ball itself was not damaged and because Popov (P) did not claim that Hayashi (D) interfered with his use and enjoyment of the ball. If there was a wrong at all, it was conversion, which is the wrongful exercise of dominion over the personal property of another. One who has neither title, nor possession, nor any right to possession may not assert a conversion claim. The key issue, therefore, is whether Popov (P) achieved possession or the right to it. "Possession," however, does not have one meaning; the meaning varies depending on the context in which it is used. Some guidelines, however, do exist, e.g., that possession requires both physical control over an item and intent to control it and exclude others from it. Here, Popov (P) clearly had the requisite intent, so the issue is whether he had exclusive dominion and control over the ball. Possession in this context is based on custom and what is physically possible. Here, "not only is it physically possible for a person to acquire unequivocal dominion and control of an abandoned baseball, but fans generally expect a claimant to have accomplished as much." Because Popov (P) did not establish by preponderance of the evidence that he would have retained control of the ball after all momentum ceased and after any incidental contact with other people or objects, he did not achieve full possession. This conclusion does not resolve the case, however, because Popov (P) was attacked illegally by the crowd, and because, therefore, it is unknown whether he would have retained control over the ball absent the crowd's actions. Because Popov (P) has a legally protected pre-possessory interest in the ball, he may advance a legitimate claim to the ball. Hayashi (D), too, was a victim of the crowd's illegal activity, but was able to extricate himself from the crowd. Although Hayashi (D) exercised complete dominion and control over the ball, the ball was encumbered by the qualified pre-possessory interest of Popov (P). Thus, awarding the ball to either of the two parties is unfair to the other. Both have a superior claim to the ball as against the world, but not against each other; they are equally entitled to the ball.

Continued on next page.

Because the court sits in equity, it may devise an equitable solution to this problem. Here, that solution is equitable division, whereby both Popov (P) and Hayashi (D) have an equal and undivided interest in the ball. Accordingly, Popov's (P) conversion claim is sustained only as to his equal and undivided interest.

ANALYSIS

The parties agreed that before Bonds hit the ball, it belonged to Major League Baseball, but that at the time it was hit, it became intentionally abandoned property. Also, to effectuate its decision, the court ordered the sale of the ball, with the proceeds being equally split between the two men. The ball ultimately sold for $450,000 – Hayashi (D) estimated that his share would only cover his legal fees.

Quicknotes

CONSTRUCTIVE TRUST A trust that arises by operation of law whereby the court imposes a trust upon property lawfully held by one party for the benefit of another, as a result of some wrongdoing by the party in possession so as to avoid unjust enrichment.

CONVERSION Act of depriving an owner of his property without permission or justification.

INJUNCTIVE RELIEF A court order issued as a remedy, requiring a person to do, or prohibiting that person from doing, a specific act.

POSSESSORY INTEREST The right to possess particular real property to the exclusion of others.

TRESPASS TO CHATTELS Action for damages sustained as a result of defendant's unlawful interference with plaintiff's personal property.

Elliff v. Texon Drilling Co.

Landowner (P) v. Oil company (D)

Tex. Sup. Ct., 210 S.W.2d 558 (1948)

NATURE OF CASE: Appeal from reversal of award of damages in negligence action.

FACT SUMMARY: Texon Drilling Co. (D) argued that it should not be liable to the Elliffs (D) after it caused severe damage to the Elliffs' oil drilling operations.

RULE OF LAW

The law of capture does not insulate an adjacent landowner from damages caused by the wrongful drainage of gas and distillate from beneath the land of another.

FACTS: Texon Drilling Co. (Texon) (D) was drilling for oil on land adjacent to the Elliffs' (P) land. The Elliffs (P) owned the surface of their land, as well as an interest in the oil and gas underlying it. They too were involved in drilling on their own land. Texon's (D) well blew out, cratered, and caught fire. The Elliffs' (P) well was destroyed as a result of this blowout, as was the surface of their land, some of their cattle, and a great portion of the underlying mineral reservoir. The Elliffs (P) brought suit for damages, claiming that the blowout was caused by Texon's (D) negligent failure to use the proper drilling mud. The trial court awarded damages. The court of appeals reversed and remanded, stating that the Elliffs (P) could not receive damages for the loss of the mineral estate based on the law of capture since they had no rights in the gas once it migrated from their land. The Elliffs (P) appealed.

ISSUE: Does the law of capture insulate an adjacent landowner from damages caused by the wrongful drainage of gas and distillate from beneath the land of another?

HOLDING AND DECISION: (Folley, J.) No. The law of capture does not insulate an adjacent landowner from damages caused by the wrongful drainage of gas and distillate from beneath the land of another. The law of capture states that minerals belong to the party that actually produces them, although part of the minerals, if they are oil or gas, may have migrated from adjoining lands. In other words, there is no liability for reasonable and legitimate drainage from the common pool. However, this does not give any owner the right to waste the gas. In this case, the waste and destruction of the Elliffs' (P) gas was not a legitimate drainage or a lawful appropriation of it. Therefore the Elliffs (P) did not lose their right or title to the gas under the law of capture. Moreover, Texon (D) had a common-law duty to exercise due care to avoid injury to the property of others. Since it breached this duty, it should be held liable. Reversed.

ANALYSIS

The court's holding takes into account that advancing technology permits the determination of the approximate amount of oil and gas located in a common pool. However, the rule of capture no longer comes into play vis-à-vis "fugitive" minerals. Instead, oil and natural gas mining is highly regulated by state and federal law.

Quicknotes

NEGLIGENCE Conduct falling below the standard of care that a reasonable person would demonstrate under similar conditions.

Christy v. Scott

Landowner (P) v. Trespasser (D)

55 U.S. 282 (1852)

NATURE OF CASE: Appeal from lower court decision finding that an ejected landowner had no rights to the land at issue against a defendant-trespasser.

FACT SUMMARY: Christy (P) was in actual possession of a tract of land when Scott (D), a trespasser with no title to the land, ejected him.

RULE OF LAW

A person in actual possession of land has strong enough rights to the land to recover it from a mere trespasser who has no right or title to the land.

FACTS: Christy (P) was in actual possession to a tract of land. Scott (D) ejected him from the land, claiming that the title given to Christy (P) was null and void. Scott (D), a trespasser, had no right or title to the land and was never in possession of it before ejecting Christy (P). Christy (P) brought this action seeking recovery of his land. The United States District Court (D. Texas) found in favor of Scott (D), essentially on the grounds that Christy's (P) title was null and void because it was obtained fraudulently from the State of Texas. The United States Supreme Court granted Christy's (P) petition for further review.

ISSUE: Does a person in actual possession of land have strong enough rights to the land to recover it from a mere trespasser who has no right or title to the land?

HOLDING AND DECISION: (Curtis, J.) Yes. A person in actual possession of land has strong enough rights to the land to recover it from a mere trespasser who has no right or title to the land. Scott (D) does not deny that he has no prior right or title to the land in question. Rather, his defense to the action is that Christy's (P) title to the land is null and void. A mere intruder cannot eject one in possession of the land and then argue that title resides with a third party. As between the two parties in this case, Christy (P), as actual possessor of the land, may recover the land against a simple trespasser. The Court does not decide whether Christy (P) has rights to the land as against the State of Texas, which is not a party to this action. Reversed and remanded.

ANALYSIS

This case underscores the primacy of actual possession within the complicated layers of property rights. One who is in actual possession will always have more rights to the land than a mere trespasser. The underlying rationale for the rule is the right to peaceable possession. The law protects actual possessors of land against all except those who have proper title to the land. One who obtains land through force will not obtain any rights to the land.

Quicknotes

ACTUAL POSSESSION Having direct, immediate, and physical control over real property. Unless the possessor is a trespasser, one in actual possession will have superior rights to the property over all others except for one with proper, legal title to the property.

POSSESSION The holding of property with the right of disposition.

TITLE The right of possession over property.

TRESPASSERS Persons present on the land of another without the knowledge or express permission of the owner, and to whom only a minimum duty of care is owed for injuries incurred while on the premises.

Armory v. Delamirie

Jewel finder (P) v. Goldsmith (D)

K.B., 93 Eng. Rep. 664 (1722)

NATURE OF CASE: Action in trover to recover the value of personal property.

FACT SUMMARY: Armory (P) found a jewel. He took the jewel to Delamirie (D), a goldsmith, for appraisal. Delamirie's (D) apprentice removed the stones, which Delamirie (D) refused to return.

RULE OF LAW

A finder of chattel has title superior to all but the rightful owner upon which he may maintain an action at law or in equity.

FACTS: Armory (P), a chimneysweeper's boy, found a jewel, which he took to Delamirie's (D) goldsmith shop to learn what it was. Delamirie's (D) apprentice, under the pretense of weighing the jewel, removed the stones from the setting and told his master the value. Delamirie (D) offered Armory (P) three halfpence for the stones, but he refused. Delamirie (D) returned the setting without the stones.

ISSUE: Could Armory (P), who lacked legal title to the chattel, maintain an action to recover its value?

HOLDING AND DECISION: (Sir John Pratt, C.J.) Yes. The finder of lost property, although he does not acquire absolute ownership, does acquire title superior to everyone else except the rightful owner. Such title is a sufficient property interest in the finder upon which he may maintain an action against anyone (except the rightful owner) who violates that interest. Additionally, Delamirie (D) was liable as he was responsible for the actions of his apprentice. As for the measure of damages, if Delamirie (D) did not show the stones were not of the finest value, their value would be so determined.

ANALYSIS

As to ownership, the finder is in a position similar to that of a bailee. The finder does not obtain absolute ownership, but does have the right of ownership against everybody except the true owner. Here, the chattel, the jewel, was subsequently converted against the finder. Yet the finder, if he should subsequently lose the chattel, may reclaim it from a subsequent finder. The finder has a choice of remedies. He may recover the chattel in specie if it is still in the converter's possession, or he may recover full value from the wrongdoer. Notice that an action in trover, which is an action at law, is to recover the value of the chattel. If it is desired to have the item returned, an action in replevin must be brought in equity.

Quicknotes

BAILEE Person holding property in trust for another party.

CHATTEL An article of personal property, as distinguished from real property; a thing personal and moveable.

Charrier v. Bell

Archaeologist (P) v. Landowner (D)

La. Ct. App., 496 So. 2d 601 (1986)

NATURE OF CASE: Appeal from denial of compensatory and declaratory relief confirming ownership.

FACT SUMMARY: After Charrier (P) uncovered Tunica Indian artifacts while excavating property without the property owner's (D) permission, descendants of the Tunica tribe claimed ownership of the artifacts.

RULE OF LAW

Ownership in burial artifacts cannot be transferred to another under the theory of abandonment.

FACTS: Charrier (P), an amateur archaeologist, located a Tunica Indian burial site on a privately held plantation. Charrier (P) received permission to excavate from the caretaker but not from the owner. He spent three years uncovering a great number of Tunica artifacts. When he tried to sell the artifacts to a museum, he found he could not do so without proving ownership. Charrier (P) brought suit against Bell (D) and the other landowners to quiet title to the artifacts. The State (D) bought the plantation and took over defense of the suit in favor of the descendants of the Tunica Indians. The trial court found the Tunica-Biloxi Indians to be the owners of the artifacts, and Charrier (P) appealed.

ISSUE: Can ownership in burial artifacts be transferred to another under the theory of abandonment?

HOLDING AND DECISION: (Ponder, J.) No. Ownership in burial artifacts cannot be transferred to another under the theory of abandonment. Charrier's (P) claim to the artifact is based on the theory that the Tunica Indians abandoned them, and he became the owner by finding them. Abandonment requires intent to abandon. Traditionally burial goods do not fall under the classification of treasures to be found. Otherwise burial grounds would be subject to despoilment. When a society buries goods with the deceased person, it is for religious, spiritual, or moral reasons, not with the intent that the next person to come along should uncover them. The artifacts were buried with the intent that they would remain there for all eternity. There is thus no intent to abandon connected with burial goods, and finding them cannot transfer them away from the rightful owners. Affirmed.

ANALYSIS

Lost property is personal property that has been parted from its rightful owner involuntarily or unintentionally left somewhere and forgotten. Abandoned property has been intentionally relinquished. As a practical matter, however, most states do not make these common-law distinctions any longer; by law, the finder is permitted to claim ownership after depositing the property with the police for a certain amount of time.

Quicknotes

COMPENSATORY RELIEF Measure of damages necessary to compensate victim for actual injuries suffered.

DECLARATORY RELIEF A judgment of the court establishing the rights of the parties.

OWNERSHIP BY OCCUPANCY Means of acquiring ownership of property by taking possession of property not owned by anyone with the intent to own it.

POSSESSION The holding of property with the right of disposition.

RES DERELICTAE Property that is relinquished by its owner so that the first person to find or occupy the property acquires ownership thereof.

RES NULLIUS The rule that the first person to find property that is not owned by anyone acquires ownership of that property.

Willcox v. Stroup

Possessor of property (P) v. State (D)

467 F.3d 409 (4th Cir. 2006)

NATURE OF CASE: Appeal from lower court decision regarding plaintiff's motion for declaratory judgment.

FACT SUMMARY: Willcox (P), the possessor of Civil War era documents worth $2.4 million, sought a declaratory judgment against South Carolina's Department of Archives (D) that he was the rightful owner of the documents.

RULE OF LAW

A rebuttable presumption exists that those in possession of property are rightly in possession, absent evidence of superior title in another.

FACTS: Willcox (P) found 444 documents in a closet in his late stepmother's home. The documents contained letters, military reports and telegrams from the Civil War and were valued at $2.4 million. Stroup, the director of South Carolina's Department of Archives and History (D), obtained a temporary restraining order to prevent Willcox (P) from selling the documents. In response, Willcox (P) filed this lawsuit seeking a declaratory judgment that he was the rightful owner. Regarding the chain of title, it appears the documents came to the Willcox family though a great, great uncle of Willcox (P). There are certain breaks in the chain and there is no evidence of how Willcox's (P) late stepmother came into possession of the documents. However, there is no evidence that the documents ever left the Willcox family for the last 140 years. The family did allow the papers to be microfilmed. [The bankruptcy court originally ruled for the state, but the district court found in favor of Willcox (P). Stroup appealed on behalf of the state (D).]

ISSUE: Does a rebuttable presumption exist that those in possession of property are rightly in possession, absent evidence of superior title in another?

HOLDING AND DECISION: (Wilkinson, J.) Yes. A rebuttable presumption exists that those in possession of property are rightly in possession, absent evidence of superior title in another. Because there is no evidence of a clear chain of title for these papers, common-law principles of property take precedence. South Carolina employs the well-known rule that one in possession of property enjoys a presumption of ownership. Only clear and convincing evidence of superior title in another will overcome the presumption. The presumption exists to resolve cases such as this where direct evidence of ownership is lacking. In addition, the presumption in favor of possessors promotes stability in society. Lastly, the public will not be harmed by this decision as the family has allowed the documents to be microfilmed for public access. Affirmed.

ANALYSIS

The decision noted at its conclusion that ownership of most state or presidential papers are covered now by statute. Prior to the twentieth century, many politicians retained personal ownership of their own papers. There was no evidence in the record of any South Carolina law that would have granted ownership of the documents in question to the state. Therefore, the case presents a fine example of the rule that possession, absent evidence of title in another, constitutes ownership.

Quicknotes

POSSESSION The holding of property with the right of disposition.

REBUTTABLE PRESUMPTION A rule of law, inferred from the existence of a particular set of facts, is conclusive in the absence of contrary evidence.

CHAPTER 3

What Can Be Owned?

Quick Reference Rules of Law

In the Matter of Baby M

Surrogate mother (D) v. Parents (P)

N.J. Sup. Ct., 537 A.2d 1227 (1988)

NATURE OF CASE: Appeal of order determining parentage and child custody.

FACT SUMMARY: Whitehead (D) reneged on an agreement to provide a baby fathered by Stern (P) and give it up to the Sterns (P).

RULE OF LAW

A "surrogacy contract" wherein a woman agrees to have a child and surrender it is void.

FACTS: Elizabeth Stern (P) did not wish to give birth due to a possible genetic defect. Nonetheless, the Sterns (P) wanted a baby. They contracted with Whitehead (D) that she would be artificially inseminated with William Stern's (P) sperm, give up the baby, and receive $10,000. Whitehead (D) had the baby, but did not want to give it up. Following a protracted series of maneuverings, the Sterns (P) obtained custody. They filed a complaint seeking to have the contract enforced and custody permanently awarded to them. The trial court found the contract valid, awarded custody to the Sterns (P), and cut off Whitehead's (D) parental rights entirely. Whitehead (D) appealed.

ISSUE: Is a "surrogacy contract" wherein a woman agrees to have a child and surrender it void?

HOLDING AND DECISION: (Wilentz, C.J.) Yes. A "surrogacy contract" wherein a woman agrees to have a child and surrender it is void. A contract of this nature conflicts with at least three categories of statutes: (1) laws prohibiting the use of money in connection with adoptions; (2) laws requiring proof of parental unfitness prior to termination of parental rights; and (3) laws that make surrender of custody and consent to adoption revocable. Further, contracts of this type conflict with nonstatutory, but nonetheless accepted, policy considerations governing child placement. First and foremost of these is that the paramount consideration in deciding where a child shall be placed be the best interests of the child. A contract such as that in question gives no weight to that consideration. Also, such contracts, by favoring the natural father over the natural mother, conflict with the policy that natural parents shall receive equal considerations. Further, it is impossible not to conclude that such contracts constitute baby selling, which public policy strongly disfavors. For these reasons, contracts such as those at issue here are void. Reversed. [The court went on to decide custody based on a best-interest-of-the-child test, and awarded custody to Mr. Stern (P), but reinstated Whitehead's (D) parental rights, including visitation.]

ANALYSIS

This was one of the country's most closely watched cases in 1987 and 1988. It was the first major case on the validity of surrogate parenting contracts. What little legislative reaction that had occurred as of the time of this writing tended to codify the court's holding. The court's decision does not prohibit voluntary arrangements performed without consideration (i.e., payment to the natural mother).

Moore v. Regents of the University of California

Patient (P) v. Medical center (D)

Cal. Sup. Ct., 793 P.2d 479 (1990)

NATURE OF CASE: Appeal from action for conversion.

FACT SUMMARY: Moore (P) claimed that Dr. Golde (D) wrongfully used cells from Moore's (P) diseased spleen and other organs for pecuniary advantage.

RULE OF LAW

A person does not have a property interest in his cell tissue.

FACTS: John Moore (P) went to UCLA Medical Center where he was diagnosed with hairy-cell leukemia. His treating physician, Dr. Golde (D), recommended that he have his spleen removed. Golde (D) was aware that the cells of the diseased spleen were valuable for research and commercial purpose; however, he secured Moore's (P) consent for the operation without disclosing this information. Dr. Golde (D) and his colleagues (D) arranged to preserve the removed cells and, through their own efforts, developed the cells into a lucrative cell line. After the surgery, Moore (P) was required to return to UCLA from his home in Seattle for additional samples of genetic materials. The materials were used for further research on the cell line again without Moore's (P) knowledge or consent. Dr. Golde (D) patented the cell line and received several hundred thousand dollars from pharmaceutical companies for products derived from the cell line. Moore (P) brought suit for conversion.

ISSUE: Does a person have a property interest in his cell tissue?

HOLDING AND DECISION: (Panelli, J.) No. A person does not have a property interest in his cell tissue. Although a person does have a right to his own likeness, the products produced from cells are based on genetic material that is common to all human beings. Thus, Moore (P) had no unique personality interest in the materials taken. California law dictates specifically how removed human tissue must be disposed of. Dr. Golde's (D) use of the tissue was in accordance with statutory requirements. If Moore (P) had desired to dispose of the cells on his own, he would have been barred by law from doing so. Once the cells were removed, he no longer had the right to possess them. Moore (P) cannot be held to have a property interest in the cells. Furthermore, public policy mitigates against a finding that would chill beneficial research. Moore (P) may sue for breach of fiduciary duty or lack of informed consent, but not for conversion.

CONCURRENCE: (Arabian, J.) Moore (P) asks the court to recognize and enforce a right to sell one's own body tissue for profit. Golde's (D) conduct was outrageous, but the legislature is the proper forum for resolution of this problem.

CONCURRENCE AND DISSENT: (Broussard, J.) The court's holding is anomalous; it prevents Moore (P) from selling his body for profit but allows Golde (D) and the Regents (D) to profit from cells wrongfully acquired.

DISSENT: (Mosk, J.) The concept of property refers to a "bundle of rights" that encompasses the right to exclude others from that property or to dispose of it by gift or sale. Certain legal constraints, however, intervene for a variety of policy reasons to limit the exercise of these rights. While these legal restrictions may limit the bundle of rights, what always remains is a protectable property interest. "Every individual has a legally protectable property interest in his own body and its products." This basic principle stems from society's ethical imperative to respect the human body and prohibit economic exploitation of one person by another. Such exploitation is akin to the institution of slavery. Our society also values fundamental fairness when it comes to dealings between people and condemns the unjust enrichment of anyone at the expense of another. Moore's (P) protectable property interest in his own tissue at minimum must match that of the defendants. Moore (P) could have contracted with researchers and pharmaceutical companies to develop the potential of his tissue. It is absurd to allow the defendants to appropriate Moore's (P) tissue saying they have a legal right to his property, while at the same time saying Moore (P) had no such right. It is unethical and immoral not to allow Moore (P) to share in the proceeds attained from his cells, without which defendants would have nothing.

ANALYSIS

Justice Mosk makes two compelling policy arguments in his dissent—one based on equity and the other on ethics. Because, he argues, Moore (P) made a crucial contribution to the cell line developed by Golde (D), he should be permitted to share in the profits. Mosk contends that when research treats the human body as a mere commodity, the dignity and respect due the

Continued on next page.

human body are sacrificed. For more on this debate, see "Danforth, Cells, Sales, and Royalties," 6 *Yale L. and Pol'y Rev.* 179 (1988).

Quicknotes

CONVERSION Act of depriving an owner of his property without permission or justification.

FIDUCIARY DUTY A legal obligation to act for the benefit of another, including subordinating one's personal interests to that of the other person.

Flynn v. Holder

Challengers to statute (P) v. Federal government (D)

684 F.3d 852 (9th Cir. 2012)

NATURE OF CASE: Appeal from lower court decision that dismissed the plaintiffs' constitutional challenge to the National Organ Transplant Act.

FACT SUMMARY: The National Organ Transplant Act bans any compensation for human organs, including bone marrow. The plaintiffs—a group of patients, physicians, and nonprofits—challenged the constitutionally of the ban.

RULE OF LAW

While the direct removal of bone marrow is prohibited by the National Organ Transplant Act (NOTA), the removal of immature bone marrow stem cells from the blood, rather than from the marrow itself, is similar to a blood donation and is not prohibited by NOTA.

FACTS: The National Organ Transplant Act (NOTA) bans any compensation for human organs, including bone marrow. The plaintiffs—a group of patients, physicians, and nonprofits—challenged the constitutionally of the ban. The plaintiffs seek to create a program that would offer $3,000 to possible bone marrow donors. Because there are millions of bone marrow cell types, the chances of a donor match are very rare. The plaintiffs seek to offer the $3,000 compensation to incentivize possible donors and increase the match ratio for those suffering from leukemia or other blood-related diseases. The older method of extracting bone marrow involved the use of a long needle that would be inserted directly into the cavity of the larger bones of the donor, such as the hipbone. A newer method is less invasive. Scientists discovered that blood stem cells are born in bone marrow and typically develop into mature blood cells before passing into the blood stream. Significantly, they also discovered that some of the bone marrow stem cells pass into the blood stream before maturing into full blood cells. A process called "apheresis" was developed to remove only the immature bone marrow stems cells from a donor's blood stream. The process involves a needle being inserted into the vein of a donor. The donor then sits for an hour or two while the stem cells are removed from his or her blood. Those immature bone marrow stem cells are then injected into the donee where they grow into healthy, cancer-free blood cells. The plaintiffs argue the ban on bone marrow transplants is a violation of Equal Protection. A federal district court dismissed their complaint. The plaintiffs appealed to the United State Court of Appeals for the Ninth Circuit.

ISSUE: While the direct removal of bone marrow is prohibited by the National Organ Transplant Act (NOTA), is the removal of immature bone marrow stem cells from the blood, rather than from the marrow itself, similar to a blood donation and therefore not prohibited by NOTA?

HOLDING AND DECISION: (Kleinfeld, J.) Yes. While the direct removal of bone marrow is prohibited by the National Organ Transplant Act (NOTA), the removal of peripheral bone marrow stem cells from the blood, rather than from the marrow itself, is similar to a blood donation and is not prohibited by NOTA. Turning first to the older method of extracting bone marrow directly, there is no question NOTA has banned compensation for extracted bone marrow. Congress had rational basis to outlaw the sale of bone marrow as well as all other organs of the body, including subparts thereof. One concern was that rich patients would induce the poor to sell their organs, even if the process was a painful one. Compensation for donors may also degrade the quality of the organs donated if potential donors lie about their medical histories. Accordingly, Congress has a rational basis for banning the sale of organs and it is not for this Court to substitute its own judgment. Separately, however, the process known as "apheresis" is not covered by NOTA. That method only involves the removal of blood from a donor, similar to the process of giving blood. Payments for blood have been common for some time and NOTA does not ban that practice. The Government (D) is incorrect in saying that the bone marrow stem cells are a "subpart" of the bone marrow. Blood contains red cells, white cells, platelets, and stem cells. To ban the removal of the stem cells alone would necessarily include a ban on blood donations themselves. Accordingly, NOTA does not ban compensation to donors for their bone marrow stem cells extracted using the apheresis method. Affirmed in part and reversed in part.

ANALYSIS

In fall 2013, the Department of Health and Human Services proposed a rule that would effectively ban the new apheresis method of extracting bone marrow stem cells from blood. If adopted, the rule would moot the

Continued on next page.

Ninth Circuit's decision in this case. As of this printing, a final rule on the issue had yet to be adopted.

Quicknotes

MOTION TO DISMISS Motion to terminate an action based on the adequacy of the pleadings, improper service or venue, etc.

RATIONAL BASIS REVIEW A test employed by the court to determine the validity of a statute in equal protection actions, whereby the court determines whether the challenged statute is rationally related to the achievement of a legitimate state interest.

Martin Luther King, Jr. Center for Social Change v. American Heritage Products

Nonprofit organization (P) v. Manufacturer (D)

Ga. Sup. Ct., 296 S.E.2d 697 (1982)

NATURE OF CASE: Certified question from Eleventh Circuit Court of Appeals to Georgia Supreme Court.

FACT SUMMARY: Martin Luther King, Jr. Center for Social Change (P) sued Bolen (D) for the unauthorized development and marketing of a plastic bust of Dr. Martin Luther King, Jr.

RULE OF LAW

Public figures have a right of publicity that survives the death of the figure, and thus is inheritable and devisable, the measure of damages for violation of which is the value of the appropriation to the user.

FACTS: Bolen (D) is the sole proprietor of a business that manufactures and sells plastic products as funeral accessories. He developed the concept of marketing a plastic bust of Martin Luther King, Jr., and formed a company in order to sell them. Although Bolen (D) sought the endorsement of Martin Luther King, Jr. Center for Social Change (the Center) (P), it refused to endorse the product. He nevertheless pursued the idea, hiring persons to prepare the model and taking out advertising. The Center (P) filed suit demanding Bolen (D) cease and desist from further marketing and development of the bust. The Eleventh Circuit Court of Appeals certified the question to the Georgia Supreme Court of whether a right of publicity exists in the state of Georgia, and whether it is devisable and inheritable.

ISSUE: Do public figures have a right of publicity that survives the death of the figure, and thus is inheritable and devisable, the measure of damages for violation of which is the value of the appropriation to the user?

HOLDING AND DECISION: (Hill, J.) Yes. Public figures have a right of publicity that survives the death of the figure, and thus is inheritable and devisable, the measure of damages for violation of which is the value of the appropriation to the user. Similar to the right of privacy in private figures, a public figure has a right in the publicity value of his likeness, the rationale for which is the prevention of unjust enrichment. Private citizens as well as public ones have a right not to have their names and photographs used for financial gain of the user without their consent. Furthermore the right of publicity is inheritable and devisable, and as such furthers the purpose of rewarding and encouraging effort and creativity. There is no requirement that the owner of the right have commercially exploited it before his death for the right to survive.

CONCURRENCE: (Weltner, J.) This new right of publicity jeopardizes the right to freedom of speech.

ANALYSIS

The right of publicity has been extended to also apply to imitations of public figures. Several California cases have held that where a well-known singer's voice is deliberately imitated in order to sell merchandise, misappropriation of the celebrity's likeness has occurred.

Quicknotes

FREEDOM OF SPEECH The right to express oneself without governmental restrictions on the content of that expression.

RIGHT OF PUBLICITY The right of a person to control the commercial exploitation of his name or likeness.

UNJUST ENRICHMENT The unlawful acquisition of money or property of another for which both law and equity require restitution is made.

Rosa and Raymond Parks Institute for Self-Development v. Target Corp.

Owner of name and likeness of historical figure (P) v. National retailer (D)

812 F.3d 824 (11th Cir. 2016)

NATURE OF CASE: Appeal from dismissal of action asserting claims for unjust enrichment, right of publicity, and misappropriation.

FACT SUMMARY: The Rosa and Raymond Parks Institute for Self-Development (Institute) (P), which owned the name and likeness of Rosa Parks, the famous civil rights figure, contended that Target Corp. (D), the national retailer, violated its rights by selling biographies, a children's book, a movie, and a plaque about, or incorporating images of, Parks without the Institute's (P) prior knowledge or consent. Target (D) asserted that its use of Parks's name and likeness were protected by the qualified privilege to communicate on matters of public concern.

RULE OF LAW

The sale of works containing an individual's name and likeness does not violate the individual's right of publicity where the works concern matters of great public interest.

FACTS: In 1955, Rosa Parks, an African American, made history, and inspired the modern Civil Rights Movement, when she refused to yield her seat on a bus to White men. Arguably, her act of resistance transformed the nation. Many years after Parks died, Target Corp. (D), the large national retailer, offered for sale several books, a television movie, and a children's book about Parks, as well as plaque about civil rights and courage that included a picture of Parks alongside Dr. Martin Luther King, Jr. None of these were identified with Target (D), and all had been created independently of Target (D). The Rosa and Raymond Parks Institute for Self-Development (Institute) (P), which owned Parks's name and likeness pursuant to a right-of-publicity assignment, brought a federal diversity action for unjust enrichment, right of publicity, and misappropriation. Target (D) defended by asserting a qualified privilege to communicate on matters of public interest. Upon Target's (D) motion for summary judgment, the district court dismissed the complaint, and the U.S. Court of Appeals for the Eleventh Circuit granted review.

ISSUE: Does the sale of works containing an individual's name and likeness violate the individual's right of publicity where the works concern matters of great public interest?

HOLDING AND DECISION: (Rosenbaum, J.) No. The sale of works containing an individual's name and likeness does not violate the individual's right of publicity where the works concern matters of great public interest. Under the law of the state applied by the district court, the misappropriation of a person's name or likeness is commonly referred to as a violation of the "right of publicity." This right is founded upon the interest of the individual in the exclusive use of the individual's identity, in so far as it is represented by the individual's name or likeness, and in so far as the use may be of benefit to the individual or to others. The right thus guards against the appropriation of the commercial value of a person's identity by using without consent the person's name, likeness, or other indicia of identity for the purpose of trade. The right, however, is not absolute. Based on the state's constitutional free speech rights, the state's courts have recognized that individual rights, including the right of publicity, must in appropriate cases yield to the qualified privilege to communicate on matters of public interest, especially in cases concerning social issues. It is beyond dispute that Parks is a figure of great historical significance and that the Civil Rights Movement is a matter of legitimate and important public interest. Given that all the works sold by Target (D) related to Parks as a historical figure or to the Civil Rights Movement, they all concerned matters of the highest public interest. Although the qualified privilege is not invincible, the Institute (P) failed to articulate any argument as to why the qualified privilege for matters of public concern would not apply to these works, in light of the conspicuous historical importance of Rosa Parks, and the court cannot conceive of any such argument. To the contrary, the use of Rosa Parks's name and likeness in the books, movie, and plaque is necessary to chronicling and discussing the history of the Civil Rights Movement—matters quintessentially embraced and protected by the qualified privilege. Indeed, it is difficult to conceive of a discussion of the Civil Rights Movement without reference to Parks and her role in it, and the applicable state law does not make discussion of these topics of public concern contingent on paying a fee. As a result, all the works are protected by the qualified privilege protecting matters of public interest. Affirmed.

Continued on next page.

ANALYSIS

The Institute's (P) additional claims of misappropriation and unjust enrichment were derivative of its right-of-publicity claim. Because the misappropriation of likeness claim was the same as its claim based on the right of publicity, it was duplicative of the right of publicity claim. And, because the court affirmed the dismissal of the right of publicity claim, it effectively dismissed the misappropriation claim. Likewise, because the court found that Target (D) did not unlawfully use Parks's name and likeness, any acquired benefit would not have been unjust, so the Institute's (P) common-law claim of unjust enrichment necessarily failed. For these reasons, the court did not address these additional claims.

Quicknotes

MISAPPROPRIATION The unlawful use of another's property or funds.

RIGHT OF PUBLICITY The right of a person to control the commercial exploitation of his name or likeness.

PUBLIC INTEREST Something in which the public has either a monetary or legal interest.

UNJUST ENRICHMENT Principle that one should not be unjustly enriched at the expense of another.

Wana the Bear v. Community Construction, Inc.

Miwok Indian (P) v. Developer (D)

Cal. Ct. App., 128 Cal. App. 3d 536, 180 Cal. Rptr. 423 (1982)

NATURE OF CASE: Appeal from judgment in action seeking to enjoin development of an area that included a Native American burial ground.

FACT SUMMARY: Wana the Bear (P) filed suit to enjoin continued development by Community Construction, Inc. (D) of property containing a burial ground used by the Miwok Indians before they were driven out of the area.

RULE OF LAW

A burial ground used as a public graveyard prior to the enactment of the cemetery law is not protected under that law as a public cemetery.

FACTS: While excavating property for development of a residential tract, Community Construction, Inc. (D) uncovered human remains on the property. Community Construction (D) continued developing the property, disinterring the remains of over 200 human beings in the process. The burial ground had been used by the Miwok Indians until they were driven out of the area between 1850 and 1870. California's applicable cemetery law was enacted in 1872. Wana the Bear (P), descendant of the Bear People Lodge of the Miwok Indians and related to some or all of the persons whose remains lay there, brought suit to enjoin further excavation and other desecration of the property. The lower court found that the burial ground was not a cemetery entitled to protection under the California cemetery law. Wana the Bear (P) appealed.

ISSUE: Is a burial ground used as a public graveyard prior to the enactment of the cemetery law protected under that law as a public cemetery?

HOLDING AND DECISION: (Blease, J.) No. A burial ground used as a public graveyard prior to the enactment of the cemetery law is not protected under that law as a public cemetery. The 1854 cemetery law applied to burial sites created prior to 1872. However, the 1854 law was not incorporated into the 1872 law. The 1872 law contained a prescriptive use condition, vesting title of the graveyard in the city or village using it only when the land was used as a burial ground continuously, without interruption, for five years. In addition, the new law further declared that no part of the code was retroactive unless expressly so declared. The Miwoks were no longer using the burial ground when the new law replaced the 1854 law. Therefore, the burial ground was not made a cemetery by the operation of the 1872 law. The legislative judgment is binding on this court in the absence of a supervening constitutional right, and none has been claimed. Affirmed.

ANALYSIS

A public cemetery is generally created by one of two methods: dedication or prescriptive use. After the decision in this case, the California legislature enacted legislation providing for the protection of Native American burial sites. Under the new legislation, when property owners find Native American remains on their property, they must notify public officials and meet with representatives of the affected tribes to negotiate for reburial of the remains and any other objects found with them.

Republic of Turkey v. Christie's Inc.

Sovereign nation (P) v. Auction house (D)

425 F. Supp. 3d 204 (S.D.N.Y. 2019)

NATURE OF CASE: Motion for summary judgment in federal diversity action for conversion, replevin, and declaratory judgment respecting a historical and cultural artifact.

FACT SUMMARY: The Republic of Turkey (Turkey) (P) claimed that a historical and cultural artifact dating back to at least 2200 B.C.E, the Idol, which allegedly had been removed illegally some time before 1961 from Turkey (P), belonged to Turkey (P) pursuant to a 1906 Decree of the Ottoman Empire, the predecessor of modern-day Turkey (P). Christie's Inc. (D), an auction house that had possession of the Idol in New York and that planned to auction it off, contended that Turkey's (P) claim was unfounded, on grounds that Turkey (P) could not show ownership of the Idol under the 1906 Decree and that, in any event, Turkey's (P) claim was time-barred.

RULE OF LAW

(1) A statute of limitations for the recovery of chattel from a good-faith purchaser accrues when the purchaser is put on notice, via a demand for return of the property, that such property is claimed to be stolen, and the purchaser refuses such demand.

(2) A law of a foreign sovereign is an ownership law that vests ownership of antiquities in the sovereign where the law by its plain language clearly and unambiguously vests ownership in the sovereign of antiquities found or taken from the sovereign's lands, and where evidence indicates that such law is enforced and treated as an ownership law.

(3) Summary judgment cannot be awarded to a defendant in an action for conversion and replevin of a foreign antiquity, brought pursuant to a foreign ownership law, where there are genuine disputes of material fact as to where and when the antiquity was excavated and exported from the foreign sovereign's lands.

FACTS: Around 1961, the Martins, American art collectors, acquired the Idol—an Anatolian marble female Idol of Kiliya-type that dates to at least 2200 B.C.E. —from J.J. Klejman Gallery. Klejman was a well-known "dealer-smuggler" who sold looted art in the 1960s. Kulaksizlar, located in the modern-day Republic of Turkey (Turkey) (P), is the only workshop known to have produced Kiliya-type idols. The Martins loaned the Idol to the Metropolitan Museum of Art (Museum), where it was on display from 1966 to 1993. The Idol then in 1993 became owned by Steinhardt (D), who loaned it back to the Museum from 1999 to 2007. Around March 2, 2017, Steinhardt (D) consigned the Idol to an auction house—Christie's Inc. (D)—for sale, and it was delivered to Christie's (D) that same day. Christie's (D) conducted provenance research and listed the Idol's provenance as tracing back to "1966 or prior," when it was acquired by the Martins. Christie's (D) listed the Idol, along with its provenance information, for its scheduled April 28, 2017, auction. Around March 26, 2017, Turkey (P) learned about the planned sale of the Idol, and on April 19, 2017, Turkey (P) sent Christie's (D) a letter claiming that the Idol was likely of Turkish origin, and, as such, was state property protected under Turkish law. Turkey (P) claimed ownership of the Idol under a 1906 Ottoman [Empire] Decree (1906 Decree); the Ottoman Empire was the predecessor of modern-day Turkey (P). The 1906 Decree provided, inter alia, that all monuments and antiquities situated in or on land belonging to the Ottoman Empire belonged to the Ottoman Empire, and that the right to discover, preserve, collect, and donate to museums such artifacts belongs to the Ottoman Empire. The 1906 Decree also defines antiquity as "[a]ny work or any kind of product without exception, by any and all types of ancient peoples which once existed in or on the lands ruled by the Ottoman Government, related to fine arts, science, literature, religion and craft." Turkey (P) commenced a federal diversity action against Steinhardt (D) and Christie's (D) on April 27, 2017, for conversion, replevin, and declaratory judgment that Turkey (P) was the Idol's owner, and immediately sought a temporary restraining order enjoining sale of the Idol at the scheduled April 28, 2017, auction. The court denied that relief, but required that Christie's (P) inform potential purchasers that Turkey (P) had asserted a claim of ownership over the Idol; and that Christie's (D) retain possession of the Idol for 60 days and "delay receipt of funds by any successful bidder" during that time. In accord with these conditions, Christie's (P) sold the Idol for $12.7 million, but the buyer never took possession of the Idol, which remained in Christie's (D) possession. The parties cross-moved for summary judgment. As a threshold matter, the court determined that New York governed Turkey's (P) claims, and that Turkish law—in particular, the 1906 Decree—governed whether Turkey (P) owned the Idol.

Continued on next page.

ISSUE:

(1) Does a statute of limitations for the recovery of chattel from a good-faith purchaser accrue when the purchaser is put on notice, via a demand for return of the property, that such property is claimed to be stolen, and the purchaser refuses such demand?

(2) Is a law of a foreign sovereign an ownership law that vests ownership of antiquities in the sovereign where the law by its plain language clearly and unambiguously vests ownership in the sovereign of antiquities found or taken from the sovereign's lands, and where evidence indicates that such law is enforced and treated as an ownership law?

(3) Can summary judgment be awarded to a defendant in an action for conversion and replevin of a foreign antiquity, brought pursuant to a foreign ownership law, where there are genuine disputes of material fact as to where and when the antiquity was excavated and exported from the foreign sovereign's lands?

HOLDING AND DECISION: (Nathan, J.)

(1) Yes. A statute of limitations for the recovery of chattel from a good-faith purchaser accrues when the purchaser is put on notice, via a demand for return of the property, that such property is claimed to be stolen, and the purchaser refuses such demand. Christie's (D) and Steinhardt (D) argued that they were entitled to summary judgment on Turkey's (P) claims because those claims were barred by the relevant three-year statute of limitations for the recovery of chattel, which applies to conversion and replevin claims, and which starts running from the accrual of the claim. However, the date of accrual varies depending on whether the current possessor is a good-faith purchaser or bad-faith possessor. A claim accrues against a bad-faith possessor immediately from the time of wrongful possession because the bad-faith possessor's possession is necessarily unlawful *ab initio*. On the other hand, conversion and replevin claims against a person who lawfully comes by a chattel accrue not upon the stealing or the taking, but upon the defendant's refusal to convey the chattel upon demand. This distinction is attributable to the fact that a good-faith purchaser's possession of stolen property is not wrongful until the purchaser is put on notice, via a demand for return of the property, that such property is stolen. It is the refusal of such a demand that transforms a previously lawful possession into an unlawful one. Here, it is undisputed that Steinhardt (D) was a good-faith purchaser. Therefore, Turkey's (P) claims accrued, and the three-year statute of limitations began to run, when it demanded the Idol and Christie's (D) and Steinhardt (D) refused, which occurred on April 19, 2017. Turkey's (P) claims are thus timely unless an exception to the demand and refusal rule applies. Because none of the exceptions to the demand and refusal rule identified by Christie's (D) and Steinhardt (D) apply, Turkey's (P) claims are timely, and Christie's (D) and Steinhardt (D) are not entitled to summary judgment on statute of limitations grounds.

(2) Yes. A law of a foreign sovereign is an ownership law that vests ownership of antiquities in the sovereign where the law by its plain language clearly and unambiguously vests ownership in the sovereign of antiquities found or taken from the sovereign's lands, and where evidence indicates that such law is enforced and treated as an ownership law. Here, the parties agree that the only Turkish law that could vest ownership of antiquities, and, therefore, the Idol, in Turkey (P), is the 1906 Decree. Whether the 1906 Decree is in fact an ownership law—and thus whether Turkey (P) can maintain the conversion and replevin claims it asserts here—is a question of the proper interpretation of foreign law for the court to decide as a matter of law. In determining whether foreign law vests ownership of antiquities in the state, courts must look first to the plain language of the relevant law. By the 1906 Decree's plain terms, movable and immovable antiquities found on both public and private lands of the Ottoman Empire were the property of the Ottoman Empire during the time of its existence, and of modern-day Turkey (P) thereafter. Where, as here, the plain language of the law is clear and unambiguous, the defendant may still present evidence that the law is nonetheless not what its plain language indicates it is, by, for example, offering evidence that people within the country may nonetheless legally keep antiquities or that the law is otherwise generally not enforced. Here, Turkey (P) presented evidence that private ownership of antiquities in Turkey (P) is prohibited under the 1906 Decree, and that the 1906 Decree is domestically enforced. This evidence confirms that the 1906 Decree is what it says it is—an ownership law. The evidence Christie's (D) and Steinhardt (D) offer—that the 1906 Decree's validity was only "reaffirmed" by the Turkish Constitutional Court in 1965, that Turkey's (P) enforcement efforts were hindered because the Decree was available only in ancient Turkish until the 1960s, and that Turkey (P) failed to adequately publicize the law, especially internationally, is insufficient to overcome the combination of Turkey's (P) evidence and the plain language of the Decree, which makes clear that the Turkish government claims ownership of all antiquities found in Turkey (P) after 1906. First, the 1965 decision only reaffirmed the status quo—namely, that the Decree remained in effect—and, merely because the Decree was not translated or publicized

Continued on next page.

has little bearing on whether it is an ownership law, as such a requirement might be relevant only in a criminal case respecting fair notice concerns. Because Christie's (D) and Steinhardt (D) have failed to present sufficient evidence that the Decree is not what its plain language indicates it is, they are not entitled to summary judgment on the ground that it does not vest any ownership rights to the Idol in Turkey (P).

(3) No. Summary judgment cannot be awarded to a defendant in an action for conversion and replevin of a foreign antiquity, brought pursuant to a foreign ownership law, where there are genuine disputes of material fact as to where and when the antiquity was excavated and exported from the foreign sovereign's lands. For Turkey (P) to establish ownership under the 1906 Decree, it must prove that the Idol was found within and exported from the boundaries of modern-day Turkey (P) while the 1906 Decree was in effect. Christie's (D) and Steinhardt (D) assert that Turkey (P) has presented no evidence of the Idol's find spot, nor of the date of its excavation and exportation. However, the record demonstrates that there are genuine disputes of material fact as to all of these issues. As to where the Idol was found, some evidence was presented that it likely was found in Kulaksizlar, since that location was the only known workshop for the production of Kiliya-type idols. Although Christie's (D) and Steinhardt (D) also point to evidence that Kiliya-type idols traveled around the eastern Mediterranean during the era of their manufacture, and thus, even if manufactured within Turkey (P), this specific Idol could have been excavated from a site outside Turkey (P), this evidence only underscores the genuine dispute as to the material fact of the Idol's find spot. Given that the only workshop known to have manufactured Kiliya-type idols is located in Turkey (P) and that, in the opinion of Turkey's archaeology expert, the Idol at issue here was excavated in Turkey (P), a reasonable juror could conclude that the Idol was found in modern-day Turkey (P). Christie's (D) and Steinhardt's (D) suggestion that Turkey (P) must further be able to establish a specific find spot—of which, they claim, there is no evidence—in order to sustain its ownership claim has no basis in either the 1906 Decree nor the relevant case law. As to when the Idol was excavated and ultimately exported, there was undisputed evidence that the Idol was acquired by the Martins around 1961. Accordingly, the Idol must have been excavated and exported from Turkey (P) prior to that time. Although Christie's (D) and Steinhardt (D) argue that Turkey (P) has presented no other evidence, either of its excavation date or of its export date, Turkey (P) has indeed put forth evidence from which a reasonable juror could infer that the Idol was excavated and exported while the 1906 Decree was in effect, since Turkey (P) offered evidence from its archaeology expert that several other prominent examples of antiquities looted from Turkey (P) appeared on the market and were acquired by museums or collectors within a year or two of their looting. Turkey (P) also presented evidence that the source from which the Martins acquired the Idol, J.J. Klejman, was a well-known "dealer-smuggler" who sold looted art in the 1960s. From this evidence, a reasonable juror could conclude that the Idol, which was in the hands of American collectors by 1961, was excavated and exported from Turkey (P) shortly before then, while the 1906 Decree was in effect. Because Turkey (P) has presented sufficient evidence of several genuine issues of material fact, Christie's (D) and Steinhardt (D) are not entitled to summary judgment. Accordingly, their summary judgment motion is denied.

ANALYSIS

Regarding the accrual of the statute of limitations for conversion and replevin claims, Christie's (D) and Steinhardt (D) argued that because Steinhardt (D) openly dealt with the Idol, Turkey (P) was precluded from invoking the demand and refusal rule. However, the law (at least in New York) is clear that a possessor openly dealing with property as the possessor's own only precludes the demand and refusal rule if the possessor knew the property was not theirs before openly dealing with it. Demand and refusal is unnecessary in such cases not because the possessor openly deals with the property as their own, but because the possessor is already on notice that it is not theirs when they do so. The act of openly dealing with it as if it were their own is relevant under those circumstances because it transforms good-faith possession into a conversion and starts the running of the statute of limitations. Accordingly, because Steinhardt (D) did not deal openly with the Idol as his own knowing it in fact was not, a demand and refusal was required to change the character of his good-faith possession.

Quicknotes

AB INITIO From its inception or beginning.

CHATTEL An article of personal property, as distinguished from real property; a thing personal and moveable.

CONVERSION The act of depriving an owner of his property without permission or justification.

DECLARATORY JUDGMENT A judgment of the court establishing the rights of the parties in a controversy that does not grant damages but is binding.

Continued on next page.

DIVERSITY ACTION An action commenced by a citizen of one state against a citizen of another state or against an alien, involving an amount in controversy set by statute, over which the federal court has jurisdiction.

GOOD-FAITH PURCHASER A party who purchases property in good faith and for valuable consideration without notice of a defect in title.

MATERIAL FACT A fact without the existence of which a contract would not have been entered.

NOTICE Communication of information to a person by one authorized or by an otherwise proper source.

REPLEVIN An action to recover personal property wrongfully taken.

SOVEREIGN A state or entity with independent authority to govern its affairs.

STATUTE OF LIMITATIONS A law prescribing the period in which a legal action may be commenced.

SUMMARY JUDGMENT Judgment rendered by a court in response to a motion made by one of the parties, claiming that the lack of a question of material fact in respect to an issue warrants disposition of the issue without consideration by the jury.

Qualitex Co. v. Jacobson Products Co.

Dry cleaning product manufacturer (P) v. Competitor (D)

514 U.S. 159 (1995)

NATURE OF CASE: Review of order reversing finding of a trademark violation.

FACT SUMMARY: Qualitex Co. (P) sought to register a trademark on a color.

RULE OF LAW
Color alone may be registered as a trademark.

FACTS: Qualitex Co. (P) manufactured and sold pads used by dry cleaners on their presses. The pads made by Qualitex Co. (P) were of a distinctive green-gold color. When Qualitex (P) discovered that Jacobson Products Co. (Jacobson) (D) was also selling pads of the same color, it brought an unfair competition action and also sought to register the color as a trademark. The district court held Jacobson (D) to be in violation of Qualitex's (P) trademark. The United States Circuit Court of Appeals for the Ninth Circuit reversed, holding that color alone could not be registered as a trademark. The United States Supreme Court accepted review.

ISSUE: May color alone be registered as a trademark?

HOLDING AND DECISION: (Breyer, J.) Yes. Color alone may be registered as a trademark. The Lanham Act, which establishes federal trademark law, is quite liberal with respect to the universe of things that can be trademarked. Any symbol that carries a secondary meaning linking it with a particular product may be trademarked. There seems to be no reason why a color cannot fall within this definition. Jacobson's (D) arguments to the contrary are mostly based on pre-Lanham Act common law. Jacobson (D) also argues that since the number of colors is finite, color should not be trademarked. It is not necessary to establish a blanket prohibition for a rare problem. Reversed.

ANALYSIS

Numerous things of tenuous tangibility have become trademarks: a bottle shape (Coca-Cola) and sound (NBC Broadcasting Co.). Given this, allowing color to be the subject of a trademark is not unusual.

Quicknotes

LANHAM ACT Name of the Trademark Act of 1946 that governs federal law regarding trademarks.

Craft Smith LLC v. EC Design LLC

Personal planner designer (D) v. Personal planner designer (P)

969 F.3d 1092 (10th Cir. 2020)

NATURE OF CASE: Appeal from summary judgment for defendants in action for copyright and trade-dress infringement.

FACT SUMMARY: EC Design LLC (P), which designed and sold personal planners with unique elements under the name "LifePlanner," contended that Craft Smith LLC (D) infringed its copyright and trade-dress rights in its LifePlanner organizers when Craft Smith (D) sold personal planners under the name "Recollections Planner," which EC Design (P) alleged had very similar elements to its LifePlanner organizers. Craft Smith (D) maintained that the elements of its Recollections Planner were sufficiently different from the LifePlanner, so that no copyright infringement occurred, and also maintained that the LifePlanner's trade dress had failed to achieve distinctiveness through secondary meaning, so that there was no trade-dress infringement.

RULE OF LAW

(1) The copyright in a literary compilation is not infringed where there is not substantial similarity between the allegedly infringing work and the elements of the copyrighted work that are legally protected.

(2) As a matter of law, a work's product-design trade dress cannot be infringed where the work's trade dress has not become distinctive through secondary meaning.

FACTS: In 2007, EC Design LLC (P) created and started to sell a personal planner under the name "LifePlanner" that had weekly and monthly calendars, which were color-coded and used a tab system, and, in addition to the calendars, the LifePlanner had colorful artwork, spaces for the user to write notes, inspirational quotations, and various other textual elements, all of which were interspersed throughout the entire planner. All these features were bound together by a single metal coil and enclosed between plastic-laminated front and back covers. A user could choose among numerous color and art variations of the LifePlanner, and occasionally layout and binding variations, on a yearly basis. Craft Smith LLC (D) entered the personal planner market in 2017 with an organizer under the name "Recollections Planner." Craft Smith's (D) planner was like the 2015 LifePlanner insofar as it was also spiral-bound, had a similar layout, and contained color-coded calendars, inspirational quotes, and artwork. However, none of the quotations or artwork (i.e., two-dimensional, or 2-D elements) were directly copied from the LifePlanner. After EC Design (P) informed Craft Smith (D) that it believed the Recollections Planner infringed the copyright and trade dress of the LifePlanner, Craft Smith (D) sought a declaratory judgment in federal district court that its planner did not infringe in these ways on EC Design's (P) planner. EC Design (P) counterclaimed for copyright and trade-dress infringement. The parties cross-moved for summary judgment, and the district court granted Craft Smith's (D) motion. The United States Court of Appeals for the Tenth Circuit granted review.

ISSUE:

(1) Is the copyright in a literary compilation infringed where there is not substantial similarity between the allegedly infringing work and the elements of the copyrighted work that are legally protected?

(2) As a matter of law, can a work's product-design trade dress be infringed where the work's trade dress has not become distinctive through secondary meaning?

HOLDING AND DECISION: (Phillips, J.)

(1) No. The copyright in a literary compilation is not infringed where there is not substantial similarity between the allegedly infringing work and the elements of the copyrighted work that are legally protected. It is undisputed that EC Design (P) has a valid compilation copyright in the LifePlanner. The next question is whether that copyright was infringed. That question is resolved by determining whether there was factual copying, and whether there is substantial similarity between the allegedly infringing work and the elements of the copyrighted work that are legally protected. Copyright protects original works of authorship fixed in any tangible medium of expression, but does not protect ideas embodied in such works. In the case of copyrighted compilations, as here, copyright protection extends to the collection and assembling of preexisting materials or of data that are selected, coordinated, or arranged in such a way that the resulting work as a whole constitutes and original work of authorship. Here, it is beyond dispute that the LifePlanner is a collection and assembly of preexisting material and that it has been selected, coordinated, and arranged. To be original and a work of authorship, it must also be independently created by the author and must possess a minimal degree of creativity—a very low threshold to satisfy. EC Design (P) contends that its LifePlanner is, among

Continued on next page.

other things, a "literary work," which means that it is a work, other than an audiovisual work, expressed in words, numbers, or other verbal or numerical symbols or indicia, regardless of the nature of the material objects, such as books, in which they are embodied. EC Design (P) correctly argues that the LifePlanner compilation qualifies as a literary work because it contains "preexisting phrases, months, weeks, days, holidays, numbers, and other data and information." The LifePlanner's original selection, coordination, and arrangement of phrases, inspirational quotations, holidays, and other numerical data qualify the LifePlanner compilation as a literary work. Thus, the LifePlanner compilation's protected expression includes the specific text selected, as it has been originally arranged throughout the LifePlanner, as well its original selection and arrangement of the specific 2-D artwork and graphics contained therein. However, copyright protection does not extend to the work's format and layout—since those elements are considered mere ideas, which copyright does not protect. Having identified the LifePlanner compilation's protected expression, the court next must determine whether that expression is "substantially similar to the accused work." Substantial similarity exists when the accused work is so similar to the plaintiff's work that an ordinary reasonable person would conclude that the defendant unlawfully appropriated the plaintiff's protectable expression by taking material of substance and value. For compilations, because the copyrightability of a factual compilation depends upon the originality in selection, coordination, or arrangement of the facts as a whole work, in an infringement action the court must compare the allegedly infringing work as a whole when determining whether the two works are substantially similar. Although EC Design (P) claims asserts that Craft Smith's (D) planner used the same types of forms, banners, and notes sections, and arranged them in the same order, as well as using tabs of the same size and identical fonts, EC Design (P) does not claim that any of its planner's artwork or text—the two most significant portions of protected expression in the LifePlanner compilation—were copied. In fact, EC Design (P) does not even claim that Craft Smith (D) employed similar artwork or similar text. Instead, EC Design (P) essentially claims that Craft Smith's planner (D) has adopted a similar format; however, the format of the LifePlanner is not part of its protectable expression. Rather, EC Design's (P) protectable expression, for example, is the selection of particular quotations and the arrangement thereof. Copyright law does not protect how EC Design (P) has laid out its LifePlanner, which is an idea, not expression. EC Design's (P) original idea of arranging a colorful organizer full of quotations and art is not protectable by copyright. Thus, when Craft Smith (D) used entirely different artwork and text, even if arranged similarly, it did not copy the LifePlanner's protected expression. These substantial differences eliminate the possibility that a reasonable juror could conclude that the protected elements of the LifePlanner are substantially similar to the Recollections Planner. Accordingly, the district court did not err in granting summary judgment as to the issue of copyright infringement to Craft Smith (D). Affirmed as to this issue.

(2) No. As a matter of law, a work's product-design trade dress cannot be infringed where the work's trade dress has not become distinctive through secondary meaning. Trade dress consists of a product's overall image and appearance, and may include features such as size, shape, color or color combinations, texture, graphics, and even particular sales techniques. Here, some of the factors EC Design (P) has identified that make up the trade dress of the LifePlanner are its plastic-laminated front and back covers, coil-bound planner pages, colored themes throughout, and overall layout. In other words, the trade dress is the total image and overall look and feel that the various pieces of the LifePlanner leave in consumers' minds. In addition, the district court concluded that the LifePlanner possesses product-design trade dress, a conclusion EC Design (P) did not challenge. This determination—that the trade dress at issue is product-design trade dress—is significant, since distinctiveness for product-design trade dress can exist only if the trade dress has acquired secondary meaning. To succeed on its trade dress claim, EC Design (P) would have to show: (1) its trade dress is inherently distinctive or has become distinctive through secondary meaning; (2) there is a likelihood of confusion among consumers as to the source of the competing products; and (3) the trade dress is nonfunctional. Because the district court granted summary judgment for Craft Smith (D) on the first requirement, distinctiveness is the sole issue on appeal. Secondary meaning requires that the trade dress have been used so long and so exclusively by one producer with reference to the producer's goods or articles that, in the trade and to that branch of the purchasing public, the trade dress has come to mean that the article is the producer's product. In other words, secondary meaning exists when the trade dress's primary significance in the minds of potential consumers is no longer as an indicator of something about the product itself but as an indicator of its source or brand. This means that the ultimate inquiry is whether in the consumer's mind the trade dress denotes a single thing coming from a single source. Whether a trade dress has acquired secondary

Continued on next page.

meaning is a question of fact and thus generally (but not always) should not be decided at the summary judgment stage as a question of law. To show secondary meaning, parties can present both direct evidence, such as consumer surveys or testimony from consumers, and circumstantial evidence. Though secondary meaning is often a question for the jury, it only becomes so if the plaintiff's evidence creates a genuine issue of material fact regarding whether the relevant trade dress has the primary significance of identifying the source of the product rather than the product itself. For product-design trade dress, this task can be difficult, because even the most unusual of product designs often exists not to identify the source, but to render the product itself more useful or more appealing, and to survive a motion for summary judgment, the plaintiff must offer evidence creating a genuine issue of material fact that the trade dress serves primarily as a source identifier. Although EC Design (P) argues that the length of use of the trade dress creates such a genuine issue of material fact, here the trade dress at issue has only been in use for a little over a year, so that, as a matter of law, it cannot have acquired secondary meaning in that short a period. Moreover, EC Design (P) has routinely altered the LifePlanner's trade dress annually, and sometimes even more frequently, so that it is hard to see how a constantly updated product's design can develop secondary meaning, even through long-term use. Even if such use could be considered long enough, many aspects of the LifePlanner trade dress are not exclusive to EC Design (P), and, in fact, several other competitors were using a variety of the features constituting the LifePlanner trade dress, not just Craft Smith (D). For these reasons, EC Design's (P) length-of-use evidence fails to create a genuine issue of material fact as to secondary meaning. EC Design (P) also presented advertising evidence that it used advertising to promote the LifePlanner's desirable features, rather than to promote a conscious connection between its trade dress and itself as the source. Such evidence not only fails to support a finding of secondary meaning, it directly undermines such a finding. Thus, this evidence, too, fails to create a genuine issue of material fact as to secondary meaning. Finally, EC Design's (P) evidence that third parties commented that the Recollections Planner was a "knockoff" of the LifePlanner does not show actual consumer confusion, nor does it show that consumers view the LifePlanner's trade dress as a source identifier, so that EC Design's (P) evidence of third-party recognition does not create a genuine issue of material fact over secondary meaning. Affirmed as to this issue. Affirmed.

ANALYSIS

Trade-dress protection exists to prevent deception and consumer confusion as to the source of products, and the secondary meaning requirement for product-design trade dress reflects the reality that consumer predisposition to equate a product's feature with a certain source typically does not exist. Instead, consumers are aware of the reality that, almost invariably, even the most unusual of product designs is intended not to identify the source, but to render the product itself more useful or more appealing. Therefore, when a competitor copies a product's design, its purpose is not necessarily to confuse consumers, but to copy the aspects of that product that make it more functional. In this way, product-design trade dress fundamentally differs from product-packaging trade dress, which can be inherently distinctive, because the very act of encasing a product in a distinctive packaging serves to identify the source of the product. As a result, a product's design is distinctive, and therefore protectible, only upon a showing of secondary meaning.

Quicknotes

SECONDARY MEANING A word or mark that becomes associated with a particular merchant or product as its source of origin.

SUMMARY JUDGMENT Judgment rendered by a court in response to a motion made by one of the parties, claiming that the lack of a question of material fact in respect to an issue warrants disposition of the issue without consideration by the jury.

TRADE DRESS The overall image of, or impression created by, a product that a court may enforce as a trademark if it determines that such image has acquired secondary meaning and that the public recognizes it as an indication of source.

Dr. Seuss Enterprises, L.P. v. ComicMix LLC

Copyright owner (P) v. Publisher (D)

983 F.3d 443 (9th Cir. 2020)

NATURE OF CASE: Appeal from summary judgment for defendant on copyright infringement claim.

FACT SUMMARY: ComicMix LLC (D) intended to publish a book titled *Oh, the Places You'll Boldly Go!* (*Boldly*), which liberally borrowed material from the very popular Dr. Seuss children's book, *Oh, the Places You'll Go!* (*Go!*), as well as other Dr. Seuss works, without permission or license, and combined that material with elements of the popular *Star Trek* franchise. Dr. Seuss Enterprises, L.P. (Seuss) (P), brought suit against ComicMix (D) for, among other things, copyright infringement. ComicMix (D) defended by asserting fair use.

RULE OF LAW

The use of copyrighted material is not a fair use where the use meets none of the non-exclusive fair-use factors set forth in 17 U.S.C. § 107(1)-(4).

FACTS: Some of the authors of episodes of *Star Trek*, the popular space-travel franchise, wanted to do a mash-up of *Star Trek* and some other well-known children's book or book series, and ultimately created a work that liberally borrowed from the extremely popular *Oh, the Places You'll Go!* (*Go!*) by Dr. Seuss and other Dr. Seuss titles. They did not obtain permission to use, or a license for, the Dr. Seuss materials. They titled the mash-up *Oh, the Places You'll Boldly Go!* (*Boldly*), and a publisher, ComicMix LLC (D), started a crowd-sourcing campaign to pay for producing the book, which ComicMix (D) intended to publish. When Dr. Seuss Enterprises, L.P. (Seuss) (P), the holder of the copyrights in Dr. Seuss's works, learned of *Boldly*, Seuss (P) demanded that ComicMix (D) cease and desist from publishing it. ComicMix (D) responded by asserting that its use of the Dr. Seuss materials was a parody and, thus, a fair use. Seuss (P), which had previously licensed *Go!* and other Dr. Seuss works for numerous types of works and merchandise, and had great commercial success doing so, brought suit against ComicMix (D) and the *Boldly* authors and others (collectively "ComicMix" (D)) for, inter alia, copyright infringement. The parties cross-moved for summary judgment, and the district court, finding *Boldly* was a fair use of *Go!*, granted summary judgment to ComicMix (D). The United States Court of Appeals for the Ninth Circuit granted review.

ISSUE: Is the use of copyrighted material a fair use where the use meets none of the non-exclusive fair-use factors set forth in 17 U.S.C. § 107(1)-(4)?

HOLDING AND DECISION: (McKeown, J.) No. The use of copyrighted material is not a fair use where the use meets none of the non-exclusive fair-use factors set forth in 17 U.S.C. § 107(1)-(4). These factors are: (1) the purpose and character of the use, including whether such use is of a commercial nature or is for nonprofit educational purposes; (2) the nature of the copyrighted work; (3) the amount and substantiality of the portion used in relation to the copyrighted work as a whole; and (4) the effect of the use upon the potential market for or value of the copyrighted work. In conducting a fair-use analysis, a court assesses each factor and weighs the results. Here, all four factors decisively weigh against ComicMix (D), and no countervailing copyright principles counsel otherwise. As to the first factor, "the purpose and character of the use, including whether such use is of a commercial nature or is for nonprofit educational purposes," courts look to whether and to what extent the new work is "transformative." Transformative use of the original work can tip the first factor in favor of fair use. A transformative work adds something new, with a further purpose or different character, altering the first with new expression, meaning, or message. Thus, the purpose and character of a parody can render it transformative, since by definition, a parody must use some elements of a prior author's composition to create a new one that, at least in part, comments on that author's works. However, contrary to ComicMix's (D) argument, *Boldly* is not a parody. ComicMix (D) does not seriously contend that *Boldly* critiques or comments on *Go!*. Rather, it claims *Boldly* is a parody because it situated the violent, sexual, sophisticated adult entertainment of *Star Trek* "in the context of Dr. Seuss's world to create a "funny" book. However, the juxtapositions of *Go!* and *Star Trek* elements do not hold *Seussian style* up to ridicule. Instead, *Boldly* evokes, rather than ridicules, *Go!*. Also rejected is ComicMix's (D) completely unconvincing, post-hoc characterization of its work as criticizing the theme of banal narcissism in *Go!*. Nor is *Boldly* otherwise transformative. ComicMix (D) argues that even if *Boldly* is not a parody, *Boldly* is transformative because it replaced Seuss characters and other elements with *Star Trek* material. However, merely adding *Star Trek* material on top of what it meticulously copied from *Go!* cannot be characterized as transformative since such use fails to further a new purpose or different character of the new work; fails to create new information, a new aesthetic, new insights and understanding, or new expression, meaning, or message in the original work, i.e., the addition of value to the original; and fails to use the quoted matter as "raw material," instead of repackaging it and "merely supersed[ing]

Continued on next page.

the objects of the original creation." Instead of possessing a further purpose or different character, *Boldly* intentionally paralleled *Go!*'s purpose. In propounding the same message as *Go!*, *Boldly* used expression from *Go!* to keep to *Go!*'s sentiment. Absent a new purpose or character, merely recontextualizing the original expression by plucking the most visually arresting excerpts of the copyrighted work is not transformative. In sum, as to this factor, it seems that *Go!* was selected to get attention or to avoid the drudgery in working up something fresh, and not for a transformative purpose. As to the second factor, the nature of the copyrighted work, it is recognized that because creative works are closer to the core of intended copyright protection than informational and functional works, fair use is more difficult to establish when the copied work is a creative work. Thus, the creative and expressive nature of *Go!* weighs against fair use. Regarding the third factor, which asks whether the amount and substantiality of the portion used in relation to the copyrighted work as a whole favors fair use, a court considers both the quantitative amount and qualitative value of the original work used in relation to the justification for that use. This factor circles back to the first factor because the extent of permissible copying varies with the purpose and character of the use. Here, the quantitative amount taken by *Boldly* is substantial—close to 60% of *Go!* and significant illustrations from other Dr. Seuss works. For each of the highly imaginative illustrations copied by ComicMix (D), it replicated, as much and as closely as possible from *Go!*, the exact composition, the particular arrangements of visual components, and the swatches of well-known illustrations. ComicMix's (D) claim that it judiciously incorporated just enough of the original to be identifiable as Seussian, or that its modest taking merely alluded to particular Dr. Seuss illustrations, is flatly contradicted by looking at and comparing the books. The qualitative value used by *Boldly* is also substantial. The qualitative analysis often asks if the copyist took the "heart," that is, the most valuable and pertinent portion, of the work. Here, ComicMix (D) took the heart of Dr. Seuss's works, as it took the "heart" of each individual copyrighted picture, and this, too, tilts the third factor against fair use. Given the absence of a parody or a transformative work, ComicMix (D) offers no justification for the commercial exploitation and the extensive and meticulous copying of *Go!*. Thus, the third factor weighs decisively against fair use. Finally, as to the fourth factor, which considers the effect of the use upon the potential market for or value of the copyrighted work, courts must address not only the extent of market harm caused by the particular actions of the alleged infringer, but also whether unrestricted and widespread conduct of the sort engaged in by the defendant would result in a substantially adverse impact on the potential market for the original and the market for derivative works. Here, ComicMix's (D) non-transformative and commercial use of Dr. Seuss's works likely leads to cognizable market harm to the original. Although not much about the fair use doctrine lends itself to absolute statements, the Supreme Court and this circuit have unequivocally placed the burden of proof on the proponent of the affirmative defense of fair use. ComicMix (D) tries to circumvent this burden by contending that fair use is not an affirmative defense and that the burden shifts to Seuss (P) to prove potential market harm, but leading precedent in this area squarely forecloses this argument, given that, since fair use is an affirmative defense, its proponent would have difficulty carrying the burden of demonstrating fair use without favorable evidence about relevant markets. Thus, ComicMix (D), as the proponent of the affirmative defense of fair use, "must bring forward favorable evidence about relevant markets," *Dr. Seuss Enters., L.P. v. Penguin Books USA, Inc.*, 109 F.3d 1394, 1403 (9th Cir. 1997), but because ComicMix's (D) position is that it does not bear the burden of proof, it does not argue the adequacy of its scant evidence. First, ComicMix (D) sidesteps the fact that it intentionally targeted and aimed to capitalize on the same graduation market as *Go!*. The planned release date for the first publication of *Boldly* was scheduled to launch "in time for school graduations." ComicMix (D) acknowledged that *Boldly*'s use of *Go!* will "resonate so much, especially as a graduation gift for folks who grew up reading Seuss." The assertion that the two works target different age groups is undermined by ComicMix's (D) own admission that *Boldly* is "safe" for five-year-olds and "a perfect gift for children and adults of all ages." Additionally, ComicMix (D) does not address a crucial right for a copyright holder—the derivative works market, an area in which Seuss (P) has engaged extensively for decades, and has already vetted and authorized multiple derivatives of *Go!*. Works like *Boldly* would curtail *Go!*'s potential market for derivative works. This is not a case where the copyist's work fills a market that the copyright owner will likely avoid, as is true for a lethal parody or a scathing theater review. In fact, ComicMix (D) hoped to get to one of the potential markets for Seuss's derivative works before Seuss (P), believing that Seuss (P) would want to publish it themselves and give ComicMix (D) a nice payday. Crucially, ComicMix (D) does not overcome the fact that Seuss (P) often collaborates with other creators, including in projects that mix different stories and characters. Seuss (P) routinely receives requests for collaborations and licenses and has entered into various collaborations that apply Seuss's (P) works to new creative contexts. Further, the law does not limit the scope of the relevant market to products that are already made or in the pipeline. The potential market exists independently of the copyright owner's present intent, and Seuss (P) has the right to the artistic decision not to saturate those markets with variations of their original, and Seuss (P) has the

Continued on next page.

right to change its mind. Finally, the unrestricted and widespread conduct of the sort engaged in by ComicMix (D) would harm Seuss's (P) market by undermining its potential market. This aspect is particularly significant here because of Seuss's (P) strong brand, and ComicMix's (D) effort to use Seuss's (P) success against it falls flat; the unrestricted and widespread conduct of the sort ComicMix (D) engaged in could result in anyone being able to produce, without Seuss's (P) permission, countless mash-ups, and incentives to pirate intellectual property. It could also disincentivize the creation of illustrated books—which is contrary to the goal of copyright to "promote the Progress of Science." U.S. Const. art. I, §8, cl. 8. In sum, ComicMix (D) created, without seeking permission or a license, a nontransformative commercial work that targeted and would usurp *Go!*'s potential market. Accordingly, ComicMix (D) did not carry its burden on the fourth factor. Based on the weighing of the statutory factors in light of the purposes of copyright, ComicMix (D) cannot sustain a fair-use defense. The district court erred in granting summary judgment in favor of ComicMix (D). Reversed.

ANALYSIS

The court emphatically rejected ComicMix's (D) argument regarding the third statutory factor that the amount it took from Dr. Seuss's works was not substantial because ComicMix (D) used only five out of almost 60 Dr. Seuss books. The court characterized this argument as "fake math" that distorted the result because ComicMix (D) identified the wrong denominator. The court stressed that the third factor looks at "the amount and substantiality of the portion used *in relation to the copyrighted work as a whole*," not to the entire corpus of the author. 17 U.S.C. § 107(3) (emphasis added), so that under ComicMix's (D) theory, the more prolific the creator, the greater license a copyist would have to copy and imitate the original works. However, nothing in copyright law supports such an argument.

Quicknotes

AFFIRMATIVE DEFENSES An assertion raised by the defendant in the answer, permitting the introduction of additional evidence to address or refute a plaintiff's allegations; affirmative defenses shift the burden of proof to the defendant to establish all the elements of the defense.

COPYRIGHT INFRINGEMENT A violation of one of the exclusive rights granted to an artist pursuant to Article I, Section 8, clause 8 of the United States Constitution over the reproduction, display, performance, distribution, and adaptation of his work for a period prescribed by statute.

DERIVATIVE WORK A work of authorship that is based on a previous work.

FAIR USE An affirmative defense to a claim of copyright infringement providing an exception from the copyright owner's exclusive rights in a work for the purposes of criticism, comment, news reporting, teaching, scholarship, or research.

SUMMARY JUDGMENT Judgment rendered by a court in response to a motion made by one of the parties, claiming that the lack of a question of material fact in respect to an issue warrants disposition of the issue without consideration by the jury.

Association for Molecular Pathology v. Myriad Genetics, Inc.

Challengers to patent (P) v. Patent holder (D)

569 U.S. 576 (2013)

NATURE OF CASE: Appeal from a decision by the United States Court of Appeals for the Federal Circuit holding that Myriad's (D) patent for two human genes was valid.

FACT SUMMARY: Using a widely known process to isolate DNA and human genes, Myriad Genetics, Inc. (D) successfully identified and isolated two specific human genes naturally occurring in the human body. Mutations in these two genes can significantly increase a woman's risk of developing breast and ovarian cancer.

RULE OF LAW

Laws of nature, natural phenomena, and abstract ideas are not patentable because they are tools of scientific and technological work that lie beyond the domain of patent protection.

FACTS: Myriad Genetics, Inc. (Myriad) (D) successfully identified and isolated two specific human genes that exist naturally in the human body. Mutations in these two genes, BRCA1 and BRCA2, can significantly increase a woman's risk of developing breast and ovarian cancer. Myriad (D) discovered the two genes using a widely recognized method of identifying such genes. Many other entities and scientists employed the same method. After discovery of the two genes that related to breast and ovarian cancer, Myriad (D) sought a patent that would give it the exclusive right to perform genetic testing on women by isolating and examining the genes at issue. Myriad (D) also sought a patent to synthetically create the two genes to allow for further research. After Myriad (D) received the patents, a group of advocacy groups, patients, and physicians known as the Association for Molecular Pathology (P) brought suit against Myriad (D), challenging the validity of the patents. A federal District Court found the patents invalid because they involved genes that occurred naturally. The United States Court of Appeals for the Federal Circuit reversed and held that Myriad's (D) patent for the two human genes was valid. The United States Supreme Court vacated that decision and returned the case to the Court of Appeals. That court disagreed over the patentability of the two genes but did find that the creation of synthetic genes was patentable. The United States Supreme Court again granted the petition for further review.

ISSUE: Are laws of nature, natural phenomena, and abstract ideas not patentable because they are tools of scientific and technological work that lie beyond the domain of patent protection?

HOLDING AND DECISION: (Thomas, J.) Yes. Laws of nature, natural phenomena, and abstract ideas are not patentable because they are tools of scientific and technological work that lie beyond the domain of patent protection. 35 U.S.C. § 101 provides that "whoever invents or discovers any new or useful . . . composition of matter, or useful improvement thereof, may obtain a patent therefor." However, laws of nature or natural phenomena are generally not patentable. Granting patents in these cases would tie up research tools and potentially inhibit further innovations. Patent law strikes a balance between creating incentives that lead to inventions and impeding the flow of knowledge and information that assists with such inventions and creations. The issue in this case is: do Myriad's (D) patents relate to "new and useful composition of matter," or naturally occurring phenomena? Regarding the two genes, BRCA1 and BRCA2, Myriad (D) did not create anything. It did discover the two genes, but the act of separating those genes and identifying them is not an act of creation. In addition, the method of identifying genes is well known and widely employed. However, Myriad's (D) creation of the two synthetic genes resembling BRCA1 and BRCA2 is patentable. Synthetic DNA or cDNA is distinct from the naturally occurring DNA from which it is derived. To create the cDNA, a lab technician must isolate only part of a DNA strand as opposed to the entire strand. This portion of a gene is therefore not something that naturally occurs. The lab technician must take steps to add nucleotides to create a synthetic DNA molecule. There is no question the lab technician is creating something new in this situation. Accordingly, Myriad's (D) patent relating to the creation of synthetic BRCA1 and BRCA2 is patentable.

ANALYSIS

This unanimous decision from the United States Supreme Court explains the well-known patent exception for things that occur naturally. The case deals with patentability, the first of five requirements an invention must meet before it can be patented. The five requirements are: (1) the subject matter must be a composition of matter or a method of manufacture; (2) the invention must be novel; (3) the invention must be nonobvious; (4) the invention must be useful; and (5) the invention must be particularly described.

Continued on next page.

Quicknotes

PATENT A limited monopoly conferred on the invention or discovery of any new or useful machine or process that is novel and nonobvious.

Juicy Whip, Inc. v. Orange Bang, Inc.

Patent holder (P) v. Alleged patent infringer (D)

185 F.3d 1364 (Fed. Cir. 1999)

NATURE OF CASE: Appeal from lower court decision finding that the plaintiff's patent was invalid because it lacked the requirement of utility.

FACT SUMMARY: Juicy Whip, Inc. (P), a manufacturer of beverage dispensers, created a dispenser that displayed a previously mixed beverage in an opaque bowl, leading consumers to believe they would receive their drinks directly from that bowl. Instead, when the operator poured the beverage, the dispenser would combine water from one bowl and syrup concentrate from a separate, hidden bowl to create the beverage.

RULE OF LAW

An invention does not lack the utility requirement for patentability simply because it deceives the public through imitation in an effort to increase product sales.

FACTS: Juicy Whip, Inc. (P), a manufacturer of beverage dispensers, created a dispenser that displayed a previously mixed beverage in an opaque bowl, leading consumers to believe they would receive their drinks directly from that bowl. Instead, when the operator poured the beverage, the dispenser would combine water from one bowl and syrup concentrate from a separate, hidden bowl to create the beverage. Juicy Whip (P) received a patent for the post-mix dispenser. The term post-mix derives from the time of the mixing. The mixing only occurs after a consumer has ordered the drink. Juicy Whip (P) brought this infringement suit against Orange Bang (D) after discovering Orange Bang (D) was using similar machines. Orange Bang (D) defended the suit on the grounds Juicy Whip (P) was deceiving its customers by appearing to dispense "pre-mix" beverages, when in actuality the beverages were of the post-mix variety. The lower court granted Orange Bang's (D) motion for summary judgment on the ground Juicy Whip's (P) hidden-bowl, post-mix dispenser lacked utility. The court found Juicy Whip's (P) only purpose was to increase sales by deceiving customers into thinking they were receiving their beverages directly from the opaque, pre-mixed bowl in front of them. Juicy Whip (P) appealed to the United States Court of Appeals for the Federal Circuit.

ISSUE: Does an invention lack the utility requirement for patentability simply because it deceives the public through imitation in an effort to increase product sales?

HOLDING AND DECISION: (Bryson, J.) No. An invention does not lack the utility requirement for patentability simply because it deceives the public through imitation in an effort to increase product sales. 35 U.S.C. § 101 provides that whoever invents or discovers any new or useful composition of matter or improvement thereof, may obtain a patent therefor. The threshold for utility or usefulness is low. An invention is useful if it can provide some identifiable benefit. A patent will fail for lack of utility only if it is totally incapable of achieving a useful result. Altering a product to make it imitate another product is itself a specific benefit that satisfies the utility requirement. Cubic zirconium is designed to appear as a diamond and imitation leather is designed to appear real. Laminated wood is designed to mimic the appearance of real wood. All of these have had valid patents. The value of these products is that they appear to be something they are not. Here, Juicy Whip's (P) post-mix dispenser satisfies the utility requirement by embodying the features of a post-mix dispenser while imitating the outward appearance of a pre-mix dispenser. The fact that Juicy Whip (P) is allegedly deceiving its customers does not override the utility of the invention. The federal Patent Office does not serve as arbiter of alleged deceptive trade practices. In addition, Orange Bang (D) has not argued there is anything illegal with the display of a drink that is not actually served to the customers. Accordingly, the district court erred in granting summary judgment to Orange Bang (D). Reversed and remanded.

ANALYSIS

The decision highlighted Justice Joseph Story's seminal patent opinion in *Lowell v. Lewis*, 15 F. Cas. 1018 (C.C.D. Mass. 1817). In that case, Justice Story, who went on to become a United States Supreme Court justice, held that inventions that are injurious to the well-being or sound morals of society are not patentable. Over the years, courts have moved away from the rigid, morals-based law regarding patents in favor of the utility test as codified in 35 U.S.C. § 101.

Quicknotes

PATENT A limited monopoly conferred on the invention or discovery of any new or useful machine or process that is novel and nonobvious.

SUMMARY JUDGMENT Judgment rendered by a court in response to a motion made by one of the parties, claiming that the lack of a question of material fact in respect to an issue warrants disposition of the issue without consideration by the jury.

eBay Inc. v. MercExchange, L.L.C.

Alleged patent infringer (D) v. Patent holder (P)

547 U.S. 388 (2006)

NATURE OF CASE: Appeal from a decision by the United States Court of Appeals for the Federal Circuit to allow patent holder's motion for a permanent injunction against a patent infringer.

FACT SUMMARY: MercExchange, L.L.C. (P) holds a valid business method patent for an electronic, internet-based market used for the sale of goods between private individuals. It brought a patent infringement suit against eBay Inc. (D) and a subsidiary, Half.com (D).

RULE OF LAW

Under the Patent Act, a court has discretion to issue an equitable injunction against a patent infringer only if the patent holder can satisfy the well-established, four-factor test for the issuance of a permanent injunction.

FACTS: MercExchange, L.L.C. (P) holds a valid business method patent for an electronic, internet-based market used for the sale of goods between private individuals. MercExchange (P) sought to license its patent to eBay, Inc. (D) but negotiations failed. MercExchange (P) then brought a patent infringement suit against eBay (D) and a subsidiary, Half.com (D), for using a similar internet-based market to sell goods. A jury in United States District Court for the Eastern District of Virginia found that MercExchange's (P) patent was valid and awarded it damages. MercExchange (P) then filed a motion for a permanent injunction to prohibit eBay (D) from employing its internet-based market. The federal district court denied the motion but the United States Court of Appeals for the Federal Circuit reversed. It held that, as a general rule, courts should issue permanent injunctions against patent infringers. The United States Supreme Court granted eBay's (D) petition for further review.

ISSUE: Under the Patent Act, does a court have discretion to issue an equitable injunction against a patent infringer only if the patent holder can satisfy the well-established, four-factor test for the issuance of a permanent injunction?

HOLDING AND DECISION: (Thomas, J.) Yes. Under the Patent Act, a court has discretion to issue an equitable injunction against a patent infringer only if the patent holder can satisfy the well-established, four-factor test for the issuance of a permanent injunction. A plaintiff must demonstrate: (1) that it has suffered an irreparable injury; (2) that remedies available at law, such as monetary damages, are inadequate to compensate for that injury; (3) that considering the balance of hardships between the plaintiff and defendant, a remedy in equity is warranted; and (4) that the public interest would not be disserved by a permanent injunction. Accordingly, a finding of a patent infringement does not automatically warrant the issuance of a permanent injunction as the circuit court contends. This Court has similarly held that a copyright infringement does not necessarily lead to a permanent injunction. Traditional equitable considerations remain paramount and each motion for a permanent injunction must be made on a case-by-case basis. Because neither the district court nor the circuit court applied the four-factor test for the issuance of permanent injunctions, the circuit court's decision is vacated. The case is remanded to the district court for a consideration of MercExchange's (P) motion for a permanent injunction based upon traditional equitable principles.

CONCURRENCE: (Roberts, C.J.) The majority is correct that courts should not automatically issue injunctions based on patent infringements. However, since the 19th century, courts in a majority of cases have issued various forms of equitable injunctive relief after finding that a patent has been infringed. While equitable considerations remain paramount, courts should look to prior decisions for guidance when issuing injunctions in patent cases.

CONCURRENCE: (Kennedy, J.) The Patent Act and the principles surrounding the issuance of a permanent injunction recognize that the existence of a right to exclude does not dictate the scope of the remedy for a violation of that right. While a review of historical practice may be beneficial, the economic function of the patent in many current cases is very different from earlier cases. Today, many companies obtain patents for the sole purpose of licensing those patents. Accordingly, once the patent is obtained, the holder then has the ability to threaten an injunction on another potential rival if it refuses to execute a license agreement. In these cases, where a violation is found, monetary damages may be more appropriate than a permanent injunction.

ANALYSIS

Justice Kennedy's concurring opinion relates to the rise of companies that exist solely to purchase patents. These companies then demand licensing fees from

Continued on next page.

other companies that have created an invention, perhaps totally unaware that a patent already exists for the product. Accordingly, even where a patent may technically be infringed, a permanent injunction should be avoided where the patent holder exists solely to obtain license fees.

Quicknotes

INJUNCTIVE RELIEF A court order issued as a remedy, requiring a person to do, or prohibiting that person from doing, a specific act.

LICENSE A right that is granted to a person allowing him or her to conduct an activity that without such permission he or she could not lawfully do, and which is unassignable and revocable at the will of the licensor.

PERMANENT INJUNCTION A remedy imposed by the court ordering a party to cease the conduct of a specific activity until the final disposition of the cause of action.

CHAPTER 4

Adverse Possession

Quick Reference Rules of Law

Brown v. Gobble

Property owner (P) v. Adjoining property owner (D)

W. Va. Sup. Ct. App., 474 S.E.2d 489 (1996)

NATURE OF CASE: Appeal from judgment in an action to enjoin interference with use of real property.

FACT SUMMARY: The Browns (P) and the Gobbles (D) disputed ownership of a two-foot-wide tract of property on the boundary of their properties.

RULE OF LAW

The doctrine of tacking allows parties claiming adverse possession to use their predecessors' conduct on the property to meet the time requirements of adverse possession.

FACTS: The Gobbles (D) purchased real property in 1985. At the time, a fence ran along the rear boundary of the property that adjoined property purchased by the Browns (P) in 1989. The Browns (P) discovered, prior to buying, that this fence actually extended two feet past the true boundary. However, the Browns (P) did not claim ownership of this two-foot-wide tract until 1994, when they decided to build a road along that property. The Gobbles (D) sought to prevent the building of the road, and the Browns (P) filed suit to enjoin this interference. The Gobbles (D) counterclaimed that they owned the two-foot-wide tract through adverse possession. The Gobbles (D) presented evidence that both the Blevins and the Fletchers, who owned the Gobbles' (D) property from 1937 through 1985, believed they owned the boundary tract and treated the property as their own. However, the trial court ruled that adverse possession had not been proved and entered judgment for the Browns (P). The Gobbles (D) appealed.

ISSUE: Does the doctrine of tacking allow parties claiming adverse possession to use their predecessors' conduct on the property to meet the time requirements of adverse possession?

HOLDING AND DECISION: (Cleckley, J.) Yes. The doctrine of tacking allows parties claiming adverse possession to use their predecessors' conduct on the property to meet the time requirements of adverse possession. In order to prove adverse possession, a party must prove the following elements: (1) the property has been held adversely; (2) there has been actual possession; (3) possession has been open and notorious; (4) possession has been exclusive; (5) possession has been continuous; and (6) the property has been held under claim or color of title. In the case at hand, the requisite period of time for adverse possession is ten years. The principle of tacking has long been recognized in adverse possession cases. This principle allows different adverse possessions to make up the requisite time for holding such possessions, so long as they are connected by privity of title or claim. Thus, although the Gobbles (D) had personally adversely held the property for only nine years, the adverse possession by the prior owners of the property, who are connected to them through the title to their property, helps to satisfy the elements of adverse possession long before the ten-year period. Accordingly, if their adverse possession was tacked onto the Gobbles' own adverse possession, the Gobbles (D) would meet the time requirement. The trial court apparently misunderstood the relationship between tacking and adverse possession. Reversed and remanded.

ANALYSIS

This decision also established the standard of proof for adverse possession claims. The court held that adverse possession must be proved by clear and convincing evidence. Although some jurisdictions require only a preponderance standard, the majority view is in accord with this decision.

Quicknotes

ADVERSE POSSESSION A means of acquiring title to real property by remaining in actual, open, continuous, exclusive possession of property for the statutory period.

AFFIRMATIVE EASEMENT The right to utilize a portion of another's real property in order to conduct a specific activity thereon.

NEGATIVE EASEMENT Refers to the duty to refrain from conducting a specific lawful activity on the servient estate because it interferes with the use of the dominant estate.

POSSESSION UNDER COLOR OF TITLE Means of acquiring title to real property by remaining in actual, open, continuous, exclusive possession of property for the statutory period.

PRESCRIPTIVE EASEMENT A manner of acquiring an easement in another's property by continuous and uninterrupted use in satisfaction of the statutory requirements of adverse possession.

TACKING Attachment of periods of adverse possession by different adverse possessors in order to fulfill the requirement of continuous possession for the period proscribed by statute.

Paine v. Sexton

Adverse possession claimant (P) v. Record owner (D)

Mass. App. Ct., 37 N.E. 3d 1103 (2015)

NATURE OF CASE: Appeal from judgment for plaintiffs in action to register ownership of wooded land on grounds of adverse possession and color of title.

FACT SUMMARY: The Paines (P), whose family operated a campground since the 1950s on around 36 acres of primarily wooded land sought to register the land as their own on the basis of adverse possession based on nonpermissive use of portions of the property for more than 20 years in a manner that was actual, open, notorious, exclusive, and adverse, as well as on adverse possession under color of title based on deeds purporting to convey title to them as to those portions of the locus where they could not show actual use. The Sextons (D), who claimed title to the land on the basis of a 2007 deed, contended that the Paines (P) could not establish their claim of adverse possession of any portion of the wooded parcels because they had not enclosed them or reduced them to cultivation, and that, in any event, the deeds under which they claimed color of title were inadequate in description to support such a claim.

RULE OF LAW

(1) To prevail on a claim of adverse possession of wild or wooded land through nonpermissive use that is open, notorious, exclusive, and adverse for the requisite statutory period of time, the adverse claimant, in addition, is not required to have entirely enclosed the parcel at issue or reduced it to cultivation.

(2) Where a claim of adverse possession under color of title is sought to be supported by a deed that references assessors' maps, in addition to including a metes and bounds description, or a description by reference to abutting parcels, the description by reference to the assessors' maps does not render the description of the parcel inadequate to support the claim.

FACTS: The Paines (P) and their family predecessors operated a commercial campground since the 1950s on around 36 acres of primarily wooded land. They created roadways, cleared campsites, built a house, and office, and toilet facilities, as well numerous other campsite amenities. They hung "no trespassing" signs around much of the campground and controlled entry to the locus by charging an amount per person and ousting those who did not pay. They advertised the campground with signage along the highway, and in newspaper advertisements and brochures distributed in local stores. In addition, they paid taxes on the property since the 1960s, although it was unclear exactly which parcels the plaintiffs paid taxes on because many of the bills did not delineate lot numbers and acreage. Despite the Paines' (P) extensive use of portions of the property, they did not enclose it entirely with fencing or reduce it to cultivation, instead maintaining areas between individual campsites in a predominantly natural state, for privacy and to preserve the wooded condition of the area. The Paines (P) also had seven deeds that had been properly registered that included references to the town assessors' maps for assistance in locating the parcels conveyed, as well as metes and bounds descriptions, or reference to abutting parcels. The Paines (P) sought to register the land as their own on the basis of adverse possession based on nonpermissive use of portions of the property for more than 20 years in a manner that was actual, open, notorious, exclusive, and adverse, as well as on adverse possession under color of title based on deeds purporting to convey title to them as to those portions of the locus where they could not show actual use. The Sextons (D), who claimed title to the land on the basis of a 2007 deed, contended that the Paines (P) could not establish their claim of adverse possession of any portion of the wooded parcels because they had not enclosed them or reduced them to cultivation, and that, in any event, the deeds under which they claimed color of title were inadequate in description to support such a claim. The land court (a trial court) ruled in the Paines' (P) favor on both the claim of adverse possession on the basis of nonpermissive use as well as the claim of adverse possession under color of title. The state's intermediate appellate court granted review.

ISSUE:

(1) To prevail on a claim of adverse possession of wild or wooded land through nonpermissive use that is open, notorious, exclusive, and adverse for the requisite statutory period of time, is the adverse claimant, in addition, required to have entirely enclosed the parcel at issue or reduced it to cultivation?

(2) Where a claim of adverse possession under color of title is sought to be supported by a deed that references assessors' maps, in addition to including a metes and bounds description, or a description by reference to abutting parcels, does the description by reference to the assessors' maps render the description of the parcel inadequate to support the claim?

HOLDING AND DECISION: (Brown, J.)

(1) No. To prevail on a claim of adverse possession of wild or wooded land through nonpermissive use that

Continued on next page.

is open, notorious, exclusive, and adverse for the requisite statutory period of time, the adverse claimant, in addition, is not required to have entirely enclosed the parcel at issue or reduced it to cultivation. The Sextons (D) contend that as regards wild or wooded land, a nonpermissive user must entirely enclose or reduce to cultivation, the parcel or parcels that are claimed through adverse possession, and that, therefore, the Paines (P) cannot prevail on their adverse possession claim. However, the strict rule applicable to wild or wooded lands is an application of the general rule of adverse possession to the circumstances presented by wild or uncultivated lands, so that the nature of the occupancy and use must be such as to place the lawful owner on notice that another person is in occupancy of the land, under an apparent claim of right; in the circumstances of wild and unimproved land, a more pronounced occupation is needed to achieve that purpose. Here, where the Paines (P) operated the locus as a commercial campground advertised as such, improved the site by clearing campsites and constructing roadways, toilet buildings, and an office, and restricted access to paying customers, the trial judge correctly ruled that their use was sufficient to place the record owners on notice that they occupied the locus under a claim of right. Affirmed as to this issue.

(2) No. Where a claim of adverse possession under color of title is sought to be supported by a deed that references assessors' maps, in addition to including a metes and bounds description or a description by reference to abutting parcels, the description by reference to the assessors' maps does not render the description of the parcel inadequate to support the claim. Pursuant to the doctrine of color of title, the activities relied upon to establish adverse possession reach not only the part of the premises actually occupied, but the entire premises described in a deed to the claimant, as the entry is deemed to be coextensive with the grant upon the ground that it is the intention of the grantee to assert such possession. The descriptions in the deeds presented by the Paines (P) are typical of those validly used to describe and convey property, and there is no reason why a supplemental reference to the assessors' maps should derogate from the validity of the more detailed description contained in the deeds. Affirmed as to this issue. Affirmed.

ANALYSIS

Regarding a description in a deed that references assessors' maps, such maps, or plans as they are sometimes called, typically show the particular lot in connection with all neighboring lands, and are easily found and open to public inspection at reasonable times under rational limitations, thus rendering them, as a practical matter, as definite and accurate a description of a given parcel as a plan in a registry of deeds.

Quicknotes

ADVERSE POSSESSION A means of acquiring title to real property by remaining in actual, open, continuous, exclusive possession of the property for the statutory period.

LOCUS Location or place.

METES AND BOUNDS A description of a property by its measured boundaries. A metes and bounds description states the angles and distances of the property from designated landmarks and in relation to adjoining properties.

POSSESSION UNDER COLOR OF TITLE A means of acquiring title to real property by remaining in actual, open, continuous, exclusive possession of property for the statutory period.

Nome 2000 v. Fagerstrom

Landowner (P) v. Adverse possessor (D)

Alaska Sup. Ct., 799 P.2d 304 (1990)

NATURE OF CASE: Suit for ejectment and counterclaim to acquire title by adverse possession.

FACT SUMMARY: Charles and Peggy Fagerstrom (D) used a parcel of land owned by Nome 2000 (P) for various purposes from 1944 to 1987 but did not build a house on it until 1978, thereby defeating their adverse possession claim, according to Nome (P).

RULE OF LAW

A determination of whether a claimant's physical acts upon the land of another are sufficiently continuous, notorious, and exclusive does not necessarily depend on the existence of significant improvements, substantial activity, or absolute exclusivity.

FACTS: Charles Fagerstrom's family (D) used a rural parcel of land owned by Nome 2000 (P) for recreational purposes beginning in 1944. In 1963, Charles and Peggy Fagerstrom married. In the 1970s, Charles and Peggy Fagerstrom (D) and their family began to make more substantial use of the land, adding improvements and spending more time there each year. In 1977, they built a reindeer shelter that occasionally housed reindeer. They also excluded trailers from the land and spent weekends there. In 1987, the Fagerstroms (D) built a cabin on the land and continued to use the land on weekends and vacations for recreational purposes. In 1987, Nome 2000 (P) brought suit to quiet title. The Fagerstroms (D) counterclaimed for title by adverse possession.

ISSUE: Does a determination of whether a claimant's physical acts upon the land of another are sufficiently continuous, notorious, and exclusive necessarily depend on the existence of significant improvements, substantial activity, or absolute exclusivity?

HOLDING AND DECISION: (Matthews, C.J.) No. A determination of whether a claimant's physical acts upon the land of another are sufficiently continuous, notorious, and exclusive does not necessarily depend on the existence of significant improvements, substantial activity, or absolute exclusivity. Use consistent with the use by any similarly situated owner is sufficient to establish claim by adverse possession. The statute requires continuous, notorious, hostile, and exclusive use of a property for ten years in order to succeed in a claim for adverse possession. Nome (P) claimed that the Fagerstroms' (D) possession only became adverse when they built the cabin in 1978, and thus they did not meet the statutory ten-year period. But the statute does not require actual improvements to the land, only sufficient use based on the type of property occupied. The land in question is rural and thus has a lower requirement of use. The Fagerstroms (D) occupied the land sufficiently that their occupation was visible in 1977. The various structures erected and the feeling of the community that the Fagerstroms (D) were the owners of the property, meets the statutory requirement of continuous, notorious, exclusive, and hostile possession. The judgment of the superior court denying the Plaintiff's motion for a direct verdict is reversed and the case is remanded to the trial court.

ANALYSIS

The court found that what the Fagerstroms (D), as Native Alaskans, believed or intended vis-à-vis the property had nothing to do with whether their possession was hostile. The hostility requirement merely means that the adverse possessor acted toward the land as if he were the owner. But the Fagerstroms (D) claim that title to a large portion of the land was only partially granted by the court. The Fagerstroms' (D) use of certain trails for hiking did not constitute dominion and control over the south portion of the land sufficient to demonstrate adverse possession.

Quicknotes

ADVERSE POSSESSION A means of acquiring title to real property by remaining in actual, open, continuous, exclusive possession of property for the statutory period.

EJECTMENT An action to oust someone in possession of real property unlawfully and to restore possession to the party lawfully entitled to it.

PRESCRIPTIVE EASEMENT A manner of acquiring an easement in another's property by continuous and uninterrupted use in satisfaction of the statutory requirements of adverse possession.

Frech v. Piontkowski

Prescriptive easement claimant (P) v. Owner of artificial body of water (D)

Conn. Sup. Ct., 994 A.2d 84 (2010)

NATURE OF CASE: Appeal from judgment granting a prescriptive easement for recreational use to landowners abutting an artificial body of water.

FACT SUMMARY: Landowners (P) abutting an artificial reservoir that was privately owned claimed that they had acquired a prescriptive easement for recreational use over the body of water. The reservoir owners (D) contended that, as a matter of law, an abutting landowner may not acquire such a prescriptive easement, and that, in any event, the abutting landowners (P) failed to prove they satisfied the requirements for obtaining a prescriptive easement.

RULE OF LAW

(1) As a matter of law, an abutting landowner may acquire a prescriptive easement for recreational use over a nonnavigable, artificial body of water.

(2) Landowners abutting an artificial, nonnavigable body of water may acquire a prescriptive easement for recreational use over the entire body of water where they have made recreational use of the body of water under a claim of right, openly and notoriously, and continuously and uninterrupted, for the requisite statutory period of time.

FACTS: A reservoir was artificially created by damming a brook, and the owners of the land underneath the reservoir became its owners. Owners of land abutting the reservoir (P) made recreational use of the entire reservoir, including boating, swimming, fishing, and skating, for well over two decades. The reservoir owners (D) never gave the abutting landowners (P) permission to do so—and the abutting landowners (P) never asked for such permission. At different times, the reservoir owners (D) posted "No Trespassing" signs in the water near the land owned by the abutting landowners (P), but each time they did so, the abutting landowners (P) would take the signs down. On a few occasions, the reservoir owners (D) ejected members of the abutting landowners' (P) families from the reservoir, but as a matter of course, the abutting landowners (P) did not respond the reservoir owners' (D) attempt to prevent them from using the reservoir. Eventually, the abutting landowners (P) brought an action for a prescriptive easement over the reservoir for recreational purposes. The reservoir owners (D) contended that, as a matter of law, an abutting landowner may not acquire such a prescriptive easement, and that, in any event, the abutting landowners (P) failed to prove they satisfied the requirements for obtaining a prescriptive easement. The trial court granted judgment for the abutting landowners (P), and the state's highest court granted review.

ISSUE:

(1) As a matter of law, may an abutting landowner acquire a prescriptive easement for recreational use over a nonnavigable, artificial body of water?

(2) May landowners abutting an artificial, nonnavigable body of water acquire a prescriptive easement for recreational use over the entire body of water where they have made recreational use of the body of water under a claim of right, openly and notoriously, and continuously and uninterrupted, for the requisite statutory period of time?

HOLDING AND DECISION: (McLachlan, J.)

(1) Yes. As a matter of law, an abutting landowner may acquire a prescriptive easement for recreational use over a nonnavigable, artificial body of water. First, the reservoir owners (D) argue that the acquisition of an easement over an artificial body of water imposes too great a burden on the servient estate by imposing on the owner the duty to maintain the artificial body of water. Second, they argue that the acquisition of an easement for recreational purposes over water presents notice issues that do not exist with respect to easements acquired over land or to easements for commercial purposes over water. Neither argument is persuasive. As to the first argument, the reservoir owners (D) rely on the principle that one who has an easement by prescription has the right to do such acts that are reasonable and necessary to effectuate the party's enjoyment of the easement unless it unreasonably increases the burden on the servient tenement. This principle, however, is relevant to the scope of an easement that has been acquired by prescription, and not to whether an easement may or may not be acquired as a matter of law. Moreover, the extent to which the servient estate will be burdened by the easement is at best unclear, since it is unclear whether the owners of the body of water would be required to maintain it in perpetuity. As to the second argument, the reservoir owners (D) contend that recreational uses of a body of water are too intermittent and do not leave adequate traces to offer

Continued on next page.

sufficient notice, and they argue that the lack of sufficient notice is inconsistent with a conclusion that adverse recreational use can be open. Whether the elements of a prescriptive easement have been proven in a particular case, however, presents a question of fact. That argument, therefore, goes to whether there is sufficient evidence to support a trial court's factual finding that a claimant's use is open, but does not call into question whether an easement by prescription for recreational purposes may be acquired as a matter of law.

(2) Yes. Landowners abutting an artificial, nonnavigable body of water may acquire a prescriptive easement for recreational use over the entire body of water where they have made recreational use of the body of water under a claim of right, openly and notoriously, and continuously and uninterrupted, for the requisite statutory period of time. A party claiming to have acquired an easement by prescription must demonstrate that the use of the property has been open, visible, continuous, and uninterrupted (in this state) for 15 years and made under a claim of right. The purpose of the open and visible requirement is to give the owner of the servient land knowledge and full opportunity to assert the owner's rights. To satisfy this requirement, the adverse use must be made in such a way that a reasonably diligent owner would learn of its existence, nature, and extent. Open generally means that the use is not made in secret or stealthily. It may also mean that it is visible or apparent. An openly visible and apparent use satisfies the requirement even if the neighbors have no actual knowledge of it. Here, the evidence supported the trial court's findings that the abutting landowners (P) and their predecessors in title had used the whole of the reservoir in an open, visible, continuous, and uninterrupted manner under a claim of right. Such use has been made without license or permission and without recognition of any rights in the reservoir owners (D) to prevent this use. The evidence showed that the abutting landowners (P), their predecessors in title, their families, and their guests, for over a period of 25 years, used the whole of the reservoir for myriad recreational purposes, and that such use would have been discovered by a diligent owner. Therese findings were sufficient to support the determination that the abutting landowners' (P) use was open and notorious. The requirement that the use be continuous is satisfied if it is proven that the use was uninterrupted for a period of at least 15 years. Here, the trial court found that the recreational uses made of the reservoir by the abutting landowners (P) continued without interruption up to the time of trial. The reservoir owners (D) contend that because the use of the reservoir was not constant, it was not continuous. Nonetheless, the use was regular, notwithstanding that in some years some uses were greater than others. Moreover, the law has not imposed a requirement that use must be constant to satisfy the requirement that use be continuous, and it has been held that, depending on the type of use involved, seasonal use may be sufficient to satisfy the continuity requirement. It is axiomatic that in determining whether a prescriptive easement has vested, the nature of the easement will dictate the type of evidence that is required to prove it. To require proof of daily or constant use for a recreational easement ignores the type of easement at issue. Thus, the evidence was sufficient to support the trial court's determination that the use was continuous. The reservoir owners (D) also contended that their actions were sufficient to interrupt the abutting landowners' (P) use of the reservoir, pointing to their posting of "No Trespassing" signs in the water, and to ejecting abutting landowners' (P) family members on a couple of occasions. The trial court found that these actions were not sufficient to interrupt the continuous use of the reservoir. A state statute provides that "[t]he owner of land over which a right-of-way or other easement is claimed or used may give notice in writing, to the person claiming or using the privilege, of his intention to dispute the right-of-way or other easement and to prevent the other party from acquiring the right; and the notice, being served and recorded… shall be deemed an interruption of the use and shall prevent the acquiring of a right thereto by the continuance of the use for any length of time thereafter." However, none of the actions taken by the reservoir owners (D) satisfied these requirements, and the evidence was sufficient to support the trial court's finding that the adverse use was uninterrupted. The reservoir owners (D) also contended that there was insufficient evidence to support the trial court's determination that the abutting landowners (P) had used the reservoir under a claim of right. The requirement that the use must be exercised under a claim of right does not necessitate proof of a claim actually made and brought to the attention of the owner. It means nothing more than a use as of right, that is, without recognition of the right of the landowner. When there is no proof of an express permission from the owner of the servient estate, on the one hand, or of an express claim of right by the person or persons using the way, on the other, the character of the use, whether adverse or permissive, can be determined as an inference from the circumstances of the parties and the nature of the use, and a trier of fact has wide latitude in drawing an inference that a use was

Continued on next page.

under a claim of right. Here, there was no testimony presented that the abutting landowners (P) asked for, or were given permission to use the reservoir and the evidence presented of their conduct with respect to the reservoir supported the trial court's determination that they used the reservoir under a claim of right. When the reservoir owners (D) placed "No Trespassing" signs in the water, the abutting landowners (P) removed the signs. They used the entire reservoir without receiving permission to do so and did not respond to the reservoir owners' (D) intermittent attempts to prevent them from using the reservoir. Although the reservoir owners (D) presented evidence that at some point the abutting landowners (P) considered, and rejected, the option of paying the reservoir owners (D) to use the reservoir, there was insufficient evidence that the abutting landowners (P) used the reservoir under a claim of right. On the contrary, the abutting landowners' (P) rejection of paying the reservoir owners (D) for the right to use the reservoir as an option after exploring that possibility supports the trial court's conclusion that the abutting landowners (P) did not recognize the reservoir owners' (D) authority to exclude them from the reservoir. For these reasons, the abutting landowners (P) satisfied the requirements for acquiring the prescriptive easement they sought. Affirmed.

ANALYSIS

In general, title may be acquired against riparian or littoral owners by prescription. Historically, property rights in lakes were significantly different from property rights in streams, and each had a different name. Rights in streams were "riparian," whereas rights in lakes were "littoral." Although rights in the Great Lakes, and other large bodies of standing water, still are treated differently from the rights of owners along the shore of smaller lakes or ponds in some jurisdictions, the two terms generally have merged and the term "riparian right" is now considered to encompass both types. In this case, it was undisputed that the reservoir owners (D) owned the land beneath the reservoir. Even though the reservoir owners' (D) deeds did not describe the reservoir by metes and bounds, the court concluded that the title to the reservoir was governed by the same principles that govern a parcel of land, so that it was possible, as a matter of law, for an abutting landowner to acquire a prescriptive easement over the reservoir.

Quicknotes

CLAIM OF RIGHT Made by a person claiming a right in property, who is in possession and intends to claim ownership of that property without regard to the record title owner.

EASEMENT The right to utilize a portion of another's real property for a specific use.

LITTORAL Relating to or situated on or near the coast or shore of an ocean, sea, or lake.

PRESCRIPTIVE EASEMENT A manner of acquiring an easement in another's property by continuous and uninterrupted use in satisfaction of the statutory requirements of adverse possession.

SERVIENT ESTATE Land subject to an easement for use by others than its owner.

Hoffman v. Bob Law, Inc.

Owner of lot in real estate development (P) v. Adjoining landowner (D)

S.D. Sup. Ct., 888 N.W.2d 569 (2016)

NATURE OF CASE: Appeal from judgment on counterclaim awarding nominal damages for, and denying injunction to remove, encroachments, in action to enjoin removal of encroachment.

FACT SUMMARY: Hoffman (P) purchased Lot 3 in a development owned by Bob Law, Inc. (Corporation) (D). After Hoffman's (P) purchase, the Corporation (D) informed Hoffman (P) that various improvements—including a septic system—mistakenly believed to have been made on Lot 3 actually encroached on a small sliver of Lot 4. The Corporation (D) owned Lot 4. Hoffman (P) sought and received a preliminary injunction prohibiting the Corporation (D) from removing the septic system. The Corporation (D) counterclaimed for trespass, money damages, and an injunction permitting removal of the encroachments.

RULE OF LAW

(1) Where an encroachment constitutes a trespass, a court may nonetheless deny an injunction to remove the encroachment where the balance of the relative hardships and equities of such removal weighs against removal of the encroachment.

(2) Where there are multiple encroachments on private property and the property owner requests an injunction to remove all the encroachments, a court may not deny the injunction as to all the encroachments on the basis of the relative hardships and equities of removing only one of the encroachments.

FACTS: Bob Law, Inc. (Corporation) (D), owned a real estate development that it developed with Rick DeJager. Construction on Lot 3 of the development began in 2003. As a consequence of construction mistakes, various improvements at the time—including installation of a septic system—believed to have been made on Lot 3 actually were placed on Lot 4. Lot 3, which had been owned by the Corporation (D), was then conveyed to DeJager and his wife, and DeJager made several more improvements that, unbeknownst to him, also encroached on Lot 4. The Corporation owned Lot 4. These encroachments included a lamp pole, concrete pad, propane tank, and encroaching portions of a retaining wall and driveway. After DeJager and his wife defaulted around 2010, the property was conveyed to the bank that held the mortgage. Hoffman (P) purchased Lot 3 from the bank in 2011. Although Hoffman (P) could have had the lot surveyed at no expense, he was in a hurry to close on the home and decided to forego a survey. Closing took place on June 10, 2011. The next day, the Corporation (D), through its owner, Law (D), contacted Hoffman and informed him that there was an encroachment on Lot 4. Law (D) proposed to move the septic system's leach field for $150,000 and to sell Hoffman (P) an easement for the septic tank for $25,000. When Hoffman (P) did not immediately accept this proposal, Law (D) threatened to dig out the septic system. Hoffman (P) brought suit to enjoin the removal of the septic system, and obtained a preliminary injunction for that purpose. The Corporation (D) counterclaimed for trespass, and sought money damages (rental value and diminution in value of the lot) as well as a mandatory injunction to remove the encroachments. The trial court, although finding that the encroachments constituted a trespass, awarded the Corporation (D) only nominal damages, as the Corporation (D) failed to present evidence of damages. The trial court also denied the requested injunction to remove the encroachments, finding that the balance of relative hardships from the removal of the septic system weighed in Hoffman's (P) favor. However, the trial court did not balance the relative hardships to remove the remaining encroachments. The Corporation (D) appealed from the denial of the injunction, and the state's highest court granted review.

ISSUE:

(1) Where an encroachment constitutes a trespass, may a court nonetheless deny an injunction to remove the encroachment where the balance of the relative hardships and equities of such removal weighs against removal of the encroachment?

(2) Where there are multiple encroachments on private property and the property owner requests an injunction to remove all the encroachments, may a court deny the injunction as to all the encroachments on the basis of the relative hardships and equities of removing only one of the encroachments?

HOLDING AND DECISION: (Zinter, J.)

(1) Yes. Where an encroachment constitutes a trespass, a court may nonetheless deny an injunction to remove the encroachment where the balance of the relative hardships and equities of such removal weighs against removal of the encroachment. Typically, when structures encroach on private property, pecuniary compensation will not afford adequate relief to the

Continued on next page.

owner of the land encroached upon. That is because denying an injunction to remove an encroachment and awarding money damages amounts to private eminent domain, and no one should be permitted to take land of another merely because they are willing to pay a market price for it. Moreover, in such cases, the encroacher could obtain a property right by adverse possession, which could result in a complete loss of title. For these reasons, an injunction was authorized in this case as a proper remedy. However, authorization for an injunction does not equate with entitlement to an injunction. In determining whether to grant or deny an injunction, a number of factors are considered, including: (1) Did the party to be enjoined cause the damage? (2) Would irreparable harm result without the injunction because of lack of an adequate and complete remedy at law? (3) Is the party to be enjoined acting in bad faith or is the injury-causing behavior an innocent mistake? (4) In balancing the equities, is the hardship to be suffered by the enjoined party disproportionate to the benefit to be gained by the injured party? Regarding factors (1) and (3), the trial court's findings that Hoffman (P) did not cause the damage and that he was not acting in bad faith are supported by the record, since the Corporation (D) was responsible for the location of the septic system and the remaining encroachments were installed by DeJager. Additionally, although Hoffman's (P) failure to obtain a survey was negligent, it did not constitute bad faith. Because, as previously explained, pecuniary compensation for the Corporation (D) would not afford adequate relief, factor (2) weighs in favor of granting an injunction. Nevertheless, factor (4) plays the dominant role in encroachment cases. On the one hand, no one should be permitted to take land of another merely because they are willing to pay a market price for it. On the other hand, requiring removal of an encroachment may constitute economic waste if the encroaching structure must be destroyed. Thus, the dominant approach in encroachment cases is to balance the relative hardships and equities and to grant or deny the injunction as the balance may seem to indicate. The balancing of equities encourages the denial of injunctive relief where the expense or hardship to be suffered by the trespasser is disproportionate to the small benefit to be gained by the injured party. A court may deny an injunction if the hardship to the trespasser—e.g., the cost to remove the encroachment and loss of value to the remaining structure—is disproportionate to any benefit gained by the landowner. In balancing the equities relating to the septic system, the trial court found that the hardship that would be suffered by Hoffman (P) would be disproportionate to any benefit to be gained by the Corporation (D) in ordering the removal of the septic system, which *in toto* would have cost around $175,000. The trial court also found that this encroachment was on a small sliver of land and that clearly there would be no way that anything could be built in that corner because of the utility lines. Further, Hoffman (P) played no role in contributing to this encroachment, as it was the Corporation (D) that excavated the hole for the septic tank at its current location while Lot 3 was still owned by the Corporation (D). Thus, balancing all of the relevant factors, the hardship to be suffered by Hoffman (P) in removing this encroachment that the Corporation (D) created would be disproportionate to any harm that would be suffered by the Corporation (D). Accordingly, the trial court did not abuse its discretion in denying the injunction to remove the septic tank. Affirmed as to this issue.

(2) No. Where there are multiple encroachments on private property and the property owner requests an injunction to remove all the encroachments, a court may not deny the injunction as to all the encroachments on the basis of the relative hardships and equities of removing only one of the encroachments. The Corporation (D) contends that even if the septic system need not be removed, Hoffman (P) should still be required to remove the lamp pole, concrete pad, propane tank, and encroaching portions of the concrete retaining wall and driveway. The Corporation (D) correctly points out that the trial court did not balance the relative hardships and equities to remove these encroachments, and that the injunction should only be denied if there is disproportionality. In this case, removal of the remaining encroachments may be unlike the removal of an entire building or structure at an enormous and disproportionate expense. Here, the remaining encroachments are separate from the main structure, and some might be removed without loss of enjoyment or damage to the home. Further, there is evidence that both parties were at least somewhat aware of the encroachments prior to June 10, 2011, when Hoffman (P) purchased the property; and Hoffman (P) was negligent in failing to have a survey conducted before purchasing the property. Accordingly, reversal as to these remaining encroachments, and remand to the trial court for a balancing of the equities and hardships, is required. Reversed and remanded as to this issue.

ANALYSIS

As this case illustrates, it is recognized that the appropriate remedy in encroachment cases may include permitting encroachments to remain such that the trespasser obtains an equitable easement. Where a court refuses

Continued on next page.

to order removal of encroachments after balancing the equities, the encroaching party receives an easement so that the landowner can recover possession of the land in the event that the structure is removed in the future. Thus, in this case, because the trial court did not err in refusing to order removal of the septic system, Hoffman (P) was effectively granted a temporary easement that will remain in effect until the encroachment is relocated by Hoffman (P) or his successors in interest.

Quicknotes

ADVERSE POSSESSION A means of acquiring title to real property by remaining in actual, open, continuous, exclusive possession of the property for the statutory period.

BAD FAITH Conduct that is intentionally misleading or deceptive.

ENCROACHMENT The unlawful intrusion onto another's property.

ENJOIN The ordering of a party to cease the conduct of a specific activity.

INJUNCTION A court order requiring a person to do, or prohibiting that person from doing, a specific act.

MONEY DAMAGES Monetary compensation sought by or awarded to a party who incurred loss as a result of a breach of contract or tortious conduct on behalf of another party.

PECUNIARY Consisting of, or pertaining to, money.

SUCCESSOR IN INTEREST One who follows another in ownership or control of property.

TRESPASS Unlawful interference with, or damage to, the real or personal property of another.

Ward v. Ward

Landowner (P) v. Daughter-in-law/tenant (D)

W. Va. Sup. Ct., 783 S.E.2d 873 (2016)

NATURE OF CASE: Appeal, in action for unlawful detainer, from judgment awarding plaintiff the right to eject occupant of property conditioned on plaintiff's paying defendant for improvements made to property.

FACT SUMMARY: Judith Ward (Judith) (P) permitted her son, Gary, and his wife, Susan (D), and their children to build and live in a log cabin on Judith's (P) property. After Gary's death, Judith (P) sought to eject Susan (D) and the children from the property. When Susan (D) refused to leave, claiming entitlement to the log cabin, Judith (P) brought an unlawful detainer action against Susan (D).

RULE OF LAW

As a condition of ejecting a tenant, a court may require a landowner to compensate the tenant for the value of improvements the tenant made to the landowner's property.

FACTS: In 1999, Judith Ward (Judith) (P) permitted her son, Gary, and his wife, Susan (D), and their children to build and live in a log cabin on Judith's (P) property. Gary and Susan (D) paid $50,000 for the log cabin kit; Judith (P) paid for the site preparation and construction. The county taxed Judith's (P) house and the log cabin separately, and Gary and Susan (D) gave Judith (P) money to cover the property taxes. Apparently, they also maintained the property on which the log cabin was built and performed certain household services for Judith (P) in lieu of rent payments. None of these arrangements were memorialized in writing. Gary and Susan (D) and their children lived on Judith's (P) property until Gary died in February 2014. Two months after Gary's death, Judith (P) served Susan (D) with a Notice to Quit, demanding that Susan (D) and her children vacate their log cabin home. Susan (D) refused to move, claiming an entitlement to the log home arising from her purchase thereof. Apparently, Susan (D) also had the mistaken belief that Judith (P) had given Gary and Susan (D) the property on which the cabin was located. Judith (P) then filed suit against Susan (D) asserting a cause of action for unlawful detainer. The trial court granted Judith's (P) motion for judgment on the pleadings. The court concluded that as the property owner of record, Judith (P) was entitled to recover her property from Susan (D), who had no ownership interest in the parcel. Nevertheless, the trial court further determined that Judith (P) would be unjustly enriched by the addition of the log cabin home to her property and, thus, required her to pay Susan (D) $50,000, i.e., the cost of the log cabin kit, for these improvements. Finally, the trial court conditioned Judith's (P) recovery of the subject property upon her payment of this sum to Susan (D) and ruled that Susan (D) was not required to vacate the premises until ten days after her receipt of these funds. From this adverse ruling, Judith (P) appealed to the state's highest court, which granted review.

ISSUE: As a condition of ejecting a tenant, may a court require a landowner to compensate the tenant for the value of improvements the tenant made to the landowner's property?

HOLDING AND DECISION: (Davis, J.) Yes. As a condition of ejecting a tenant, a court may require a landowner to compensate the tenant for the value of improvements the tenant made to the landowner's property. It is clear that Judith (P) is the sole owner of the parcel at issue and that Susan (D) has no ownership interest therein. It is also clear that Judith (P) acquiesced in the building of the log cabin and that Susan (D) and Gary paid for the cabin kit. Because she is the property's owner of record, Judith (P) has the right to possess and occupy her property and to eject persons therefrom if she no longer consents to their occupancy. However, it is equally apparent that the construction of a log cabin home upon Judith's (P) property is a significant and valuable improvement thereto for which Judith (P) has not paid. When an ejected tenant has made improvements to the owner's property, state law requires that the owner compensate the tenant for the value of such improvements to avoid the owner's unjust enrichment. Moreover, where, as here, the tenant is not a purchaser of the property but nevertheless believes that they had an ownership interest therein when they made the improvements, the owner must compensate the tenant for the value of such improvements if the owner was aware of the improvements and did not tell the tenant not to make them. Finally, an ejected tenant who is entitled to recoup the value of the improvements the tenant made upon the property under a mistaken belief of ownership has a lien upon such property until the owner compensates the tenant for the value of such improvements. Because Susan (D) had the mistaken belief that Judith (P) had gifted the property on which the log cabin was located to Gary and Susan (D), and because Judith (P) knew of the cabin, and expressly acquiesced thereto and approved thereof for at least 15 years, the trial court correctly determined that although Judith (P) was entitled to eject Susan (D) and the children from Judith's (P) property, Judith

Continued on next page.

(P) was required to compensate Susan (D) for the value of the cabin, which will remain on Judith's property. In this regard, the trial court based its valuation of the cabin on the purchase price of the kit—$50,000—but no record was made of the cabin's current value, so the issue of the cabin's current value is remanded to the trial court to develop a full factual record of that value. Accordingly, the trial court's $50,000 damages award is reversed and remanded. Finally, given that Susan (D) is entitled to assert a lien against Judith's (P) property for the value of the improvements that she is required to abandon, the trial court did not err by requiring Judith (P) to pay Susan (D) the value of such improvements as a condition precedent to the restoration of Judith's (P) property, and, therefore, the portion of the trial court's order imposing such a requirement is affirmed. [Affirmed, in part; reversed, in part; and remanded.]

ANALYSIS

The measure of damages in an unjust enrichment claim is the greater of the enhanced market value of the property or the cost of the improvements to the property. Accordingly, the court indicated that some of the factors to be determined on remand included: how much Susan (D) and Gary expended in building and maintaining the cabin through ordinary household repairs and upkeep; the amount of property taxes Susan (D) and Gary paid for this portion of Judith's (P) lot; the costs that Susan and Gary incurred in caring for the property upon which the log home was situated; and any other factors that would be indicative of the log cabin's valuation.

Quicknotes

CONDITION PRECEDENT The happening of an uncertain occurrence which is necessary before a particular right or interest may be obtained or an action performed.

DETAINER The unlawful withholding of real or personal property from an individual who is lawfully entitled to it.

O'Keeffe v. Snyder

Artist (P) v. Adverse possessor (D)

N.J. Sup. Ct., 416 A.2d 862 (1980)

NATURE OF CASE: Appeal from reversal of award of replevin.

FACT SUMMARY: Snyder (D) contended that he had acquired three of O'Keeffe's (P) paintings by adverse possession.

RULE OF LAW

The discovery rule controls in actions involving the adverse possession of chattels.

FACTS: The painter Georgia O'Keeffe (P) brought an action against Snyder (D) for replevin or return of three small pictures painted by O'Keeffe (P). In her complaint, filed in March 1976, O'Keeffe (P) alleged that she was the owner of the paintings, and that they had been stolen from a New York art gallery in 1946. Snyder (D) asserted that he was a purchaser for value of the paintings, that he had acquired title by adverse possession, and that O'Keeffe's (P) action was barred by the expiration of the six-year period of limitations pertaining to an action in replevin. The appellate court, in reversing the trial court, concluded that the paintings were stolen, the defenses of expiration of the statute of limitations and title by adverse possession were identical, and that Snyder (D) had not proved the elements of adverse possession.

ISSUE: Does the discovery rule control in actions involving the adverse possession of chattels?

HOLDING AND DECISION: (Pollock, J.) Yes. The discovery rule provides that, in an appropriate case, a cause of action will not accrue until the injured party discovers, or by exercise of reasonable diligence and intelligence should have discovered, facts that form the basis of a cause of action. Here, O'Keeffe's (P) cause of action accrued when she first knew, or reasonably should have known through the exercise of due diligence, of the cause of action, including the identity of the possessor of the paintings. The focus of the inquiry will no longer be whether the possessor has met the tests of adverse possession, but whether the owner has acted with due diligence in pursuing his or her personal property. Under the discovery rule, if an artist diligently seeks the recovery of a lost or stolen painting but cannot find it or discover the identity of the possessor, the statute of limitations will not begin to run. Under the discovery rule, the burden is on the owner as the one seeking the benefit of the rule to establish facts that would justify deferring the beginning of the period of limitations. However, if the period of limitations does begin to run, the expiration of the six-year statutory limitation period should vest title as effectively under the discovery rule as under the doctrine of adverse possession. Reversed and remanded for further proceedings.

ANALYSIS

Prior to the ruling in this case, the discovery rule had been applied primarily in tort actions where the injuries allegedly suffered by the plaintiff were difficult to discover. The court in this case, after reviewing the difficulty of applying principles of adverse possession to cases involving artwork, ruled that the application of the discovery rule would mitigate the unjust results that would flow from strict adherence to the rules of adverse possession.

Quicknotes

ADVERSE POSSESSION A means of acquiring title to real property by remaining in actual, open, continuous, exclusive possession of property for the statutory period.

CHATTEL An article of personal property, as distinguished from real property; a thing personal and moveable.

DUE DILIGENCE The standard of care as would be taken by a reasonable person in accordance with the attendant facts and circumstances.

REPLEVIN An action to recover personal property wrongfully taken.

CHAPTER 5

Nuisance: Resolving Conflicts Between Free Use and Quiet Enjoyment

Quick Reference Rules of Law

Dobbs v. Wiggins

Neighbor (P) v. Owner of dog kennel (D)

Ill. App. Ct., 401 Ill. App. 3d 367 (2010)

NATURE OF CASE: Appeal from lower court decision finding that barking from an adjoining dog kennel constituted a private nuisance.

FACT SUMMARY: Dobbs (P) and another landowner brought suit against Wiggins (D), alleging that the loud barking from almost 100 dogs in his adjoining kennel constituted a private nuisance.

RULE OF LAW

A private nuisance is a substantial invasion of another's interest in the use and enjoyment of his land.

FACTS: Wiggins (D) operated an active dog kennel on his property. He started the kennel in 1995 and by 2007 he had almost 100 dogs on his property. The Dobbses (P) lived on land next to Wiggins's (D) property. The Dobbses (P) and another neighbor began to complain about the barking noise from the dogs in 2007. After Wiggins (D) did not decrease the number of dogs, the Dobbses (P) brought this suit against Wiggins (D) alleging that the chronic barking constituted a private nuisance. At a bench trial, several other neighbors also testified as to the constant barking. The trial court ruled in favor of the Dobbses (P), finding that the barking dogs resulted in an invasion of the Dobbses' (P) interest in the use and enjoyment of their land. The court then ordered Wiggins (D) to reduce the number of dogs from the 69 he kenneled at the time of trial to six. The court also ordered Wiggins (D) to kennel those dogs on the southern portion of his property, away from the Dobbses' (P) property. Wiggins (D) appealed to an intermediate court of appeals.

ISSUE: Is a private nuisance a substantial invasion of another's interest in the use and enjoyment of his land?

HOLDING AND DECISION: (Stewart, J.) Yes. A private nuisance is a substantial invasion of another's interest in the use and enjoyment of his land. The invasion can be intentional or negligent but must be unreasonable. The nuisance must be so physically offensive to the senses that it makes life uncomfortable. Private nuisances can include noise, smoke, and odors produced from one person's land that reaches adjoining lands. Whether some activity constitutes a private nuisance is typically a question of fact for a judge in a bench trial or a jury. In any action to enjoin an alleged nuisance, a reviewing court must balance the harm done to the plaintiffs against the utility of the defendant's business and the suitability of the land for that business. The lower court properly concluded that the barking was substantial. It also properly concluded that Wiggins (D), by virtue of the large number of dogs he kenneled, knew that the barking was certain to result in the invasion of others' use and enjoyment in their lands. The court then determined that the noise nuisance was unreasonable. It found that even though Wiggins (D) made efforts to control the noise, the barking did not abate. It also gave weight to the Dobbses' (P) longer ownership in the neighborhood. Accordingly, the lower court properly concluded the barking constituted a nuisance. However, the court erred when it ordered Wiggins (D) to reduce the number of dogs from 69 to six. The evidence at trial was insufficient to support a finding that Wiggins (D) must reduce the number of dogs to that amount. The evidence at trial revealed that Wiggins (D) began kenneling dogs on his property in 1995. For roughly ten years, he received no complaints about the kennel. There simply was no sufficient evidence to determine what should be the maximum number of dogs Wiggins (D) could kennel. Accordingly, the matter is remanded to the lower court for a determination as to the proper scope of the injunction against Wiggins (D). Affirmed in part, reversed in part, and remanded.

ANALYSIS

In any matter involving an injunction, there are always two issues. The first issue is whether the plaintiff has a legal right that the other party has violated. Here, that right was the Dobbses' (P) right to the quiet enjoyment of their land. The second issue to be determined in an injunction case is the scope of remedy. If a right has been violated, a reviewing court will seek to fashion an injunction that protects the plaintiff's right but does so in a manner that is the least restrictive on the defendant's use of his or her own land.

Quicknotes

PERMANENT INJUNCTION A remedy imposed by the court ordering a party to cease the conduct of a specific activity until the final disposition of the cause of action.

PRIVATE NUISANCE An unlawful use of property interfering with the enjoyment of the private rights of an individual or a small number of persons.

Boomer v. Atlantic Cement Company

Landowners (P) v. Cement plant (D)

N.Y. Ct. App., 26 N.Y.2d 219, 257 N.E.2d 870 (1970)

NATURE OF CASE: Action to enjoin maintenance of nuisance and for damages.

FACT SUMMARY: A trial court refused to issue an injunction that would close down a neighboring cement plant but awarded permanent damages instead.

RULE OF LAW

Where the issuance of an injunction to enjoin the maintenance of a business would shut down a business, permanent damages may be issued as an alternative.

FACTS: A group of landowners (P), complaining of injury to their property from dirt, smoke, and vibration emanating from a neighboring cement plant (D), brought an action to enjoin the continued operation of the plant and for damages. The trial court held that the plant constituted a nuisance and found substantial damage but because an injunction would shut down the plant's operation, the court refused to issue one. Permanent damages of $185,000 were awarded the group of landowners (P) instead.

ISSUE: Where the issuance of an injunction to enjoin the maintenance of a business would shut down a business, may permanent damages be issued as an alternative?

HOLDING AND DECISION: (Bergan, J.) Yes. Where the issuance of an injunction to enjoin the maintenance of a business would shut down a business, permanent damages may be issued as an alternative. Although the rule in New York is that a nuisance will be enjoined even when there is a marked disparity shown in economic consequence between the effect of the injunction and the effect of the nuisance, an injunction should not be applied if the result is to close down a plant. Permanent damages may be awarded as an alternative. Another alternative would be to grant the injunction but postpone its effect to a specified future date to give opportunity for technical advances to permit the company (D) to eliminate the nuisance. However, there is no assurance that any significant technical improvement would occur. Moreover, the problem is universal and can only be solved by an industry-wide effort. Permanent damages would themselves be a spur to conduct more research. Future owners of this land would not be able to recover additional damages, since the award is to the land. Reversed and remanded.

DISSENT: (Jasen, J.) The majority approach is licensing a continuing wrong. Furthermore, permanent damages alleviate the need for more research and decrease incentive.

ANALYSIS

The reasoning advanced here has been carried one step further by other courts. In *Pennsylvania Coal Co. v. Sanderson*, 113 Pa. St. 126, 6 A. 453 (1886), a suit for damages was frowned upon by the Supreme Court, which said, "To encourage the development of the great natural resources of a country, trifling inconveniences to particular persons must sometimes give way to the necessities of a great community."

Quicknotes

INJUNCTION A court order requiring a person to do or prohibiting that person from doing a specific act.

NUISANCE An unlawful use of property that interferes with the lawful use of another's property.

TEMPORARY DAMAGES Monetary compensation awarded by the court to a party for injuries sustained as the result of another party's occasional wrongful actions.

Johnson v. Paynesville Farmers Union Cooperative Oil Co.

Organic farmer (P) v. Nonorganic farmers (D)

Minn. Sup. Ct., 817 N.W.2d 693 (2012)

NATURE OF CASE: Appeal from intermediate appellate court's decision that reinstated the plaintiff's nuisance, negligence, and trespass claims against a nonorganic farmer located next to the plaintiff's organic farm.

FACT SUMMARY: Johnson (P), owner of an organic farm, alleged that on several occasions, the Paynesville Farmers Union Cooperative Oil Co. (Cooperative) (D) sprayed pesticides onto its fields that allegedly drifted over and onto Johnson's (P) fields.

RULE OF LAW

(1) A trespass is the wrongful and unlawful entry upon the plaintiff's property by a defendant and the plaintiff need not prove actual damages.

(2) Disruption and inconvenience caused by a private nuisance are actionable damages for which a property owner may recover.

FACTS: Johnson (P), owner of an organic farm, alleged that on several occasions, the Paynesville Farmers Union Cooperative Oil Co. (Cooperative) (D) sprayed pesticides onto its fields that allegedly drifted over and onto Johnson's (P) fields. Under the Organic Foods Production Act and the National Organic Program, an organic farmer cannot market its products as "organic" unless the farmer's fields have not had any prohibited substances applied to them in the prior three years. After Cooperative (D) sprayed pesticides that drifted onto Johnson's (P) soybean fields, Johnson (P) was compelled to notify the Minnesota Department of Agriculture (the Department). The Department tested the soybean fields and found that while pesticides were present in the soybeans, they were within acceptable levels. However, the Department still ordered Johnson (P) to clear ten acres of his soybean field and not to sell anything from that area for another three years. Another occurrence led to the presence of pesticides on Johnson's (P) alfalfa fields. Johnson (P) had to clear those fields and not sell products from those fields for another three years. Johnson (P) brought claims of trespass, nuisance, and negligence against Cooperative (D). The trial court granted summary judgment to Cooperative (D) on the ground Johnson (P) did not prove he suffered any actual damages. An intermediate appellate court reversed and reinstated Johnson's (P) claims. The Minnesota Supreme Court granted Cooperative's (D) petition for further review.

ISSUE:

(1) Is a trespass the wrongful and unlawful entry upon the plaintiff's property by a defendant and does the plaintiff not need to prove actual damages?

(2) Are disruption and inconvenience caused by a private nuisance actionable damages for which a property owner may recover?

HOLDING AND DECISION: (Gildea, C.J.)

(1) Yes. A trespass is the wrongful and unlawful entry upon the plaintiff's property by a defendant and the plaintiff need not prove actual damages. Johnson (P) petitions this court to adopt other states' expansion of the tort of trespass. Other states have held that a trespass claim may be based on particulate matter entering onto the plaintiff's property. Those states also include a necessary showing of actual damages caused by the unwelcome particulate matter. This is inconsistent with the law in Minnesota, as well as the law of most other states. A property owner need not prove actual damages as a result of a trespass. In addition, a trespass typically results from a person intentionally entering upon the land of another. The trespass must include some physical or tangible act. Invasions by particulates in the air may affect the owner's right to use and enjoy his land, but they do not require the landowner to share his land with a trespasser or some physical, trespassing object. Accordingly, the trial court was correct to dismiss Johnson's (P) claim of trespass.

(2) Yes. Disruption and inconvenience caused by a private nuisance are actionable damages for which a property owner may recover. The trial court properly dismissed the nuisance claims as they related to Johnson's (P) claims that he was forced to take several of his fields out of production. The Department of Agriculture improperly ordered Johnson (P) to destroy those crops. While pesticides were present, they were under the minimal threshold and Johnson (P) still would have been able to sell those products as organic. Accordingly, his claims should have been against the state of Minnesota and not the Cooperative (D). However, Johnson (P) also claimed the pesticide sprays actually spurred weed growth around his crops. This forced him to take

Continued on next page.

extra measures to prevent weed growth in the years following the occurrences. Johnson (P) himself complained that the pesticide spray caused him to suffer cotton mouth, swollen throat, and headaches. These types of disruptions and inconveniences are actionable under nuisance law. Accordingly, Johnson's (P) claim for nuisance may continue and the trial court should not have granted full summary judgment to the Cooperative (D). Affirmed in part and reversed in part.

ANALYSIS

The Minnesota Supreme Court sought in this decision to retain the distinction between a trespass claim and a private nuisance claim. A trespass is more of an intentional tort that includes a physical entry upon the land, causing the landowner to share his land with someone or something tangible. A nuisance claim deals more with indirect or intangible interference with the landowner's use and enjoyment of his land.

Quicknotes

PRIVATE NUISANCE An unlawful use of property interfering with the enjoyment of the private rights of an individual or a small number of persons.

TRESPASS Unlawful interference with, or damage to, the real or personal property of another.

Fontainebleau Hotel Corp. v. Forty-Five Twenty-Five, Inc.

Hotel (P) v. Neighbor hotel (D)

Fla. Dist. Ct. App., 114 So. 2d 357 (1959)

NATURE OF CASE: Interlocutory appeal from issuance of an injunction.

FACT SUMMARY: Forty-Five Twenty-Five, Inc. (Forty-Five) (P) sought to enjoin the Fontainebleau Hotel's (D) construction of an addition that would block all sunshine from Forty-Five's (P) hotel.

RULE OF LAW

There is no legal right to the free flow of light or air from an adjoining parcel of land.

FACTS: Forty-Five Twenty-Five, Inc. (Forty-Five) (P) owned the Eden Roc Hotel (Eden Roc) (P), which was subsequently built next to the Fontainebleau (D). Fontainebleau Hotel Corp. (Fontainebleau) (D) commenced construction on an addition which, when completed, would be 14 stories tall and completely block all light from Eden Roc's (P) swimming pool area. Forty-Five (P) sought an injunction to halt construction on the tower, claiming it would interfere with their pre-existing light and air easement. The lower court issued an injunction, and Fontainebleau (D) appealed.

ISSUE: Is there a legal right to the free flow of light or air from an adjoining parcel of land?

HOLDING AND DECISION: (Per curiam) No. There is no legal right to the free flow of light or air from an adjoining parcel of land. Forty-Five (P) claims the right to an injunction based on the law of nuisance. However, nuisance law states that one property holder cannot use his property right to harm the lawful rights of an adjacent landholder. No court has ever found that a property owner has a legal right to air or sunlight. Absent a legal right to the light, Forty-Five (P) has not made a claim in nuisance. Order granting injunction reversed.

ANALYSIS

Should the fact that the Fontainebleau (D) apparently erected the addition where it did out of spite and malice have any effect on the court's decision? To enjoin the addition as a so-called "spite fence," Forty-Five (P) would have to prove that the addition's sole purpose was to irritate; in other words, that the addition had no social utility whatsoever. In mixed motive cases, however, courts will almost certainly deny the injunction.

Quicknotes

EASEMENT The right to utilize a portion of another's real property for a specific use.

INJUNCTION A remedy imposed by the court ordering a party to cease the conduct of a specific activity.

NUISANCE An unlawful use of property that interferes with the lawful use of another's property.

Prah v. Maretti

Homeowner (P) v. Neighbor (D)

Wis. Sup. Ct., 321 N.W.2d 182 (1982)

NATURE OF CASE: Appeal from summary judgment denying relief from a proposed obstruction of sunlight.

FACT SUMMARY: Prah (P) sued to enjoin Maretti (D) from building on his land so as to block the flow of sunlight to Prah's (P) solar heated house.

RULE OF LAW

The doctrine of prior appropriation applies to the use of sunlight as a protectable resource.

FACTS: In 1978, Prah (P) built a house that was equipped to use solar energy. Subsequently, Maretti (D) proposed to build a house that would have obstructed the free flow of sunlight onto Prah's (P) land and therefore interfered with his solar energy system. He sued to enjoin the construction contending he had begun using sunlight as a resource prior to Maretti's (D) plans and therefore under the doctrine of prior appropriation he had a protectable right in the sunlight. He then asserted that Maretti's (D) construction constituted a private nuisance. The trial court granted Maretti's (D) motion for a summary judgment holding that prior appropriation doctrine did not apply and no easement in light and air could be recognized. Prah (P) appealed.

ISSUE: Does the doctrine of prior appropriation apply to the use of sunlight as a protectable resource?

HOLDING AND DECISION: (Abrahamson, J.) Yes. The doctrine of prior appropriation applies to the use of sunlight as a protectable resource. Because of the development of technology allowing the practical use of solar energy, sunlight has taken on an enhanced value. At early American common law, sunlight was valued for the aesthetic purposes only, and it was left that an adjacent landowner's ability to use his land as he wished outweighed this aesthetic value; and no easement of light and air was recognized. However, given this new technology, sunlight must be regarded as a valuable resource and the doctrine of prior appropriation applies to protect those who first exploit the resource. Consequently, Prah (P) could maintain an action for nuisance. A factual question is presented whether Prah's (P) use was reasonable, therefore summary judgment should not have been granted. Reversed.

DISSENT: (Callow, J.) The facts of the present case do not give rise to a cause of action for private nuisance. The majority has failed to establish the obsolescence of the policies behind the restrictions in protecting a landowner's access to sunlight in spite fence cases. The majority's policy arguments are more properly directed to a case involving a public, not a private nuisance. This court should not intrude on an area of legislative responsibility. A private nuisance involves an "invasion," and the obstruction involved in the present case does not appear to fall within the definition of invasion. Maretti's (D) actions were lawful and should not be considered intentional and unreasonable. The "sensitive use" of the property by Prah (P) should not convert this otherwise lawful use into a public private nuisance, especially where Prah (P) has taken no efforts to protect his investment. The prospective application of its decision is also troubling.

ANALYSIS

Some states, such as New Mexico, have enacted statutes that create property rights in access to solar energy. Local governments are given the power under which statutes to enact zoning regulations concerning solar rights. The New Mexico statute provides regulations protecting access in the absence of local regulations. Also, in order to be protected, solar rights as other property rights must be recorded.

Quicknotes

EASEMENT OF "LIGHTS" An interest in land granted for the unobstructed passage of light and air, from English common law.

NUISANCE An unlawful use of property that interferes with the lawful use of another's property.

Armstrong v. Francis Corp.

Landowner (P) v. Land developer (D)

N.J. Sup. Ct., 120 A.2d 4 (1956)

NATURE OF CASE: Appeal from decision enjoining landowner from artificially discharging waste waters from his land.

FACT SUMMARY: Francis Corp. (D) drained off excess water from its land by means of culverts and pipes, thereby causing severe injury to its neighbor's (P) property.

RULE OF LAW

A possessor of land is not privileged to discharge upon adjoining land, by artificial means, large quantities of surface water in a concentrated flow otherwise than through natural drainways, regardless of the means by which the surface water is collected and discharged.

FACTS: Francis (D) wanted to develop a tract of land for residential subdivision. To drain off excess water, Francis (D) constructed a series of underground pipes and culverts. Water from this system emptied into a natural stream that ran across the lands of Armstrong (P) and Klemp (P). Because of the increased flow of water, the stream often flooded and caused considerable erosion or silting on surrounding banks. In addition, the stream, being polluted by Francis's (D) pipes, became discolored and evil-smelling and lost all fish. Armstrong (P) and Klemp (P) sued to have Francis (D), on its own cost, pipe the rest of its water discharge. The lower court agreed and ordered Francis (D) to pipe the remainder of the discharge. Francis (D) appeals on the grounds he has a right to discharge the water onto adjoining lands.

ISSUE: Is a possessor of land privileged to discharge upon adjoining land, by artificial means, large quantities of surface water in a concentrated flow otherwise than through natural drainways, regardless of the means by which the surface water is collected and discharged?

HOLDING AND DECISION: (Brennan, J.) No. A possessor of land is not privileged to discharge upon adjoining land, by artificial means, large quantities of surface water in a concentrated flow otherwise than through natural drainways, regardless of the means by which the surface water is collected and discharged. Most states adopt the rule that, since surface water is the "common enemy" of necessary development, the landowner has an absolute right to discharge it upon adjoining land regardless of the harm caused his neighbors by the means he employs. However, no state applies this harsh rule literally. Courts will read in a "reasonable use" approach that has the particular virtue of flexibility. The issue of reasonableness includes such factors as the amount of harm caused, the foreseeability of the harm that results, the purpose or motive with which the possessor acted, and other relevant matter. Affirmed.

ANALYSIS

The competing approach with the "common enemy" rule is the civil law rule, which holds that a possessor has no privilege, under any circumstances, to interfere with the surface water on his land so as to cause it to flow upon adjoining land in a manner or quantity substantially different from its natural flow. Even here, however, courts will read in a "reasonable use" exception to permit minor alterations.

Quicknotes

CIVIL LAW RULE Rule of law pertaining to an individual's private rights; rule based upon statutory law rather than court decisions.

COMMON ENEMY RULE The right of a landowner to conduct activities on his land so as to ward against the intrusion of surface water without regard to the effect of such activities on other landowners.

Noone v. Price

Homeowner (P) v. Neighbor (D)

W. Va. Sup. Ct. App., 298 S.E.2d 218 (1982)

NATURE OF CASE: Appeal from grant of summary judgment denying damages for eroding lateral support of land.

FACT SUMMARY: Noone (P) contended Price (D) breached her duty to supply lateral support for Noone's (P) hillside home by allowing a retaining wall to fall into disrepair.

RULE OF LAW

An adjacent landowner is strictly liable for acts of commission and omission that result in the withdrawal of lateral support to her neighbor's land in its natural state.

FACTS: In 1912, a house was built at the base of a hill, along with a stone and cement wall located at the base of the hillside. In 1928, Union Carbide built a house on the hillside, above the wall. After several years, the wall fell into disrepair. In 1955, Price (D) purchased the house at the base of the hill. She made no repairs to the wall. Noone (P) bought the house above on the hillside in 1960. Subsequently, Noone (P) discovered that his house was slipping down the hillside, and sued Price (D), contending the wall was constructed to supply lateral support to his property, and that its disrepair caused the slippage. Price (D) moved for summary judgment, contending Noone (P) was negligent in failing to protect his own property and estopped from suing because he had purchased his house with knowledge of the wall's deteriorating condition. The trial court agreed and granted summary judgment to Price (D). Noone appealed.

ISSUE: Is an adjacent landowner strictly liable for acts of commission and omission that result in the withdrawal of lateral support to her neighbor's land in its natural state?

HOLDING AND DECISION: (Neely, J.) Yes. An adjacent landowner is strictly liable for acts of commission and omission that result in the withdrawal of lateral support to her neighbor's land in its natural state. However, if as a result of the additional weight of a building so much strain is placed on the lateral support that it will not hold, then in the absence of negligence, the adjacent landowner is not liable for any resulting damages. At the time the retaining wall was built, there were no structures on Noone's (P) land. Therefore, the wall needed to support only the land in its natural state. The builder was not required to provide support sufficient to withstand the erection of any building on the land. Price (D), as the successor in interest, was not obligated to strengthen the wall to support Noone's (P) house. If Noone (P) is to recover, he must do so by proving that the disrepair of the wall would have inevitably led to the subsidence of his land in its natural condition, without the house upon it. Because this is a factual question, the entry of summary judgment was in error. Reversed.

ANALYSIS

This case illustrates the scope of the duty to supply lateral support. The duty is absolute as to the land in its natural state, but to recover for damages to a building, negligence must be shown. A negligent withdrawal of support is actionable even if the land would not have slipped but for the presence of the added weight of a building. In determining whether negligence exists, the type of withdrawal, the nature of the soil, and whether notice of the proposed withdrawal was given are all relevant.

Quicknotes

LATERAL SUPPORT Right of a landowner to have his land supported by adjoining property.

NEGLIGENCE Conduct falling below the standard of care that a reasonable person would demonstrate under similar conditions.

STRICT LIABILITY Liability for all injuries proximately caused by a party's conducting of certain inherently dangerous activities without regard to negligence or fault.

Friendswood Development Co. v. Smith-Southwest Industries, Inc.

Landowner (D) v. Landowner (P)

Tex. Sup. Ct., 576 S.W.2d 21 (1978)

NATURE OF CASE: Appeal from summary judgment in class action in tort.

FACT SUMMARY: Friendswood Development Co. (D) pumped a great deal of subsurface water from their land, causing subsidence in adjoining plots of land.

RULE OF LAW

A person is liable for damages caused by drawing water from his own land only to the extent that his activity was negligent.

FACTS: Friendswood Development Co. (Friendswood) (D) pumped water from their land for sale to industrial users. Friendswood (D) pumped vast quantities despite an engineer report stating that withdrawal of such quantities would cause subsidence in the area surrounding the pumping. Southwest Industries (P) filed suit, claiming that Friendswood's (D) negligent withdrawal of excessive quantities of ground water was the cause in fact of severe subsidence on their lands. The appellate court refused to grant Friendswood's (D) request for summary judgment. Friendswood (D) appealed.

ISSUE: Is a person liable for damages caused by drawing water from his own land limited to the extent that his activity was negligent?

HOLDING AND DECISION: (Daniel, J.) Yes. A person is liable for damages caused by drawing water from his own land only to the extent that his activity was negligent. Under the common law, a landowner had absolute right to withdraw the water lying beneath his land. Under this rule, a landowner could not be held liable for any damage to neighboring property that resulted from activity on his own land. However, modern lawmakers have moved away from this harsh rule to hold a landowner liable for the damage to the extent his activity was negligent. Nonetheless, the case law to date has upheld the common law. Thus it would be unjust to apply a new standard to Friendswood (D) at this time. From this day forward, however, landowners will be held liable for damages caused by the negligent, willfully wasteful, or malicious withdrawal of subterranean waters. Reversed.

DISSENT: (Pope, J.) The principal opinion incorrectly applies the common law in regard to water rights and then declares that stare decisis dictates their conclusion. Smith-Southwest (P) raised absolutely no claim, and sought no damages, in relation to Friendswood's (D) capture and sale of the ground water. The complaint is that Friendswood's (D) action caused the subsidence of their land, and a landowner's right to lateral support for his adjacent land is an absolute right. Our prior holdings involving mining and oil now stand in contradiction to the present holding. A landowner may assert a cause of action against one destroying the lateral support to maintain his land in its natural state when the destruction is knowingly caused, or when the landowner can prove negligence or nuisance.

ANALYSIS

Restatement (Second) of Torts § 818 gives landowners absolute right to subadjacent support. This strict liability approach, however, is the rule in only a few states such as Washington. See *Muskatell v. City of Seattle*, 116 P.2d 363 (1941).

Quicknotes

NEGLIGENCE Conduct falling below the standard of care that a reasonable person would demonstrate under similar conditions.

NUISANCE An unlawful use of property that interferes with the lawful use of another's property.

STARE DECISIS Doctrine whereby courts follow legal precedent unless there is good cause for departure.

CHAPTER 6

Land Use and Natural Resources Regulation

Quick Reference Rules of Law

Village of Euclid v. Ambler Realty Co.

Municipal corporation (D) v. Tract owner (P)

272 U.S. 365 (1926)

NATURE OF CASE: Action to enjoin enforcement of a zoning ordinance.

FACT SUMMARY: Euclid (D) zoned property of Ambler Realty (P) in a manner that materially reduced its potential value.

RULE OF LAW

A zoning ordinance, as a valid exercise of the police power, will only be declared unconstitutional where its provisions are clearly arbitrary and unreasonable, having no substantial relation to the public health, safety, morals, or general welfare.

FACTS: Ambler Realty (P) was the owner of 68 acres in the Village of Euclid (Euclid) (D). The 68 acres is surrounded primarily by residential neighborhoods, but a major thoroughfare abuts it to the south and a railroad abuts it to the north. Euclid (D) instituted zoning ordinances placing use, height, and area restrictions. Restrictions were placed on Ambler Realty's (P) property prohibiting (1) apartment houses, hotels, churches, schools, or any other public or semi-public buildings for the first 620 feet from Euclid Avenue, the above-described major thoroughfare; and (2) industry, theatres, banks, shops, etc., for the next 130 feet after that. As a result of this zoning, the value of Ambler Realty's (P) property has declined from $10,000 per acre to $2,500 per acre. Ambler Realty (P) brought an action to enjoin Euclid (D) from enforcing the ordinance on the ground that it constitutes a violation of Fourteenth Amendment due process. From a decree in favor of Ambler Realty (P), Euclid (D) appealed, contending that the ordinance was a valid exercise of the police power of the state.

ISSUE: Is a zoning ordinance unconstitutional as a deprivation of property without due process because it results in a diminution of value in the property zoned?

HOLDING AND DECISION: (Sutherland, J.) No. A zoning ordinance, as a valid exercise of the police power, will only be declared unconstitutional where its provisions are clearly arbitrary and unreasonable, having no substantial relation to the public health, safety, morals, or general welfare. Zoning ordinances, and all similar laws and regulations, must find their justification in some aspect of the police power, asserted for the public welfare. Until recent years, urban life was comparatively simple; but with the great increase and concentration of population, problems have developed that require new restrictions on the use and occupation of private lands in urban communities. There is no serious difference of opinion on the state power to avoid the nuisances that industry may cause in a residential area. As for residential regulation, many considerations point toward their validity. Segregation of residential business and industrial buildings makes it easier to provide appropriate fire apparatus, for example. Further, it is often observed that the construction of one type of building destroys an area for other types. In light of these considerations, the court is not prepared to say that the end of public welfare here is not sufficient to justify the imposition of this ordinance. It clearly cannot be said that it ". . . passes the bounds of reason and assumes the character of a merely arbitrary fiat." The decree must be reversed.

ANALYSIS

Village of Euclid v. Ambler Realty is the landmark United States Supreme Court decision on zoning ordinances as valid exercises of the police power. Essentially, any zoning ordinance that is tied to public health, safety, morals, or welfare will be upheld unless clearly arbitrary and unreasonable. So-called *Euclidian* Zoning, which resulted from this decision, usually consists in the division of areas into zones, in which building use, height, and area are regulated in a manner designed to guarantee homogeneity of building patterns. All too often, however, zoning operates not so much to protect the public interest as to protect the vested interests in a community. Building restrictions may all too easily be used as an economic sanction by which social segregation is perpetuated. (Barring low-cost housing keeps out economically deprived segment of the population.) Note, however, that *Euclid* did not foreclose the possibility that government land-use regulations may constitute a "taking" that requires compensation. In *Pennsylvania Coal Co. v. Mahon*, 260 U.S. 393 (1922), the United States Supreme Court held that an anti-mining restriction, which totally destroyed the interest of the party who owned only the mineral rights, constituted a taking as to that person for which compensation had to be paid. In the *Mahon* case, the diminution in value of the party's property was total, and was thus clearly a "taking."

Quicknotes

INJUNCTION A court order requiring a person to do or prohibiting that person from doing a specific act.

Continued on next page.

POLICE POWER Power of a government to impose restrictions on the rights of private persons, as long as those restrictions are reasonably related to the promotion and protection of public health, safety, morals, and the general welfare.

PUBLIC WELFARE The well-being of the general community.

TAKING A governmental action that substantially deprives an owner of the use and enjoyment of his or her property, requiring compensation.

ZONING ORDINANCE A statute that divides land into defined areas and that regulates the form and use of buildings and structures within those areas.

Town of Belleville v. Parrillo's, Inc.

City (P) v. Discotheque (D)

N.J. Sup. Ct., 416 A.2d 388 (1980)

NATURE OF CASE: Appeal from the reversal of a conviction for continued operation of a nonconforming business whose usage underwent a change.

FACT SUMMARY: When Parrillo's, Inc. (D) changed its existing nonconforming use from a restaurant to a discotheque, the Town of Belleville (P) filed charges that led to a conviction of Parrillo's (D) owners. However, the appellate division reversed the conviction, prompting this appeal.

RULE OF LAW

An existing nonconforming use may continue only where it is a continuance of substantially the same kind of use as that to which the premises were devoted when the zoning ordinance was passed.

FACTS: Parrillo's, Inc. (D) already operated as a restaurant when the Town of Belleville (Town) (P) enacted a zoning ordinance designating the area in which Parrillo's (D) was located as a residence zone. Parrillo's (D) owners later made certain renovations to the premises, and then opened as a discotheque. Shortly after opening under the new format, Parrillo's (D) owners applied for a discotheque license as required by the Town's (P) ordinance regulating dance halls. Although the application was denied, Parrillo's (D) continued business as usual. The Town (P) filed charges that culminated in a conviction and a court-imposed fine. On a trial de novo after appeal, Parrillo's (D) was again found guilty. The court concluded that there had been a prohibited change in the use of the premises. The appellate division reversed. The Town (P) appealed.

ISSUE: May an existing nonconforming use continue only where it is a continuance of substantially the same kind of use as that to which the premises were devoted when the zoning ordinance was passed?

HOLDING AND DECISION: (Clifford, J.) Yes. An existing nonconforming use may continue only where it is a continuance of substantially the same kind of use as that to which the premises were devoted when the zoning ordinance was passed. Parrillo's (D) conversion of the premises from a restaurant to a discotheque resulted in a substantial, and therefore impermissible, change. The entire character of the business has been altered. What was once a restaurant is now a dance hall. Measured by the zoning ordinance, the general welfare of the neighborhood has been demonstrably affected adversely by the conversion of Parrillo's (D) business. Reversed.

ANALYSIS

Because nonconforming uses are inconsistent with the objectives of uniform zoning, the courts have required that consistent with the property rights of those affected and with substantial justice, they should be reduced to conformity as quickly as is compatible with justice. In that regard, the courts have permitted municipalities to impose limitations upon nonconforming uses. The method generally used to limit nonconforming uses is to prevent any increase or change in the nonconformity.

Quicknotes

NONCONFORMING USE The use of a structure that is rendered unlawful by the promulgation or revision of a zoning ordinance.

ZONING ORDINANCE A statute that divides land into defined areas and that regulates the form and use of buildings and structures within those areas.

Stone v. City of Wilton

Landowner (P) v. City (D)

Iowa Sup. Ct., 331 N.W.2d 398 (1983)

NATURE OF CASE: Appeal from the dismissal of a petition for declaratory judgment, injunctive relief, and damages in an action involving rezoning.

FACT SUMMARY: When the City of Wilton (D) considered a rezoning recommendation that would affect Stone's (P) property and his plan to construct a multi-family housing project, he filed a petition with the court, contending he had a vested right in developing his land.

RULE OF LAW

The validity of a police power enactment, such as zoning, depends on its reasonableness.

FACTS: Stone (P) purchased land to develop a low-income, federally subsidized housing project consisting of several multi-family units. About one-fourth of the land was zoned single-family residential, while the remainder was zoned multi-family residential. After purchasing the land, Stone (P) incurred expenses for an architect and an engineer. Stone (P) also secured a Farmers' Home Administration (FHA) loan commitment for construction of the project. Later, the planning and zoning commission recommended rezoning part of the city to single-family residential due to alleged inadequacies of sewer, water, and electrical services. The rezoning recommendation affected all of Stone's (P) property. When the City of Wilton (D) denied Stone's (P) application for a building permit due to the pending rezoning recommendation, he filed a petition with the court. Stone (P) also contended that he had a vested right in developing his property. This appeal followed the trial court's ruling.

ISSUE: Does the validity of a police power enactment, such as zoning, depend on its reasonableness?

HOLDING AND DECISION: (McGiverin, J.) Yes. The validity of a police power enactment, such as zoning, depends on its reasonableness. A city's comprehensive plan is always subject to reasonable revisions designed to meet the ever-changing needs and conditions of a community. Here, the city council (D) rationally decided to rezone this section of the city to further the public welfare in accordance with a comprehensive plan. In addition, Stone's (P) efforts and expenditures prior to rezoning were not so substantial as to create vested rights in the completion of the housing project. Finally, the rezoning only deprived Stone (P) of the land's most beneficial use, which does not render it an unconstitutional taking. This court cannot substitute its view of reasonableness for that of the city council (D). Thus, the ordinance is valid and applicable to Stone's (P) land and project. Affirmed.

ANALYSIS

The Wilton (D) city council was faced with a number of competing concerns in regard to the proper zoning of the area where Stone's (P) land was situated. Because legislative bodies are faced with balancing such competing concerns, courts refrain from reviewing the merits of their decisions if at least a debatable question exists as to the reasonableness of their action. However, where a discriminatory purpose is a motivating factor in the decision, such judicial deference is no longer justified.

Quicknotes

DECLARATORY JUDGMENT A judgment of the rights between opposing parties that is binding, but does not award coercive relief (i.e., damages).

POLICE POWERS The power of a state or local government to regulate private conduct for the health, safety, and welfare of the general public.

ZONING ORDINANCE A statute that divides land into defined areas and that regulates the form and use of buildings and structures within those areas.

Krummenacher v. Minnetonka

Landowner (P) v. Municipality (D)

Minn. Sup. Ct., 783 N.W.2d 721 (2010)

NATURE OF CASE: Appeal from lower court decisions finding that a municipality properly granted a variance to a landowner seeking to add a second story to a garage.

FACT SUMMARY: The City of Minnetonka (D) granted a variance to JoAnne K. Liebeler (D), allowing her to add a second story to a detached garage. Beat L. Krummenacher (P), a neighbor of Liebeler's (D), brought suit against Minnetonka (D) and Liebeler (D) on the grounds the variance was granted in violation of current statutory law.

RULE OF LAW

To obtain a use variance, an applicant must demonstrate undue hardship by satisfying the following three factors: (1) the property cannot be put to reasonable use if a variance is not allowed; (2) the landowner's plight is not due to conditions created by the landowner; and (3) the variance, if granted, will not alter the character of the neighborhood.

FACTS: The City of Minnetonka (Minnetonka) (D) granted a variance to JoAnne K. Liebeler (D), allowing her to add a second story to a detached garage. The detached garage, built in the 1940s, was a permissible, nonconforming use because it was only set back 17 feet from the road. A new zoning ordinance required such structures to be set back 50 feet. Liebeler (D) sought to add a second story that would include a yoga studio and craft room. Beat L. Krummenacher (P), a neighbor of Liebeler's (D), objected because of the new height of the structure. Minnetonka's (D) Planning Commission and City Council approved the project. Krummenacher (P) brought suit against Minnetonka (D) and Liebeler (D) on the grounds the variance was granted in violation of current statutory law. Krummenacher (P) argued that a municipality can only allow a variance if the property in question cannot be put to any reasonable use without the variance. Krummenacher (P) argued that Liebeler (D) already had a reasonable use for the garage—as storage for vehicles and bicycles. The trial court and an intermediate appellate court affirmed Minnetonka's (D) approvals. The Minnesota Supreme Court granted Krummenacher's (P) petition for further review.

ISSUE: To obtain a use variance, must an applicant demonstrate undue hardship by satisfying the following three factors: (1) the property cannot be put to reasonable use if a variance is not allowed; (2) the landowner's plight is not due to conditions created by the landowner; and (3) the variance, if granted, will not alter the character of the neighborhood?

HOLDING AND DECISION: (Gildea, J.) Yes. To obtain a use variance, an applicant must demonstrate undue hardship by satisfying the following three factors: (1) the property cannot be put to reasonable use if a variance is not allowed; (2) the landowner's plight is not due to conditions created by the landowner; and (3) the variance, if granted, will not alter the character of the neighborhood. Municipalities have broad discretion to grant or deny variances. Courts review those decisions to determine if jurisdiction was proper and whether the municipality acted arbitrarily or capriciously. Krummenacher (P) argues that a municipality can only allow a variance if the property in question cannot be put to any reasonable use without the variance. A prior appellate court decision required property owners to prove only that the owner will use the property in a reasonable manner currently prohibited by an ordinance. This is known as the "reasonable manner" standard. The statute, however, requires the applicant to show that the property cannot be put to any reasonable use without the variance. Simply allowing the variance if the proposed use is reasonable would water down the statute. Because this decision announces a new standard for variances, the matter is remanded to the trial court to determine if the variance complies with the new, stricter standard. Reversed and remanded.

ANALYSIS

In this decision Minnesota sought to rein in municipalities that grant variances without any regard to applicable legal standards. Local municipalities in all states often grant variances simply based on whether the improvements would complement the character of the particular neighborhood. This decision effectively will only allow variances if the structure could not be used in any reasonable manner without the variance.

Quicknotes

UNDUE HARDSHIP Excessive suffering or adversity, especially referring to financial positions that are likely to continue in spite of good faith efforts to overcome the situation.

VARIANCE Exemption from the application of zoning laws.

Village of Willowbrook v. Olech

Municipal government (D) v. Landowner (P)

528 U.S. 562 (2000)

NATURE OF CASE: Appeal from reversal of a dismissal in an equal protection claim.

FACT SUMMARY: Olech (P) brought suit against the Village of Willowbrook (D) alleging an equal protection violation in relation to an easement.

RULE OF LAW

An equal protection claim may be made by a "class of one" in instances where the plaintiff has been intentionally treated differently from similarly situated individuals and where there is no rational basis for the disparity in treatment.

FACTS: Olech (P) wanted to connect her property to the Village of Willowbrook's (Village's) (P) water supply, but the Village (D) conditioned the connection on the grant of a 33-foot easement. Olech (P) objected because surrounding landowners were only subjected to a 15-foot easement. Olech (P) brought an action in the federal court alleging that the demand for the additional 18-feet of easement violated the Equal Protection Clause of the Fourteenth Amendment. Olech (P) claimed that the Village (D) was seeking revenge because Olech (P) had previously won a lawsuit against the Village (D). Olech (P) alleged that the Village (D) intentionally sought to deprive her of her rights. The district court dismissed pursuant to Rule 12(b)(6) for failure to state a claim, but the Seventh Circuit Court of Appeals reversed finding that Olech (P) sufficiently pled that the Village (D) was motivated solely by a spiteful effort to get even wholly unrelated to any legitimate state objective. The United States Supreme Court granted certiorari to determine if the Equal Protection Clause could give rise to a cause of action on behalf of a "class of one."

ISSUE: May an equal protection claim be made by a "class of one" in instances where the plaintiff has been intentionally treated differently from similarly situated individuals and where there is no rational basis for the disparity in treatment?

HOLDING AND DECISION: (Per curiam) Yes. An equal protection claim may be made by a "class of one" in instances where the plaintiff has been intentionally treated differently from similarly situated individuals and where there is no rational basis for the disparity in treatment. The purpose of the Equal Protection Clause is to secure every person within the state's jurisdiction against intentional and arbitrary discrimination. Olech's (P) complaint properly pled that the Village (D) intentionally demanded an easement far greater than that of similarly situated property owners and that the demanded was irrational and wholly arbitrary. The decision of the Seventh Circuit Court of Appeals is affirmed.

CONCURRENCE: (Breyer, J.) Olech (P) alleged an extra factor, "ill will" or "illegitimate animus" that is sufficient to minimize any concern about transforming run-of-the-mill zoning cases into cases of a constitutional right.

ANALYSIS

Different classifications of individuals receive different applications of the Equal Protection Clause. If the person alleging discrimination is a member of a "suspect class," such as race or religion, then the government action must survive a strict scrutiny analysis. Under those circumstances the government action or a statute must be narrowly tailored to promote a compelling governmental interest. If a person is a member of a "quasi-suspect class" such as gender, then intermediary review applies and the government action must bear a substantial relationship to an important government objective. If a person is not a member of either of these classes, then only rational basis review applies and the government action must only be rationally related to a legitimate governmental purpose. In this instance, the question was whether Olech (P) belonged to any type of class to have standing to bring an action pursuant to the Equal Protection Clause. The Court found that one person could be a representative class as long as similarly situated persons received different treatment and defined the appropriate standard of review as being the rational basis test.

Quicknotes

EASEMENT The right to utilize a portion of another's real property for a specific use.

EQUAL PROTECTION CLAUSE A constitutional provision that each person be guaranteed the same protection of the laws enjoyed by other persons in like circumstances.

RATIONAL BASIS REVIEW Test employed by the court to determine the validity of a statute in equal protection actions, whereby the court determines whether the challenged statute is rationally related to the achievement of a legitimate state interest.

Southern Burlington County NAACP v. Township of Mount Laurel

Civil rights organization (P) v. Town (D)

N.J. Sup. Ct., 336 A.2d 713 (1975)

NATURE OF CASE: Appeal from invalidation of zoning ordinance.

FACT SUMMARY: The trial court held that a bona fide attempt by a municipality to provide zoned land for low-cost housing fulfilled its constitutional obligations.

RULE OF LAW

Municipal land-use regulations must provide a realistic opportunity for low- and moderate-income housing.

FACTS: The National Association for the Advancement of Colored People (NAACP) (P) sued the Township of Mount Laurel (Mount Laurel) (D), contending the municipality's zoning scheme violated the New Jersey constitution by failing to provide for low-income housing outside of depressed areas. The New Jersey Supreme Court invalidated the ordinances and remanded for further proceedings. The trial court held that it was sufficient that Mount Laurel (D) had made a bona fide attempt to comply with the Supreme Court decision and upheld the new ordinance enacted in response. The NAACP (P) appealed, contending a mere attempt to provide such zoning did not discharge Mount Laurel's (D) constitutional obligations.

ISSUE: Must municipal land-use regulations provide a realistic opportunity for low- and moderate-income housing?

HOLDING AND DECISION: (Hall, J.) Yes. Municipal land-use regulations must provide a realistic opportunity for low- and moderate-income housing. Such obligation extends beyond attempting to provide for such housing. The housing must be in direct proportion to the percentage of lower income residents in the city. To reach this goal, affirmative governmental action may be required. The elimination of some obstacles and the creation of a new zoning scheme may be frustrated by other restrictions that effectively deprive the poor of adequate housing. Therefore, the zoning scheme that merely manifested intent to abide by the original Supreme Court holding was insufficient to discharge Mount Laurel's (D) constitutional obligations. Reversed.

ANALYSIS

The rationale behind the *Mount Laurel* case is that the use of all land is controlled by the state. The state has constitutional obligations to all its residents whether rich or poor. Municipalities, as state subjects, must set aside a fair share of its land for lower-income housing. They cannot allocate only dilapidated land for the poor and retain valuable land for the rich exclusively. While this rationale appears clear in theory, in execution it has proven very difficult. The main difficulty is in developing an equitable formula for determining "fair share." Until a definitive formula is developed, this will prevent widespread application of this rule.

Quicknotes

BONA FIDE In good faith.

ZONING ORDINANCE A statute that divides land into defined areas and that regulates the form and use of buildings and structures within those areas.

Village of Belle Terre v. Boraas

Long Island village (D) v. Lessees (P)

416 U.S. 1 (1974)

NATURE OF CASE: Appeal from an action seeking a declaratory judgment and an injunction.

FACT SUMMARY: Boraas (P) and other co-lessees of a house in the Village of Belle Terre (D) brought this action for an injunction and a judgment declaring an ordinance restricting land use to one-family dwellings unconstitutional.

RULE OF LAW

Zoning legislation does not violate the Equal Protection Clause if it is reasonable, not arbitrary, and bears a rational relationship to a permissible state objective.

FACTS: The Village of Belle Terre (Village) (D) had restricted land use to one-family dwellings. The word "family" as used in the ordinance meant one or more persons related by blood or a number of persons not exceeding two living together as a single housekeeping unit though not related by blood. The Dickmans (P), owners of a house in the Village (D), leased it to two single males, a single female, and three others, Boraas (P) among them. The Village (D) served the Dickmans (P) with an "Order to Remedy Violations" of the ordinance. Thereupon, Boraas (P) and two of the other tenants, as well as the Dickmans (P), brought this action seeking an injunction and a judgment declaring the ordinance unconstitutional as violative of the Equal Protection Clause. The district court held the ordinance constitutional and the court of appeals reversed. The Village (D) appealed to the United States Supreme Court.

ISSUE: Does zoning legislation violate the Equal Protection Clause if it is reasonable, not arbitrary, and bears a rational relationship to a permissible state objective?

HOLDING AND DECISION: (Douglas, J.) No. Zoning legislation does not violate the Equal Protection Clause if it is reasonable, not arbitrary, and bears a rational relationship to a permissable state objective. The ordinance now before the Court does not discriminate against unmarried couples in violation of the Equal Protection Clause. The ordinance is not aimed at transients so as to interfere with a person's right to travel. It involves no procedural disparity inflicted on some but not on others. It involves no fundamental right guaranteed by the Constitution. Economic and social legislation does not violate the Equal Protection Clause if the law is reasonable, not arbitrary, and bears a rational relationship to a permissible state objective. Boraas (P) argues that if two unmarried people can constitute a family under the ordinance, there is no reason why three or four may not. But every line drawn by a legislature leaves some out that might well have been included. That exercise of discretion, however, is a legislative, not a judicial, function. A quiet place where yards are wide, people few, and motor vehicles restricted are legitimate guidelines in a land-use project addressed to family needs. This goal is a permissible one. The police power is not confined to elimination of filth, stench, and unhealthy places. It is ample to lay out zones where family values make the area a sanctuary for people. Therefore, the decision of the court of appeals is reversed.

DISSENT: (Marshall, J.) The disputed classification burdens the tenants' fundamental rights of association and privacy guaranteed by the First and Fourteenth Amendments. Therefore, strict equal protection scrutiny should be applied. The First Amendment provides some limitation on zoning laws, which, for example, seek to restrict occupancy to individuals adhering to particular religious, political, or scientific beliefs. Zoning officials properly concern themselves with the uses of land and can restrict the number of persons who reside in certain dwellings. But they cannot validly consider who those persons are or how they choose to live.

ANALYSIS

The freedom of association is often inextricably entwined with the constitutionally guaranteed right of privacy. In *Meyer v. Nebraska*, 262 U.S. 390 (1923), the Supreme Court held that the right to establish a home is an essential part of the liberty guaranteed by the Fourteenth Amendment. In *Stanley v. Georgia*, 394 U.S. 557 (1996), in the concurring opinion, Justice Goldberg stated that the Constitution secures to an individual a freedom to satisfy his intellectual and emotional needs in the privacy of his own home. Both these cases were used in the dissent to support the argument of discrimination.

Quicknotes

EQUAL PROTECTION CLAUSE A constitutional provision that each person be guaranteed the same protection of the laws enjoyed by other persons in like circumstances.

FREEDOM OF ASSOCIATION The right to peaceably assemble.

RIGHT TO PRIVACY Those personal liberties or relationships that are protected against unwarranted governmental interference.

Moore v. City of East Cleveland

Extended family (D) v. City (P)

431 U.S. 494 (1977)

NATURE OF CASE: Appeal from an action challenging the constitutionality of a housing ordinance.

FACT SUMMARY: Inez Moore (D), who lived with her own son and two grandsons, first cousins to each other, was directed to remove her grandson John from her home in compliance with a housing ordinance of East Cleveland, Ohio (P).

RULE OF LAW

Any zoning ordinance that infringes on a person's freedom of choice in matters of marriage and family life is subject to the strict scrutiny of the Due Process Clause of the Fourteenth Amendment.

FACTS: Inez Moore (D) lived in her East Cleveland, Ohio, home together with her son and her two grandsons. The two boys were first cousins. Moore (D) received a notice of violation of a housing ordinance from the City (P) stating that John, her grandson, was an illegal occupant and directing her to comply with the ordinance. The City's (P) housing ordinance limited occupancy of a dwelling unit to members of a single family, but contained an unusual and complicated definitional section that recognized as a family only a few categories of related individuals. Moore's (D) family did not fit into any of these categories. When Moore (D) failed to remove her grandson from her home, the City (P) filed a criminal charge. Moore (D) moved to dismiss, claiming that the ordinance was constitutionally invalid on its face. The motion was overruled, and, upon conviction, Moore (D) was sentenced to five days in jail and a fine. The Ohio Court of Appeals affirmed and the Ohio Supreme Court refused review. Moore (D) appealed to the United States Supreme Court.

ISSUE: Is any zoning ordinance that infringes on a person's freedom of choice in matters of marriage and family life subject to the strict scrutiny of the Due Process Clause of the Fourteenth Amendment?

HOLDING AND DECISION: (Powell, J.) Yes. Any zoning ordinance that infringes on a person's freedom of choice in matters of marriage and family life is subject to the strict scrutiny of the Due Process Clause of the Fourteenth Amendment. This Court has long recognized that freedom of personal choice in matters of marriage and family life is one of the liberties protected by the Due Process Clause of the Fourteenth Amendment. When government intrudes on choices concerning family living arrangements, this Court must scrutinize carefully the importance of the governmental interests advanced and the extent to which they are served by the challenged regulation. When thus examined, the Cleveland ordinance cannot survive. The City (P) sought to justify it as a means of preventing overcrowding, minimizing traffic and parking congestion, and avoiding an undue financial burden on the school system. Although these are legitimate goals, the ordinance serves them marginally at best. For example, the ordinance permits any family consisting only of husband, wife, and unmarried children to live together, even if the family contains a half-dozen licensed drivers, each with his own car. At the same time, it forbids an adult brother and sister to share a household, even if both faithfully use public transportation. The ordinance would permit a grandmother to live with a single dependent son and children, even if his school-age children number a dozen, yet it forces Moore (D) to find another dwelling for her grandson, simply because of the presence of his uncle and cousin in the same household. The decision of the Ohio Court of Appeals is, therefore, reversed.

CONCURRENCE: (Brennan, J.) The Constitution will not tolerate the imposition of one sector of the public's preference for nuclear families by the government upon the rest of society. The tradition of the extended family has a rich history in this country and has allowed waves of immigrants to come to this country and find shelter with their cousins or other relatives. Prohibiting these types of families and living arrangements intrudes upon the family associational rights that have been central to our society.

CONCURRENCE: (Stevens, J.) Long before the Constitution, the common law protected a landowner's right to use his or her property as he or she saw fit. While cities and towns may create permissible zoning plans, those plans and schemes must be exercised within constitutional limits.

DISSENT: (Stewart, J.) To suggest that the biological fact of common ancestry necessarily gives related persons constitutional rights of association superior to those of unrelated persons is to misunderstand the nature of the associational freedoms that the Constitution protects. Freedom of association has been constitutionally recognized because it is often indispensable to effectuation of explicit First Amendment guarantees. The association in this case is not for any purpose relating to the promotion of speech, assembly, the press, or religion.

Continued on next page.

DISSENT: (White, J.) While Mrs. Moore's (D) interest in having a grandchild live with her is a liberty protected by the Due Process Clause, the requirements of that clause are satisfied because the ordinance was duly enacted by the municipality and is not lacking a specific purpose. The municipality has the power to maintain the character of the neighborhood for single families. Accordingly, there must be some limit on the definition of family and the number of people who may reside in a single-family home. The Moores (D) are also free to live in other parts of the Cleveland metropolitan area, outside of East Cleveland.

ANALYSIS

The United States Supreme Court relied on *Pierce v. Society of Sisters*, 268 U.S. 535 (1925), to support its decision here. *Pierce* struck down an Oregon law requiring all children to attend the state's public schools, holding that the Constitution excludes any general power of the state to standardize its children by forcing them to accept instruction from public teachers only. The Court, in *Moore*, reasoned that by the same token the Constitution prevents East Cleveland (P) from standardizing its children and its adults by forcing all to live in certain narrowly defined family patterns.

Quicknotes

DUE PROCESS CLAUSE Clauses, found in the Fifth and Fourteenth Amendments to the United States Constitution, providing that no person shall be deprived of "life, liberty, or property, without due process of law."

FREEDOM OF ASSOCIATION The right to peaceably assemble.

TAKING A governmental action that substantially deprives an owner of the use and enjoyment of his or her property, requiring compensation.

Anderson v. City of Issaquah

Developer (P) v. Municipality (D)

Wash. Ct. App., 70 Wash. App. 64, 851 P.2d 744 (1993)

NATURE OF CASE: Appeal from denial of building permit.

FACT SUMMARY: The building code of the City of Issaquah, Washington (D), included criteria with respect to building design that were strictly subjective in nature.

RULE OF LAW

A building code cannot consist of design criteria that are strictly subjective in nature.

FACTS: The City of Issaquah, Washington (City) (D), included, as part of its municipal building code, certain design criteria to be followed in new building developments. The code mandated, inter alia, that buildings be "harmonious" with surrounding architecture and that building proportions be "appropriate." Anderson (P), intending to develop certain commercial property, submitted his building design to the Development Commission. During several hearings, the members expressed dissatisfaction with the design, although the members themselves did not seem to agree on what could be done to make the design more acceptable. After several revisions, Anderson (P) submitted his final plans, which were not approved. Anderson (P) appealed to the city council, which also denied approval. Anderson (P) filed suit seeking an injunction mandating approval. The trial court dismissed the complaint, and Anderson (P) appealed.

ISSUE: Can a building code consist of design criteria that are strictly subjective in nature?

HOLDING AND DECISION: (Kennedy, J.) No. A building code cannot consist of design criteria that are strictly subjective in nature. A statute that either forbids or requires the doing of an act in terms so vague that persons of common intelligence must necessarily guess at its meaning and differ as to its application violates due process. It is inherent in due process that laws be crafted in such a fashion that a person can reasonably be able to understand them. Terms that are totally subjective cannot meet this standard. The ordinance at issue here is an example of this. It mandates that design be "harmonious" and "appropriate." Obviously, what might or might not meet these standards is strictly in the eye of the beholder. This is borne out by the fact that the individual Commission members seemed to have had differing ideas as to what Anderson (P) had to do to bring his design into compliance, which left him in a totally impossible situation. Since the ordinance was clearly unconstitutionally vague, the City (D) should have issued the building permit. So ordered.

ANALYSIS

Private developments, such as condominium complexes, often have similar design criteria and their own architectural committees. Courts, as a general rule, have been much more deferential to decisions of private developments. Of course, the state constitution applies to state actions only, so the Due Process Clause is generally inapplicable in such situations.

Quicknotes

BUILDING CODE Local ordinances that govern requirements for residential housing.

DUE PROCESS CLAUSE Clauses, found in the Fifth and Fourteenth Amendments to the United States Constitution, providing that no person shall be deprived of "life, liberty, or property, without due process of law."

INJUNCTION A court order requiring a person to do or prohibiting that person from doing a specific act.

STATE ACTION Actions brought pursuant to the Fourteenth Amendment claiming the government violated the plaintiff's civil rights.

Westchester Day School v. Village of Mamaroneck

Religious elementary school (P) v. Town (D)

504 F.3d 338 (2d Cir. 2007)

NATURE OF CASE: Appeal from lower court decision finding that a local town improperly denied a school's application to expand its operations.

FACT SUMMARY: The Westchester Day School (P), an Orthodox Jewish co-educational day school, sought to expand its buildings on its large campus. The Village of Mamaroneck's (D) Zoning Board of Appeals rejected the application in its entirety.

RULE OF LAW

While the neutral application of legitimate zoning regulations may not constitute an improper substantial burden placed upon a religious organization, a substantial burden may exist if the municipality imposed the land-use restrictions arbitrarily, capriciously, or unlawfully.

FACTS: The Westchester Day School (WDS) (P), an Orthodox Jewish co-educational day school, sought to expand its buildings on its large campus. The project included a $12 million dollar expansion plan that would update current buildings and expand others. All of the classes, regardless of subject, include an aspect of religious and Judaic concepts to reinforce the school's core religious and educational purposes. After a vocal group of residents opposed the plan, the Village of Mamaroneck's (D) Zoning Board of appeals rejected the project in its entirety. It also denied WDS (P) the opportunity to propose modifications to the project that would address concerns over increased traffic and parking. WDS (P) brought suit against Mamaroneck (D) on the grounds the permit denial ran afoul of the federal Religious Land Use and Institutionalized Persons Act (RLUIPA). This act prohibits a local government from imposing a zoning regulation that constitutes a substantial burden upon any religious organizations. After a bench trial, a federal district court agreed and ordered Mamaroneck (D) to approve the project. Mamaroneck (D) appealed to the United States Court of Appeals for the Second Circuit.

ISSUE: While the neutral application of legitimate zoning regulations may not constitute an improper substantial burden placed upon a religious organization, may a substantial burden exist if the municipality imposed the land-use restrictions arbitrarily, capriciously, or unlawfully?

HOLDING AND DECISION: (Cardamone, J.) Yes. While the neutral application of legitimate zoning regulations may not constitute an improper substantial burden placed upon a religious organization, a substantial burden may exist if the municipality imposed the land-use restrictions arbitrarily, capriciously, or unlawfully. Specifically, the federal Religious Land Use and Institutionalized Persons Act (RLUIPA) prohibits governments from imposing a zoning regulation upon a religious organization or entity in a manner that constitutes a substantial burden, unless the government meets two conditions. First, the burden must be in furtherance of a compelling government interest and second, the burden must be the least restrictive means of furthering that particular interest. The trial court properly concluded that WDS's (P) improvements to the school involved religious education or practice. The larger issue is whether the Mamaroneck (D) imposed a substantial burden on WDS (P). A denial of a religious institution's application to expand may constitute a substantial burden but all facts must be considered. If the denial allows the opportunity to revise the plans in response to public health and safety concerns, this type of denial may not constitute a substantial burden. In addition, there must be a close nexus between the impeded conduct, here, the expansion of the school, and the institution's religious exercise. However, the test is not an "effects test." Municipalities are free to impose neutral zoning regulations upon religious entities in the same manner as other private institutions. The crux is that such applications of zoning laws upon religious entities must not be imposed because of the religious nature of the entity. This type of arbitrary application of the zoning laws may evidence a discriminatory bias against the religious entity. In this case, the district court properly found that Mamaroneck's (D) reasons to deny the project did not bear substantial relation to any public health or safety concerns. The Zoning Board's (D) conclusions relating to the traffic and parking concerns were incorrect and contradicted by their own experts at trial. Accordingly, because the Zoning Board (D) did not have substantial evidence to support its decision, its actions were arbitrary and capricious. This same lack of evidence also reveals the Zoning Board (D) failed to demonstrate that it had a compelling reason to deny the application. Affirmed.

ANALYSIS

The Religious Land Use and Institutionalized Persons Act uses similar strict scrutiny test employed by courts to review freedom of religion or other First Amendment-based challenges. Any government regulation that

Continued on next page.

infringes freedoms of religion, speech, or the press must further a compelling governmental interest and be narrowly tailored to achieve the intended results. In most cases, once a court determines that strict scrutiny will apply, the governmental regulation at issue will likely be found unconstitutional.

Quicknotes

ARBITRARY AND CAPRICIOUS STANDARD Standard imposed in reviewing the decision of an agency or court when the decision may have been made in disregard of the facts or law.

STRICT SCRUTINY The method by which courts determine the constitutionality of a law, when a law affects a fundamental right. Under the test, the legislature must have had a compelling interest to enact the law and measures prescribed by the law must be the least restrictive means possible to accomplish its goal.

ZONING Municipal statutory scheme dividing an area into districts in order to regulate the use or building of structures within those districts.

ZONING ORDINANCE A statute that divides land into defined areas and that regulates the form and use of buildings and structures within those areas.

CHAPTER 7

Servitudes: Rules Governing Contractual Restrictions on Land Use

Quick Reference Rules of Law

PAGE

1. *Green v. Lupo.* An easement is not personal if there is anything in the grant to suggest that it was intended to be tied to the land retained or conveyed. *101*

2. *Cox v. Glenbrook Co.* Where the grant is unclear, the extent of the easement must be construed as broadly as necessary to carry out the purposes for which it was granted. *102*

3. *Lobato v. Taylor.* An implied easement by estoppel may exist when: (1) a landowner permits another to use his land in a manner that would make it foreseeable that the user would substantially rely upon the permission granted; (2) the user substantially changed position in reasonable reliance that the permission would not be revoked; and (3) revocation of the permitted use would create a significant injustice. *103*

4. *Granite Properties Limited Partnership v. Manns.* If a previous use is continuous and apparent, the degree of necessity required to create an implied easement is reduced. *105*

5. *Finn v. Williams.* An easement by necessity is created when an owner conveys a portion of his land that has no outlet except over the retained land of the grantor or over the land of strangers. *106*

6. *Neponsit Property Owners' Association, Inc. v. Emigrant Industrial Savings Bank.* A covenant in the original deed subjecting land to an annual charge for improvements to the surrounding residential tract is enforceable by the property owners' association against subsequent purchasers if: (1) grantor and grantee intended that the covenant run with the land; (2) the covenant touches or concerns the land with which it runs; and (3) privity of estate between the party claiming benefit of the covenant and the party who rests under the burden of such covenant. *107*

7. *Evans v. Pollock.* Where there is a general plan or scheme in a development whereby certain restrictions apply only to well-defined similarly situated lots, the doctrine of implied reciprocal negative easements may be applied to such lots, notwithstanding that not all lots in the development are so restricted. *109*

8. *Appel v. Presley Cos.* Provisions allowing amendment of subdivision restrictions are subject to a requirement of reasonableness. *110*

9. *Davidson Brothers, Inc. v. D. Katz & Sons, Inc.* A covenant cannot be sustained if it is inconsistent with the public interest or detrimental to the public good. *111*

10. *Nahrstedt v. Lakeside Village Condominium Association, Inc.* A recorded use restriction imposed by a common interest development in California must be enforced uniformly against all residents of the development unless the restriction is unreasonable. *112*

11. *Apple Valley Gardens Association, Inc. v. MacHutta.* (1) A condominium association may prohibit the rental of condominium units through an amendment to its bylaws, rather than such a restriction having to be placed in the condominium's declaration. (2) A statement in a condominium declaration that a lease or rental agreement for a unit will not relieve the unit's owner from the financial obligations otherwise imposed by the declaration does not create an affirmative right to rent units. *114*

12. *Trustees of the Cambridge Point Condominium Trust v. Cambridge Point, LLC.* (1) A condominium bylaw provision requiring unit-owner consent before the unit-owners' association can initiate litigation is not per se void. (2) A bylaw provision filed by a condominium complex's developers that makes it effectively impossible for the *116*

Green v. Lupo

Landowner (P) v. Transferee (D)

Wash Ct. App., 647 P.2d 51 (1982)

NATURE OF CASE: Appeal from refusal to enforce an agreement to grant an easement.

FACT SUMMARY: Green (P) granted Lupo (D) a deed release upon the sale of his property on the condition that when Lupo (D) acquired title he would grant Green (P) an easement.

RULE OF LAW

An easement is not personal if there is anything in the grant to suggest that it was intended to be tied to the land retained or conveyed.

FACTS: Green (P) originally owned an entire parcel of land. Later he transferred a portion of the land to Lupo (D). Lupo (D) asked Green (P) for a deed release he needed in order to obtain financing to build a home. Green (P) granted the release on the condition that Lupo (D) grant him an easement for ingress and egress when he acquired title. Lupo (D) agreed. Green (P) turned his parcel into a mobile home park, and the occupants used the part of the land designated as the easement as a runway for motorcycles. In protest of Green's (P) use, Lupo (D) refused to transfer the easement as promised when he acquired title. Green (P) brought suit to specifically enforce the grant of the easement. The trial court found that the easement was personal and enjoined the motorcycles' use of it. Green (P) appealed.

ISSUE: Is an easement personal if there is anything in the grant to suggest that it was intended to be tied to the land retained or conveyed?

HOLDING AND DECISION: (Petrich, C.J.) No. An easement is not personal if there is anything in the grant to suggest that it was intended to be tied to the land retained or conveyed. There is a presumption against personal easements. The written instrument granting Lupo (D) his easement states the easement would be granted to Green (P) for ingress and egress to their property. Thus the easement was granted to gain access to a particular piece of land and is thus appurtenant, not personal. The lower court erred in ordering the cycles banned. Reversed and remanded.

ANALYSIS

The appeal was actually based on the admissibility of parol evidence. The court found that parol evidence is always admissible to demonstrate intent when the written instrument is unclear.

Quicknotes

EASEMENT APPURTENANT A burden attached to real property that either benefits or burdens the owner's right to utilize that property.

EASEMENT The right to utilize a portion of another's real property for a specific use.

PAROL EVIDENCE Evidence given verbally; extraneous evidence.

Cox v. Glenbrook Co.

Developer (P) v. Easement grantor (D)

Nev. Sup. Ct., 371 P.2d 647 (1962)

NATURE OF CASE: Appeal from request for declaratory judgment.

FACT SUMMARY: Glenbrook Co. (D) owned land subject to an easement for access from Cox's (P) land; the parties contested the extent of the easement.

RULE OF LAW

Where the grant is unclear, the extent of the easement must be construed as broadly as necessary to carry out the purposes for which it was granted.

FACTS: The Quill property was surrounded on four sides by land owned by others. There was an easement granted through the Glenbrook Co. (D) property to provide ingress and egress to the Quill property. The Quill property changed hands several times before it ended up in the hands of Cox (P). Cox (P) planned to develop the land as resort area. To achieve this goal, Cox (P) would have to expand the existing easement from a one-lane dirt road to a paved, two-way road. Both parties brought suit for declaratory judgment as to the extent of the easement. The trial court found that the easement was limited to those uses necessary for access by a single family. Cox (P) appealed.

ISSUE: Where the grant is unclear, must the extent of the easement be construed as broadly as necessary to carry out the purposes for which it was granted?

HOLDING AND DECISION: (Thompson, J.) Yes. Where the grant is unclear, the extent of the easement must be construed as broad as necessary to carry out the purposes for which it was granted. The trial court's construction of the limits on the easement erroneously makes the easement personal. As broadly as necessary for family use defines the easement by the person holding it rather than the land it benefits. The grant was intended to give ingress and egress to the land. This intent does not support doubling the size of the road and paving it. The easement is limited to the size and nature at the time of the grant.

ANALYSIS

Another way appurtenant easements are limited is by the nature of the servient estate. An easement cannot cause unwarranted interference or burden on the servient estate. The court found that mere grading of the road in this case would not pose such a burden, but that widening the road would.

Quicknotes

DOMINANT ESTATE Property whose owners benefit from the use of another's property.

EASEMENT The right to utilize a portion of another's real property for a specific use.

SERVIENT ESTATE Property that is burdened in some aspect for the benefit of a dominant estate.

Lobato v. Taylor

Easement holders (P) v. Landowner (D)

Colo. Sup. Ct., 71 P.3d 938 (2002) *(en banc)*

NATURE OF CASE: Appeal from lower court decisions finding that prior easement holders had no rights to a certain large tract of land owned by defendant.

FACT SUMMARY: For more than 100 years, local landowners had been able to use a mountainous tract of land in Colorado to procure water, firewood, and timber. In 1960, Taylor (D) purchased the land and began denying the adjoining landowners their prior rights to the land.

RULE OF LAW

An implied easement by estoppel may exist when: (1) a landowner permits another to use his land in a manner that would make it foreseeable that the user would substantially rely upon the permission granted; (2) the user substantially changed position in reasonable reliance that the permission would not be revoked; and (3) revocation of the permitted use would create a significant injustice.

FACTS: The history of the easement rights in this case date back to the Mexican-American War of the 1840s. At the conclusion of the war, Mexico ceded significant lands to the United States, including California, Nevada, and a portion of Colorado. One of the holders of a large tract of land in Colorado was Charles (Carlos) Beaubien. He began granting small strips of land to new settlers while also leaving aside common areas of the tract that would be used collectively by the new settlers for grazing and as a source of timber, firewood, fish, and game. In 1863, he executed the Beaubien Document, which attempted to formally establish the settlers' rights in the common areas of the land. Beaubien's heirs eventually sold the property to William Gilpin. That transaction stated that Gilpin took the land subject to the rights of the settlers to use the open, uncultivated and common areas of the tract. In 1960, Jack Taylor (D) purchased the common land known then as the mountainous tract. Taylor's (D) deed specifically stated his land was subject to the claims of the local people to use the land for pasture, firewood, and lumber. Taylor (D) immediately began fencing off the area and stationing guards around the property to deny the locals use of the property. In 1981, a number of local landowners (P) filed this suit, seeking easement rights they had enjoyed on the land prior to Taylor's (D) purchase of the property. The trial court and an intermediate court of appeals denied their claims. The landowners (P) appealed to the Colorado Supreme Court.

ISSUE: May an implied easement by estoppel exist when: (1) a landowner permits another to use his land in a manner that would make it foreseeable that the user would substantially rely upon the permission granted; (2) the user substantially changed position in reasonable reliance that the permission would not be revoked; and (3) revocation of the permitted use would create a significant injustice?

HOLDING AND DECISION: (Mullarkey, C.J.) Yes. An implied easement by estoppel may exist when: (1) a landowner permits another to use his land in a manner that would make it foreseeable that the user would substantially rely upon the permission granted; (2) the user substantially changed position in reasonable reliance that the permission would not be revoked; and (3) revocation of the permitted use would create a significant injustice. The landowners have satisfied each of the elements for an easement by estoppel. First, the prior landowners of Taylor's (D) property allowed the settlers to use the land in a manner that made it foreseeable that the settlers would substantially rely upon the permitted usage not being revoked. Their reliance was reasonable because the rights to use the common land were necessary for their survival. There is no dispute settlers were induced to come to this area by the promise they would have access to the common land and everything it could provide for them. The settlers needed wood to heat their homes and the ability to hunt game to feed their families. The second element is also satisfied. The evidence is clear that settlers left their homes in the East and settled in Colorado in reliance upon Beaubien's promise of access. The final element—the creation of an injustice if the rights are revoked—is also present. These rights existed for over 100 years, were properly stated in various real estate transactions, and Taylor (D) was fully aware of these rights. A revocation of these rights would constitute an injustice. The final issue is to establish the extent of the rights. The landowners should continue to have the rights as stated in the original Beaubien Document. These are the rights to firewood, timber, and for grazing of cattle. This court rejects the landowners' rights to hunting, fishing, and recreation. Reversed in part and affirmed in part.

CONCURRENCE AND DISSENT (Martinez, J.) The majority is correct that the landowners should continue to have the same easement rights to Taylor's

Continued on next page.

(D) land as they existed for over 100 years. However, the rights should be all-encompassing and include the right to fish, hunt, and recreate. The evidence in the record reveals that landowners had these rights as well at least from the mid-1800s.

DISSENT: (Kourlis, J.) The adjoining landowners' claims should be rejected on the ground the Beaubien Document was not valid. In 1863, Colorado law required any document conveying a real estate interest to include a specific description of the property and the names of the grantees. The document failed to do both. An easement by prescription also did not arise because there was evidence Beaubien intended others to rely upon his promise he would grant them rights to the common land.

ANALYSIS

First, the easements discussed here dealt with easements for *profits à prendre*, i.e., profits from the land such as wood, fish, and game. These were not easement simply for access rights. Most jurisdictions analyze easements for profit and easement for access under the same legal standards. Second, the decision briefly discussed easements created by prior use. An easement from a prior use may be found where the easement exists prior to the partition of the land. The easement must be obvious or apparent and necessary for enjoyment of the land. The court found the adjoining landowners also satisfied the elements for creation of this second type of implied easement.

Quicknotes

EASEMENT BY ESTOPPEL Easement that arises when a landlord imposes a servitude on his property and another person reasonably relies on the existence of such servitude in undertaking, or forbearing from undertaking, a particular act.

EASEMENT BY IMPLICATION An easement that is not expressly stated in a deed, but which is inferred upon conveyance, that a portion of one parcel had been used to benefit the other parcel and that upon sale the buyer of the benefited parcel could reasonably expect such benefits to continue.

Granite Properties Limited Partnership v. Manns

Property seller (P) v. Purchaser (D)

Ill. Sup. Ct., 512 N.E.2d 1230 (1987)

NATURE OF CASE: Appeal from grant of injunction preventing interference with use of easement.

FACT SUMMARY: Granite Properties Limited Partnership (P) argued that it had acquired, by implied reservation, easements over two driveways providing access to its properties when it sold an adjoining parcel of land to Manns (D).

RULE OF LAW

If a previous use is continuous and apparent, the degree of necessity required to create an implied easement is reduced.

FACTS: Granite Properties Limited Partnership (Granite) (P) held three contiguous parcels in common ownership from 1963 to 1982, when it sold the middle parcel to Manns (D). About five times a week, trucks servicing a shopping center located on Granite's (P) easternmost parcel used a driveway located partially on Manns's (D) property. Another driveway, also located on Manns's (D) property, serviced an apartment building on Granite's (P) property to the west. Manns (D) saw the driveways, which had been used by Granite (P) since the 1960s, before he bought the middle parcel. After his purchase, finding no recorded easements following a title search, Manns (D) notified Granite (P) to discontinue its use of the driveways. Granite (P) subsequently brought an action to enjoin Manns (D) from interfering with Granite's (P) use and enjoyment of the two driveways. The trial court denied injunctive relief as to the shopping center driveway, but found an implied easement for Granite (P) as to the apartment complex driveway. The appellate court found acquired easements for both driveways. Manns (D) appealed.

ISSUE: If a previous use is continuous and apparent, is the degree of necessity required to create an implied easement reduced?

HOLDING AND DECISION: (Ryan, J.) Yes. If a previous use is continuous and apparent, the degree of necessity required to create an implied easement is reduced. An easement implied from a prior existing use arises when an owner of two or more adjoining parcels sells part of the property without mentioning any incidental benefit one parcel may convey on another. This benefit must be obvious, continuous, and permanent, and the claimed easement must be necessary to the enjoyment of the parcel retained by the grantor. Proof of the prior use is evidence that the parties probably intended an easement. In this case, any alternatives to the two driveways would be expensive and impractical. Given the strong evidence of Granite's (P) prior use of the driveways and Manns's (D) knowledge thereof, the evidence was sufficient to fulfill the elastic necessity requirement. Affirmed.

ANALYSIS

There is one other type of implied easement – the easement by necessity. The easement by necessity usually arises when an owner of land conveys to another an inner portion that is entirely surrounded by lands owned either by the grantor or the grantor plus strangers. Unless a contrary intent is manifested, the grantee is found to have a right-of-way across the retained land of the grantor for ingress and egress to the land-locked parcel.

Quicknotes

EASEMENT The right to utilize a portion of another's real property for a specific use.

IMPLIED EASEMENT An easement that is not expressly stated in a deed, but which is inferred upon conveyance, that a portion of one parcel had been used to benefit the other parcel and that upon sale the buyer of the benefited parcel could reasonably expect such benefits to continue.

Finn v. Williams

Landlocked landowner (P) v. Surrounding landowner (D)

Ill. Sup. Ct., 33 N.E.2d 226 (1941)

NATURE OF CASE: Appeal from judgment establishing an easement by necessity.

FACT SUMMARY: Finn's (P) land was entirely landlocked after its purchase from Williams (D).

RULE OF LAW

An easement by necessity is created when an owner conveys a portion of his land that has no outlet except over the retained land of the grantor or over the land of strangers.

FACTS: Charles Williams owned 140 acres of land. In 1895, he conveyed 40 acres of his holdings to Bacon, and in 1937, Finn (P) acquired title to those 40 acres. Zelphia Williams (D) inherited the remaining 100 acres from Charles, who was her husband. The 40 acres acquired by Finn (P) were entirely landlocked, but for many years access was gained over private roads of strangers and a road over the Williams land. In 1939, Williams (D) refused Finn (P) any further access over her land. By that time all of the other private roads leading out had been closed. Finn (P) was unable to take his stock and produce to market and had to walk to the highway on a footpath carrying what produce he could.

ISSUE: Is an easement by necessity created when an owner conveys a portion of his land that has no outlet except over the retained land of the grantor or over the land of strangers?

HOLDING AND DECISION: (Wilson, J.) Yes. An easement by necessity is created when an owner conveys a portion of his land that has no outlet except over the retained land of the grantor or over the land of strangers. If at one time there had been unity of title, the easement by necessity will pass with each transfer as appurtenant to the dominant estate and may be exercised at any time by the holder. It makes no difference that the easement was not used earlier. The easement came into existence when the unity of title was split. Where an owner of land conveys a parcel that has no outlet except over the remaining lands of the grantor or over the land of strangers, a right of way by necessity exists over the remaining lands of the grantor. When permission to go over the land of strangers is denied, the subsequent grantees of the dominant estate may avail themselves of the dominant easement implied in the deed severing the dominant and servient estates. Affirmed.

ANALYSIS

A landlocked parcel of land was about the only situation that the common-law courts would recognize as creating an easement by necessity. This was the strict necessity view of such easements. In recent years, some American courts have refused to create an easement by necessity even for landlocked parcels. Their reasoning was that to do so would be to sanction a form of private eminent domain. Since only a governmental unit holds the power of eminent domain, it was the obligation of the landlocked owner to prevail upon the appropriate governmental unit to condemn a right of way and build a public road.

Quicknotes

EASEMENT APPURTENANT A burden attached to real property that either benefits or burdens the owner's right to utilize that property.

EASEMENT BY NECESSITY An easement that arises by operation of law without which the owner of the benefited property is deprived of the use and enjoyment of his property.

EMINENT DOMAIN The governmental power to take private property for public use so long as just compensation is paid therefore.

Neponsit Property Owners' Association, Inc. v. Emigrant Industrial Savings Bank

Covenantor's assignees (P) v. Subsequent purchaser (D)

N.Y. Ct. App., 15 N.E.2d 793 (1938)

NATURE OF CASE: Action to foreclose a lien upon land.

FACT SUMMARY: Neponsit Property Owners (P) claim Emigrant Industrial Savings Bank's (D) deed to certain property conveyed such property subject to a covenant contained in the original deed that provided for the payment by all subsequent purchasers of an annual improvements charge.

RULE OF LAW

A covenant in the original deed subjecting land to an annual charge for improvements to the surrounding residential tract is enforceable by the property owners' association against subsequent purchasers if: (1) grantor and grantee intended that the covenant run with the land; (2) the covenant touches or concerns the land with which it runs; and (3) privity of estate between the party claiming benefit of the covenant and the party who rests under the burden of such covenant.

FACTS: Neponsit Property Owners' (P) assignor, Neponsit Realty Company, conveyed the land now owned by Emigrant Industrial Savings Bank (Emigrant Bank) (D) to R. Deyer and wife by deed. That original deed contained a covenant providing: (1) that the conveyed land should be subject to an annual charge for improvements upon the entire residential tract then being developed; (2) that such charge should be a lien; (3) such charge should be payable by all subsequent purchasers to the company or its assigns, including a property owners' association that might thereafter be organized; and (4) such covenant runs with the land. Neponsit Property Owners (P) brought action based upon the above covenant to foreclose a lien upon the land that Emigrant Bank (D) now owns, having purchased it at a judicial sale. Emigrant Bank (D) appealed from an order denying their motion for judgment on the pleadings.

ISSUE: Does a covenant in the original deed subjecting land to an annual charge for improvements run with the land and create a lien that is enforceable against subsequent owners by Neponsit Property Owners (P)?

HOLDING AND DECISION: (Lehman, J.) Yes. A covenant in the original deed subjecting land to an annual charge for improvements will run with the land and will be enforceable against a subsequent purchaser if: (1) the grantor and grantee intend that the covenant run with the land; (2) the covenant touches or concerns the land with which it runs; and (3) there is privity of estate between the party claiming benefit of the covenant and the party who rests under the burden of the covenant. In the instant case, the grantor and grantee manifested their intent that the covenant run with the land by so stating in the original deed. The covenant touches or concerns the land in substance if not in form, i.e., the covenant alters the legal rights of ownership of the land, by providing that the burden of paying the cost of maintaining public improvements is inseparably attached to the land that enjoys the benefits of such improvements. The concept of privity of estate between parties usually requires that the party claiming benefit from the enforcement of a covenant own the property that benefits from such enforcement. Although Neponsit Property Owners (P), the corporation, does not own the property that would benefit from enforcement, the corporation is acting as the agent of property owners and should therefore be considered in privity in substance if not in form. Since the covenant complies with the legal requirements for one that runs with the land and is enforceable against subsequent purchasers, the order that denied Emigrant Bank's (D) motion for judgment on the pleadings is affirmed.

ANALYSIS

It has been suggested that the technical requirements that determine the enforceability of covenants as to future parties, e.g., *Neponsit*, might well be abandoned and that the intention of the covenanting parties be the sole criterion. This suggestion is supported by the following developments: (1) the benefit of a contract may now be assigned, or even created, initially for the benefit of a third person; (2) recording systems, though imperfect, afford much protection to the purchaser of land against outstanding burdens of which he may be unaware. It should be noted, however, that the unrestricted enforcement of covenants may seriously impair the usefulness of land. A student reading this case should keep in mind that *Neponsit* is not concerned with the enforcement of covenants between original covenanting parties. That question of enforceability is left to the contracts course.

Continued on next page.

Quicknotes

COVENANT A written promise to do, or to refrain from doing, a particular activity.

FORECLOSURE An action to recover the amount due on a mortgage of real property where the owner has failed to pay their debt, terminating the owner's interest in the property, which must then be sold to satisfy the debt.

JUDICIAL SALE A sale of property by a sheriff pursuant to a judgment.

LIEN A claim against the property of another in order to secure the payment of a debt.

PRIVITY OF ESTATE Common or successive relation to the same right in property.

"RUN WITH THE LAND" Covenants that are binding on successor in interest to the property to which they are attached.

Evans v. Pollock

Owner of restricted property in subdivision (P) v. Owner of unrestricted property in subdivision (D)

Tex. Sup. Ct., 796 S.W.2d 465 (1990)

NATURE OF CASE: Appeal from reversal of judgment against defendants in action for declaratory, equitable, and injunctive relief seeking to impose restrictions on land under the implied reciprocal negative easement doctrine.

FACT SUMMARY: Evans (P), whose lakefront property in a subdivision was restricted, sought to enjoin the commercial use of unrestricted lots within the subdivision under the implied reciprocal negative easement doctrine.

RULE OF LAW

Where there is a general plan or scheme in a development whereby certain restrictions apply only to well-defined similarly situated lots, the doctrine of implied reciprocal negative easements may be applied to such lots, notwithstanding that not all lots in the development are so restricted.

FACTS: Evans (P) owned lakefront property in a subdivision. Evans's (P) property was restricted, as were a majority of other lakefront properties. However, the lakefront properties that had been retained by the subdivision developers were unrestricted. The deeds for a majority of the plats contained restrictive covenants that prohibited commercial use, limited construction to single-family homes, and provided that the restrictions could be altered by a "3/4 vote" of lakefront properties. Pollock (D) sought to buy some of the unrestricted lots from the developers' devisees for use as a marina, a private club, and condominiums. Evans (P) and other property owners brought suit under the implied reciprocal negative easement doctrine seeking to enjoin the sale of the unrestricted land without imposition of the restrictions, and also seeking a declaration that the restrictive covenants on their properties were implied by reciprocity on the other similarly situated properties that had been retained by the developers. The trial court found that the restrictions were intended to apply to all the lakefront lots in the subdivision, but not to certain hilltop properties. The state's intermediate court reversed, ruling that for the implied reciprocal negative easement doctrine to apply, the developers had to have intended that the entire subdivision be restricted. The state's highest court granted review.

ISSUE: Where there is a general plan or scheme in a development whereby certain restrictions apply only to well-defined similarly situated lots, may the the doctrine of implied reciprocal negative easements be applied to such lots, notwithstanding that not all lots in the development are so restricted?

HOLDING AND DECISION: (Ray, J.) Yes. Where there is a general plan or scheme in a development whereby certain restrictions apply only to well-defined similarly situated lots, the doctrine of implied reciprocal negative easements may be applied to such lots, notwithstanding that not all lots in the development are so restricted. Evans (P) and the other plaintiffs are asking that reciprocal negative easements be implied on the land Pollock (D) seeks to buy. Such restrictions may be implied on a showing that the developer had a general development scheme for the subdivision where certain similarly situated lots would be restricted, but other lots would not be restricted. Contrary to the intermediate appellate court's ruling, the developer need not have intended that all lots in the development be restricted for the doctrine of implied reciprocal negative easements to apply. Here, the restricted lots were all similarly situated lakefront properties. Accordingly, the restrictions that apply to those lots may be applied to the lakefront property that Pollock (D) seeks to purchase. Reversed and remanded.

ANALYSIS

Note that the doctrine of implied reciprocal negative servitudes binds the buyers even though the grantor omits to include the mutual restrictions in subsequent deeds. The state of California, for one, has refused to recognize the doctrine on the grounds that it fails to protect buyer expectations, fosters uncertainty, and circumvents the orderly development of subdivisions. Instead, state law requires that only restrictive covenants must be in writing or on the deed in order to be enforceable.

Quicknotes

NEGATIVE EASEMENT Refers to the duty to refrain from conducting a specific lawful activity on the servient estate because it interferes with the use of the dominant estate.

RECIPROCAL NEGATIVE EASEMENT When a landowner sells part of his or land and restricts the purchaser's use of that part of the land, an easement is created. The restriction is also placed on the part of the land retained by the landowner.

RESTRICTIVE COVENANT A promise contained in a deed to limit the uses to which the property will be made.

Appel v. Presley Cos.

Homeowner (P) v. Developer (D)

N.M. Sup. Ct., 806 P.2d 1054 (1991)

NATURE OF CASE: Appeal from suit for permanent injunction.

FACT SUMMARY: The Appels (P) sought a permanent injunction to prevent Presley (D) from building four townhouses on a tract in their subdivision.

RULE OF LAW

Provisions allowing amendment of subdivision restrictions are subject to a requirement of reasonableness.

FACTS: The Appels (P) owned a home in a subdivision owned by Presley (D). Presley (D) proposed to replat the property in order to build townhouses on the subdivision, which consisted of single-family dwellings. The Appels (P) brought suit to enjoin such replatting and building claiming breach of restrictive covenants, negligent and fraudulent misrepresentation, and unfair trade practices, as well as seeking an injunction of development on the property. Judgment was entered for Presley (D) and the Appels (P) appealed.

ISSUE: Are provisions allowing amendment of subdivision restrictions subject to a requirement of reasonableness?

HOLDING AND DECISION: (Franchini, J.) Yes. Provisions allowing amendment of subdivision restrictions are subject to a requirement of reasonableness. A court of equity will not enforce restrictions if the circumstances render them inequitable. The determination of whether the restrictions were reasonable or destroyed the value of the property is a factual matter, and thus summary judgment must be reversed and the cause is remanded.

ANALYSIS

Note that there is an inherent inconsistency in the establishment of restrictive covenants upon which purchasers may rely, and the reservation of the right to change such restrictions. Thus such amendments may be upheld, so long as the developer exercises them reasonably.

Quicknotes

EQUITABLE Just; fair.

PERMANENT INJUNCTION A remedy imposed by the court ordering a party to cease the conduct of a specific activity until the final disposition of the cause of action.

RESTRICTIVE COVENANT A promise contained in a deed to limit the uses to which the property will be made.

SUBDIVISION PLOT A parcel of land that is divided into portions to be resold or developed.

SUMMARY JUDGMENT Judgment rendered by a court in response to a motion by one of the parties, claiming that the lack of a question of material fact in respect to an issue warrants disposition of the issue without consideration by the jury.

Davidson Brothers, Inc. v. D. Katz & Sons, Inc.

Seller (P) v. Buyer (D)

N.J. Super. Ct. App. Div. 643 A.2d 642 (1994), *on remand from* N.J. Sup. Ct., 579 A.2d 288 (1990)

NATURE OF CASE: Appeal from decision rendering a restrictive covenant unenforceable.

FACT SUMMARY: The trial court, applying a reasonableness test, determined that a covenant prohibiting the use as a supermarket of property in downtown New Brunswick was unenforceable.

RULE OF LAW

A covenant cannot be sustained if it is inconsistent with the public interest or detrimental to the public good.

FACTS: Davidson Brothers, Inc. (Davidson) (P), a supermarket operator in N.J., opened a store on George Street in downtown New Brunswick. The store was later closed because it had opened another location two miles away. Davidson sold the George Street location to D. Katz & Sons, Inc. (Katz) (D), a rug merchant. The deed contained a covenant prohibiting its use as a supermarket. The city acquired the property from Katz (D) and attempted to procure another supermarket. The Housing Authority leased the store to C-Town for $1 per year on the condition they make certain improvements. Davidson (P) brought suit to enforce the covenant. The trial court, applying a reasonableness test promulgated by the New Jersey Supreme Court, determined that a covenant prohibiting the use as a supermarket of property in downtown New Brunswick was unenforceable. Davidson (P) appealed.

ISSUE: Can a covenant be sustained if it is inconsistent with the public interest or detrimental to the public good?

HOLDING AND DECISION: (D'Annunzio, J.) No. A covenant cannot be sustained if it is inconsistent with the public interest or detrimental to the public good. New Jersey courts have refused to enforce covenants that violate public policy. The rehabilitation of inner cities is a public policy of the state often expressed in relevant legislation. The covenant was so contrary to public policy that it should not be recognized as a valid, enforceable obligation. Affirmed.

ANALYSIS

The closing of the George Street location created an extreme hardship on the residents of downtown New Brunswick. Experts and testimony were introduced to show that many persons had no access to motor vehicles and that lack of markets in downtown areas make food more expensive for inner city residents.

Quicknotes

COVENANT A written promise to do, or to refrain from doing, a particular activity.

DEED A signed writing transferring title to real property from one person to another.

Nahrstedt v. Lakeside Village Condominium Association, Inc.

Cat lover (P) v. Homeowners association (D)

Cal. Sup. Ct., 878 P.2d 1275 (1994)

NATURE OF CASE: Suit challenging the validity of a provision in a common interest development's covenants, conditions, and restrictions that prohibited the keeping of pets in the development.

FACT SUMMARY: A resident of a common interest development in California kept three cats in her condominium in violation of the development's governing covenants, conditions, and restrictions. The homeowners association therefore assessed continuing penalties against her for the violations.

RULE OF LAW

A recorded use restriction imposed by a common interest development in California must be enforced uniformly against all residents of the development unless the restriction is unreasonable.

FACTS: Nahrstedt (P) owned and lived in a condominium in Lakeside Village, a 530-unit common interest development in Los Angeles County overseen by the Lakeside Village Condominium Association (the homeowners association) (D). Nahrstedt's (P) ownership of her condominium gave her membership in the homeowners association (D). One of the homeowners association's (D) duties was to enforce Lakeside Village's governing, duly recorded covenants, conditions and restrictions (CC&Rs). One clause of the CC&Rs provided that "[n]o animals (which shall include dogs and cats) . . . shall be kept in any unit." Nahrstedt (P), who alleged that she did not know of the pet restriction when she bought her condominium, lived in her unit with her three cats, but she did not let her cats have free run of Lakeside Village's common areas. When the homeowners association (D) learned that Nahrstedt (P) was keeping the cats in her home, it started assessing monthly fines against her for violating the CC&Rs. Nahrstedt (P) sued the homeowners association (D), asking the trial court to invalidate the assessments already imposed against her, to enjoin the homeowners association (D) from making such assessments against her in the future, and to declare the pet restriction in the CC&Rs "unreasonable" as applied to situations involving non-disturbing, essentially entirely in-home pet ownership like hers. The homeowners association (D) filed a demurrer to Nahrstedt's (P) complaint [i.e., the homeowners association (D) moved to dismiss her complaint for failing to state a claim upon which relief could be granted]. The trial court agreed with the homeowners association (D) and dismissed Nahrstedt's (P) complaint. On Nahrstedt's (P) appeal, the intermediate appellate court reversed the trial court's judgment, agreeing with Nahrstedt (P) that the reasonableness of a recorded use restriction in a common interest development must be determined on a case-by-case basis. The homeowners association (D) petitioned the California Supreme Court for further review.

ISSUE: Must a recorded use restriction imposed by a common interest development in California be enforced uniformly against all residents of the development unless the restriction is unreasonable?

HOLDING AND DECISION: (Kennard, J.) Yes. A recorded use restriction imposed by a common interest development in California must be enforced uniformly against all residents of the development unless the restriction is unreasonable. Homeowners in a common interest development sacrifice certain freedoms in exchange for, among other things, their ability to enforce restrictive covenants against other homeowners in the development. These restrictions are enforceable, though, only if they qualify as equitable servitudes or as covenants running with the land. In Section 1354(a) of the California Civil Code, California's legislature has established the test for determining whether a common interest development's use restrictions are enforceable: under Section 1354(a), a recorded declaration's use restrictions are "enforceable . . . unless unreasonable." Some states have reached similar conclusions through the courts. For example, in *Hidden Harbour Estates v. Basso*, 393 So. 2d 637 (Fla. Ct. App. 1981), a Florida appellate court held that a recorded declaration's stated use restrictions are entitled to a heavy presumption of validity, so much so that even somewhat unreasonable restrictions should nevertheless be enforced. The *Hidden Harbour Estates* court concluded further that arbitrary restrictions or those that violate public policy or a fundamental constitutional right should not be enforced. In a case involving a pet restriction, *Noble v. Murphy*, 612 N.E.2d 266 (Mass. App. Ct. 1993), the court agreed with the *Hidden Harbour Estates* rationale that otherwise-valid use restrictions should be enforced unless they violate constitutional rights or public policy. This court concludes, then, that recorded restrictive covenants should not be enforced when they violate public policy, as in *Shelley v. Kramer*, 334 U.S. 1 (1948) (racial restriction), or when they are arbitrary and bear no rational relation to a purpose involving the land. In such cases, the harm resulting from enforcement of arbitrary use restrictions or restrictions that violate fundamental public policy always outweighs any benefit that such restrictions might

Continued on next page.

confer. Such principles also inform Section 1354(a) of the California Civil Code, which this court interprets as requiring enforcement of use restrictions unless they are arbitrary, violate public policy, or impose burdens outweighing any benefit. This presumption of validity for recorded restrictive covenants means that homeowners associations can enforce their covenants without fear of instigating litigation. The presumption also relieves the judicial system from making case-by-case determinations of whether covenants are reasonable as applied to a particular homeowner. The presumption thus in turn means that homeowners in common interest developments will have the assurance that their covenants will be enforced uniformly and predictably. In this particular case, the appellate court failed to apply the pertinent rules governing equitable servitudes and erroneously relied on two opinions, *Portola Hills Community Assn. v. James*, 5 Cal. Rptr. 2d 580 (Cal. Ct. App. 1993), and *Bernardo Villas Management Corp. v. Black*, 235 Cal. Rptr. 509 (Cal. Ct. App. 1987), both of which are hereby disapproved because those courts did not use appropriately deferential review of the covenants at issue in those cases. Whether a use restriction is reasonable or unreasonable must be determined by referring to the entire common interest development, not by referring to the particular facts of a specific complaining homeowner. More specifically, the court holds that the Lakeside Village pet restriction is not arbitrary because it rationally promotes the other owners' legitimate concerns about health, sanitation, and noise; Nahrstedt (P) has failed to allege that the restriction's burden is so disproportionate to the legitimate benefits that the pet restriction is unreasonable. Moreover, no fundamental public policy requires that pets be kept in a condominium development, and no constitutional provision or California statute grants the right to keep pets in such a situation, either. Reversed and remanded.

DISSENT: (Arabian, J.) The majority's reasoning has technical merit, but the application of that analysis to these facts reveals a narrow understanding of the relationship between the law and the human spirit. The pet restriction at issue here violates Section 1354(a). It is arbitrary and unreasonable, within the meaning of Section 1354(a), because it imposes an undue burden on owners who keep their pets within their units and do not permit their pets to disturb the use of other homeowners' properties. The restriction's burden on such homeowners outweighs those homeowners' quality of life in the common interest development, and indeed the restriction only worsens the breakdown of our social fabric. All that the majority has done today is to accept, uncritically, the homeowners association's (D) assurances that uniform enforcement will promote all owners' "health and happiness." The first question in an appropriately probing inquiry should be to recognize that the burden on the particular use at issue here goes well beyond the impersonal and mundane issues normally covered by restrictive covenants. The majority instead asks only whether the use restriction at issue was stated in the original recorded declaration. If it was, it now shall be presumed valid unless it violates public policy. Such a standard means that almost all recorded use restrictions are valid, a status that only the commandments issued by Moses have enjoyed before today. Further, the proscribed activity here, pet ownership that is wholly confined to one's own home, deprives homeowners of the American dream, a notion that has always included the ownership and full enjoyment of one's home. Courts should rule with more humanity and strive to create harmony, not division, within the populace.

ANALYSIS

Despite the emotionalism of Justice Arabian's dissent, and despite the intermediate appellate court's contrary ruling (relying on two now-invalidated opinions), today this case seems relatively easy for all the reasons cited by the majority. Public policy argues heavily against Nahrstedt's (P) position because that position would create great instability within homeowners associations, and because the burden of deciding enforceability of use restrictions on a case-by-case basis would substantially increase the caseloads of a judicial system that is already over-burdened. Under the rationale of *Nahrstedt* and cases like it, homeowners now can know that, when they sign a development's recorded covenants and use restrictions, those covenants and restrictions will almost certainly be enforced.

Quicknotes

CC&RS Covenants, conditions, and restrictions that residents of a condominium development agree to abide by when they take ownership of a unit in that development.

DECLARATORY RELIEF A judgment of the court establishing the rights of the parties.

Apple Valley Gardens Association, Inc. v. MacHutta

Condominium association (P) v. Condominium unit owner (D)

Wis. Sup. Ct., 763 N.W.2d 126 (2009)

NATURE OF CASE: Appeal from affirmance of summary judgment in favor of plaintiff condominium association seeking declaratory judgment that an amendment to its bylaws was enforceable.

FACT SUMMARY: The MacHuttas (D), who founded and owned units in the Apple Valley Gardens Association, Inc. (Association) (P), a condominium complex, and who for over 20 years rented out one of their units, continued to rent out that unit over the Association's (P) objections, notwithstanding a bylaw amendment that prohibited the rental of units. The MacHuttas (D) contended that the prohibition on rentals was ineffective because it had not been added to the condominium's declaration. The Association (P) sought a declaratory judgment that the bylaw amendment was enforceable.

RULE OF LAW

(1) A condominium association may prohibit the rental of condominium units through an amendment to its bylaws, rather than such a restriction having to be placed in the condominium's declaration.

(2) A statement in a condominium declaration that a lease or rental agreement for a unit will not relieve the unit's owner from the financial obligations otherwise imposed by the declaration does not create an affirmative right to rent units.

FACTS: In 1979, the MacHuttas (D) collectively built, developed, declared, and incorporated Apple Valley Gardens Association, Inc. (Association) (P), a condominium complex. The condominium declaration stated that its overriding purpose was for single-family use only. It also declared that owners who leased their units would remain financially responsible to the Association (P). The MacHuttas (D) had two units and rented one of them to tenants. In 2002, the Association (P) amended its bylaws to prohibit the renting of units. In 2004, over the Association's (P) objections, the MacHuttas (D) rented out the unit to new tenants, claiming the bylaw amendment was ineffective because it had not been added to the condominium declaration. The Association (P) brought suit for a declaratory judgment that the bylaw amendment was enforceable. The trial court granted summary judgment to the Association (P), the state's intermediate appellate court affirmed, and the state's highest court granted review.

ISSUE:

(1) May a condominium association prohibit the rental of condominium units through an amendment to its bylaws, rather than such a restriction having to be placed in the condominium's declaration?

(2) Does a statement in a condominium declaration that a lease or rental agreement for a unit will not relieve the unit's owner from the financial obligations otherwise imposed by the declaration create an affirmative right to rent units?

HOLDING AND DECISION: (Gableman, J.)

(1) Yes. A condominium association may prohibit the rental of condominium units through an amendment to its bylaws, rather than such a restriction having to be placed in the condominium's declaration. Contrary to the MacHuttas' (D) contention, restrictions, including restrictions on the ability of owners to rent their units, may be enacted through the bylaws. Although state statute requires that a condominium declaration contain a statement of the purposes for which the building and each of the units are intended and restricted as to use, such use restrictions are general in nature, and nothing in the statute or any other state statute requires that all restrictions on use must be identified in the declaration. Similarly, no statute suggests that a prohibition on the rental of condominium units must be placed in the declaration to be effective. Declarations are not required to be exhaustive as to permissible uses of condominium units. Instead, state statute permits the addition to a condominium association's bylaws of restrictions respecting the use and maintenance of units. This statute does not place limitations on the types of restrictions that can be implemented through bylaw amendments. Therefore, provided use restrictions do not conflict with the declaration or with state or federal law, they are valid and enforceable. Although these statutes thus empower condominium associations to take actions that limit the rights of individual owners, condominium ownership is a statutory creation that obligates individual owners to relinquish rights they might otherwise enjoy in other types of real property ownership; when purchasing a condominium unit, individual owners agree to be bound by the declaration and bylaws as they may be amended from time to time. Merely because lenders and purchasers rely on recorded declarations is irrelevant.

Continued on next page.

If lenders and purchasers wish to know whether and under what conditions a condominium unit may be rented out, they may easily inquire of both the declaration and the bylaws. Even so, the association, if not prohibited by the declaration, could choose to withdraw an owner's ability to rent out the owner's unit at a later date. This is one of the sacrifices of condominium ownership under the current statutory scheme. Affirmed as to this issue.

(2) No. A statement in a condominium declaration that a lease or rental agreement for a unit will not relieve the unit's owner from the financial obligations otherwise imposed by the declaration does not create an affirmative right to rent units. Here, the declaration, in a paragraph titled "PURPOSE—RESTRICTION ON USE," recites that owners who lease their units are still financially responsible to the Association (P). While this provision certainly does not foreclose the possibility of rentals, and contemplates the possibility that units might be rented, the provision does not create an affirmative right to rent. When read in context, the provision neither grants a right to rent one's unit nor prohibits it. The gravamen of the sentence has nothing to do with a right to rent. Rather, its purpose is to emphasize the unyielding nature of the owners' financial obligations whether a unit owner rents or occupies a unit. Further, another paragraph in the declaration authorizes the Association (P) to make reasonable rules and regulations governing the use of the units—which is exactly what the Association (P) did. Accordingly, the 2002 bylaws amendment does not conflict with the declaration and is enforceable against the MacHuttas (D). Affirmed as to this issue. Affirmed.

DISSENT: (Prosser, J.) More than 20 years after the condominium complex was established by the MacHuttas (D), the Association (P) membership amended the bylaws to require that all units be owner-occupied. The 2002 amendment added: "No residential unit owner shall rent, lease or otherwise so devise any residential unit or any part therein." This amendment significantly altered a unit owner's rights to the use of the owner's property. Inasmuch as most owners of multiple units cannot afford to occupy more than one unit in the same condominium complex, they are effectively forced to sell some of their property. The declaration itself did not impair a unit owner's property right to lease or rent a condominium unit, and, by its language, the declaration recognized that right, as do state statutes. Because the MacHuttas' (D) unbroken practice since the filing of the declaration was to rent some of the condominium units, the amended bylaws conflicted with the declaration as it was intended and consistently interpreted. State statute also provides, critically, that if there is any conflict between any provisions of a declaration and any provisions of the bylaws, the provisions of the declaration control. To contend that there is no conflict between any provision in the declaration and any provision in the amended bylaws simply ignores reality. Yet, to concede "any conflict" decides the case for the MacHuttas (D). When a unit owner's right to rent is abrogated by an amendment to the condominium bylaws, the owner's investment and the owner's ability to relocate temporarily for employment or family can be seriously affected. The abrogation can also adversely affect the rights of third parties, such as mortgagees. Although the state's condominium law permits these rights and interests to be adversely affected, such an adverse effect must be in accordance with the declaration and the statutes. That did not happen here.

ANALYSIS

As this case illustrates, condominium law is different from basic property law in that condominium property owners have shared responsibilities and are often subject to restrictions that traditional property owners are not. For example, the right to rent is inherent in the "exclusive ownership" of real property, but may be restricted in common interest developments such as condominiums. Nonetheless, restrictions on the use of property are not favored in the law, and where doubt exists about a restriction, that doubt should be resolved in favor of the free use of property. However, where such restrictions do not conflict with the declaration or with state or federal law, they will be enforced.

Quicknotes

DECLARATORY JUDGMENT A judgment of the court establishing the rights of the parties in a controversy that does not grant damages but is binding.

GRAVAMEN The material part of a cause of action setting forth the injury that is sought to be redressed.

SUMMARY JUDGMENT Judgment rendered by a court in response to a motion made by one of the parties, claiming that the lack of a question of material fact in respect to an issue warrants disposition of the issue without consideration by the jury.

Trustees of the Cambridge Point Condominium Trust v. Cambridge Point, LLC

Condominium board of trustees (P) v. Condominium's developer (D)

Mass. Sup. Ct., 88 N.E.3d 1142 (2018)

NATURE OF CASE: Direct appeal from dismissal of action by condominium board of trustees against the condominium's developer for negligence, breach of the implied warranty of habitability, negligent misrepresentation, fraudulent misrepresentation and concealment, breach of fiduciary duty, and a declaration that a provision of the condominium bylaws requiring 80% approval of unit holders prior to bringing litigation involving common areas and facilities was void.

FACT SUMMARY: The board of trustees (trustees) (P) of the Cambridge Point Condominium Trust (trust) wanted to bring suit against Cambridge Point, LLC (developers) (D), the condominium complex's developers, when it was discovered that multiple design and construction defects were causing significant leaking and mold problems throughout the complex. However, a bylaw that the developers (D) had filed when they registered the condominium complex required that the trustees (P) obtain 80% approval of the unit owners prior to instituting such litigation, and, because the developers (D) and their affiliates had retained more than 20% of the units, it was effectively impossible for the trustees (P) to obtain such approval. The trustees (P) nevertheless brought suit against the developers (D) on multiple grounds, and sought a declaration that the litigation bylaw was void, either per se, or as a matter of public policy in this particular instance.

RULE OF LAW

(1) A condominium bylaw provision requiring unit-owner consent before the unit-owners' association can initiate litigation is not per se void.

(2) A bylaw provision filed by a condominium complex's developers that makes it effectively impossible for the condominium trust to obtain redress from the developers for defective construction of common areas is void as contravening public policy.

FACTS: In 2007, Cambridge Point, LLC (developers) (D), as the declarant of a predominantly residential condominium complex, filed in the registry of deeds a master deed, a declaration of trust, and the bylaws of the Cambridge Point Condominium Trust (trust). The trust's board of trustees (trustees) (P) was responsible for administering the affairs of the trust. Among the powers and duties committed to the trustees (P) was the authority under § 1(o) of the bylaws to "conduct[] litigation as to any course of action involving the common areas and facilities." However, this authority was limited by a condition precedent that required the trustees (P), before initiating any litigation against anyone who was not a unit owner, (1) to deliver a copy of the proposed complaint to all unit owners; (2) to specify a monetary limit of the amount to be paid as legal fees and costs in the proposed litigation; (3) to inform all unit owners that, if they consented to the initiation of the litigation, they would forthwith be separately assessed this amount of legal fees and costs as a special assessment; and (4) within 60 days after a copy of the proposed complaint had been delivered to the unit owners, to receive the written consent of not less than 80% of all unit owners to bring the litigation. Moreover, the developers (D) and their affiliates had in fact reserved for themselves, and continued to own, enough units to prevent an 80% supermajority of unit owners to authorize the trust to institute a lawsuit. In 2012, the trust began receiving complaints from unit owners about pervasive water leaks, which were infiltrating and damaging the building envelope, eventually causing a mold infestation both on the exterior sheathing of the building envelope and within individual units. An investigation conducted by an engineering firm in 2013 identified myriad design and construction defects with the condominium. When the trust's demands that the developers (D) repair the defective construction proved futile, the trust sought out a contractor to repair the building, who estimated the costs of repair as exceeding $2 million. In 2014, after having delivered to the unit owners the proposed complaint and a statement of the estimated legal fees and costs of the litigation, but without having received the written consent of at least 80% of the unit owners, the trustees (P) filed suit against the developers (D) alleging negligence, breach of the implied warranty of habitability, negligent misrepresentation, fraudulent misrepresentation and concealment, and breach of fiduciary duty. The trustees (P) also sought a judgment declaring that § 1(o) of the bylaws was void. The trial court dismissed the suit, and the state's highest court granted direct appellate review.

ISSUE:

(1) Is a condominium bylaw provision requiring unit-owner consent before the unit-owners' association can initiate litigation per se void?

Continued on next page.

(2) Is a bylaw provision filed by a condominium complex's developers that makes it effectively impossible for the condominium trust to obtain redress from the developers for defective construction of common areas void as contravening public policy?

HOLDING AND DECISION: (Gants, C.J.)

(1) No. A condominium bylaw provision requiring unit-owner consent before the unit-owners' association can initiate litigation is not per se void. Under the state's condominium law, the board of trustees of a condominium trust has the exclusive right to conduct litigation regarding defects or other problems in the common areas. Here, the trustees (P) contend, in essence, that, because the condominium law provides that they are the only party that may commence litigation to obtain compensation for damages arising from construction and design defects in the common areas, the law implicitly prohibits any bylaw provision that requires the trustees to obtain the consent of the unit owners before filing suit. This argument is unpersuasive. The condominium law is "essentially an enabling statute, setting out a framework for the development of condominiums in the [state], while providing developers and unit owners with planning flexibility." *Scully v. Tillery*, 926 N.E.2d 154 (Mass. 2010). It sets forth certain minimum requirements for the establishment of condominiums, but those matters that are not specifically addressed in the statute are to be worked out by the involved parties. Matters not specifically addressed by the condominium law may be undertaken through the condominium bylaws, provided they are not inconsistent with the law or the master deed. Although the condominium law declares that the "organization of unit owners," such the trust here, has the power to manage, and otherwise deal with common areas and facilities of the condominium, it does not grant unbridled authority to the trust with respect to every management decision that affects common areas and facilities. For example, it requires the agreement of at least 75% of the unit owners to repair or restore a condominium in the event it suffers a casualty loss that exceeds 10% of the condominium's value. It also provides that improvements to the common areas and facilities may not be treated as a "common expense" borne collectively by the unit owners unless at least 75% of the unit owners agree to make the improvements. The existence of such provisions in the condominium law suggests that the state's legislature did not believe that a condominium trust's power to manage the common areas and facilities is necessarily inconsistent with a requirement of unit-owner consent for certain management decisions. The trustees (P) contend that, because the legislature included provisions in the condominium law requiring unit-owner consent under some circumstances, but failed to include any comparable provision governing the initiation of litigation, it can be inferred that the legislature intended to prohibit any bylaw requiring unit-owner consent for litigation. "However, the maxim of negative implication—that the express inclusion of one thing implies the exclusion of another—requires great caution in its application," *Halebian v. Berv*, 931 N.E.2d 985 (Mass. 2010), and such caution is especially appropriate here, given the enabling nature of the condominium law and the wide latitude and flexibility it provides developers and unit owners to craft arrangements not specifically addressed by the act. Therefore, it cannot reasonably be inferred that because the condominium law requires unit-owner consent for some management decisions, the legislature intended to prohibit any bylaw requiring unit-owner consent for other management decisions, including the decision to commence litigation concerning common areas or facilities. Such an inference would require a clearer indication of legislative intent than mere negative implication. For these reasons, a bylaw provision requiring unit-owner consent to initiate litigation is not per se void on the grounds that it is "inconsistent" with the state's condominium law.

(2) Yes. A bylaw provision filed by a condominium complex's developers that makes it effectively impossible for the condominium trust to obtain redress from the developers for defective construction of common areas is void as contravening public policy. Regarding the bylaw provision's requirement of the consent of at least 80% of all unit owners makes it effectively impossible for the trustees (P) to sue the developers (D) of a condominium for damages arising from the defective construction and design of common areas or facilities where, as here, the developers (D) or their affiliates retain an ownership interest in at least 20% of the units; the developers (D) are not likely to agree to sue themselves. Moreover, if the trustees (P) cannot file suit against the developers (D), no one can, because the trustees' (P) authority to bring such a suit is "exclusive" as to the common areas and facilities of the condominium. Even if the developers (D) or their affiliates did not retain a 20% ownership interest, the litigation bylaw provisions, in their entirety, make it extraordinarily difficult for the trustees (P) to sue the developers (D) for defective construction and design of common areas or facilities. Because the trustees (P) must obtain the affirmative consent of at least 80% of all unit owners, any unit owner who fails to respond to the request

Continued on next page.

for written consent is treated as if they refused such consent, regardless of whether the unit owner is ill, has rented out the unit and is presently unavailable, or is simply unwilling to make a decision. The litigation bylaw also provides that the entirety of the legal fees and costs to be incurred from litigation must be "separately assessed as a special assessment effective forthwith" upon consent, even though the legal fees and costs would be incurred and billed during the life of the litigation. Further, the trustees (P) have only a brief time frame of 60 days to obtain the required written consent from the unit owners. Cumulatively, these requirements function as a formidable hurdle that the trustees (P) are required to surmount before commencing litigation against the developers (D). It has long been recognized that the public interest in freedom of contract is sometimes outweighed by public policy, and that in such cases a contract will not be enforced. Consequently, it must be considered, as a clear matter of legislative acts or judicial decisions, whether a bylaw that makes it extraordinarily difficult—and in this case, effectively impossible—to obtain redress for a developer's defective construction and design of common areas and facilities is void because it is contrary to public policy. The state has a well-established public policy in favor of the safety and habitability of homes, as reflected in the implied warranty of habitability under common law—which has been extended by judicial decision to the sale of a new home—and in the legislative enactment of building codes. The purpose of this implied warranty is to protect a purchaser of a new home from latent defects that create substantial questions of safety and habitability. The policy reasons underpinning the implied warranty of habitability in the purchase of a new home apply equally to the purchase of a new condominium unit. A developer of a condominium is not only subject to the implied warranty of habitability but also must comply with the minimum standards prescribed by the building code, which are designed to safeguard public health, safety, and general welfare. Where a claim arises from a building code violation, that claim cannot be waived because such a waiver could "do violence to the public policy underlying the legislative enactment." *Canal Elec. Co. v. Westinghouse Elec. Corp.*, 548 N.E.2d 182 (1990). Thus, it is clear from legislative acts and judicial decisions that the state's public policy strongly favors the safety and habitability of homes. To effectuate this public policy, the courts have consistently recognized the rights of individuals to obtain legal redress when their homes fail to meet minimum standards, and that such rights cannot be waived. This clear expression of public policy leads to the conclusion that a condominium bylaw provision that effectively limits the ability of unit owners to obtain legal redress for violations of these rights must be carefully scrutinized to determine whether it contravenes that public policy. For example, if a bylaw were to provide that the unit owners waive all claims against the developers for any defects in construction, such a bylaw surely would be declared void as contravening public policy to the extent that it sought to waive the unwaivable claims based on the implied warranty of habitability and policies underlying building codes reflected in the state's unfair trade practices act. Such a sweeping waiver surely would not be enforced to the extent that it would shield the developers from claims of gross negligence. Here, however, the litigation bylaw provision is even more sweeping than such a hypothetical bylaw provision because, as here, where the developers (D) and their affiliates control more than 20% of the units, this provision effectively prevents the trustees (P) from bringing any claim in litigation against the developers (D) for defects in construction or design, regardless of whether the claim is for a breach of the implied warranty of habitability, a building code violation under the unfair trade practice act, or any other claim (including gross negligence, fraud, or intentional misconduct). Moreover, the litigation bylaw at issue is more unfair than such a hypothetical provision because practical effect would likely not be immediately apparent to a reasonable prospective purchaser, who would not necessarily understand from its terms the absence of—or severe impediments to—legal recourse because the prospective purchaser would not know how many condominium units the developers (D) intended to retain, and for how long. Without this information, a prospective purchaser could not know whether the litigation bylaw is simply a provision that requires consent from 80% of the unit owners before initiating litigation or a provision that, in effect, will shield the developers (D) from any and all legal claims by the trustees (P). It is overreaching for a developer to impose a condition precedent that, for all practical purposes, makes it extraordinarily difficult or even impossible for the trustees to initiate any litigation against the developers regarding the common areas and facilities of a condominium. Such a provision has all the same flaws as a waiver of liability provision—which clearly is void as contravening public policy—but without the transparency of such a provision. Accordingly, the litigation bylaw, viewed in light of the totality of the circumstances, is void because it contravenes public policy.

Continued on next page.

ANALYSIS

Under the common law, the implied warranty of habitability attached only to residential leases. However, in Massachusetts, the state's highest court (which ruled in the case at bar) extended this warranty to the sale of new homes and new condominiums by builder-vendors. The purpose of this implied warranty is to protect a purchaser of a new home from latent defects that create substantial questions of safety and habitability. In a rental of any premises for dwelling purposes, under a written or oral lease, for a specified time or at will, there is an implied warranty that the premises are fit for human occupation, and although the precise scope of the warranty depends on the circumstances of the case, a home that is unsafe because it deviates from fundamental aspects of the applicable building codes, is structurally unsound, or fails to keep out the elements because of defects of construction would breach the implied warranty. The implied warranty of habitability cannot be waived or disclaimed, because to permit the disclaimer of a warranty protecting a purchaser from the consequences of latent defects would defeat the very purpose of such a warranty.

Quicknotes

BREACH The violation of an obligation imposed pursuant to contract or law, by acting or failing to act.

CONTRAVENE To oppose; to act contrary to.

FRAUDULENT MISREPRESENTATION A statement or conduct by one party to another that constitutes a false representation of fact.

IMPLIED WARRANTY OF HABITABILITY A warranty implied by a landlord that the premises are suitable, and will remain suitable, for habitation.

NEGLIGENCE Conduct falling below the standard of care that a reasonable person would demonstrate under similar conditions.

NEGLIGENT MISREPRESENTATION A misrepresentation that is made pursuant to a business relationship, in violation of an obligation owed, upon which the plaintiff relies to his detriment.

VOID Null; incapable of being enforced.

Shelley v. Kraemer

Property owners (D) v. Neighbors (P)

334 U.S. 1 (1948)

NATURE OF CASE: On writ of certiorari in action to enjoin a sale of property.

FACT SUMMARY: The Kraemers (P) sought to oust the Shelleys (D), a Black family, from their recently purchased property on the grounds that it was subject to a racially restrictive covenant.

RULE OF LAW

The Equal Protection Clause of the Fourteenth Amendment prohibits judicial enforcement by state courts of restrictive covenants based on race or color.

FACTS: In 1945, the Shelleys (D), a Black family, purchased property that, unknown to them, was subject to a racially restrictive covenant signed in 1911 for a 50-year period by the majority of property owners on the block. The Kraemers (P), also owners of property subject to the covenant, sued in the state court to restrain the Shelleys (D) from taking possession and to revest the title in others. The state court denied relief on the grounds that the covenant had never been finalized. However, the Missouri Supreme Court reversed. The United States Supreme Court granted the Shelleys (D) certiorari. They argued that the Equal Protection Clause of the Fourteenth Amendment prevented the judicial enforcement by state courts of racially restrictive covenants.

ISSUE: Does the Equal Protection Clause of the Fourteenth Amendment prohibit judicial enforcement by state courts of racially restrictive covenants?

HOLDING AND DECISION: (Vinson, C.J.) Yes. The Equal Protection Clause of the Fourteenth Amendment prohibits judicial enforcement by state courts of racially restrictive covenants. Equality in the enjoyment of property rights was clearly among the civil rights intended to be protected from discriminatory state action by the framers of the Fourteenth Amendment. And although past cases have struck down such discrimination when enacted by state legislatures or city councils, it may not be said that such discrimination, as in the instant case, may escape on the grounds that it was only an agreement between private individuals. Indeed, was it no more than that, no violation would exist. However, in this case state action is clearly present by reason of the active intervention of the state court to enforce the covenant. As early as 1880, in *Ex parte Virginia*, 100 U.S 339, 347, this Court found state action in violation of the Fourteenth Amendment when a state judge restricted jury service to Whites. Nor is the amendment ineffective simply because this action was taken according to the state's common-law policy. We hold that in granting judicial enforcement of these restrictive covenants, the state has denied the Shelleys (D) equal protection of the laws. Reversed.

ANALYSIS

In the 1961 case of *Burton v. Wilmington Parking Authority*, 365 U.S. 715, a state agency had built and owned a parking garage, and rented space in the garage to a private restaurant. The United States Supreme Court held that the restaurant's exclusion of Black people from service amounted to state action under the Fourteenth Amendment. The test announced was that of significant state involvement in private discrimination.

Quicknotes

EQUAL PROTECTION A constitutional guarantee that no person shall be denied the same protection of the laws enjoyed by other persons in life circumstances.

RESTRICTIVE COVENANT A promise contained in a deed to limit the uses to which the property will be made.

STATE ACTION Actions brought pursuant to the Fourteenth Amendment claiming that the government violated the plaintiff's civil rights.

Northwest Real Estate Co. v. Serio

Property seller (D) v. Buyer (P)

Md. Ct. App. 144 A. 245 (1929)

NATURE OF CASE: Action for specific performance to compel the sale of real property.

FACT SUMMARY: Northwest Real Estate (D) prevented the sale of property to the Serios (P) based on a covenant restricting the alienation of the property.

RULE OF LAW

Covenants restraining a grantee's ability to sell property are inconsistent with a grant of fee simple and are thus invalid.

FACTS: Northwest Real Estate (Northwest) (D) included a covenant in a deed preventing its grantees from selling a property before a certain date without its consent. The grantees attempted to sell the property to the Serios (P) before the required date, and Northwest (D) refused to consent. The Serios (P) sued Northwest (D) for specific performance of the contract for sale and the circuit court found for them.

ISSUE: Are covenants restraining a grantee's ability to sell property inconsistent with a grant of fee simple and thus invalid?

HOLDING AND DECISION: (Urner, J.) Yes. Covenants restraining a grantee's ability to sell property are inconsistent with a grant of fee simple and thus invalid. Freedom to alienate is essential to a grant of title in fee simple. The restriction imposed on the deed by Northwest (D) was designed to temporarily deprive the grantees of the unrestrained power of alienation and was clearly repugnant to the fee simple title conveyed by the grants. Affirmed.

DISSENT: (Bond, C.J.) The court's holding would hinder a developer's plan to create a city as a single large enterprise and thus is contrary to public policy.

ANALYSIS

The purpose of the covenant in question was to develop a high-class neighborhood. By retaining the right to approve of sales, developers can attempt to keep out "undesirables."

Quicknotes

FEE SIMPLE An estate in land characterized by ownership of the entire property for an unlimited duration and by absolute power over distribution.

RESTRAINT AGAINST ALIENATION A provision restricting the transferee's ability to convey interests in the conveyed property.

SPECIFIC PERFORMANCE An equitable remedy whereby the court requires the parties to perform their obligations pursuant to a contract.

El Di, Inc. v. Town of Bethany Beach

Restaurant operator (D) v. City (P)

Del. Sup. Ct., 477 A.2d 1066 (1984)

NATURE OF CASE: Appeal of injunction enforcing a restrictive covenant.

FACT SUMMARY: Bethany Beach (P) sought to enforce a restrictive covenant prohibiting the sale of alcoholic beverages, even though the nature of the neighborhood had changed greatly since the creation of the covenant.

RULE OF LAW
A restrictive covenant will not be enforced where a fundamental change in the nature of the neighborhood has made the purpose sought by the covenant unattainable.

FACTS: The Town of Bethany Beach (P) was originally established by a church and was intended to be a quiet, residential community. The property originally forming the town had a restrictive covenant placed on it preventing commercial use and the sale of alcoholic beverages. Over the years, the community grew. The covenant against non-residential use was ignored; in fact, the original center of town was zoned for commercial use. In 1981, El Di, Inc. (D), operator of a restaurant, applied for and received a license to sell alcohol, which it began to do. Bethany Beach (P) obtained an injunction enforcing the restrictive covenant. El Di (D) appealed.

ISSUE: Will a restrictive covenant be enforced where a fundamental change in the nature of the neighborhood has made the purpose sought by the covenant unattainable?

HOLDING AND DECISION: (Herrmann, C.J.) No. A restrictive covenant will not be enforced where a fundamental change in the nature of the neighborhood has made the purpose sought by the covenant unattainable. Courts will not enforce a restrictive covenant to no purpose. Here, the purpose of the covenant was to ensure that Bethany Beach (P) remained a quiet, residential community. This has not occurred, however. Rather, commercial development has occurred, and the town is now a seaside resort. Therefore, the community is no longer that envisioned by its founders, and the covenant has outlived its purpose. Reversed.

DISSENT: (Christie, J.) Despite its growth, Bethany Beach (P) still remains a quiet family-oriented community, justifying the continued enforcement of the restrictions. The tolerance of public consumption of alcohol does not negate the prohibition on its sale.

ANALYSIS

"Changed conditions" is conceptually distinct from "abandonment," another rationale for extinguishment of servitude. The former refers to changes in the community outside the restricted land. Abandonment occurs when the use of the dominant tenement is altered so as to make enforcement of the covenant unreasonable.

Quicknotes

PERMANENT INJUNCTION A remedy imposed by the court ordering a party to cease the conduct of a specific activity until the final disposition of the cause of action.

RESTRICTIVE COVENANT A promise contained in a deed to limit the uses to which the property will be made.

Blakeley v. Gorin

Property owner (P) v. Adjacent apartment owner (D)

Mass. Sup. Jud. Ct., 313 N.E.2d 903 (1974)

NATURE OF CASE: Appeal from action to remove building restrictions.

FACT SUMMARY: Blakeley (P) wanted to build a hotel to be connected by a passageway over an alley with an existing structure owned by him.

RULE OF LAW

Building restrictions will not be specifically enforced, even when they convey an actual and substantial benefit to the person seeking enforcement, if they impede reasonable use of the land for its most suitable purposes.

FACTS: Massachusetts placed certain restrictions on land sold to private parties. Blakeley (P) owned property subject to these restrictions. One parcel had a hotel built on it. Behind the property, separated by an alley, Blakeley (P) owned a vacant lot. Blakeley (P) wanted to build an addition to the hotel on this lot and to connect the two buildings by a walkway over the alley. Gorin (D), who owned an eight-story apartment building adjacent to the vacant lot, objected to the building of the walkway, alleging that it would infringe on light and air rights. Gorin (D) also alleged that the new construction would violate the no mercantile restriction and the 16-foot distance requirement between abutting buildings contained in the original deeds issued by Massachusetts. The court found that the restrictions were no longer valid and should not be enforced since they would unreasonably impede the most reasonable use of the property. The court found authority for its position under a state law that allowed the court to deny specific enforcement of outdated restrictions or that money damages could, where appropriate be awarded in lieu of enforcement. Gorin (D) appealed, alleging that the statute allowed for a taking of property rights without compensation, and he had been denied damages for loss of air and light rights.

ISSUE: Will building restrictions be specifically enforced when they convey an actual and substantial benefit to the person seeking enforcement if they impede reasonable use of the land for its most suitable purposes?

HOLDING AND DECISION: (Hennessey, J.) No. Building restrictions will not be specifically enforced, even when they convey an actual and substantial benefit to the person seeking enforcement, if they impede reasonable use of the land for its most suitable purposes. The legislature may provide that outdated or unnecessary building restrictions may be denied specific enforcement by the court. If the person asserting that the restriction should be enforced can establish damages, a money award in lieu of enforcement may be allowed. Any mercantile businesses established in the new structure are merely subsidiary to the primary business of operating the hotel. They will have no effect on the property owner. The passageway between the buildings does constitute an infringement on Gorin's (D) property rights, but it is not so substantial as to require enforcement of the restriction. Rather than deprive Blakeley (P) of the best and most reasonable use of his property, money damages are sufficient to compensate him. Private building restrictions are not the equivalent of constitutionally protected rights. Reasonable government regulation and control are permissible if it serves a valid public purpose. The valid public purpose served by the new hotel is the beneficial effect on the city's tax base. Reversed and remanded for a determination of damages to be awarded.

DISSENT: (Quirico, J.) The statute allowing nonenforcement of private restrictions is unconstitutional as applied herein. It allows private parties to deprive others of valuable property rights for a very large number of reasons.

ANALYSIS

Normally, if any of the following conditions exist, building restrictions/covenants may be avoided (depending on the jurisdiction): (1) change in the neighborhood's character rendering the restriction unfair/unnecessary, (2) conduct of the party imposing the condition constituting waiver, (3) the party claiming enforcement owns no land in the parcel subdivision and the restrictions are not required to achieve a common plan, and/or (4) the restriction serves no public/private interest and would inhibit growth of the neighborhood and/or best use of the land.

Quicknotes

INFRINGEMENT Conduct in violation of a statute or contract that interferes with another's rights pursuant to law.

RESTRICTIVE COVENANT A promise contained in a deed to limit the uses to which the property will be made.

CHAPTER 8

Concurrent, Family, and Entity Property

Quick Reference Rules of Law

Carr v. Deking

Property owner (P) v. Lessee (D)

Wash. Ct. App., 765 P.2d 40 (1988)

NATURE OF CASE: Appeal from decision declaring that a valid lease existed between one cotenant and a third party.

FACT SUMMARY: George Carr, owner of a parcel of land with his son, Joel Carr (P), as tenants in common, executed a written lease agreement with Deking (D) without Joel's (P) authorization.

RULE OF LAW

A cotenant may lawfully lease his own interest in the common property to another without the consent of the other tenant and without the other tenant joining in the lease.

FACTS: George Carr and his son, Joel Carr (P), owned a parcel of land as tenants in common. From 1974 to 1986 they leased the land to Deking (D) pursuant to a year-to-year oral agreement, receiving one-third of the annual crop as rent. In 1986, Joel Carr (P) informed Deking (D) he wanted cash rent in place of crop rent. Shortly thereafter, George Carr (P) executed a written lease agreement with Deking (D) without his son's authorization. Joel Carr (P) commenced this action to declare that no valid lease existed and that Deking (D) had no right to farm the land.

ISSUE: May a cotenant lawfully lease his own interest in the common property to another without the consent of the other tenant and without the other tenant joining in the lease?

HOLDING AND DECISION: (Green, J.) Yes. A cotenant may lawfully lease his own interest in the common property to another without the consent of the other tenant and without the other tenant joining in the lease. It is established law that each tenant in common of real property may use, benefit from, and possess the entire property subject only to the equal rights of the other cotenant. While a cotenant may lawfully lease his interest to another without the consent of the other cotenant, the nonjoining cotenant is not bound by the lease to the third person. The lessee, in effect, "steps into the shoes" of the leasing cotenant and becomes a tenant in common for the duration of the lease. A cotenant that does not join in the lease may not demand exclusive possession against the lessee, but may only demand to be let into the co-possession. Under these circumstances, the lease with Deking (D) is valid, and Carr (P) is not entitled to eject him. The proper remedy for Carr (P) to seek if he does not wish to let Deking (D) into the co-possession is that of physical partition. Until the land is partitioned, Deking (D) is entitled to farm the land pursuant to the terms of the lease. The trial court's judgment denying the eviction is affirmed. On remand, the trial court must determine Carr's (P) intentions as to whether he wants to accept the new lease with Deking (D) or if Carr (P), as a cotenant, desires a return to the terms of his prior oral lease with Deking (D).

ANALYSIS

It is well settled that each tenant in common of real property may use, benefit, and possess the entire property subject only to the equal rights of cotenants. Thus, a cotenant may lawfully lease his own interest in the common property to another without the consent of the other tenant and without his joining in the lease.

Quicknotes

EJECTMENT An action to oust someone in possession of real property unlawfully and to restore possession to the party lawfully entitled to it.

PARTITION The division of property held by co-owners, granting each sole ownership of his or her share.

TENANCY IN COMMON An interest in property held by two or more people, each with equal right to its use and possession. Interests may be partitioned, sold, conveyed, or devised.

Tenhet v. Boswell

Property owner (P) v. Lessee (D)

Cal. Sup. Ct., 554 P.2d 330 (1976)

NATURE OF CASE: Joint tenant's action to have a lease declared invalid.

FACT SUMMARY: Johnson, a joint tenant with Tenhet (P), leased his interest in the joint tenancy property to Boswell (D) for a term of years and died during that term.

RULE OF LAW

(1) A lease entered into by a joint tenant does not sever the joint tenancy.

(2) A lease entered into by a joint tenant expires upon the death of that tenant.

FACTS: Johnson and Tenhet (P) owned a parcel of property as joint tenants. Without Tenhet's (P) knowledge or consent, Johnson leased the property to Boswell (D) for a period of ten years. Johnson died three months after execution of the lease, and Tenhet (P) sought to establish her sole right to possession of the property as the surviving joint tenant. After an unsuccessful demand upon Johnson (D) to vacate the premises, Tenhet (P) brought an action to have the lease declared invalid.

ISSUE:

(1) Does a lease entered into by a joint tenant sever the joint tenancy?

(2) Does a lease entered into by a joint tenant expire upon the death of that tenant?

HOLDING AND DECISION: (Mosk, J.)

(1) No. A lease entered into by a joint tenant does not sever the joint tenancy. A joint interest is one owned by two or more individuals in equal shares. Four unities are required to create a joint tenancy: unity of interest, unity of time, unity of title, and unity of possession. There is but one estate, which is taken jointly, and destruction of one of the unities destroys the joint tenancy. A joint tenancy carries with it the right of survivorship that is an expectancy that is not irrevocably fixed, but rather depends on survival without a prior breach of any of the unities. A partial alienation of one of the joint tenants interests, i.e., the lease, does not breach any of the four unities because it only conveys, at most, a life estate *pur autre vie*. Thus, it is only valid during that joint tenant's lifetime.

(2) Yes. A lease entered into by a joint tenant expires upon the death of that tenant. A joint tenancy must be expressly declared by a written instrument or a tenancy in common results. Likewise, severing a joint tenancy requires a demonstration of a clear and unambiguous intent to terminate the estate. This would have required written conversion into a tenancy in common, or a conveyance of the property to a third person and a splitting of the proceeds. A joint tenancy can also be severed by the actions of one of the joint tenants by conveying his entire interest in the property to another, or by bringing an action to partition the property. In this instance, nothing was done to sever the joint tenancy. Because the joint tenants did nothing to sever their joint tenancy, the most Johnson could have conveyed in the lease was a life estate *pur autre vie*. This interest in the property, however, dies with the joint tenant and any encumbrances placed on the property by this tenant are unenforceable as to the other.

ANALYSIS

California Civil Code § 683 provides in part, "A joint interest is one owned by two or more persons in equal shares, by a title created by a single will or transfer, when expressly declared in the will or transfer to be a joint tenancy." This statute, requiring an express declaration for the creation of joint interests, does not abrogate the common-law rule that four unities are essential to an estate in joint tenancy: unity of interest, unity of time, unity of title, and unity of possession.

Quicknotes

FEE SIMPLE An estate in land characterized by ownership of the entire property for an unlimited duration and by absolute power over distribution.

JOINT TENANCY An interest in property whereby a single interest is owned by two or more persons and created by a single instrument; joint tenants possess equal interests in the use of the entire property and the last survivor is entitled to absolute ownership.

LIFE ESTATE An interest in land measured by the life of the tenant or a third party.

RIGHT OF SURVIVORSHIP Between two or more persons, such as in a joint tenancy relationship, the right to the property of a deceased passes to the survivor.

TENANCY IN COMMON An interest in property held by two or more people, each with equal right to its use and possession. Interests may be partitioned, sold, conveyed, or devised.

Sawada v. Endo

Injured car accident victims (P) v. Driver of car (D)

Haw. Sup. Ct., 561 P.2d 1291 (1977)

NATURE OF CASE: Appeal from refusal to set aside a conveyance of land.

FACT SUMMARY: The Sawadas (P), who were injured when struck by a car driven by Endo (D) and unable to obtain satisfaction of their judgments from Endo's (D) personal property, sought to set aside a conveyance by Endo (D) and his wife of some land that had been held by them as tenants by the entirety.

RULE OF LAW

The interest of one spouse in real property, held in tenancy by the entirety, is not subject to levy and execution by his or her individual creditors absent consent of both spouses.

FACTS: In 1968, Endo (D) struck Masako and Helen Sawada (P) while driving his car. After Helen Sawada (P) filed suit, Endo (D) and his wife conveyed to their sons some real property that they held as tenants by the entirety. Masako Sawada (P) filed suit, and both she and Helen Sawada (P) obtained judgments against Endo (D). Unable to satisfy the judgments from Endo's (D) personal property, the Sawadas (P) sought to set aside the conveyance of land. The court refused to do so, and the Sawadas (P) appealed.

ISSUE: Is the interest of one spouse in real property, held in tenancy by the entirety, subject to levy and execution by his or her individual creditors absent consent of both spouses?

HOLDING AND DECISION: (Menor, J.) No. The interest of one spouse in real property, held in tenancy by the entirety, is not subject to levy and execution by his or her individual creditors absent consent of both spouses. The tenancy by the entirety is an estate held by a husband and wife in single ownership; both and each hold the whole estate. At common law this unity was unequal and the husband maintained exclusive control and dominion of the possession and profits of the estate. The husband had the right to convey the estate in its entirety subject only to the possibility that the wife may become entitled to it upon surviving him, and the estate in its entirety was also subject to levy by the husband's individual creditors. Following the passage of the Married Women's Property Acts, this estate became indivisible except by joint action of the spouses. These Acts did not abrogate this type of estate, but rather placed the wife on an equal level with the husband with regard to ownership of the entire estate. Now, neither the husband nor wife has a separate divisible interest in the property that can be conveyed or reached by execution. A joint tenancy may be severed by voluntary alienation, partition, or by levy and execution. A tenancy by the entireties may not. The spouses can jointly convey the property free of any judgment liens against the husband or wife as individuals. This is in accord with the purpose of the estate; to protect a spouse from the other spouse's improvident debts. The tenancy of the entirety carries an indestructible right of survivorship, an inability for one spouse to alienate his interest in the estate, and broad immunity from the claims of separate creditors. Since the land in question was held by Endo (D) and his wife in tenancy by the entirety, it was immune from claims by Endo's (D) separate creditors, the Sawadas (P). Affirmed.

DISSENT: (Kidwell, J.) The effect of the Married Women's Act, if properly interpreted, was not to take from the husband his common-law right to transfer his interest but to give the wife the same right to alienate her interest in the estate. Thus, judgment creditors of either spouse should be able to levy and execute on the separate interests, at least to the extent of the husband's or wife's right of survivorship.

ANALYSIS

About half the states continue to recognize tenancy by the entirety as a valid institution. The majority of these states are aligned with *Sawada v. Endo* on the interpretation of the Married Women's Act: one spouse alone cannot assign his or her interest in a tenancy by the entirety. This is of great significance for general creditors, as they can only reach property that the debtors can voluntarily assign. This consequence of tenancy by the entirety is one of its primary attractions.

Quicknotes

FEE SIMPLE An estate in land characterized by ownership of the entire property for an unlimited duration and by absolute power over distribution.

HOMESTEAD A dwelling house and its surrounding property.

JOINT TENANCY An interest in property whereby a single interest is owned by two or more persons and created by a single instrument; joint tenants possess equal interests in the use of the entire property and the last survivor is entitled to absolute ownership.

TENANCY BY THE ENTIRETY The ownership of property by a husband and wife whereby they hold undivided interests in the property with right of survivorship.

Ark Land Company v. Harper

Coal mining company (P) v. Property heirs (D)

W. Va. Sup. Ct. App., 599 S.E.2d 754 (2004)

NATURE OF CASE: Appeal of order directing the partition and sale of property.

FACT SUMMARY: A company tried to acquire land owned by a family and the company in order to mine it for coal, and when they refused, sought to have the land partitioned.

RULE OF LAW

In a partition proceeding in which a party opposes the sale of property, the economic value of the property is not the exclusive test for deciding whether to partition in kind or by sale.

FACTS: The Caudill family (D) owned 75 acres of West Virginia land for nearly 100 years. The property consists of a farmhouse, several small barns, and a garden. In 2001, Ark Land Company (P) bought a 67.5 percent undivided interest in the land by purchasing property interests of several Caudill family members (D). When the remaining heirs refused to sell their interests, Ark Land (P) filed a complaint to have the land partitioned and sold. The court found that the property could not be partitioned in kind and ordered the partition and sale of the property.

ISSUE: In a partition proceeding in which a party opposes the sale of property, is the economic value of the property the exclusive test for deciding whether to partition in kind or by sale?

HOLDING AND DECISION: (Davis, J.) No. In a partition proceeding in which a party opposes the sale of property, the economic value of the property is not the exclusive test for deciding whether to partition in kind or by sale. In this case, the Caudill heirs (D) were not concerned with money, but with their emotional desire to keep their ancestral family home within the family. Economic and sentimental attachment must be considered in actions to partition. In addition, an expert testified that the house could be partitioned from the property so as to not deprive Ark Land (P) of any coal, and the circuit court erroneously dismissed this uncontradicted fact because of the increased costs that Ark Land (P) would incur as a result of partition in kind. Its economic burden is not determinative, however, because such a rule would allow commercial entities to always evict pre-existing co-owners since a commercial entity will always be able to show that its interest will always increase the property's value. Reversed and remanded.

CONCURRENCE AND DISSENT: (Maynard, C.J.) Evidence of long-standing ownership along with emotional attachment to property are factors that should be considered and, in some cases, control the decision of whether to partition in kind or sale, but in this case, the evidence does not support the application of those factors. None of the Caudill family members (D) lived in the property for years, except for weekend retreats, and only a minority of the family has refused to sell its interest. Also, the majority may not have ruled the way it did if the company were pursuing some other use than coal mining, which it views as not important, economically.

ANALYSIS

Most jurisdictions will order partition in kind where possible because of the devastating effect partition by sale can have on property owners, particularly in cases such as this one, where a family home is at stake. That said, a critical economic requirement that might benefit many people could support a court's decision to order a partition by sale.

Quicknotes

PARTITION IN KIND A separation of undivided interests in land so that the parties may possess their interests separately.

PARTITION SALE A court-ordered sale of property held in joint tenancy, as a cotenant or in tenancy by the entirety, if the property is incapable of being divided; the income is distributed in proportion to the parties' interests in the sold property.

Wilbur v. DeLapp

Unmarried cohabitant (P) v. Unmarried cohabitant (D)

Or. Ct. App., 850 P.2d 1151 (1993)

NATURE OF CASE: Cross appeals from judgment dividing assets acquired during nonmarital cohabitation.

FACT SUMMARY: After Wilbur (P) and DeLapp (D) separated after living together as an unmarried couple, they disagreed about the appropriate division of the property they had acquired during their time of cohabitation.

RULE OF LAW

When parties who have lived together in a nonmarital domestic relationship separate, a court's division of the property acquired during the time of cohabitation may be guided by the parties' intent as well as equity.

FACTS: Wilbur (P) and DeLapp (D) lived together in a nonmarital domestic relationship for 18 years. During most of the parties' relationship, DeLapp (D) was employed by the state and was primarily responsible for paying the couple's living expenses. Wilbur's (P) main contribution was as a homemaker, although she worked during part of the relationship and contributed that money to household expenses. She also contributed an inheritance of approximately $5,000, as well as approximately $3,000 from the settlement of a dissolution of a prior marriage. When she began drawing social security, she contributed those funds to household expenses. Earlier in their relationship, DeLapp (D) obtained a loan from the Department of Veterans Affairs and purchased, in his name only, the house in which the parties lived until their separation. Wilbur (P) sold some jewelry to pay for repairs that were necessary for the house to qualify for the loan. DeLapp (D) paid the mortgage and all utility bills except for the telephone bill. Together, they purchased and held title to a travel trailer and a membership in an outdoor club called Trail's End. Soon before they separated, DeLapp (D) bought a lot in a town, La Pine, that was a distance away from where the couple lived. According to Wilbur (P), they bought the land for use during their retirement, but DeLapp (D) asserted that he purchased the land for his own use. At the time of separation, DeLapp (D) had accumulated approximately $33,000 in his Public Employees Retirement System (PERS) retirement account, for which Wilbur (P) was the named beneficiary until the couple's separation. Wilbur (P) had minimal savings. After the separation, DeLapp (D) lived in the house and Wilbur (P) lived in the travel trailer. Wilbur (P) brought suit to divide the couple's assets. At the time of trial, DeLapp (D) earned a gross income of $2,500 per month, and Wilbur (P) continued to draw social security of about $670 per month. The trial court concluded that the parties' home was treated as "joint property" over the years, that Wilbur (P) made substantial economic and noneconomic contributions to the home, and that the parties' actions showed an intent to share the property equally. Accordingly, the court declared the parties to be equal cotenants in the house. The trial court also granted a $15,000 judgment to Wilbur (P), which it found represented her one-half interest in the PERS account. It also awarded the parties' travel trailer and their Trail's End membership to the parties jointly. The La Pine property was awarded to DeLapp (D). The parties cross-appealed from the trial court's judgment. DeLapp (D) asserted that the trial court erred in equally dividing the house and his PERS retirement account between the parties. Wilbur (P) asserted that the trial court erred by not awarding her an equal interest in the La Pine property. She also asked that the judgment to partition the property the parties held jointly be modified to prevent the need for another lawsuit. The state's intermediate appellate court granted review.

ISSUE: When parties who have lived together in a nonmarital domestic relationship separate, may a court's division of the property acquired during the time of cohabitation be guided by the parties' intent as well as equity?

HOLDING AND DECISION: (Deits, J.) Yes. When parties who have lived together in a nonmarital domestic relationship separate, a court's division of the property acquired during the time of cohabitation may be guided by the parties' intent as well as equity. Although precedent requires that in resolving a property dispute between persons who have been living together in a nonmarital domestic relationship, the property should be distributed on the basis of the express or implied intent of the parties, a court is not precluded from exercising its equitable powers to reach a fair result based on the circumstances of a particular case. Because the parties were not married and the state does not recognize common-law marriage, the parties are not subject to the statutes governing the distribution of marital property, including the presumption of equal contribution to property acquired during the marriage. Here, DeLapp (D) held legal title to the house and was solely responsible for the mortgage payments. Legal ownership of the property, however, is not dispositive. Wilbur (P) contributed, financially and otherwise, to improving and maintaining

Continued on next page.

the home. From this, it can be inferred that the parties intended that Wilbur (P) have an interest in the house. As a matter of equity, she is entitled to a one-half interest in the house. Regarding the PERS account, although Wilbur (P) did not have a legal entitlement thereto at the time of trial, she is entitled to an award that recognizes her contribution to the parties' financial circumstances, including their provisions for retirement. The parties planned to retire together and conducted their financial affairs accordingly. DeLapp (D) told others that he intended to take care of Wilbur (P) in her advanced years and, for that purpose, she was the beneficiary of his PERS account up until the time of the separation. Wilbur (P) did not have any retirement funds, given that she was the homemaker and had a limited opportunity to accrue a retirement fund of her own. Her contribution to the relationship assisted DeLapp (D) in his career and allowed for a more comfortable standard of living. Most of the money that Wilbur (P) received during the time at issue was spent on household expenses. Therefore, the trial court correctly recognized that she held an interest in DeLapp's (D) PERS fund. Wilbur (P) contended that there was mutual intent to use the La Pine property as a place to live during retirement, and that but for her contribution to the partnership, DeLapp (D) would not have been financially able to buy the property. In view of all of these circumstances, and based on the intent of the parties that can be inferred from the circumstances and as a matter of equity, Wilbur (P) is entitled to a judgment of $16,000, to represent her contribution to the parties' financial provisions for retirement. However, the trial court's award of the La Pine property to DeLapp (D) is left undisturbed. Because it is in the parties' best interest to disentangle their affairs as much as possible, and partition avoided, this court will divide the property at issue. The trial court's order is modified accordingly. In addition to his full interest in the La Pine property, DeLapp (D) is awarded the house. Wilbur (P) is to receive an offsetting award equal to one-half the equity in the house at the time of trial. The outstanding mortgage is approximately $38,000, and the fair market value, according to the parties' testimony, is approximately $48,000. Therefore, Wilbur (P) is entitled to an additional judgment of $5,000. The award of $1,350 to Wilbur (P) that represented back rent is vacated. Wilbur (P) is also entitled to the travel trailer and the Trail's End membership, with a corresponding offset to DeLapp (D) for his one-half interest in each. The travel trailer is valued at $6,500 and the membership at $2,000. Both are paid in full. DeLapp (D) is entitled to half that amount, or $4,250. Considering Wilbur's (P) awards of $16,000 and $5,000 and DeLapp's (D) corresponding offsets of $4,250, Wilbur (P) is awarded a judgment of $16,750. On appeal and cross-appeal, the trial court's judgment is modified to award DeLapp (D) the full interest in the house and La Pine property and to award Wilbur (P) the full interest in the travel trailer and Trail's End membership, in addition to a money judgment of $16,750, payable by DeLapp (D) in annual installments of $3,000, plus 9% annual interest.

ANALYSIS

Although some jurisdictions base property division awards on a nonmarried couples' intent, as such intent can be inferred from all the circumstances, many do not, and many jurisdictions will not distribute nonmarital assets absent express written contracts for such distribution upon separation. Contrary to the result in the case at bar, in many cases where a party seeks an interest in nonmarital property, courts will recognize title to property without any offset for non-monetary contributions to the relationship, which many courts treat as gifts that cannot form the basis of property or contract rights. See Antognini, *The Law of Nonmarriage,* 58 B.C. L. Rev. 1 (2017).

Quicknotes

COMMON-LAW MARRIAGE A marriage that is not solemnized but is established by an agreement to enter into a marital relationship, followed by cohabitation.

EQUITY Fairness; justice; the determination of a matter consistent with principles of fairness and not in strict compliance with rules of law.

Tompkins v. Jackson

Unmarried cohabitant (P) v. Unmarried cohabitant (D)

N.Y. Sup. Ct. [trial court], 880 N.Y.S.2d 876 (2009)

NATURE OF CASE: Motion for summary judgment in action by one unmarried cohabitant against another unmarried cohabitant for breach of contract, unjust enrichment, and specific performance.

FACT SUMMARY: Tompkins (P), who lived and had a child with Jackson (D), a rap artist (also known as "50 Cent") who became financially successful, contended that notwithstanding that they were not married, Jackson (D) had promised to take care of her "for life." After the relationship soured and Jackson (D) sought to evict Tompkins (P) from a house Jackson (D) owned, Tompkins (P) brought suit, seeking lifetime financial support from Jackson (D) on the basis of alleged oral promises he had made to her, asserting claims for, inter alia, breach of contract, unjust enrichment, and specific performance.

RULE OF LAW

(1) An oral agreement between two unmarried cohabitants for one to take care of the other for life in exchange for the other promising to perform household duties and take care of the parties' children is not enforceable.

(2) Recovery in quantum meruit on an implied contract between two unmarried cohabitants for one to take care of the other for life in exchange for the other promising to perform household duties and take care of the parties' children is precluded by the Statute of Frauds.

(3) An email promising to "give" a plaintiff "the house" by placing "the house" in the plaintiff's name does not satisfy the Statute of Frauds' requirement that an agreement to sell or transfer title to real estate must be in writing and signed by the party to be charged.

(4) A plaintiff's shopping and negotiating the price for real estate, without any contribution of money or effort to the financing or maintenance of the real estate, does not warrant the imposition of a constructive trust over the real estate for the plaintiff's benefit.

(5) A claim for unjust enrichment is not viable where it is based on the giving and receiving of love, affection, and gifts ordinarily associated with live-in lovers cohabitating with one another.

(6) A claim for breach of a joint venture is not stated where the plaintiff fails to adduce facts sufficient to establish the plaintiff's contribution of property, skills, or control over the venture or a sharing of possible financial losses.

FACTS: Tompkins (P) and Jackson (D) (who later became a rap celebrity known as "50 Cent") began dating in 1995, when Tompkins (P) was in college and Jackson (D) was recently paroled. In 1996, they had a son together. According to Tompkins (P), Jackson (D) made oral promises to her around this time to take care of her for the rest of her life if he became a successful rap artist. Between 1997 and 2000, the parties lived in Jackson's (D) grandmother's house in New York, where Tompkins (P) cooked, cleaned, laundered the parties' clothing, and purchased groceries for Jackson (D) and their son. During this time, Tompkins (P) financially supported Jackson (D), and provided him with money to pay for studio time and to establish his own studio, Rotten Apple Records. In 2000, Jackson (D) was nearly fatally shot. Tompkins (P) stayed with him while he was hospitalized, and, upon his discharge, the parties relocated to Tompkins's (P) mother's house in Pennsylvania, where Tompkins (P) nursed Jackson (D) back to health over the course of five months. In 2003, the parties moved to their own apartment in Pennsylvania, where they resided for the next four years. Also in 2003, Jackson (D) signed a lucrative music deal, and he began paying some of the couple's bills and gave Tompkins (P) some money he made from touring. He also gave her an ATM card, an American Express card, and blank checks drawn against his record company. Throughout the years they were together, Jackson (D) gave Tompkins (P) numerous gifts and money and paid for services and goods for Tompkins (P) and members of her family. Jackson (D) also bought a mansion in Connecticut where he could reside and record music. Tompkins (P) visited him there on weekends and during summers. Although he invited Tompkins (P) to move to Connecticut, she declined because she wanted to be close to her family. In 2005, they moved to an apartment in Bayside, New York, so Tompkins (P) could look for a house for them to share. She found a house in Dix Hills, New York (the Dix Hill home). Before the closing, Jackson (D) orally agreed that the house would be in Tompkins's (P) name. He also sent her an email saying, "You can have the house I'll have them put it in your name." However, on the day of the closing, in January 2007, Jackson's (D) representative failed to put her name on the closing documents. After Tompkins (P) stopped the closing and called Jackson (D) about this, and after Jackson (D) talked with the representative, Tompkins (P) was told the closing documents would not list her as the owner, but that the property would be retransferred in her name in a few weeks. The closing continued, and Tompkins (P) was given

Continued on next page.

the keys. Following the closing, Tompkins (P) and her grandmother packed all of Tompkins's (P) and Jackson's (D) belongings for the parties' move into the house Over the next two weeks, Jackson (D) and Tompkins (P) lived together. However, Jackson (D) moved out because Tompkins (P) and Jackson (D) got into a physical altercation where he hit Tompkins (P), who was upset because the house was supposed to be in her name, and at the last minute, at the closing, he changed his mind. In 2008, Jackson (D) filed a petition in Family Court to establish his child support obligations, and later he filed a petition in Housing Court to evict Tompkins (P) from the Dix Hills home. The Family Court directed that Jackson (D) pay $6,700 in child support, which included a housing allowance. The Housing Court granted Jackson (D) possession of the Dix Hills home and issued a warrant of eviction against Tompkins (P). Thereafter, Tompkins (P) commenced a suit against Jackson (D) for, inter alia, a temporary stay of her eviction, which was granted, and damages for breach of contract, unjust enrichment, and specific performance. Subsequently, the Dix Hills home burned down. Jackson (D) moved for summary judgment on all the claims. He maintained that Tompkins's (P) breach of contract claim was actually a claim for palimony, and failed because: (1) no oral contract ever existed; (2) the purported contract was barred by the Statute of Frauds and Statute of Limitations; and (3) the purported contract lacked the requisite specificity, mutual assent, and definition. In support of his motion, Jackson (D) denied having any conversation with Tompkins (P) wherein he agreed to take care of her for the rest of her or his life, and stated that if he so intended he would have married her. He denied that he entered into a joint venture agreement in founding Rotten Apple Records, denied that he promised to put the Dix Hills house in her name, and denied that she supported and cared for him. He claimed that he encouraged her to find meaningful employment, and he did not recall writing the email saying that Tompkins (P) could have the house but thought that the email referred to the Bayside property, not the Dix Hills house. The trial court considered the motion.

ISSUE:

(1) Is an oral agreement between two unmarried cohabitants for one to take care of the other for life in exchange for the other promising to perform household duties and take care of the parties' children enforceable?

(2) Is recovery in quantum meruit on an implied contract between two unmarried cohabitants for one to take care of the other for life in exchange for the other promising to perform household duties and take care of the parties' children precluded by the Statute of Frauds?

(3) Does an email promising to "give" a plaintiff "the house" by placing "the house" in the plaintiff's name satisfy the Statute of Frauds' requirement that an agreement to sell or transfer title to real estate must be in writing and signed by the party to be charged?

(4) Does a plaintiff's shopping and negotiating the price for real estate, without any contribution of money or effort to the financing or maintenance of the real estate, warrant the imposition of a constructive trust over the real estate for the plaintiff's benefit?

(5) Is a claim for unjust enrichment viable where it is based on the giving and receiving of love, affection, and gifts ordinarily associated with live-in lovers cohabitating with one another?

(6) Is a claim for breach of a joint venture stated where the plaintiff fails to adduce facts sufficient to establish the plaintiff's contribution of property, skills, or control over the venture or a sharing of possible financial losses?

HOLDING AND DECISION: (Edmead, J.)

(1) No. An oral agreement between two unmarried cohabitants for one to take care of the other for life in exchange for the other promising to perform household duties and take care of the parties' children is not enforceable. Tompkins (P) and Jackson (D) were in love when they allegedly entered the oral agreement at issue. According to Tompkins (P), Jackson (D) agreed to vigorously pursue a professional recording career while she maintained their home and supported him mentally, emotionally, and financially, so that through their combined efforts he would become successful and they would equally share the wealth that would come from his success. Allegedly, Jackson (D) agreed to support Tompkins (P) for life, even if the parties broke up and ceased cohabitating. An implied contract to compensate for those things that are ordinarily done by one person for another as a matter of regard and affection is not recognized in the state, and, in the context of a cohabiting relationship, is against public policy. The services for which Tompkins (P) seeks compensation arise out of the nature of the relationship of the parties to one another. The services involved—to devote time and attention to Jackson (D), to act as companion, to accompany him to social events, and to perform household duties—are of a nature that would ordinarily be exchanged without expectation of pay. Providing loving care and assistance to her boyfriend and the father of their son before and after he was shot and seriously injured, does not transform her relationship to one founded on contract. To conclude otherwise would transform the parties' personal, yet informal, relationship to that of a marriage. Further, even if such an oral agreement were recognized in the state, Tompkins (P) would still bear the burden of proving that the agreement was in fact

Continued on next page.

made, and what its specific terms were. A contract to merely take care someone for life, without more, is insufficiently specific as to its terms. For all these reasons, the alleged oral agreement is unenforceable, as are any claims based on it, and all these claims are dismissed.

(2) Yes. Recovery in quantum meruit on an implied contract between two unmarried cohabitants for one to take care of the other for life in exchange for the other promising to perform household duties and take care of the parties' children is precluded by the Statute of Frauds. First, because the services Tompkins (P) performed are of a nature that would ordinarily be exchanged without expectation of pay, an implied contract to compensate for such services cannot stand. Second, such an oral agreement is precluded by the Statute of Frauds, which requires any agreement that by its terms is not to be performed within one year from the making thereof to be in writing. It is clear that Jackson's (D) alleged oral promise to take care of Tompkins (P) for the rest of her life was incapable of performance before the end of her lifetime, and, therefore, her claim is barred by the Statute of Frauds, and dismissed.

(3) No. An email promising to "give" a plaintiff "the house" by placing "the house" in the plaintiff's name does not satisfy the Statute of Frauds' requirement that an agreement to sell or transfer title to real estate must be in writing and signed by the party to be charged. As to Jackson's (D) alleged agreement to transfer title of the Dix Hills home to Tompkins (P), at the time she was living in Bayside, Jackson (D) executed the sales contract for the Dix Hills home. Jackson (D) thereafter sent Tompkins (P) an email indicating that she "can have the house" and that he would have "them put it in your name." At first blush, it appears that Jackson (D) intended to purchase the Dix Hills home for Tompkins (P) and place title to the house in her name. However, this sole email, in the absence of any other related correspondence, is insufficient to create an interest in Tompkins (P) in the Dix Hills home, and cannot be enforced against Jackson (D). Because the Statute of Frauds is implicated in such an alleged agreement, the issue is whether the email constitutes a sufficient writing, signed by Jackson (D), to satisfy the Statute of Frauds. The email, and the promises therein, are insufficient for Statute of Frauds purposes, because the email fails to identify the specific house to which Jackson (D) was referring or the date on which the promised transfer would take place. Accordingly, the email is insufficient on its face, especially given that Jackson (D) owned several houses at the time, to satisfy the Statute of Frauds. The alleged oral agreement to convey Jackson's (D) interest in the Dix Hills home is therefore unenforceable, and all claims related thereto are dismissed.

(4) No. A plaintiff's shopping and negotiating the price for real estate, without any contribution of money or effort to the financing or maintenance of the real estate, does not warrant the imposition of a constructive trust over the real estate for the plaintiff's benefit. Although the Statute of Frauds does not constitute a defense to a constructive trust, the evidence in this case fails to establish that Tompkins (P) is entitled to an order imposing a constructive trust over the Dix Hills home or the proceeds from the insurance policy covering the home. To impose a constructive trust, there must be a showing of "(1) a confidential or fiduciary relation, (2) a promise, (3) a transfer in reliance thereon and (4) unjust enrichment." *McGrath v. Hilding*, 41 N.Y.2d 625 (1977). The transfer element may be satisfied by a showing that funds, time, and effort are contributed in reliance on a promise to share in the result, but here, there is no evidence that Tompkins (P) contributed any efforts or money toward the purchase, maintenance, or improvement of the Dix Hills home. All she did was "show up" at the closing and, thereafter, lived in the Dix Hills home without any documented efforts towards purchasing or improving it. Merely shopping for the house, and possibly negotiating its price, is insufficient to imposing a constructive trust, as that is not the kind of contribution of money or labor that is required. Therefore, Therefore, the claim for constructive trust of all of Jackson's (D) assets, including the Dix Hills home and the insurance proceeds, is insufficient to defeat the Statute of Frauds defense to the oral agreement to place title of the home in Tompkins's (P) name, and is dismissed.

(5) No. A claim for unjust enrichment is not viable where it is based on the giving and receiving of love, affection, and gifts ordinarily associated with live-in lovers cohabitating with one another. Although courts have equitable powers to create an implied contract based in equity, it must be shown that a defendant was (i) enriched; (ii) that the enrichment was at plaintiff's expense; and (iii) that equity and good conscience require defendant to return the money or the property to the plaintiff. Here, given the relationship between the parties and overall circumstances, it cannot be said, as a matter of equity, that Jackson (D) was enriched, or, even if he were, that equity and good conscience would require restitution to Tompkins (P). Jackson (D) paid for goods and services, like movies, clothing, dinners, and groceries for Tompkins (P) on countless occasions, and conferred ample economic benefits on

Continued on next page.

Tompkins (P) and members of her family in addition. These were the kinds of exchanges rendered between two cohabitants, not for remuneration, but because they value each other's company, or because they find it caring, convenient, or rewarding to do so. Accordingly, "it cannot be said that under these particular circumstances equity and good conscience cry out for fiscal adjustment." *Soderholm v. Kosty*, 177 Misc. 2d 403 (1998). Moreover, merely because Jackson (D) derived benefit from Tompkins's (P) acts does not mean that he was unjustly enriched. Finally, it cannot be ignored that Jackson (D) will be required to pay Tompkins (P) child support for many years to come in an amount that will enable her and her children (Tompkins (P) has a daughter who is not Jackson's (P) child) to live in a home equal in value to the Dix Hills home, without working. Thus, Tompkins (P) and her daughter will reap the benefits of living in a home at Jackson's (D) expense for years to come. For these reasons, any claim sounding in unjust enrichment is dismissed.

(6) No. A claim for breach of a joint venture is not stated where the plaintiff fails to adduce facts sufficient to establish the plaintiff's contribution of property, skills, or control over the venture or a sharing of possible financial losses. "An agreement to distribute the proceeds of an enterprise upon a percentage basis does not give rise to a joint venture if the enterprise does not represent a joinder of property, skills and risks." *Steinbeck v. Gerosa*, 4 N.Y.2d 302, 175 N.Y.S.2d 1 (1958). Here, it is undisputed the parties did not discuss the sharing of losses, and there was no evidence that Tompkins (P) contributed any skills, or had control of any aspect of any joint venture, including that of Rotten Apple Records. Therefore, her claims for breach and specific performance of the joint venture and accounting are dismissed.

The motion for dismissal of the complaint is granted in its entirety.

ANALYSIS

Most, if not all, of the court's ruling in the case can be viewed through the perspective that, as a matter of human experience, personal services will frequently be rendered by two people cohabitating with each other because they value each other's company or because they find it a convenient or rewarding thing to do. For courts to attempt through hindsight to sort out the intentions of the parties and affix jural significance to conduct carried out within an essentially private and generally noncontractual relationship runs too great a risk of error; there is substantially greater risk of emotion-laden afterthought, not to mention fraud, in attempting to ascertain by implication what services, if any, were rendered gratuitously and what compensation, if any, the parties intended to be paid. The court's decision stands as a reminder that where compensation for services, even between two cohabitants who love each other at the time, is intended, such intention should be memorialized in a written contract or document that spells out the details of the parties' understanding if that understanding is to be enforced by the courts.

Quicknotes

BREACH The violation of an obligation imposed pursuant to contract or law, by acting or failing to act.

BREACH OF CONTRACT Unlawful failure by a party to perform its obligations pursuant to contract.

COHABITATION The state of living together as partners in life.

CONSTRUCTIVE TRUST A trust that arises by operation of law whereby the court imposes a trust upon property lawfully held by one party for the benefit of another, as a result of some wrongdoing by the party in possession so as to avoid unjust enrichment.

IMPLIED CONTRACT An agreement between parties that may be inferred from their general course of conduct.

JOINT VENTURE Venture undertaken based on an express or implied agreement among the members, with a common purpose and interest, and an equal power of control.

JURAL Legal.

MUTUAL ASSENT A requirement of a valid contract that the parties possess a mutuality of assent as manifested by the terms of the agreement and not by a hidden intent.

PALIMONY Support payments made from one person to another following the termination of a nonmarital relationship.

QUANTUM MERUIT Equitable doctrine allowing recovery for labor and materials provided by one party, even though no contract was entered into, in order to avoid unjust enrichment by the benefited party.

SPECIFIC PERFORMANCE An equitable remedy whereby the court requires the parties to perform their obligations pursuant to a contract.

STATUTE OF FRAUDS A statute that requires specified types of contracts to be in writing in order to be binding.

STATUTE OF LIMITATIONS A law prescribing the period in which a legal action may be commenced.

UNJUST ENRICHMENT The principle of retaining a benefit given to one by another, without compensating the giver, in situations where compensation is reasonably expected.

CHAPTER 9

Present Estates and Future Interests

Quick Reference Rules of Law

Wood v. Board of County Commissioners of Fremont County

Land grantor (P) v. Grantee (D)

Wyo. Sup. Ct., 759 P.2d 1250 (1988)

NATURE OF CASE: Appeal from summary judgment for defense in action for reversion.

FACT SUMMARY: Wood (P) claimed that a grant of land to the Board of Commissioners of Fremont County (D) was subject to a condition subsequent that the land be used as a hospital.

RULE OF LAW

A grant of fee simple determinable must clearly state that the estate will terminate if not used in accordance with the grant.

FACTS: Wood (P) gave a parcel of land to the Board of Commissioners of Fremont County (County) (D). The transfer stated that the purpose of the grant was that it be used for a hospital, but it did not express what would happen to the estate if it were not so used. The County (D) operated a hospital on the land for nearly 40 years before putting it up for sale. Wood (P) then brought suit, claiming a right to a reversion in the grant, which became effective when the land ceased to be used for the intended purpose. The trial court granted summary judgment to the County (D). Wood (P) appealed.

ISSUE: Must a grant of fee simple determinable clearly state that the estate will terminate if not used in accordance with the grant?

HOLDING AND DECISION: (Brown, C.J.) Yes. A grant of fee simple determinable must clearly state that the estate will terminate if not used in accordance with the grant. A fee simple determinable is characterized by its expiration upon the happening of an uncertain event. However, the grant must clearly state that the estate will expire automatically upon the happening of the uncertain event. The grant from Wood clearly stated the condition but failed to state that the grant would not continue to be valid if the condition were not met. Nor did Wood (P) grant a fee simple subject to a condition subsequent, because the grant made no clear provision for termination. Wood (P) retained no interest in the property. The trial court is affirmed.

ANALYSIS

There is a presumption against forfeiture in the law. Thus any grant purporting to cause such forfeiture will be strictly construed against the grantor absent clear intent otherwise. Although the grantor's intent, if realizable, typically prevails, ambiguous grants give rise to public policy considerations—in the above case, the free alienability of property.

Quicknotes

FEE SIMPLE DETERMINABLE A fee simple interest in property that may last forever or until the happening of a specified event.

REVERSION An interest retained by a grantor of property in the land transferred, which is created when the owner conveys less of an interest than he or she owns and which returns to the grantor upon the termination of the conveyed estate.

Edwards v. Bradley

Mother (D) v. Daughter (P)

Va. Sup. Ct., 315 S.E.2d 196 (1984)

NATURE OF CASE: Appeal from suit for injunction on the sale of property.

FACT SUMMARY: Bradley (P) brought suit against her mother's estate seeking to enjoin the sale of certain property devised by her grandmother.

RULE OF LAW

A conditional limitation imposed on a life estate is valid.

FACTS: Lilliston (testatrix) died testate leaving her farms to her daughter, Edwards (D), on the basis that she not sell the property. In such case her interest would be forfeited. Edwards (D) sought to have her children and their spouses sign an agreement to consent to her selling the farm. Edwards's daughter Bradley (P) declined and Edwards (D) died testate, leaving her $1. Bradley (P) filed a complaint against the executors and her siblings seeking to enjoin the sale of the farm. The trial court ruled that Edwards (D) owned a life estate. Edwards's executors appealed (D), claiming a fee simple interest.

ISSUE: Is a conditional limitation imposed on a life estate valid?

HOLDING AND DECISION: (Cochran, J.) Yes. A conditional limitation imposed on a life estate is valid. The draftsman clearly did not use the words "fee simple"; however, such words are not necessary in order to create a fee simple estate where real estate is devised without words of limitation unless a contrary intent appears in the will. This is the case here. The testatrix clearly intended to create a life estate in Edwards (D) with a fee simple remainder in her children. Affirmed.

ANALYSIS

Note that the court recognized the testatrix created a spendthrift trust in other portions of her will, and could have chosen that vehicle here if she intended to. The court will uphold the apparent intent of the testatrix if possible where it does not otherwise violate another rule of law.

Quicknotes

DEVISE The conferring of a gift of real or personal property by means of a testamentary instrument.

FEE SIMPLE An estate in land characterized by ownership of the entire property for an unlimited duration and by absolute power over distribution.

LIFE ESTATE Interest in land measured by the life of the tenant or a third party.

REMAINDER An interest in land that remains after the termination of the immediately preceding estate.

McIntyre v. Scarbrough

Life tenant (D) v. Property owners (P)

Ga. Sup. Ct., 471 S.E.2d 199 (1996)

NATURE OF CASE: Petition to establish title and terminate a life estate.

FACT SUMMARY: The Scarbroughs (P) brought a petition to establish title and to terminate Ms. McIntyre's (D) interest in a portion of the land they purchased from her.

RULE OF LAW

A life tenant is entitled to the full use and enjoyment of the property if in such use he or she exercises the ordinary care of a prudent person for its preservation and protection and commits no acts that would permanently injure the remainder interest.

FACTS: The Scarbroughs (P) purchased a tract of land from McIntyre (D) by warranty deed, with the reservation of a life estate for McIntyre (D) of 1.2 acres of the land for her natural life. She (D) was also to be responsible for the maintenance and upkeep of the property, all improvements thereon, and the payment of ad valorem taxes. The Scarbroughs (P) brought a petition to establish title and terminate the life estate and moved for summary judgment, claiming waste and violation of the warranty deed. The trial court first denied summary judgment, then reversed on the basis that McIntyre (D) failed to exercise ordinary care for the preservation of the property and thereby forfeited her interest to the remaindermen, who are entitled to immediate possession.

ISSUE: Is a life tenant entitled to the full use and enjoyment of the property if in such use he or she exercises the ordinary care of a prudent person for its preservation and protection and commits no acts that would permanently injure the remainder interest?

HOLDING AND DECISION: (Thompson, J.) Yes. A life tenant is entitled to the full use and enjoyment of the property if in such use he or she exercises the ordinary care of a prudent person for its preservation and protection and commits no acts that would permanently injure the remainder interest. This court has held that failure to pay burdens imposed by law on the property during the term constitutes such lack of ordinary care as a prudent person should exercise for its protection and preservation and would tend to divest the fee interest by subjecting it to sale. Here McIntyre (D) failed to pay the ad valorem property taxes on the tract for the years 1991–1993 or the improvements for the years 1992–1994, which was also a requirement of the warranty deed. Such failure results in forfeiture of the life estate as a matter of law. Affirmed.

DISSENT: (Benham, C.J.) The issue of waste is ordinarily one for the jury to decide. The question of whether McIntyre's (D) conduct with regard to the life estate was so egregiously wasteful as to warrant forfeiture of her interest in the property was inappropriate for summary judgment and should have been submitted to the jury.

ANALYSIS

The court here concluded that while the trial court too narrowly construed the definition of occupancy, it correctly determined that the life estate was terminated under the doctrine of waste. The trial court defined occupancy as "dwelling" in the subject premises. This court recognized that the term "occupy" is more expansive and encompasses those situations in which a person holds possession of property for use.

Quicknotes

LIFE ESTATE Interest in land measured by the life of the tenant or a third party.

LIFE TENANT An individual whose estate in real property is measured either by his own life or by that of another.

REMAINDER INTEREST An interest in land that remains after the termination of the immediately preceding estate.

Phillips v. Estate of Holzmann

Testamentary transferee (D) v. Decedent's estate (P)

Fla. Dist. Ct. App., 740 So. 2d 1 (1998)

NATURE OF CASE: Appeal from order requiring return of moneys transferred under will to decedent's estate.

FACT SUMMARY: Holzmann, in her will, transferred money to her friend, Phillips (D), for the purpose of taking care of Holzmann's dogs upon her death. Holzmann's estate (P) contended that Phillips (D) had to return the money to the estate (P) because the dogs had to be put down shortly after Holzmann died, so that the purpose for the transferred funds no longer existed.

RULE OF LAW

Where the purpose of a testamentary honorary trust fails, a resulting trust is created for the benefit of the settlor's estate's residual beneficiaries, so that the transferee of the honorary trust funds must return the funds to the settlor's estate.

FACTS: Holzmann, in her will, transferred $25,000 to her friend, Phillips (D), for the purpose of taking care of Holzmann's two dogs upon her death. Shortly after Holzmann died, her dogs had to be put down for health reasons. Holzmann's estate (P) brought suit seeking the return of the money transferred to Phillips (D), contending that the purpose for the transferred funds no longer existed. The trial court agreed and ordered Phillips (D) to return the funds to the estate (P), finding that the transferred funds initially constituted an "honorary trust," the purpose of which failed once the dogs were put down, so that the trust became a "resulting trust" for the benefit of the estate's (P) residual beneficiaries. The state's intermediate appellate court granted review.

ISSUE: Where the purpose of a testamentary honorary trust fails, is a resulting trust created for the benefit of the settlor's estate's residual beneficiaries, so that the transferee of the honorary trust funds must return the funds to the settlor's estate?

HOLDING AND DECISION: (Gersten, J.) Yes. Where the purpose of a testamentary honorary trust fails, a resulting trust is created for the benefit of the settlor's estate's residual beneficiaries, so that the transferee of the honorary trust funds must return the funds to the settlor's estate. The guiding principle for interpreting a will is the testator's intent. Here, Holzmann, the testator, intended that the money at issue would be used for the benefit of her dogs. This noncharitable purpose thus established an honorary trust, which is not a true trust—there is no beneficiary capable of enforcing its terms. Nonetheless, the Restatement (Second) of Trusts § 124 (1959) takes the position that the transferee has the power to apply the property to the designated purpose, but cannot be compelled to do so. If the transferee does not apply the property to its designated purpose, the transferee holds it upon a resulting trust for the settlor or the settlor's estate. The court adopts this position regarding honorary trusts. Because the Holzmann's dogs were put to sleep, Phillips (D) could not apply the $25,000.00 to the designated purpose. A resulting trust was thereby created and the trial court properly ordered Phillips (D) to return the property to the estate. Affirmed.

ANALYSIS

The Uniform Trust Code (UTC), some version of which has been adopted by all states, provides for the creation of a trust for the care of an animal or animals. Section 408 of the UTC provides that a trust may be created to provide for the care of an animal alive during the settlor's lifetime. The trust terminates upon the death of the animal or, if the trust was created to provide for the care of more than one animal alive during the settlor's lifetime, upon the death of the last surviving animal. Such a trust may be enforced by a person appointed in the terms of the trust or, if no person is so appointed, by a person appointed by the court, and a person having an interest in the welfare of the animal may request the court to appoint a person to enforce the trust or to remove a person appointed. The UTC further provides that the property in such a trust may be applied only to its intended use, except to the extent a court determines that the value of the trust property exceeds the amount required for the intended use. Except as otherwise provided in the terms of the trust, property not required for the intended use must be distributed to the settlor, if then living. Otherwise, the property must go to the settlor's successors in interest.

Quicknotes

BENEFICIARY A third party who is the recipient of the benefit of a transaction undertaken by another.

DECEDENT A person who is dead.

TESTAMENTARY Of or relating to a will or trust.

TRUST The holding of property by one party for the benefit of another.

Evans v. Abney

State, municipality, and residents (D) v. Board managers of local park (P)

396 U.S. 435 (1970)

NATURE OF CASE: Appeal from state supreme court decision finding that because a trust settlor's intention of creating a Whites-only public park could no longer be carried out lawfully, the park should close and the trust property should revert to the heirs of the trust settlor.

FACT SUMMARY: In 1911, Senator A. O. Bacon of Georgia conveyed property in trust to Macon, Georgia, to be used as a public park for Whites only. In a prior decision, the United States Supreme Court ruled the park's Whites-only designation was discriminatory. The Georgia Supreme Court then ruled that because Bacon's intentions could no longer be carried out lawfully, the park should close and the trust property should revert to the heirs of the trust settlor.

RULE OF LAW

When a valid charitable bequest may no longer be carried out in the same manner as provided by the testator or donor, a court sitting in equity may revise the bequest in such a manner it adheres as closely as possible to the testator's or donor's intention.

FACTS: In 1911, Senator A. O. Bacon of Georgia conveyed property in trust to Macon, Georgia, to be used as a public park for Whites only. Just six years prior, the Georgia legislature modified a statute to allow for the dedication of land for use by one race only. Macon (D) initially operated the park for Whites only. However, it then opened the park to all residents. In response, several of the Board of Managers of the park brought this suit to remove the city as trustee and to appoint new trustees, who presumably would run the park again as Whites-only. The case eventually reached the United States Supreme Court after African American residents intervened to keep the park open. In the prior decision, *Evans v. Newton*, 382 U.S. 296 (1966), the Court ruled the park's Whites-only designation was discriminatory. On remand, the African American residents and the Georgia Attorney General's office argued that the state court should apply the doctrine of cy pres and modify the trust to allow all residents to use the park. The Georgia Supreme Court ruled, however, that because Bacon's intentions could no longer be carried out lawfully, the park should close and the trust property should revert to Bacon's heirs, 224 Ga. 826, 165 S.E.2d 160 (1968). The United States Supreme Court granted the state Attorney General's petition for further review.

ISSUE: When a valid charitable bequest may no longer be carried out in the same manner as provided by the testator or donor, may a court sitting in equity revise the bequest in such a manner it adheres as closely as possible to the testator's or donor's intention?

HOLDING AND DECISION: (Black, J.) Yes. When a valid charitable bequest may no longer be carried out in the same manner as provided by the testator or donor, a court sitting in equity may revise the bequest in such a manner it adheres as closely as possible to the testator's or donor's intention. Most states follow this doctrine, known as cy pres. When the testator's fundamental purpose is thwarted or no longer possible and trust funds or property remain, courts are free to modify the trust document for the public's benefit. However, the doctrine of cy pres is not applicable in all cases. Where the evidence is clear via the trust document that the settlor of the trust only desires a certain outcome, the trust may cease and trust property may revert to the heirs of the trust when that outcome becomes impossible. Here, Senator Brown was clear that he had limitations for the public park. He specifically stated that the park should not be used for anything other than a Whites-only public park. His trust stated that he did not believe that Whites and African Americans could coexist. The Georgia trial courts and Georgia Supreme Court concluded that Bacon's limitation on use of the park was quite clear and that no modification was allowed. Trusts and wills are matters of state law. These state court decisions respecting a particular trust present no violation of any constitutionally protected rights. Separately, this case is distinguishable from a case where a city closes a public park. In that case, there is state action that could lead to a colorable constitutional claim, such as an equal protection violation. Here, the state courts are interpreting a private trust and no state action is present. Affirmed.

DISSENT: (Brennan, J.) State action is present in this case via a number of avenues. First, the city accepted title to the park and operated it for fifty years as a desegregated public park. Second, a state court decision to prevent willing parties to associate with one another is itself a form of state action. Third, the Georgia legislature itself enabled Bacon to create this Whites-only park when it modified state statutes to allow the practice. This is also a form of state action. Accordingly, the petitioners have

Continued on next page.

stated a colorable claim for an equal protection violation. A city should not be able to close a public park when forced to desegregate it.

ANALYSIS

Whenever the United States Supreme Court grants certiorari to parties appealing a state court decision, the case must include a significant federal issue. Here, the presence of a possible equal protection violation was likely enough for the court to grant the petition for review. However, the crux of this case, an interpretation of trust law, is essentially a state law matter.

Quicknotes

CERTIORARI A discretionary writ issued by a superior court to an inferior court in order to review the lower court's decisions; the United States Supreme Court's writ ordering such review.

COLORABLE CLAIM A claim sufficient to withstand a motion to dismiss; a claim valid on its face without the resolution of factual disputes.

CY PRES DOCTRINE Equitable doctrine applied in order to give effect to an instrument as close to the drafter's intent as possible without violating the law, which effect would be unlawful if strictly enforced.

Symphony Space, Inc. v. Pergola Properties, Inc.

Buyer (P) v. Seller (D)

N.Y. Ct. App., 669 N.E.2d 799 (1996)

NATURE OF CASE: Suit for declaratory judgment.

FACT SUMMARY: Symphony Space, Inc. (P) sought a declaratory judgment that an option clause in its agreement to purchase property from Broadwest Realty Corp. was unenforceable in violation of the Rule Against Perpetuities.

RULE OF LAW

Commercial option agreements are not exempted from the Rule Against Perpetuities.

FACTS: Symphony Space, Inc. (Symphony) (P), a non-profit organization dedicated to the arts, leased a theatre from Broadwest Realty Corp (Broadwest). Broadwest sold the building to Symphony (P) and leased back the income-producing property, minus the theatre, for one year. The purpose of the agreement was to provide Symphony (P) with a tax exemption. The agreement also contained an option clause allowing Broadwest to purchase the property during specified periods. Pergola Properties, Inc. (Pergola) (D), a nominee of Broadwest, notified Symphony (P) of its intent to exercise the option, and Symphony (P) brought suit seeking a declaratory judgment that the option violated New York's Rule Against Perpetuities. The Appellate Division held the clause unenforceable.

ISSUE: Are commercial option agreements exempted from the Rule Against Perpetuities?

HOLDING AND DECISION: (Kaye, C.J.) No. Commercial option agreements are not exempted from the Rule Against Perpetuities. Options to purchase are to be treated differently than preemptive rights, which impede transferability only minimally in contrast to purchase options, which vest substantial control over the alienability of the property upon the option holder. Only where the preemptive right arises in a governmental or commercial agreement is the minor restraint offset by the holder's incentive to improve the property. The option agreement here creates the type of control over the transferability over property that the rule against remote vesting has sought to prevent. An option "appurtenant" to purchase land that originates in a lease provision that is not exercisable after the expiration of the lease, and is incapable of separation from the lease agreement, is still generally valid even though the holder's interest may vest beyond the perpetuities period. Here the option does not qualify as an option appurtenant, since it significantly deters the development of the property. The order of the Appellate Division should be affirmed, with costs, and the certified question answered in the affirmative.

ANALYSIS

The exception to the Rule Against Perpetuities for preemptive rights was developed in order to provide an incentive for the development of property. At common law, options to purchase land were subject to the rule, since they worked as a disincentive to such development. Although such options are typically found in commercial contracts, they are still subject to the rule against remote vesting.

Quicknotes

FREE ALIENABILITY Unrestricted transferability.

OPTION A contract pursuant to which a seller agrees that property will be available for the buyer to purchase at a specified price and within a certain time period.

RULE AGAINST PERPETUITIES The doctrine that a future interest that is incapable of vesting within twenty-one years of lives in being at the time it is created is immediately void.

VESTING Attaining of the right to pension or other employer-contribution benefits when, the employee satisfies the minimum requirements necessary in order to be entitled to the receipt of such benefits in the future.

Estate of Guidotti

Wife (P) v. Trustee (D)

Cal. Ct. App., 109 Cal. Rptr. 2d 674 (2001)

NATURE OF CASE: Appeal from lower court decision finding that testator could permissibly terminate income support to his wife in the event she remarried after his death.

FACT SUMMARY: Earl Guidotti's will created a testamentary trust for the benefit of his wife, Darlene Guidotti (P). The trust document stated she would receive the net income from the trust for life unless and until she remarried.

RULE OF LAW

Conditions in testamentary instruments that impose restraints on marriage are typically void as against public policy, unless the intent of the provision was not to forbid marriage but only to provide support until the surviving spouse remarries.

FACTS: Earl Guidotti's will created a testamentary trust for the benefit of his wife, Darlene Guidotti (P). The trust document stated she would receive the net income from the trust for life unless and until she remarried or cohabited with another man as though they were man and wife. Earl passed away in 1999. In 2000, Darlene (P) petitioned the court to reform the will. Darlene (P) did so because the provision terminating her income interest upon her remarriage precluded her from obtaining the federal estate tax marital deduction. At the lower court, Darlene (P) produced evidence from the attorney who drafted Earl's will. The attorney declared that Earl was very jealous of Darlene (P) and desired that she not remarry. The attorney included the income termination provision in the will even though he thought it might be void as against public policy. The lower court found that the provision was not a restraint on marriage. Rather it found the intent of the provision was only to provide for Darlene (P) until she did remarry. Darlene (P) appealed to an intermediate appellate court.

ISSUE: Are conditions in testamentary instruments that impose restraints on marriage typically void as against public policy, unless the intent of the provision was not to forbid marriage but only to provide support until the surviving spouse remarries?

HOLDING AND DECISION: (Gilbert, J.) Yes. Conditions in testamentary instruments that impose restraints on marriage are typically void as against public policy, unless the intent of the provision was not to forbid marriage but only to provide support until the surviving spouse remarries. The interpretation of written instruments, from contracts to wills, is typically a question of law. A reviewing court may construe testamentary instruments provided that any extrinsic evidence is not conflicting with the documents. The intention of the testator is paramount and courts will strive to construe testamentary instruments in a manner consistent with that intent. California, as well as most states, invalidate provisions in wills that impose a restraint on marriage of a surviving spouse or heir. In this case, the evidence from Earl's attorney is dispositive that Earl's provision barring Darlene (P) from remarriage is an improper restraint on marriage. The attorney declared that Earl was jealous of Darlene (P). It is clear Earl did not simply wish to provide for Darlene (P) until the time she remarried. Rather, he sought, impermissibly, to bar her from marriage entirely. The case is remanded to the trial court with the order that the will should be reformed consistent with this opinion. Reversed and remanded.

ANALYSIS

There is a fine distinction between impermissible provisions restraining marriage and permissible provisions that seek to provide support until a surviving spouse remarries. The determining factor is the intent of the testator. Typically, extrinsic evidence will be required to determine that intent. Often the best evidence will come from the attorney who drafted the testamentary instrument.

Quicknotes

EXTRINSIC EVIDENCE Evidence that is not contained within the text of a document or contract, but which is derived from the parties' statements or the circumstances under which the agreement was made.

TESTAMENTARY INSTRUMENT Instrument that takes effect upon the death of the maker.

CHAPTER 10

Leaseholds

Quick Reference Rules of Law

Vásquez v. Glassboro Service Association, Inc.

Farmworker (P) v. Employer (D)

N.J. Sup. Ct., 415 A.2d 1156 (1980)

NATURE OF CASE: Appeal from a judgment in an action seeking to enjoin farm owners from depriving farmworkers of the use of their quarters except through judicial process.

FACT SUMMARY: After Vásquez's (P) employment as a migrant farmworker was terminated, he was not allowed to remain overnight in the employer-provided barracks until he could find alternative housing.

RULE OF LAW

When a migrant farmworker's employment is terminated, he or she may be removed from employer-provided housing only through a judicial proceeding.

FACTS: Glassboro Service Association, Inc. (Glassboro) (D) contracted to bring migrant farmworkers to New Jersey from Puerto Rico, supplying living quarters for those workers at its labor camp. No extra charge was imposed for such housing. Vásquez (P), who was recruited in Puerto Rico, worked for Glassboro (D). Later, Glassboro's (D) foreman told Vásquez (P) that his work was unsatisfactory and that he was to be discharged. After a hearing and discharge, Vásquez (P) was not allowed to remain in the camp overnight. Unable to speak English and without funds to return to Puerto Rico, Vásquez (P) sought the assistance of the Farmworkers Corporation. He also consulted with the Farmworkers Rights Project, which filed a complaint, seeking an order permitting Vásquez (P) to reenter his living quarters and enjoining Glassboro (D) from depriving him of the use of the quarters except through judicial process.

ISSUE: When a migrant farmworker's employment is terminated, may he or she be removed from employer-provided housing without a judicial proceeding?

HOLDING AND DECISION: (Pollock, J.) No. When a migrant farmworker's employment is terminated, he or she may not be removed from employer-provided housing without a judicial proceeding. The contract under which Vásquez (P) was brought from Puerto Rico is a contract of adhesion. The unconscionability of the contract inheres not only in its failure to provide a worker with a reasonable opportunity to find alternative housing, but in its disregard for his welfare after termination of his employment. In the absence of any concern demonstrated for the worker in the contract, public policy requires the implication of a provision for a reasonable time to find alternative housing. By abolishing self-help in such situations, the court provides a forum for an equitable resolution of a controversy between a farm labor service and a migrant farmworker on termination of employment.

ANALYSIS

A migrant farmworker has even less bargaining power than a residential tenant. Although Vásquez (P) had found housing at the time of this court decision, other workers had been evicted, some at odd hours of the night. The lack of alternative housing emphasized the inequality between Glassboro (D) and the migrant farmworkers. Once his employment ended, a farmworker lost not only his job but his shelter. Moreover, a migrant farmworker is not a tenant under the applicable New Jersey statute.

Quicknotes

COVENANT OF HABITABILITY A warranty implied by a landlord that the premises are suitable, and will remain suitable, for habitation.

EJECTMENT An action to oust someone in possession of real property unlawfully and to restore possession to the party lawfully entitled to it.

EJUSDEM GENERIS Belonging to the same class or type; rule of construction applied when general words follow a specified class of persons or items, then the words are not to be applied in their broad meaning but are to apply only to those persons or items listed.

RESTRICTIVE COVENANT A promise contained in a deed to limit the uses to which the property will be made.

TENANT An individual who enjoys the use and occupation of the property of another for a specified period.

Kendall v. Ernest Pestana, Inc.

Prospective buyer (P) v. Leaseholder (D)

Cal. Sup. Ct., 709 P.2d 837 (1985)

NATURE OF CASE: Appeal from judgment in an action for declaratory and injunctive relief for a landlord's refusal to consent to a lease assignment.

FACT SUMMARY: When Ernest Pestana, Inc. (Pestana) (D) refused to allow Bixler to assign his interest in a commercial leasehold to Kendall (P) and two others, they filed suit, seeking a declaration that Pestana's (D) refusal was unreasonable.

RULE OF LAW

Where a lease provides for assignment only with the prior consent of the lessor, such consent may be withheld only where the lessor has a commercially reasonable objection to the assignment.

FACTS: Ernest Pestana, Inc. (Pestana) (D) held an assigned lease interest in hangar space at the San Jose Municipal Airport. The original holders of the lease had also entered into a 25-year sublease with Bixler, who was to use the premises for an airplane maintenance business. Bixler later decided to sell the business to Kendall (P) and two others. The proposed sale included the existing lease. Kendall (P) had a stronger financial statement and greater net worth than Bixler and was willing to be bound by the terms of the lease. However, Pestana (D) refused to consent to the assignment, maintaining that it had an absolute right arbitrarily to refuse any such request. Kendall (P) and the others brought suit, seeking a declaration that Pestana's (D) refusal was unreasonable and an unlawful restraint on the freedom of alienation. This appeal followed the lower court's decision.

ISSUE: Where a lease provides for assignment only with the prior consent of the lessor, may such consent be withheld only where the lessor has a commercially reasonable objection to the assignment?

HOLDING AND DECISION: (Broussard, J.) Yes. Where a lease provides for assignment only with the prior consent of the lessor, such consent may be withheld only where the lessor has a commercially reasonable objection to the assignment. Some of the factors that the trier of fact may properly consider in applying the standards of good faith and commercial reasonableness are: (1) financial responsibility of the proposed assignee, (2) suitability of the use for the particular property, (3) legality of the proposed use, (4) need for alteration of the premises, and (5) the nature of the occupancy. Pestana (D) is trying to get more than it bargained for in the lease. A lessor is free to build periodic rent increases into a lease, as was done here. Any increased value of the property beyond this belongs to the lessor only in the sense that the lessor's reversionary estate will benefit from it upon the expiration of the lease. The minority rule applied here is the preferable one.

DISSENT: (Lucas, J.) The weight of authority should be followed, which allows the commercial lessor to withhold his consent to an assignment or sublease arbitrarily or without reasonable cause.

ANALYSIS

The impetus for change in the majority rule has come from two directions, reflecting the dual nature of a lease as a conveyance of a leasehold interest and a contract. The Restatement (Second) of Property adopts the minority rule on the validity of approval clauses in leases, requiring that withholding of consent be reasonable. In addition, where a contract confers on one party a discretionary power affecting the rights of the other, a duty is imposed to exercise that discretion in good faith and in accordance with fair dealing.

Quicknotes

LEASEHOLD INTEREST The interest of a landlord or tenant pursuant to a lease agreement.

RESTRAINT AGAINST ALIENATION A provision restricting the transferee's ability to convey interests in the conveyed property.

Slavin v. Rent Control Board of Brookline

Landlord (P) v. Rent control board (D)

Mass. Sup. Jud. Ct., 548 N.E.2d 1226 (1990)

NATURE OF CASE: Appeal from a ruling refusing to issue an eviction certificate requested by a landlord.

FACT SUMMARY: When Slavin (P) sought a certificate of eviction in an attempt to evict a tenant for violation of a lease provision requiring the landlord's consent for another person to occupy the premises, the Rent Control Board of Brookline (D) refused to issue the certificate on the ground that Slavin (P) had acted unreasonably.

RULE OF LAW

A lease provision requiring the landlord's consent to an assignment or sublease permits the landlord to refuse arbitrarily or unreasonably.

FACTS: Slavin (P) applied to the Rent Control Board of Brookline (the Board) (D) for a certificate of eviction, seeking to evict a tenant, Myers (D), on the ground that Myers (D) violated an obligation of his tenancy by allowing an unauthorized person to occupy his apartment without first obtaining Slavin's (P) written consent as stipulated in the lease. The Board (D) refused to issue the certificate on the ground that Slavin (P) had acted unreasonably because she had categorically refused to allow Myers (D) to bring in someone new after the original cotenant had moved out. Thus, Myers (D) could not be said to have violated the lease. Slavin (P) appealed.

ISSUE: Does a lease provision requiring the landlord's consent to an assignment or sublease permit the landlord to refuse arbitrarily or unreasonably?

HOLDING AND DECISION: (O'Connor, J.) Yes. A lease provision requiring the landlord's consent to an assignment or sublease permits the landlord to refuse arbitrarily or unreasonably. All but two of the cases cited by the Board (D) involved a commercial, not a residential lease. In several of the cases, the court specifically states that its holding is limited to the commercial lease context. In *68 Beacon St., Inc. v. Sohier*, 194 N.E. 303 (Mass. 1935), this court ruled that a commercial lease provision requiring a landlord's consent prior to an assignment, with no limitation on the landlord's ability to refuse, is not an unreasonable restraint on alienation. In light of that decision and in the absence of a demonstrable trend involving residential leases in other jurisdictions, there appears no need to impose on residential landlords a reasonableness requirement. The question is one of public policy, which the legislature is free to address. Reversed.

ANALYSIS

The court noted that in *Kruger v. Page Management Co.*, 432 N.Y.S.2d 295 (Sup. Ct. 1980)—the only purely residential lease case cited by the Board (D)—the reasonableness requirement in New York has been statutorily imposed. Valid arguments can be made in support of a reasonableness rule in the residential context. But there are also valid counter-arguments, not the least of which is that such a rule would be likely to engender a plethora of litigation about whether the landlord's withholding of consent was reasonable.

Quicknotes

RENT CONTROL A municipal ordinance limiting the maximum rent that may be lawfully charged for rental property.

RESTRAINT AGAINST ALIENATION A provision restricting the transferee's ability to convey interests in the conveyed property.

Sommer v. Kridel

Apartment owner (P) v. Lessee (D)

N.J. Sup. Ct., 378 A.2d 767 (1977)

NATURE OF CASE: Appeal from intermediate appellate court's decision in favor of defendant.

FACT SUMMARY: Sommer (P) did not attempt to re-let the premises he had leased to Kridel (D), even though the opportunity to do so existed and Kridel (D) had specifically informed Sommer (P) that he was unable to go through with the leasing for personal reasons and asked for acceptance of his surrender.

RULE OF LAW

If a lessee has affected a "surrender" of the leased premises, the landlord is under an obligation to make a reasonable effort to mitigate damages by attempting to re-let the premises.

FACTS: Sommer (P) and Riverview Realty Co. (Riverview) (P) were both landlords who leased to tenants, Kridel (D) and Perosio (D), respectively, who were forced by personal circumstances to attempt "surrenders." Sommer (P) received a letter explaining the situations and stating Kridel's (D) desire to surrender. Neither landlord made an attempt to re-let their vacated units, even though a party expressed interest in renting the unit from Sommer (P). Instead, both landlords brought suits to recover damages from their respective "defaulting" tenants. Noting that Sommer (P) never responded to Kridel's (D) written offer of surrender and finding that such was tantamount to an acceptance of that offer, the court found that Kridel's (D) tenancy had been terminated along with his obligation to pay rent. From an appellate reversal of the judgment dismissing Sommer's (P) complaint and the counterclaim for return of the security deposit, Sommer (P) appealed. His appeal was consolidated with that of Perosio (D), there having been an appellate affirmance of the trial court decision granting Riverview (P) summary judgment.

ISSUE: If a lessee has affected a "surrender" of the leased property, is the landlord under an obligation to make a reasonable effort to mitigate damages by attempting to re-let the premises when a lessee "surrenders" same?

HOLDING AND DECISION: (Pashman, J.) Yes. If a lessee has affected a "surrender" of the leased premises, the landlord is under an obligation to make a reasonable effort to mitigate damages by attempting to re-let the premises. Such mitigation of damages is the landlord's duty when he seeks to recover rents due from a defaulting tenant. While the historical rule, and that still followed in a majority of states, is that no such duty exists, the modern trend is in favor of finding such a duty. This trend is based on the recognition that a lease is no longer simply a conveyance giving the tenant control over an estate and making his abandonment of as little concern to the landlord as would be the tenant's abandonment of property he owned outright and not simply for a term. Leases now also are of contractual nature; the changes in society have created diverse problems that have come to be dealt with by utilizing specific clauses in residential leases to fit each particular set of circumstances. Thus, a contractual ingredient has been reintroduced into the law of estates for years. Contractual obligations bespeak a duty to mitigate damages, and in the case of a residential lease, this is accomplished, upon "surrender" by the lessee, by an attempt to re-let the premises. As the landlord is in a better position to prove that he has used reasonable diligence in attempting to re-let the premises, the burden of proof on that issue lies with him. The facts show that Sommer (P) was not diligent in that regard; thus, that judgment must be reversed. As to Riverview (P), the lack of a factual determination as to any attempt to re-let requires that the case be remanded for a determination of whether a reasonable attempt to mitigate damages was made.

ANALYSIS

Some courts have found that such mitigation is not required when a landlord simply sues to recover unpaid rent. For example, in *Winshall v. Ampco Auto Parks, Inc.*, 417 F. Supp. 334 (E.D. Mich. 1976), the court specifically held that mitigation was a concept applicable only to suits for damages and then went on to state that an action to recover unpaid rent was not a suit for damages.

Quicknotes

IMPLIED WARRANTY OF HABITABILITY A warranty implied by a landlord that the premises are suitable, and will remain suitable, for habitation.

MITIGATION OF DAMAGES A plaintiff's implied obligation to reduce the damages incurred by taking reasonable steps to prevent additional injury.

Minjak Co. v. Randolph

Landlord (P) v. Tenant (D)

N.Y. App. Div., 528 N.Y.S.2d 554 (1988)

NATURE OF CASE: Appeal from reversal of an award in tenant's favor of rent abatement and punitive damages in a landlord's action for nonpayment of rent.

FACT SUMMARY: After Randolph (D) and Kikuchi (D) withheld their rent due to the condition of the loft space they were leasing, Minjak Co. (P), the landlord, brought this action for nonpayment, and Randolph (D) and Kikuchi (D) counterclaimed for breach of warranty of habitability.

RULE OF LAW

A tenant may assert the defense of constructive eviction for the nonpayment of rent, even if he or she has abandoned only a portion of the demised premises due to the landlord's acts.

FACTS: Randolph (D) and Kikuchi (D) leased a loft in a building owned by Minjak Co. (P). Two-thirds of the loft space was used as a music studio by Kikuchi (D), and the remainder of the space was used as their residence. At one point, water poured into the bedroom and closets from the tenant's loft above them. After Minjak (P) started construction on the building, huge clouds of dust came pouring into the loft, settling everywhere. Kikuchi's (D) musical equipment had to be covered at all times to protect it from the dust. When Randolph (D) and Kikuchi (D) withheld their rent payments, Minjak (P) commenced a summary nonpayment proceeding against them. Randolph (D) and Kikuchi (D) counterclaimed for breach of warranty of habitability. After trial, the jury awarded Randolph (D) and Kikuchi (D) a rent abatement as compensatory damages on the theory of constructive eviction, along with punitive damages. The appellate term reversed. This appeal followed.

ISSUE: May a tenant assert the defense of constructive eviction for the nonpayment of rent, even if he or she has abandoned only a portion of the demised premises due to the landlord's acts?

HOLDING AND DECISION: (Memorandum Decision) Yes. A tenant may assert the defense of constructive eviction for the nonpayment of rent, even if he or she has abandoned only a portion of the demised premises due to the landlord's acts. The evidence fully supported a finding that Randolph (D) and Kikuchi (D) had to abandon the music studio portion of the loft due to the Minjak's (P) wrongful acts. Moreover, the record supports the jury's finding of morally culpable conduct allowing punitive damages in light of the dangerous and offensive manner in which the landlord permitted the construction work to be performed. Accordingly, the award of punitive damages is sustained.

ANALYSIS

The appellate term held that the doctrine of constructive eviction could not provide a defense to the nonpayment proceeding because Randolph (D) and Kikuchi (D) had not abandoned possession of the demised premises. However, the appellate division found that compelling considerations of social policy and fairness dictated the rule it applied here. Punitive damages may be awarded in breach of warranty of habitability cases where the landlord's actions were intentional and malicious.

Quicknotes

ABATEMENT A decrease or lessening of something; in equity, a suspension or dismissal of a cause of action.

CONSTRUCTIVE EVICTION An action, whereby the landlord renders the property unsuitable for occupancy, either in whole or in part, so the tenant is forced to leave the premises.

PUNITIVE DAMAGES Damages exceeding the actual injury suffered for the purposes of punishment, deterrence, and comfort to plaintiff.

WARRANTY OF HABITABILITY An implied warranty owed by a landlord to a tenant to provide leased premises is properly maintained in a habitable condition prior to leasing the premises and during the duration of the lease.

Javins v. First National Realty Corp.

Tenant (D) v. Landlord (P)

428 F.2d 1071 (D.C. Cir. 1970)

NATURE OF CASE: Appeal from actions to recover past-due rents.

FACT SUMMARY: Javins (D) refused to pay rent due to numerous housing code violations.

RULE OF LAW

Leases of urban dwelling units contain an implied warranty of habitability, and breach of this warranty gives rise to the usual remedies for breach of contract.

FACTS: Javins (D) and other tenants refused to pay rent due to approximately 1,500 housing code violations in the building. The landlord, First National Realty (First National) (P), brought suit to recover possession and past-due rent. The trial court refused Javins's (D) offer of proof as to the violations, finding that their presence was not a defense. Judgment was rendered for First National (P).

ISSUE: Do leases of urban dwelling units contain an implied warranty of habitability, the breach of which gives rise to the usual remedies for breach of contract?

HOLDING AND DECISION: (Wright, J.) Yes. Leases of urban dwelling units contain an implied warranty of habitability, and breach of this warranty gives rise to the usual remedies for breach of contract. The old common-law rule that the lessor is not obligated to effectuate repairs unless he covenants to do so in the lease is outdated and must be rejected. The value of the lease to a tenant is that it gives him a place to live; a home suitable for occupation. Because a lease contract specifies a time period during which the tenant has a right to use the apartment for shelter, there is a legitimate expectancy that the apartment be fit for habitation during the term of the contract. The common law must recognize the landlord's obligation to keep the premises in a habitable condition. Beyond the common law, the district's housing code also requires an implied warranty of habitability. The code establishes the standards for such housing and delineates the penalties for violations. The code specifically provides that every premise be maintained and kept in a state of repair to provide decent living conditions for the occupants. In the instant case, the landlord sued for possession for nonpayment of rent. However, the tenant's obligation to pay is dependent on the landlord's performance of his obligations, including maintaining the premises in a habitable condition. The case is remanded to determine what violations in the code existed during the time when the tenants withheld rent. The trial court must also determine if the tenant's obligation to pay rent was suspended, in full or in part, by the landlord's breach of the implied warranty. Should it be determined that any rental obligation exists, no judgment for possession shall be entered unless the tenant refuses to pay such obligation.

ANALYSIS

The implied warranty of habitability is found to be coextensive with the requirements of the housing code in some jurisdictions. In others it is mere evidence of breach of warranty. The breach of one covenant by the landlord excuses the tenant's counter-performance (breaches of mutually dependent covenants). The lease is treated as a contract rather than as a conveyance of real property under these theories. Some states require that the rent withheld be placed in an escrow account pending repairs.

Quicknotes

BREACH OF CONTRACT Unlawful failure by a party to perform its obligations pursuant to contract.

REMEDY Compensation for violation of a right or for injuries sustained.

IMPLIED WARRANTY OF HABITABILITY A warranty implied by a landlord that the premises are suitable, and will remain suitable, for habitation.

WARRANTY OF HABITABILITY An implied warranty owed by a landlord to a tenant to provide leased premises is properly maintained in a habitable condition prior to leasing the premises and during the duration of the lease.

CHAPTER 11

Real Estate Transactions

Quick Reference Rules of Law

Burns v. McCormick

Caretakers (P) v. Heir contesting promise (D)

N.Y. Ct. App., 135 N.E. 273 (1922)

NATURE OF CASE: Appeal from decision denying specific performance.

FACT SUMMARY: The Burnses (P) agreed to take care of Halsey (now deceased) for life in exchange for Halsey's house and furnishings after his death.

RULE OF LAW

Acts of part performance are not solely and unequivocally referable to a contract for the sale of land.

FACTS: Halsey told the Burnses (P) that if they would board and care for him during his life, he would give them his house and furniture at his death. Halsey died without will, deed, or memorandum of the alleged transfer. The Burnses (P) sued for specific performance of the oral contract, and other parties in interest raised the Statute of Frauds. McCormick (D) was successful and the trial court denied specific performance. The Burnses (P) appealed.

ISSUE: Are acts of part performance solely and unequivocally referable to a contract for the sale of land?

HOLDING AND DECISION: (Cardozo, J.) No. Acts of part performance are not solely and unequivocally referable to a contract for the sale of land. In general, the Statute of Frauds requires a written contract for the conveyance of real property. In order for performance alone to satisfy the Statute of Frauds, the performance must be unequivocally referable to the agreement. Not every act of part performance will move a court in equity to grant specific performance, even though legal remedies are deemed to be inadequate. The board and care of Halsey by the Burnses (P) could have been in exchange for rent or explained in any number of different ways. The performance in this case is not unequivocally referable to an agreement to convey the property and without more the Statue of Frauds cannot be satisfied. The trial court decision is affirmed.

ANALYSIS

Hardship, estoppel, and numerous casual remarks by a decedent may be recognized in various jurisdictions as proving the existence of the alleged oral contract to pass property after death. Some jurisdictions, notably California, have held that hardship alone may remove an oral contract from the statute through estoppel. However, a majority of courts still strictly construe the Statute of Frauds and the doctrine of part performance.

Quicknotes

SPECIFIC PERFORMANCE Equitable remedy whereby the court requires the parties to perform their obligations pursuant to a contract.

STATUTE OF FRAUDS A statute that requires specified types of contracts to be in writing in order to be binding.

Hurtubise v. McPherson

Adjoining landowner (P) v. Adjoining landowner (D)

Mass. Ct. App., 951 N.E.2d 994 (2011)

NATURE OF CASE: Appeal from judgment ordering specific performance of an oral agreement for a land swap.

FACT SUMMARY: McPherson (D), whose land adjoined that of Hurtubise (P), contended that the oral agreement they had for a land swap was unenforceable under the Statute of Frauds, notwithstanding that Hurtubise (P) had relied thereon to his detriment, and that, in any event, the terms of the agreement were too indefinite to be specifically enforced.

RULE OF LAW

(1) An oral agreement for a land trade is specifically enforceable where the plaintiff seeking to enforce the agreement has taken possession of the land and made valuable and permanent improvements thereon, thus estopping the defendant, on grounds of equity and fairness, from raising the Statute of Frauds as a defense.

(2) An agreement for a land trade is specifically enforceable where, although the dimensions and detailed boundaries of the parcels to be traded were not detailed by the parties in the agreement, the parcels can be reasonably identified from the attending circumstances.

FACTS: Hurtubise (P) and McPherson (D) owned adjoining tracts of land in a town. Hurtubise (P) operated a storage business on his property, and wanted to build an additional storage shed along the border between his property and McPherson's (D) property. Hurtubise (P) realized that he could not meet the setback requirements of the local zoning ordinance unless he acquired land from McPherson (D). Hurtubise (P) approached McPherson (D), explained his need, and proposed a land trade, offering to convey to McPherson (D) a portion of the front of his (Hurtubise's (P)) property in exchange for the portion of McPherson's (D) land on which Hurtubise (P) intended to erect the new storage shed. McPherson (D) agreed to the proposal and the parties shook hands. Hurtubise (P) proceeded with his plans for construction of the new building. He obtained a building permit and began to excavate along the border of McPherson's (D) lot. During the two months of construction, Hurtubise (P) saw McPherson (D) at the site. McPherson (D) never objected to the location of the new building. Hurtubise (P) eventually constructed a 300-by-30-foot storage shed for $39,690. After construction, Hurtubise (P) sent McPherson (D) a plan outlining the details of the land swap. The plan showed that the new storage shed extended onto McPherson's (D) lot by approximately ten feet. McPherson (D) objected and accused Hurtubise (P) of taking more land than he initially had represented. McPherson (D) informed Hurtubise (P) that a payment of $250,000 would resolve the dispute. The judge found that that amount grossly exceeded the value of the property at issue. Hurtubise (P) refused to pay McPherson (D), who then notified the town that Hurtubise's (P) new building encroached on his property. The town's building commissioner revoked Hurtubise's (P) building permit and ordered him to cease occupancy of the storage shed. After McPherson (D) threatened to demolish the building, Hurtubise (P) brought suit for specific performance of the oral agreement. In response, McPherson (D) raised the Statute of Frauds as an affirmative defense. The trial court ruled for Hurtubise (P), and McPherson (D) appealed. The state's intermediate appellate court granted review.

ISSUE:

(1) Is an oral agreement for a land trade specifically enforceable where the plaintiff seeking to enforce the agreement has taken possession of the land and made valuable and permanent improvements thereon, thus estopping the defendant from raising the Statute of Frauds as a defense on grounds of equity and fairness?

(2) Is an agreement for a land trade specifically enforceable where, although the dimensions and detailed boundaries of the parcels to be traded were not detailed by the parties in the agreement, the parcels can be reasonably identified from the attending circumstances?

HOLDING AND DECISION: (Sikora, J.)

(1) Yes. An agreement for a land trade is specifically enforceable where the plaintiff seeking to enforce the agreement has taken possession of the land and made valuable and permanent improvements thereon, thus estopping the defendant, on grounds of equity and fairness, from raising the Statute of Frauds as a defense. As a black letter rule, the Statute of Frauds bars suit on a contract for the sale of lands or of any interest in or concerning them unless the promise, contract, or agreement is in writing and signed by the party to be charged therewith. However, an equitable

Continued on next page.

exception puts some flexibility into the joints of the Statute, so that such an agreement "may be specifically enforced notwithstanding failure to comply with the Statute of Frauds if it is established that the party seeking enforcement, in reasonable reliance on the contract and on the continuing assent of the party against whom enforcement is sought, has so changed his position that injustice can be avoided only by specific enforcement." *Hickey v. Green*, 442 N.E.2d 37, 38 (Mass. 1982). Each case must be assessed on its particular facts to determine if this exception should apply. Here, the requirements for the exception to apply are met, since Hurtubise (P) occupied a parcel of McPherson's (D) land and undertook the expense of construction in reliance upon McPherson's (D) apparent agreement, while McPherson (D) watched in apparent silent acquiescence as Hurtubise's (P) reliance unfolded through two months of construction and $39,690 of expenditures. Under such circumstances, McPherson's (D) silence misled Hurtubise (P) to his harm, and, therefore, McPherson (D) is estopped from setting up the Statute of Frauds as a defense to specific performance.

(2) Yes. An oral agreement for a land trade is specifically enforceable where, although the dimensions and detailed boundaries of the parcels to be traded were not detailed by the parties in the agreement, the parcels can be reasonably identified from the attending circumstances. Generally, "the essential terms of a contract must be sufficiently definite so that the nature and extent of the obligations of the parties can be ascertained." *Simons v. American Dry Ginger Ale Co.*, 140 N.E.2d 649, 652 (Mass. 1957). "However, a contract is not to be held unenforceable 'if, when applied to the transaction and construed in the light of the attending circumstances,' the meaning can be ascertained with reasonable certainty." *Id.* Here, the parcels can be reasonably identified from the attending circumstances. The parcel to be subtracted from McPherson's (D) land was visible to him. Over a period of two months, he observed without objection the gradual formation of the footprint and the body of Hurtubise's (P) building on McPherson's (D) property. The reciprocal parcel coming from Hurtubise's (P) lot also received an adequate description, as he designated an area near the front of his property, close to an abutting road and existing fence, and near the house on McPherson's (D) land. Hurtubise also presented a trial exhibit showing the reciprocal parcel he proposed. Accordingly, the trial judge reasonably inferred that its area should equate with the storage building parcel and that its location should be at or near the place designated by Hurtubise's (P) testimony. In these circumstances, indefiniteness does not prevent specific enforcement. Affirmed.

ANALYSIS

According to the Restatement (Second) of Contracts § 129 comment a (1981), the equitable exception to the requirements of the Statute of Frauds applied by the courts in this case was established by English courts of equity soon after the enactment of the Statute of Frauds in 1677. The exception permits courts with equitable powers to exercise discretion with appropriate caution in light of all the circumstances. As in this case, the application of the exception largely depends on the degree of reliance on the oral agreement by the party pursuing specific enforcement, in light of all the circumstances.

Quicknotes

BUILDING PERMIT A permit that is issued by local government entities, authorizing the building of new structures or expanding or changing existing ones.

ESTOP Prevent or bar.

SPECIFIC PERFORMANCE An equitable remedy whereby the court requires the parties to perform their obligations pursuant to a contract.

STATUTE OF FRAUDS A statute that requires specified types of contracts to be in writing in order to be binding.

ZONING Municipal statutory scheme dividing an area into districts in order to regulate the use or building of structures within those districts.

ZONING ORDINANCE A statute that divides land into defined areas and that regulates the form and use of buildings and structures within those areas.

Johnson v. Davis

Seller (D) v. Purchaser (P)

Fla. Sup. Ct., 480 So. 2d 625 (1985)

NATURE OF CASE: Appeal from trial court decision finding fraudulent misrepresentation and granting respondents the return of their deposit.

FACT SUMMARY: The Davises (P) agreed to purchase the Johnsons' (D) home after the Johnsons (D) assured them that buckling around a family room window and stains on the ceiling resulted from a minor problem that had long since been fixed.

RULE OF LAW

Where the seller of a home knows of facts materially affecting the value of the property that are not readily observable and are not known to the buyer, the seller is under a duty to disclose them to the buyer.

FACTS: In May of 1982, the Davises (P) entered into a contract to buy the Johnsons' (D) home. The contract required a $5,000 deposit payment and an additional $26,000 deposit payment within five days. Before making the additional $26,000 payment, the Davises (P) noticed ceiling stains and buckling around a family room window. The Johnsons (D) assured them that these problems resulted from a minor problem that had long since been fixed. Several days later during a heavy rain, water came gushing into the house through various parts of the family room. Two roofers hired by the Johnsons (D) concluded that the problem could be solved for under $1,000. Three roofers hired by the Davises (P) determined that the roof was inherently defective and any repairs would be temporary because the roof was slipping. The Davises (P) filed a complaint alleging breach of contract, fraud, and misrepresentation and sought recession of the contract and return of their deposit. The trial court ruled for the Davises (P), and the Johnsons (D) appealed.

ISSUE: Where the seller of a home knows of facts materially affecting the value of the property that are not readily observable and are not known to the buyer, is he under a duty to disclose them to the buyer?

HOLDING AND DECISION: (Adkins, J.) Yes. Where the seller of a home knows of facts materially affecting the value of the property that are not readily observable and are not known to the buyer, he is under a duty to disclose them to the buyer. This duty is equally applicable to all forms of real property, new and used. In the case at bar, the evidence shows that the Johnsons (D) knew of and failed to disclose that there had been problems with the roof of the house. The Davises (P) detrimentally relied on this concealment. Affirmed.

DISSENT: (Boyd, C.J.) Homeowners who attempt to sell their houses are typically in no better position to measure the quality, value, or desirability of their houses than are the prospective purchasers with whom they come into contact. This ruling will give rise to a flood of litigation and will facilitate unjust outcomes in many cases.

ANALYSIS

In the state of Florida, relief for a fraudulent misrepresentation may be granted only when the following elements are present: (1) a false statement concerning a material fact; (2) the representor's knowledge that the representation is false; (3) an intention that the representation induce another to act on it; and (4) consequent injury by the party acting in reliance on the representation. Those opposed to this sort of regulation argue that it is unnecessary since prudent purchasers inspect property, with expert advice if necessary, before they agree to buy, and prudent lenders require inspections before agreeing to provide purchase money.

Quicknotes

FRAUDULENT MISREPRESENTATION A statement or conduct by one party to another that constitutes a false representation of fact.

Commonwealth v. Fremont Investment & Loan

Massachusetts (P) v. Industrial Bank (D)

Mass. Sup. Jud. Ct., 897 N.E.2d 548 (2008)

NATURE OF CASE: Appeal from trial court's granting of preliminary injunction to state.

FACT SUMMARY: Fremont Investment & Loan (D) was selling subprime, adjustable rate mortgages to thousands of residents in Massachusetts. The Massachusetts Attorney General's (P) office brought suit alleging the sale of such mortgages was a violation of the Massachusetts Consumer Protection Act.

RULE OF LAW

Mortgage loans with the following four characteristics would likely be "unfair" under Massachusetts' Consumer Protection Act: (1) the loans were adjustable with a preliminary rate for three years; (2) the initial rate was typically three points lower than the usual mortgage rate on 30-year loans; (3) the debt-to-income ratio would exceed 50 percent after the introductory period expired; and (4) the loan-to-value ratio was 100 percent.

FACTS: Fremont Investment & Loan (Fremont) (D) was selling loans to thousands of residents in Massachusetts. There is no dispute the loans in question all had the four characteristics as mentioned above. In March 2007, Fremont (D) entered into an agreement with the Federal Deposit Insurance Corporation (FDIC) to cease granting subprime loans to customers without considering whether the customer would be able to pay the monthly loan amounts after the rate increased. Subsequently, Massachusetts (P) entered into a similar agreement with Fremont (D). Accordingly, Fremont (D) had to give the Massachusetts Attorney General's (P) office 90 days notice before any foreclosures. If the Attorney General (P) objected, Fremont (D) would attempt to resolve the matter short of foreclosure. As it turned out, the Attorney General (P) objected to all foreclosure requests. It then filed this action to enjoin Fremont (D) from foreclosing on such loans because the loans were "unfair" under Chapter 93A of the Massachusetts Consumer Protection Statute. The judge granted the preliminary injunction. The court ordered Fremont (D) to give notice to the Attorney General (P) prior to foreclosures and ordered it to resolve any foreclosure issues with the Attorney General (P). If there was no resolution, Fremont (D) had to go to court for an order of foreclosure. Fremont (D) appealed on the grounds that its loans were customary in the industry and therefore not unfair.

ISSUE: Are mortgage loans with the following four characteristics likely to be "unfair" under Massachusetts' Consumer Protection Act: (1) the loans were adjustable with a preliminary rate for three years; (2) the initial rate was typically three points lower than the usual mortgage rate on 30-year loans; (3) the debt-to-income ratio would exceed 50 percent after the introductory period expired; and (4) the loan-to-value ratio was 100 percent?

HOLDING AND DECISION: (Botsford, J.) Yes. Mortgage loans with the following four characteristics would likely be "unfair" under Massachusetts' Consumer Protection Act: (1) the loans were adjustable with a preliminary rate for three years; (2) the initial rate was typically three points lower than the usual mortgage rate on 30-year loans; (3) the debt-to-income ratio would exceed 50 percent after the introductory period expired; and (4) the loan-to-value ratio was 100 percent. First, Fremont's (D) argument that the adjustable rate mortgage (ARM) loans were not unfair because it was standard practice in the industry is without merit. The record at the preliminary injunction stage revealed that Fremont (D) knew or should have known that loans that had the four characteristics stated above would most likely be difficult to repay. In addition, the record reveals that Fremont (D) did not attempt to determine if borrowers would be able to pay the monthly loan amounts after the rate increased. Federal Deposit Insurance Corporation's actions in this matter underscore its belief that these loans constitute unsafe and unsound banking practices. Regarding the Massachusetts Predatory Home Loan Practices Act, Fremont (D) is correct that the statute technically does not apply because that statute only applies to high cost home mortgage loans. However, the judge used the statute for policy support to conclude that loans are unfair where the lender should know the borrower will be unable to repay the loan. Lastly, that the loans in question are technically allowed by state and federal regulations does not mean they are not unfair. It has long been held that a determination of whether conduct is permitted by statute is just one aspect of the fairness analysis. It is not dispositive. The preliminary injunction is affirmed and the case remanded.

ANALYSIS

This case is an example of a successful government action against the subprime lenders in the wake of the mortgage crisis. However, surprisingly, other states have

Continued on next page.

not followed Massachusetts's tactic of using a local consumer protection act. Rather, a handful of other states have brought actions against subprime lenders under the federal Securities Act of 1933.

Quicknotes

MORTGAGE An interest in land created by a written instrument providing security for the payment of a debt or the performance of a duty.

PRELIMINARY INJUNCTION A judicial mandate issued to require or restrain a party from certain conduct; used to preserve a trial's subject matter or to prevent threatened injury.

U.S. Bank National Association v. Ibanez

Purported mortgage holder (P) v. Homeowner (D)

Mass. Sup. Jud. Ct., 941 N.E.2d 40 (2011)

NATURE OF CASE: Appeal from lower court decision finding that purported mortgage holders, attempting to foreclose on two properties, failed to demonstrate they actually held the mortgage on the properties at issue.

FACT SUMMARY: U.S. Bank National Association (P) and Wells Fargo (P) foreclosed on two properties. The mortgages on each of the properties had been sold and assigned multiple times during their existence. After the foreclosure process, U.S. Bank National Association (P) and Wells Fargo (P) brought actions in state court seeking a declaration that they were the owners in fee simple of the two properties.

RULE OF LAW

Any foreclosure proceeding initiated by a party that lacks the jurisdiction and authority to conduct the foreclosure shall be null and void.

FACTS: Antonio Ibanez (D) purchased a home in Springfield, Massachusetts, for $103,500, with a loan secured by a mortgage to the lender, Rose Mortgage, Inc. The mortgage was then assigned multiple times to different mortgage companies. In 2006, the latest holder of the mortgage pooled it with 1,200 other mortgages into a trust known as a mortgage-backed security. This process, known as a securitization, allowed these trusts to be bought and sold by investors. Eventually, U.S. Bank National Association (U.S. Bank) purchased a mortgage-backed security that allegedly included Ibanez's (D) mortgage. That transaction occurred via a private placement memorandum. That document states the trust would include all mortgages placed into it and those mortgages would be reflected on an attached schedule of mortgages. A similar scenario played out with a mortgage taken out by Mark and Tammy LaRace (D). It was also pooled into a mortgage-backed security and eventually purchased by Wells Fargo (P). U.S. Bank (P) and Wells Fargo (P) foreclosed on the two properties in 2007, a process that does not require judicial approval. The foreclosure process included the properties being placed up for sale and then purchased by U.S. Bank (P) and Wells Fargo (P), respectively. (There is no dispute both homeowners defaulted on their loans.) After the foreclosure process, U.S. Bank (P) and Wells Fargo (P) brought actions in state court seeking a declaration that they were the owners in fee simple of the two properties. At the trial court level, the judge found both plaintiffs failed to prove they had the authority to foreclose on the properties. Specifically, using U.S. Bank (P) as an example, that entity did not provide the court with a schedule or any documentation that the Ibanez (D) mortgage was actually included in the mortgage-backed security that U.S. Bank (P) purchased in 2006. U.S. Bank (P) and Wells Fargo (P) appealed and the case was transferred to the Massachusetts Supreme Judicial Court.

ISSUE: Is any foreclosure proceeding initiated by a party that lacks the jurisdiction and authority to conduct the foreclosure null and void?

HOLDING AND DECISION: (Gants, J.) Yes. Any foreclosure proceeding initiated by a party that lacks the jurisdiction and authority to conduct the foreclosure shall be null and void. In these actions to quiet title to property, U.S. Bank (P) and Wells Fargo (P) have the burden of proving they were the fee simple owners of the properties. To do so, they (Ps) need to demonstrate that they properly adhered to the statutory foreclosure process in Massachusetts. Massachusetts, like many states, does not require judicial approval before an entity forecloses on a property. The mortgagor/homeowner may petition a court to enjoin the foreclosure if he or she desires. Any mortgage includes a power of sale. However, one who sells under a power of sale must strictly follow the terms. Powers of sale have restrictions on who can actually foreclose on the property. A power of sale can be exercised only by a mortgagee or its successors or assigns. U.S. Bank (P) claims that the private placement memorandum it received when it purchased the mortgage-backed security in 2006 made U.S. Bank (P) the holder of the Ibanez (D) mortgage. However, U.S. Bank (P) did not provide the lower court with a schedule or any documentation that the Ibanez (D) mortgage was actually included in the mortgage-backed security that U.S. Bank (P) purchased in 2006. Read closely, the private placement memorandum reveals an intent that certain mortgages would be included in the pool, but there simply was no evidence attached to that document stating which mortgages were included, if any. The last assignment on the record of Ibanez's (D) mortgage was to an entity called Option One. Accordingly, U.S. Bank (P) did not have the authority to foreclose on the mortgage. Wells Fargo (D) similarly could not demonstrate it actually held the mortgage on the LaRace (D) property. Affirmed.

CONCURRENCE: (Cordy, J.) Assignments of mortgages need not be recorded to be effective. However, the assignment or similar transaction must actually occur. In these complicated mortgage-backed security

Continued on next page.

transactions, the onus is on the mortgage holders to demonstrate that the assignment has passed to them before a foreclosure can proceed.

ANALYSIS

This litigation and others like it were spawned after the housing crisis began in 2008. With the rate of foreclosures skyrocketing around the country, courts began to examine more closely the complicated array of transactions that occur after a homeowner takes out a mortgage. This particular decision resulted in a large number of foreclosures being placed into legal limbo until the foreclosing parties could remedy the defects in the various transactions. Although assignment of a mortgage does not have to be recorded, it does have to actually occur via some written instrument, which neither bank in this case could prove was the case.

Quicknotes

FORECLOSURE An action to recover the amount due on a mortgage of real property where the owner has failed to meet the mortgage obligations, terminating the owner's interest in the property, which must then be sold to satisfy the debt.

MORTGAGE An interest in land created by a written instrument providing security for the payment of a debt or the performance of a duty.

MORTGAGEE Party to whom an interest in property is given in order to secure a loan.

MORTGAGOR Party who grants an interest in property in order to secure a loan.

Continued on next page.

Baskurt v. Beal

Purchasers of real property (D) v. Foreclosed party (D)

Alaska Sup. Ct., 101 P.3d 1041 (2004)

NATURE OF CASE: Appeal from lower court decision finding that purchase and sale of foreclosed property should be voided.

FACT SUMMARY: After the foreclosure of Beal's (P) property, three individuals, including the holder of the promissory note that secured Beal's original loan, purchased Beal's (P) property for less than 15 percent of its market value.

RULE OF LAW

While inadequacy of price is typically not sufficient to set aside a foreclosure sale, a court may invalidate the sale if the sale price is so inadequate as to shock the conscience of the court or the inadequate sales price is coupled with other irregularities in the foreclosure sale process.

FACTS: Marion and Mortimer Moore sold two pieces of property to Annette Beal (P) via a quitclaim deed. Beal (P) purchased Parcel A for $95,000 and secured it with a promissory note payable to Mortimer Moore. She purchased Parcel B for $135,000 and secured that parcel with a promissory note payable to Mortimer's former wife, Marion. The promissory notes were further secured by a deed of trust that covered both parcels of land. That document stated the Beal (P), the trustor, was aware that default on either of the two promissory notes would constitute default on the other note as well. The Trustee, Sarah Baskurt (D) (the Moores' daughter), would then be able to sell the property either in whole or in part at a public auction to the highest bidder. Beal (P) paid off the $95,000 amount to Mortimer Moore in 1994 with a lump sum payment. She then paid 80 percent of the $135,000 loan to Marion but began defaulting on the loan. The outstanding balance was $26,780.81. In the fall of 1999, Baskurt (D) commenced foreclosure proceedings on both Parcel A and Parcel B. A foreclosure sale took place on April 26, 2000. Baskurt (D) and two other partners were present and placed the only bid on the properties. Their successful bid amount was $26,781.81 for both properties, one dollar more than the amount Beal (P) owed on the loan. The sale amount was for approximately 15 percent of the properties' fair market value. Beal (P) then filed this action to set aside the foreclosure sale as void due to the inadequate sales price. A lower court agreed and voided the sale. Baskurt (P) and her partners appealed.

ISSUE: While inadequacy of price is typically not sufficient to set aside a foreclosure sale, may a court invalidate the sale if the sale price is so inadequate as to shock the conscience of the court or the inadequate sales price is coupled with other irregularities in the foreclosure sale process?

HOLDING AND DECISION: (Matthews, J.) Yes. While inadequacy of price is typically not sufficient to set aside a foreclosure sale, a court may invalidate the sale if the sale price is so inadequate as to shock the conscience of the court or the inadequate sales price is coupled with other irregularities in the foreclosure sale process. A trustee of a deed of trust securing real property may foreclose and sell the property. However, defects in the sale process may render the sale voidable. One potential defect is inadequacy of price. Gross inadequacy is measured by reference to the fair market value of the property. Jurisdictions vary on what percentage of fair market value would constitute a gross inadequacy. The Restatement uses a figure of 20 percent. In addition, a trustee of a deed of trust has a fiduciary responsibility to both the trustor of the property (Beal) and the beneficiary (Marion Moore). A trustee must take steps to avoid the sacrifice of the trustor's property unnecessarily. That did not occur in this case. First, the sales price for Parcel A and B was only 15 percent of the fair market value of roughly $225,000. The court below was correct that the sale price was grossly inadequate. Second, Baskurt (D) failed in her fiduciary duty to protect Beal's (P) interest in her property by foreclosing on both parcels, even though Beal (P) had paid off the $95,000 note relating to Parcel A. Baskurt (D) acted unreasonably by failing to sell only Parcel B. Accordingly, due to the inadequate sale price for the property and Baskurt's (D) failure to protect Beal's (P) interests in Parcel A, the lower court was correct to void the sale. Affirmed.

ANALYSIS

Over the course of the past several years, many states have responded to the housing crisis in the United States by enacting new legislation to strengthen the rights of property owners faced with foreclosure. The legislative requirements vary from state to state, but most include requirements of public notice, providing the homeowner with the opportunity to obtain another lender and bid on the property, and preventing mortgagees from obtaining unjust enrichment resulting from a successful low bid on the property.

Continued on next page.

Quicknotes

FIDUCIARY DUTY A legal obligation to act for the benefit of another, including subordinating one's personal interests to that of the other person.

FORECLOSURE SALE Termination of an interest in property, usually initiated by a lienholder upon failure to tender mortgage payments, resulting in the sale of the property in order to satisfy the debt.

TRUSTOR The creator of a trust.

Sebastian v. Floyd

Buyer (D) v. Seller (P)

Ky. Sup. Ct., 585 S.W.2d 381 (1979)

NATURE OF CASE: Appeal from judgment enforcing forfeiture.

FACT SUMMARY: Sebastian (D) sought to have an installment land contract treated as a mortgage after he defaulted.

RULE OF LAW

The seller's interest in an installment land sale contract should be treated as a lien in order to protect the buyer from unfair forfeiture.

FACTS: Sebastian (D) contracted to buy real property from Floyd (P) for $3,800 down and the balance of $10,900 in monthly installments at 8 percent interest. The agreement contained a forfeiture clause providing that if Sebastian (D) defaulted on any payments, Floyd (P) could terminate the contract and retain all previous payments as liquidated damages. Sebastian (D) defaulted after paying out a total of $5,480 ($4,300 of principal). Floyd (P) sued to enforce the forfeiture. The trial court ruled for Floyd (P), and Sebastian (D) appealed.

ISSUE: Should the seller's interest in an installment land sale contract be treated as a lien in order to protect the buyer from unfair forfeiture?

HOLDING AND DECISION: (Aker, J.) Yes. The seller's interest in an installment land sale contract should be treated as a lien in order to protect the buyer from unfair forfeiture. In a typical installment land contract, legal title to the property remains with the seller until the buyer has paid the entire contract price, but equitable title is transferred at the outset of the agreement. There is no practical difference between this type of contract and a purchase money mortgage in which the buyer gets legal title immediately and the seller holds a lien on the property as security. However, under a mortgage, the buyer's interest in the property is not forfeited at default. Instead, the buyer is entitled to any remaining equity in the property after the seller has been paid the contract amount and any expenses. Since this arrangement protects both the buyer and seller, an installment land contract should be treated as giving the seller a lien on the property. Therefore, in the present case, the forfeiture clause may not be enforced by Floyd (P), and Sebastian (D) is entitled to any equity interest in the property that remains after Floyd (P) exercises his lien. Reversed.

ANALYSIS

Other states treat only some installment land contracts as mortgages based on a range of factors, including the buyer's equity in the property and the length of the default period. See *Grombone v. Krekel*, 754 P.2d 777 (Colo. Ct. App. 1988). In that case, the court of appeals held the decision to be within the lower court's discretion pending an analysis of those factors.

Quicknotes

FORFEITURE The loss of a right or interest as a penalty for failing to fulfill an obligation.

INSTALLMENT CONTRACT A contract pursuant to which the parties are to render performance or payment in periodic intervals.

LIQUIDATED DAMAGES An amount of money specified in a contract representing the damages owed in the event of breach.

PURCHASE MONEY MORTGAGE A mortgage or other security in property taken in order to ensure the performance of a duty undertaken pursuant to the purchase of such property.

Koenig v. Van Reken

Seller (P) v. Buyer (D)

Mich. Ct. App., 279 N.W.2d 590 (1979)

NATURE OF CASE: Appeal from a dismissal of complaint.

FACT SUMMARY: Koenig (P) claimed an equitable mortgage should be imposed because she did not intend to grant an absolute deed to Van Reken (D).

RULE OF LAW

A conveyance of property by deed may be treated as a mortgage if it appears that the parties did not intend to make an absolute transfer.

FACTS: Koenig (P) owned a home with a market value of $60,000. There were three mortgages on the property totaling $26,000. Koenig (P) was unable to pay the property taxes and the mortgage payments. Van Reken (D) then approached Koenig (P) and proposed a complex arrangement whereby Van Reken (D) would purchase the property, redeem it from tax sale and foreclosure, and give Koenig (P) a lease with an option to repurchase the property. The lease agreement provided that Koenig (P) would pay $300 per month for three years, after which she could repurchase the premises for $32,000. Van Reken (D) prepared all of the contracts and deeds and Koenig (P) was unrepresented by counsel. After almost two years under the agreement, Koenig (P) defaulted and was evicted. Koenig (P) brought suit to impose an equitable mortgage based on the agreement with Van Reken (D). [The lower court dismissed Koenig's (P) complaint. Koenig (P) appealed that decision.]

ISSUE: May conveyances of property by deed be treated as mortgages if it appears that the parties did not intend to make an absolute transfer?

HOLDING AND DECISION: (Brennan, J.) Yes. Conveyances of property by deed may be treated as mortgages if it appears that the parties did not intend to make an absolute transfer. The intention of the parties determines whether an absolute deed should be construed as a mortgage. This intention may be determined by looking at the circumstances of the transaction and the relative positions of the parties. If the adverse financial position of the seller is combined with an inadequate purchase price, a deed should be considered a mortgage. In the present case, Koenig (P) was in financial distress and entered into an agreement whereby her $30,000 in equity was conveyed for less than $4,000. This indicates that the conveyance was not meant to be absolute and that an equitable mortgage should be imposed. The granting of the motion to dismiss was improper. Reversed.

ANALYSIS

Equitable mortgages are not affected by the Statute of Frauds. Other courts have identified other factors that should be considered when imposing an equitable mortgage, such as the relationship of the parties, the sophistication of the parties, and who retained possession.

Quicknotes

EQUITABLE MORTGAGE A lien upon real property, enforceable in equity but not at law, in order to ensure that a specific sum of money is paid or a particular performance is rendered.

QUITCLAIM DEED A deed whereby the grantor conveys whatever interest he or she may have in the property without any warranties or covenants as to title.

WARRANTY DEED A deed that guarantees that the conveyor possesses the title that he purports to convey.

Sabo v. Horvath

Purchaser who recorded deed (D) v. Purchaser who did not record (P)

Alaska Sup. Ct., 559 P.2d 1038 (1976)

NATURE OF CASE: Action to determine title to real property

FACT SUMMARY: Horvath (P) recorded his deed prior to a patent being granted the seller so that the recorded deed was outside the chain of title.

RULE OF LAW

A deed outside the chain of title is not constructive notice and a subsequently recorded deed will take priority.

FACTS: Lowery filed for a federal land patent on real property he was homesteading in Alaska. Prior to the issuance of the patent, Lowery conveyed his interest in the land to Horvath (P) by quitclaim deed. Horvath (P) recorded the deed, which was then outside the chain of record title since Lowery had not yet obtained patent title to the land. After patent title was obtained, Horvath (P) did not re-record the deed. Lowery subsequently "sold" the land a second time to Sabo (D) by quitclaim deed. Sabo (D) recorded his deed. Sabo (D) had no notice of the earlier conveyance. Horvath (P) brought a quiet title action. Sabo (D) alleged that a deed recorded out of chain of title was not constructive notice and that under the state's notice recording law he had no notice of the earlier sale and should be given preference.

ISSUE: Is a deed recorded outside the chain of title given preference to a subsequent bona fide purchaser without actual notice?

HOLDING AND DECISION: (Boochever, C.J.) No. A deed outside the chain of title is not constructive notice and a subsequently recorded deed will take priority. The purpose of our recording statute is to protect innocent purchasers without notice of an earlier unrecorded sale. Normally, a recordation gives the subsequent purchaser constructive notice of the earlier conveyance. However, we hold that a deed recorded outside the chain of title is not constructive notice to an innocent purchaser for value without actual notice. It is less burdensome for one recording outside the chain of title to re-record than to force purchasers to check all conveyances outside the chain of the title. Quitclaim deedholders are entitled to protection under the recording statutes (the majority rule). While Horvath (P) originally received Lowery's equitable interest in the land, his failure to re-record after the patent was granted requires us to find for Sabo (D).

ANALYSIS

Sabo would be useful only where the jurisdiction does not use a tract index system. Under a tract index system, every document affecting land is recorded. Some jurisdictions hold that the grantee of a quitclaim deed is not a bona fide purchaser. In *Crossly v. Campion Mining Co.*, 1 Alaska 391 (1901), a quitclaim grantee with knowledge of a superior unrecorded claim was held not to be in good faith.

Quicknotes

ACTION TO QUIET TITLE Equitable action to resolve conflicting claims to an interest in real property.

BONA FIDE PURCHASER A party who purchases property in good faith and for valuable consideration without notice of a defect in title.

CONSTRUCTIVE NOTICE Knowledge of a fact imputed to an individual who was under a duty to inquire and who could have learned of the fact through the exercise of reasonable prudence.

QUITCLAIM DEED A deed whereby the grantor conveys whatever interest he or she may have in the property without any warranties or covenants as to title.

Brock v. Yale Mortgage Corporation

Husband (P) v. Former wife (D) and Mortgage lender (D)

Ga. Sup. Ct., 700 S.E.2d 583 (2010)

NATURE OF CASE: Appeal from lower court decision finding that husband ratified a forged quitclaim deed that his former wife drafted granting her full title to the property.

FACT SUMMARY: To avoid foreclosure, Brock's (P) wife, Joyce (D), forged a quitclaim deed that granted her full title to their home. Without Brock's (P) knowledge, she then took out a new mortgage with Yale Mortgage Company (Yale) (D). When Brock (P) and Joyce (D) divorced several years later, their settlement agreement acknowledged the existence of a liability on the home in the amount of the loan from Yale (D).

RULE OF LAW
One holding property with another as tenants in common cannot convey the other person's interests in the property without his or her consent.

FACTS: Brock (P) and his wife, Joyce (D), did not have a joint checking account. Each month he would give her money to make the monthly mortgage payments on their home. On several different occasions, Joyce (D) spent the money in other ways. Eventually, foreclosure proceedings were commenced against the property, all with Brock (P) having no knowledge of any of the proceedings. To avoid foreclosure, Joyce (D) forged a quitclaim deed that granted her full title to their home. Again without Brock's (P) knowledge, Joyce (D) then took out a new mortgage with Yale Mortgage Company (Yale) (D). The new mortgage was secured via a promissory note and another deed in favor of Yale (D). The parties divorced several years later after Brock (P) alleged that Joyce (D) removed $200,000 from his checking account. At some point, Brock (P) became aware of the forged deed and the Yale (D) mortgage. The parties' divorce settlement agreement acknowledged the existence of a liability on the home in the amount of the loan from Yale (D). Brock (P) commenced this action to void the forged deed and set aside the subsequent deed granted to Yale (D) as part of the new mortgage transaction. The lower court found that Brock (P) ratified the forged deed by virtue of the provision in the divorce settlement agreement acknowledging the existence of a liability in the property. Brock (P) appealed.

ISSUE: Can one holding property with another as tenants in common convey the other person's interests in the property without his or her consent?

HOLDING AND DECISION: (Hunstein, C.J.) No. One holding property with another as tenants in common cannot convey the other person's interests in the property without his or her consent. A deed may be voided if it is proven to be a forgery. While a tenant in common cannot encumber other tenants without their consent, one tenant may encumber his own interest in the property. If a tenant purports to convey the entire property, the forged deed will still affect his own interest but will not bind the others. Accordingly, the forged deed resulted in Yale (D) receiving only a one-half interest in the property. Yale (D) argues it is a bona fide purchaser. Typically, a bona fide purchaser is protected against any outstanding interests of which, the purchaser is not aware. However, a bona fide purchaser cannot obtain title to property via a forged deed, which is a nullity. Accordingly, Yale (D) cannot obtain title over the entire property using that argument. Turning to the ratification issue, a forged signature may become binding if ratified by the person whose name was fraudulently signed. The lower court found that the settlement agreement was evidence of Brock's (P) acknowledgment and ratification of the quitclaim deed and the mortgage transaction to Yale (D). However, the provision states only that the parties acknowledge "Joyce has incurred a $50,000 liability on the property." While the parties may have been contemplating the Yale (D) mortgage, there is no specific identifying information confirming that is the case. Accordingly, this factual dispute needs to be determined in light of any available extrinsic evidence. Affirmed in part, reversed in part, and remanded for further proceedings.

ANALYSIS

A bona fide purchaser who receives a valid title to property will typically have greater rights to property over other claimants of which the purchaser was not aware. These situations arise where an heir or other claimant fails to record his or her interest properly in the local registry or there is some other defect in the title. However, as noted here, to gain status as a bona fide purchaser, the purchaser cannot have simply received a forged deed.

Quicknotes

BONA FIDE PURCHASER A party who purchases property in good faith and for valuable consideration without notice of a defect in title.

FORGERY The false preparation or modification of a written document with intent to defraud another.

RATIFICATION Affirmation of a prior action taken by either the individual himself or by an agent on behalf of the principal, which is then treated as if it had been initially authorized by the principal.

McCoy v. Love

[Parties not identified.]

Fla. Sup. Ct., 382 So. 2d 647 (1980)

NATURE OF CASE: Appeal from finding that a deed was voidable.

FACT SUMMARY: Russell drew up a fraudulent sales contract wherein Elliott (P) unknowingly conveyed all of her interest in mineral rights to Russell.

RULE OF LAW

Fraud in the inducement renders a legally effective deed merely voidable and not void.

FACTS: Elliott (P), who was unable to read or write, agreed to sell Russell a small portion of her mineral rights in a property. Russell drew up a sales contract wherein Elliott (P) unknowingly conveyed all of her interest to Russell. Russell notified Elliott (P) that a mistake had been made, but in the meantime sold part of Elliott's (P) mineral rights to other parties, including Love (D). Elliott (P) remained ignorant of these subsequent transactions until she wanted to sell more of her mineral rights and a title search revealed them. She sued for cancellation of the deed. The trial court concluded that the deed was void and granted summary judgment to Elliott (P). On appeal, the district court held the deed voidable rather than void. Elliott (P) appealed.

ISSUE: Does fraud in the inducement render a legally effective deed merely voidable and not void?

HOLDING AND DECISION: (Boyd, J.) Yes. Fraud in the inducement renders a legally effective deed merely voidable and not void. Where all essential legal requisites of a deed are present, it conveys legal title. In this case, Elliott (P) knew she was executing and delivering a deed of mineral rights. She was responsible for informing herself of its legal effect. The district court was correct in holding that the deed was merely voidable and that it conveyed a legal title to Russell. The case should be remanded for trial on the factual issue of whether Love (D) and the other buyers were bona fide purchasers.

ANALYSIS

A deed is either void or voidable if obtained by forgery or fraud. The deed will be set aside at the previous owner's request if no further conveyances have occurred. Where the property has been conveyed to a bona fide purchaser (BFP), if the deed is void, no title is conveyed to the grantee; thus, the grantee cannot convey the title to another. If the deed is considered merely voidable by an owner who had a fraud perpetrated against him, a subsequent BFP will obtain good title.

Quicknotes

BONA FIDE PURCHASER A party who purchases property in good faith and for valuable consideration without notice of a defect in title.

FRAUD A false representation of facts with the intent that another will rely on the misrepresentation to his detriment.

INDUCEMENT Incentive or benefit motivating a party to enter into a contractual relationship.

CHAPTER 12

Fair Housing Law

Quick Reference Rules of Law

Fair Housing Council of San Fernando Valley v. Roommate.com, LLC

Federal agency (P) v. Internet-based company (D)

666 F.3d 1216 (9th Cir. 2012)

NATURE OF CASE: Appeal from lower court decision finding that website's requirement that applicants disclose their sex, sexual orientation, and familial status while searching for roommates violated the Fair Housing Act.

FACT SUMMARY: The Fair Housing Council of San Fernando Valley (P) sued Roommate.com, LLC (D) in federal court alleging that the website's requirement that applicants disclose their sex, sexual orientation, and familial status and the website's subsequent use of that information to match roommates violated the Fair Housing Act.

RULE OF LAW

The Fair Housing Act, which prohibits discrimination on the basis of race, color, religion, sex, familial status, and national origin in the sale or renting of a dwelling, does not apply to a tenant's choice of a roommate within the dwelling.

FACTS: Roommate.com, LLC (D) operates an internet-based business that helps people find roommates. Users of the website create a site profile indicating their sex, sexual orientation, and familial status. Users list their preferences for a roommate using the same criteria. Based upon the selected criteria, Roommate.com (D) then provides a list of potential roommate matches. The Fair Housing Council of San Fernando Valley (P) sued Roommate.com (D) in federal court. The suit alleged that the website's requirement that applicants disclose their sex, sexual orientation, and familial status and subsequent use of that information to match roommates violated the Fair Housing Act. The federal district court agreed and enjoined Roommate.com's (D) practice of using these characteristics to pair up roommates. Roommate.com (D) appealed to the United States Court of Appeals for the Ninth Circuit.

ISSUE: Does the Fair Housing Act, which prohibits discrimination on the basis of race, color, religion, sex, familial status, and national origin in the sale or renting of a dwelling, apply to a tenant's choice of a roommate within the dwelling?

HOLDING AND DECISION: (Kozinski, C.J.) No. The Fair Housing Act (FHA), which prohibits discrimination on the basis of race, color, religion, sex, familial status, and national origin in the sale or renting of a dwelling, does not apply to a tenant's choice of a roommate within the dwelling. The central issue in this case is the scope of the statutory phrase, "sale or rental of a dwelling." The FHA defines a dwelling as a single living unit such as a house or an apartment. It would be difficult to divide these single unit spaces into separate dwellings for the purposes of the statute. While the statute prohibits discrimination in the sale or renting of a living unit, it does not cover the choice of one's roommate inside that dwelling. Essentially, the coverage of the statute stops at the front door. A business transaction to buy or lease property is different from an arrangement by two people who wish to live together. In addition, constitutional concerns prohibit the statute from reaching one's choice of a roommate. The freedom to enter and carry on certain private or intimate relationships is a fundamental right protected by the Bill of Rights. To determine if a certain relationship is constitutionally protected, courts will examine the size, purpose, selectivity, and whether others are excluded from the relationship. The roommate relationship qualified. People are selective about their roommates. Roommates share living spaces, bathrooms, and sometimes bedrooms. Because of a potential roommate's access to one's living space, the choice of a roommate implicates significant privacy and safety considerations. A government's ability to regulate and restrict a person's ability to choose a roommate thus improperly invades one's private home. The Constitution and Bill of Rights clearly protect a person from these unwarranted government intrusions into one's home. Restricting one's ability to choose a roommate based upon compatible lifestyles would be an invasion of privacy. For example, single women often seek other women for roommates out of security concerns. This type of private engagement should not be prohibited. Because the FHA does not apply to the sharing of individual dwelling units, Roommate.com's practice of pairing up roommates based on their sex, sexual orientation, and familial status is not prohibited. Reversed.

ANALYSIS

As further support, the decision also notes in dicta that, whenever possible, federal and state statutes will be interpreted to avoid any constitutional concerns. Courts will attempt to construe statutes to avoid these concerns unless the interpretation is clearly contrary to the statue. In this case, adopting the narrow interpretation that a dwelling is a single, indivisible unit allowed the court to avoid the constitutional issues such as invasion

Continued on next page.

of privacy or interference with a protected intimate relationship.

Quicknotes

FAIR HOUSING ACT 42 U.S.C. § 3601 Prohibits housing discrimination on the basis of race, color, religion, sex, familial status, or national origin.

FUNDAMENTAL RIGHT A liberty that is either expressly or impliedly provided for in the United States Constitution, the deprivation or burdening of which is subject to a heightened standard of review.

Asbury v. Brougham

Black renter (P) v. Housing complex (D)

866 F.2d 1276 (10th Cir. 1989)

NATURE OF CASE: Appeal from award of damages for illegal discrimination.

FACT SUMMARY: Asbury (P) claimed that she was denied an opportunity to rent a home at Brougham Estates (D) because she was Black.

RULE OF LAW

The Fair Housing Act is violated where the plaintiff proves a prima facie case of intent to discriminate based on race and the defendant is unable to demonstrate legitimate nondiscriminatory reasons.

FACTS: Asbury (P), a Black woman, went to Brougham Estates (Brougham) (D), a housing complex, looking to rent a home. Asbury (P) was told that there were no vacancies and was refused an application. The following day, a White woman inquired about the same housing and was told that there were immediate openings. Other evidence presented at trial also indicated that White persons were given different information than Asbury (P). Brougham Estates (D) responded that there was no appropriate housing available for Asbury (P) at the time she inquired. The jury awarded damages, including punitive damages, against Brougham (D) to Asbury (P), and Brougham (D) appealed.

ISSUE: Is the Fair Housing Act violated where the plaintiff proves a prima facie case of intent to discriminate based on race and the defendant is unable to demonstrate legitimate nondiscriminatory reasons?

HOLDING AND DECISION: (Parker, J.) Yes. The Fair Housing Act is violated where the plaintiff proves a prima facie case of intent to discriminate based on race and the defendant is unable to demonstrate legitimate nondiscriminatory reasons. Under the Fair Housing Act and § 1982, persons may not use race as a factor to discriminate against minority applicants for rental housing. The plaintiff has the burden of bringing proof of a prima facie case. Then the defendant has the burden of showing that the refusal to rent or provide information was motivated by legitimate nonracial reasons. Finally, the burden shifts back to the plaintiff to demonstrate that the reasons claimed by the defendant were not the true considerations. Asbury (P) made her prima facie case by proving that she was denied access to housing although it remained available to White applicants. Brougham Estates' (D) defense that Asbury (P) was not qualified for housing was rebutted by evidence that exceptions were often made for persons in her position and she was not even provided with the conditions for obtaining an exception. Thus, the jury had a valid basis for deciding that Brougham Estates' (D) reasons were not legitimate. Affirmed.

ANALYSIS

The award of punitive damages against Brougham (D), the owner of the complex, was upheld despite his assertion that he could not be held responsible for the actions of his employees. The court found that there was ample evidence that Brougham (D) had adopted the discriminatory policy and ratified the employees' actions.

Quicknotes

COMPENSATORY DAMAGES Measure of damages necessary to compensate victim for actual injuries suffered.

PRIMA FACIE CASE An action where the plaintiff introduces sufficient evidence to submit the issue to the judge or jury for determination.

PUNITIVE DAMAGES Damages exceeding the actual injury suffered for the purposes of punishment, deterrence, and comfort to plaintiff.

Quigley v. Winter

Tenant (P) v. Landlord (D)

598 F.3d 938 (8th Cir. 2010)

NATURE OF CASE: Appeal from jury verdict finding that, among other things, landlord's sexual harassment of plaintiff created a hostile housing environment, entitling the plaintiff to compensatory and punitive damages.

FACT SUMMARY: Quigley (P), a mother of four, rented an apartment from Winter (D) via a Section 8 housing voucher from the federal government. Quigley (P) alleged that Winter (D) sexually harassed her on many different occasions in and around her apartment, forcing Quigley (P) to terminate her lease and move out.

RULE OF LAW

A claim of a hostile housing environment created by sexual harassment may be demonstrated by evidence that a landlord or property owner subjected a tenant to unwelcome sexual harassment sufficiently severe so as to interfere with or deprive the tenant of his or her rights to use or enjoy the home.

FACTS: Quigley (P), a mother of four, rented an apartment from Winter (D) via a Section 8 housing voucher from the federal government. Quigley (P) alleged that Winter (D) sexually harassed her on many different occasions in and around her apartment. The harassment included two occasions of unwanted touching, various sexually suggestive comments, calls to Quigley's (P) home in the middle of the night, and repeated unannounced visits and unapproved entrances into Quigley's (P) apartment. Winter's (D) behavior eventually forced Quigley (P) to terminate her lease and move out. Quigley (P) filed a complaint in federal district court alleging sexual harassment, sex discrimination, and coercion and intimidation with her (P) rights in violation of the Fair Housing Act (FHA). Winter (D) filed a counterclaim alleging that Quigley (P) breached her lease when she vacated the apartment early. A jury found in favor of Quigley (P) on all counts and awarded her $13,685 in compensatory damages and $250,000 in punitive damages. The district court then lowered the punitive damage amount to $20,527.50. Both parties appealed to the United States Appeals Court for the Eighth Circuit.

ISSUE: May a claim of a hostile housing environment created by sexual harassment be demonstrated by evidence that a landlord or property owner subjected a tenant to unwelcome sexual harassment sufficiently severe so as to interfere with or deprive the tenant of his or her rights to use or enjoy the home?

HOLDING AND DECISION: (Riley, J.) Yes. A claim of a hostile housing environment created by sexual harassment may be demonstrated by evidence that a landlord or property owner subjected a tenant to unwelcome sexual harassment sufficiently severe so as to interfere with or deprive the tenant of his or her rights to use or enjoy the home. First, as a matter of law, a claim for hostile housing environment based on sexual harassment is allowed under the FHA and several other circuit courts have concluded the same. Winter (D) claims the evidence to establish the claim was insufficient at trial. Based upon the factual evidence presented at trial regarding the multiple instances of sexual harassment, the court concludes Quigley (P) presented sufficient evidence to support the claim. All of these instances occurred in and around Quigley's (P) own home, making the conduct even more egregious. The jury also found that Quigley (P) proved the separate legal claim of "quid pro quo" sexual harassment. For this claim, Quigley (P) must have shown that she was a member of a protected class, she was subjected to harassment based on sexual advances, and her submission to the advances was an implied condition of receiving some type of benefit. Here, Quigley (P) produced evidence that when she inquired with Winter (D) as to whether she would receive her security deposit back, Winter (D) put his hand on her stomach and said, "My eagle eyes have not seen everything yet." The jury could properly infer that Winter (D) was conditioning the return of the security deposit upon seeing more of Quigley's (P) body. This Court will not overturn that decision by the jury. Turning to Quigley's (P) third claim, 42 U.S.C. § 3617 prohibits use of coercion and intimidation to deny or limit benefits to a person in connection with the rental of a dwelling. Based upon the same evidence noted above supporting her hostile environment claim, Quigley (P) produced enough evidence to support her coercion claim. Lastly, the district court reduced the punitive damage award by too large of a degree. Punitive damages are appropriate in federal civil actions when the defendant's conduct included evil motive or intent or reckless indifference to federally protected rights. Here, Winter (D) admitted at trial he knew sexual harassment was unlawful. The only question on appeal is the reasonableness of the jury's damage award. To assess reasonableness, courts should consider: (1) the degree of reprehensibility of the defendant's conduct; (2) the ratio between compensatory damages and the punitive damages; and (3) any civil or criminal penalties that could be imposed for the conduct in question. There

Continued on next page.

is no question Winter's (D) conduct was reprehensible. It occurred multiple times, in Quigley's (P) home and often in the presence of her children. Turning to the ratio, the jury's $250,000 punitive damages award was 18 times the amount of compensatory damages. The court agrees with the trial court that this was excessive. The last factor is the amount of any civil or criminal penalties. A provision of the FHA states any person interfering with one's rights under the FHA may be subject to a penalty of $55,000 for first time offences. Accordingly, the court finds the compensatory damages should be multiplied by four. This will result in a punitive damages award of $54,750. Affirmed in part and reversed in part.

ANALYSIS

The United States Supreme Court has recently issued several decisions that have limited the possibility of large punitive damage amounts in federal civil cases. The Court has said a four to one ratio of punitive damages to compensatory damages will normally suffice. The Court also stated that awards with a ratio higher than ten to one may be presumptively unconstitutional because they violate the Due Process Clauses of the Fifth and Fourteenth Amendment.

Quicknotes

PUNITIVE DAMAGES Damages exceeding the actual injury suffered for the purposes of punishment of the defendant, deterrence of the wrongful behavior, or comfort to the plaintiff.

SEXUAL HARASSMENT The practice of subjecting persons to oppressive conduct on account of their gender.

Human Rights Commission v. LaBrie, Inc.

Mobile park homeowner (P) v. Mobile park owner (D)

Vt. Sup. Ct., 668 A.2d 659 (1995)

NATURE OF CASE: Appeal in a case alleging discrimination in housing.

FACT SUMMARY: The McCarthys (P) claimed the LaBries (D) unlawfully discriminated against them by prohibiting them to reside in their mobile home park with minor children.

RULE OF LAW

Privately imposed occupancy limits that limit or exclude persons with minor children are unreasonable and in violation of state and federal law.

FACTS: The LaBries (D) purchased a mobile home park. They changed the occupancy provisions of their leases to provide that no tenants be permitted to have children under the age of 18 reside in their mobile home. The McCarthys (P) purchased a home in the park; however, they were later forced to sell when Mrs. McCarthy learned she was pregnant. The McCarthys (P) brought suit against the LaBries (D), claiming violations of the Fair Housing and Public Accommodations Act by discriminating against persons intending to occupy a dwelling with one or more minor children. The court found in favor of plaintiffs and the LaBries (D) appealed.

ISSUE: Are privately imposed occupancy limits that limit or exclude persons with minor children unreasonable and in violation of state and federal law?

HOLDING AND DECISION: (Allen, C.J.) Yes. Privately imposed occupancy limits that limit or exclude persons with minor children are unreasonable and in violation of state and federal law. In addition, the LaBries' (D) argument that the occupancy limit is based on legitimate water and septic capacity considerations is without merit. The trial court properly rejected this argument on the grounds the LaBries (D) failed to present evidence that an increase in the number of occupants in the units would adversely affect their water and septic capacities. We agree with the trial court that this argument is merely a pretext to prohibit minors from the mobile home park. A privately enforced occupancy limit must at a minimum be reasonable. Defendants failed to make this showing. Affirmed.

ANALYSIS

The defendants were guilty here of both disparate treatment and disparate impact discrimination. While such discrimination may be proven by extrinsic evidence, here there was direct evidence of the fact that no minor children had moved into the park. Moreover, the court held that the affirmative defense asserted by the LaBries (D) that an increase in occupancy would overburden their septic systems was unproven.

Quicknotes

AFFIRMATIVE DEFENSE A manner of defending oneself against a claim not by denying the truth of the charge but by the introduction of some evidence challenging the plaintiff's right to bring the claim.

DISPARATE TREATMENT Unequal treatment of employees or of applicants for employment without justification.

EXTRINSIC EVIDENCE Evidence that is not contained within the text of a document or contract but that is derived from the parties' statements or the circumstances under which the agreement was made.

State ex rel. Sprague v. City of Madison

Lessee (P) v. City (D)

Wis. Ct. App., 555 N.W.2d 409 (1996)

NATURE OF CASE: Appeal in a case alleging sexual discrimination in violation of municipal law.

FACT SUMMARY: Sprague (P) brought suit against Hacklander-Ready and Rowe for their retraction of an offer to rent her a room based on her sexual orientation.

RULE OF LAW

A statute is ambiguous if it may be construed in different ways by reasonably informed persons or its literal meaning produces an absurd or unreasonable result.

FACTS: Hacklander-Ready leased a four-bedroom house. She had the owner's permission to lease rooms out to other persons to help her in paying the rent. She leased a room to Rowe, and they placed ads to find tenants to replace two women who were moving out. They agreed to rent a room to Sprague (P) and were aware of her sexual orientation. However, they retracted their offer on the basis that they were uncomfortable living with a person of her sexual orientation. Sprague (P) filed a complaint with the Madison Equal Opportunity Commission alleging discrimination on the basis of sexual orientation in violation of Madison General Ordinances. The trial court found Ready and Rowe in violation of the statute and they appealed.

ISSUE: Is a statute ambiguous if it may be construed in different ways by reasonably informed persons or its literal meaning produces an absurd or unreasonable result?

HOLDING AND DECISION: (Sundby, J.) Yes. A statute is ambiguous if it may be construed in different ways by reasonably informed persons or its literal meaning produces an absurd or unreasonable result. This is not the case here. The statute unambiguously prohibits any person having right of rental to refuse to rent to any person because of the person's sexual orientation. Hacklander-Ready has the right to rent the property to others and the sole reason she and Rowe withdrew their offer was due to Sprague's (P) sexual orientation. Affirmed.

ANALYSIS

Note that all jurisdictions have ordinances that expressly prohibit discrimination in housing based on sexual orientation. Moreover, the definition of "family" for purposes of statutory construction may also differ from jurisdiction to jurisdiction. Some jurisdictions extend the definition to include a homosexual partner.

Quicknotes

AMBIGUOUS TERMS Contract terms that are capable of more than one interpretation.

SEXUAL HARASSMENT An employment practice subjecting persons to oppressive conduct on account of their gender.

DiLiddo v. Oxford Street Realty, Inc.

Tenant (P) v. Landlord (D)

Mass. Sup. Jud. Ct., 876 N.E.2d 421 (2007)

NATURE OF CASE: Appeal from granting of summary judgment in favor of defendant.

FACT SUMMARY: DiLiddo (P) sought to rent an apartment from Oxford Street Realty, Inc. (Oxford) (D) using a state assisted housing program, which required landlords to execute a form lease. Oxford (D) objected to the terms of the lease.

RULE OF LAW

In Massachusetts, a landlord may not refuse to rent an apartment to a participant in a state assisted housing program for temporary housing simply because the landlord considers certain terms of the program's standard lease form economically unfavorable.

FACTS: The Massachusetts Legislature created a program in 1995 whereby the state would subsidize temporary housing costs for qualified disabled persons of low income. The enabling statute created an alternate housing voucher program (AHVP) as well as a standard form lease for such short-term tenancies. The lease allowed tenants to provide one month's notice of termination if the tenant found more suitable, permanent housing. DiLiddo (P), disabled from an auto accident, sought to rent an apartment owned by Oxford Street Realty, Inc. (Oxford) (D). Oxford (D) objected on the grounds the one-month termination provision in favor of the tenant placed an unreasonable financial burden on the landlord. DiLiddo (P) brought suit, alleging that Oxford's (D) actions were discriminatory and in violation of state law that prohibited landlords from discriminating against tenants who receive public housing assistance or because of any requirement of the public assistance program. [The lower court granted Oxford (D) summary judgment and DiLiddo (P) appealed.]

ISSUE: In Massachusetts, may a landlord refuse to rent an apartment to a participant in a state assisted housing program for temporary housing simply because the landlord considers certain terms of the program's standard lease form economically unfavorable?

HOLDING AND DECISION: (Marshall, C.J.) No. In Massachusetts, a landlord may not refuse to rent an apartment to a participant in a state assisted housing program for temporary housing simply because the landlord considers certain terms of the program's standard lease form economically unfavorable. M.G.L. c. 151 Section 4(10) prohibits landlords from discriminating against tenants who receive public subsidies or because of any requirements of the subsidy program. The question here is whether the alternate housing voucher program's (AHVP's) one-month notice of termination provision is a "requirement" of the AHVP program, therefore barring landlords from refusing to execute the lease. We hold the language of Chapter 151B is unambiguous. The landlord may not object to the lease's notice of termination provision because the provision constitutes a requirement of the subsidy program. In addition, the statute does not require the plaintiff to proffer evidence of a discriminatory animus. On this point, Chapter 151B does not require such a showing. Accordingly, Oxford's (D) objections to the lease run afoul of Chapter 151B. [The court reversed the summary judgment in favor of Oxford (D) and ordered judgment in favor of DiLiddo (P) as to liability.]

ANALYSIS

This case represented the first time the Massachusetts Supreme Judicial Court interpreted this particular statute in over twenty years. Essentially, the court held that landlords could no longer use economic reasons as grounds to reject tenants who receive public subsidies.

Quicknotes

SUMMARY JUDGMENT Judgment rendered by a court in response to a motion made by one of the parties, claiming that the lack of a question of material fact in respect to an issue warrants disposition of the issue without consideration by the jury.

MHANY Management v. County of Nassau

Affordable housing developer (P) v. County (D)

819 F.3d 581 (2d Cir. 2016)

NATURE OF CASE: Appeal from judgment finding, inter alia, disparate treatment violations by a municipality of the Fair Housing Act/Title VIII of the Civil Rights Act of 1968.

FACT SUMMARY: The Village of Garden City (D), which claimed to have non-racially motivated reasons for changing zoning for a development from multi-family to single family, contended that it did not violate § 804 of the Fair Housing Act (FHA), also known as Title VIII of the Civil Rights Act of 1968, which prohibits, inter alia, discriminatory zoning on the basis of race or color. Garden City (D) also challenged the district court's finding that it had violated the FHA's disparate impact prong, asserting that the court erred in failing to apply the test for discriminatory impact issued by the Secretary of Housing and Urban Development (HUD).

RULE OF LAW

(1) Under § 804 of the Fair Housing Act (FHA), also known as Title VIII of the Civil Rights Act of 1968, a district court may find intentional racial discrimination on the basis of the negative racial impact a municipality's zoning decision will have, and on the basis of the sequence of events that led the municipality to reach its decision in response to public opposition to the prospect of affordable housing.

(2) Where the Secretary of Housing and Urban Development (HUD) has issued a burden-shifting disparate impact test under the Fair Housing Act (FHA), a federal court must apply that test where courts in the circuit have not held that the FHA is unambiguous to disparate impact.

FACTS: The Village of Garden City (Garden City) (D) is a municipality located in Nassau County (D), New York. Only about 2.6 percent of Garden City's (D) population was made up of minorities, and Garden City (D) had no affordable housing, because the Garden City (D) community and leadership had repeatedly resisted the building of such housing. However, several of the communities surrounding Garden City (D) were "majority-minority," communities in which minorities made up a majority of the population. Desiring to raise money, Nassau County (D) planned to sell a multi-acre site it owned in Garden City (D) for development, and the county requested that Garden City (D) rezone the site. Garden City (D), led by a subcommittee of its Board of Trustees (the P-Zone Committee), hired planning firm, BFJ, to advise the best way to rezone the site. BFJ proposed applying "multi-family residential group" or "R-M" zoning controls to this property. R-M zoning would have allowed for the construction of up to 311 residential apartment units on the site, or 75 single-family homes. BFJ asserted that this rezoning would "be likely to generate a net tax benefit to the Village." When BFJ presented its proposal to the public for the first time, residents raised concerns about the impact of the rezoning on traffic and schools, so BFJ further analyzed these issues, and concluded that R-M zoning would still be the best zoning option. Around a year after the rezoning process had started, the P–Zone Committee adopted BFJ's recommendation for R-M zoning for the approval of the Board of Trustees, which unanimously accepted the recommendation a few months later. When the rezoning proposal was presented to the public, residents expressed a strong desire to preserve the single-family nature of Garden City (D), and were effectively opposed to the idea of multi-family housing. In response to public pressure, BFJ and Garden City (D) began modifying the rezoning proposal, and scrapped the R-M zoning proposal altogether within a few months. Instead, BFJ proposed rezoning the vast majority of the site "Residential-Townhouse" (R-T), an entirely new zoning classification. This proposal restricted development of multi-family housing to less than 15 percent of the site, and only by permit. Whereas the previous proposed rezoning took more than a year to come before the Board, the shift to R-T zoning moved rapidly through Garden City's (D) government. Residents supported the change to R-T zoning, the Board approved it very quickly, and it was enacted within weeks. Once the R-T zoning was in place, Nassau County (D) solicited bids for development, with a $30 million floor on bids. Affordable housing developers (P) concluded that it was not financially feasible to build affordable housing under R-T zoning restrictions at any acquisition price. The contract was awarded to Fairhaven Properties, Inc. (Fairhaven), a developer of single-family homes, for $56.5 million, the highest bid. Fairhaven proposed the development of 87 single-family detached homes, and did not include any townhouses. After the contract was awarded to Fairhaven, an affordable housing developer (NYAHC) (P) prepared four proposals, or "pro formas," for development at the site under the R-M zoning designation, with the percentage of affordable and/or Section 8 housing units of the 311 total rental units ranging from 15 percent to 25 percent. Its expert analyzed each proposal in conjunction

Continued on next page.

with the racial/ethnic distribution of the available pool of renters and determined that, had NYAHC (P) been able to build housing under any of the four proposals in accordance with the rejected R-M zoning designation, the pool of renters likely to occupy all units, including market-rate, affordable, and Section 8 units, would have likely been between 18 percent and 32 percent minority, with minority households numbering between 56 and 101. Under the proposal predicting 18 percent minority population, NYAHC (P) would have been able to bid $56.1 million for the site. The expert also opined that the likely racial composition of the pool of homeowners who could afford to purchase single-family units potentially developed by Fairhaven would be between three and six minority households. Thus, while the NYAHC (P) proposals would likely increase racial diversity in Garden City (D), the Fairhaven proposal would likely leave the racial composition of Garden City (D) "unchanged." Affordable housing developers (P) brought suit in federal district court under § 804 of the Fair Housing Act (FHA), also known as Title VIII of the Civil Rights Act of 1968, which prohibits, inter alia, discriminatory zoning on the basis of race or color, alleging that Garden City's (D) rezoning was discriminatory. The district court concluded, inter alia, that Garden City's (D) decision to abandon R-M zoning in favor of R-T zoning was made with discriminatory intent and was a knowing response to the vocal and racially influenced opposition among Garden City's (D) citizenry. The district court also determined that Garden City (D) was in violation of the FHA's disparate impact prong. In so doing, the district court applied the circuit's traditional test for disparate impact, rather than a test issued by the Secretary of Housing and Urban Development (HUD). Under both tests, a plaintiff must first establish a prima facie case by showing (1) the occurrence of certain outwardly neutral practices, and (2) a significantly adverse or disproportionate impact on persons of a particular type produced by the defendant's facially neutral acts or practices. Once a plaintiff has presented a prima facie case of disparate impact, the burden shifts to the defendant to prove its actions furthered, in theory and in practice, a legitimate, bona fide governmental interest. Under the circuit's test, the defendant must also prove that no alternative would serve that interest with less discriminatory effect. However, under the Secretary's test, if the defendant meets its burden, the burden of proof shifts back to the plaintiff to show that the substantial, legitimate, nondiscriminatory interests supporting the challenged practice could be served by another practice that has a less discriminatory effect. Garden City (D) appealed, contending that the district court's findings and rulings were erroneous, and that the district court should have applied the Secretary's test, not the traditional circuit test, and should have shifted the burden back to the plaintiffs to show that Garden City's (D) legitimate government interests could be served by means that had a less discriminatory effect. The court of appeals granted review.

ISSUE:

(1) Under § 804 of the Fair Housing Act (FHA), also known as Title VIII of the Civil Rights Act of 1968, may a district court find intentional racial discrimination on the basis of the negative racial impact a municipality's zoning decision will have, and on the basis of the sequence of events that led the municipality to reach its decision in response to public opposition to the prospect of affordable housing?

(2) Where the Secretary of Housing and Urban Development (HUD) has issued a burden-shifting disparate impact test under the Fair Housing Act (FHA), must a federal court apply that test where courts in the circuit have not held that the FHA is unambiguous as to disparate impact?

HOLDING AND DECISION: (Pooler, J.)

(1) Yes. Under § 804 of the Fair Housing Act (FHA), also known as Title VIII of the Civil Rights Act of 1968, a district court may find intentional racial discrimination on the basis of the negative racial impact a municipality's zoning decision will have, and on the basis of the sequence of events that led the municipality to reach its decision in response to public opposition to the prospect of affordable housing. The district court did not err here. A plaintiff can establish a prima facie case of disparate treatment by showing that animus against the protected group was a significant factor in the position taken by the municipal decision-makers themselves or by those to whom the decision-makers were knowingly responsive. Here, the district court premised its findings of intentional racial discrimination on statistical evidence that the original R-M proposal would have created a pool of potential renters with a significantly larger percentage of minority households than the pool of potential renters for the zoning proposal ultimately adopted as law by Garden City (D), and, more importantly, on the fact that after constant support for the R-M zoning proposal, BFJ and the Board abruptly reversed course in response to vocal citizen opposition to the possibility of multi-family housing, including complaints that affordable housing with undesirable residents could be built under this zoning. The district court permissibly focused on the suddenness of this change. Although the P–Zone Committee had consistently recommended R-M zoning for 18 months, R-T zoning went from proposal to enactment in a matter of weeks, and the

Continued on next page.

court noted that BFJ's consideration of R-T zoning was not nearly as comprehensive and deliberative as that for R-M zoning. Garden City (D) counters that because the interested stakeholders had discussed the zoning for over a year, there was no need to spend additional time discussing the same issues once they settled on a preferable lower-density approach, so that the quick approval of R-T zoning was actually just efficient local government. Although this may be one reasonable interpretation of the facts, the district court was nevertheless entitled to draw the contrary inference that the abandonment of R-M zoning was an abrupt change and that the not nearly as deliberative adoption of R-T zoning was suspect. The district court also considered numerous instances of strong citizen opposition to the R-M zoning on grounds that it would introduce affordable housing, and, with it, undesirable elements, into the municipality. The district court, viewing this opposition in light of (1) the racial makeup of Garden City (D), (2) the lack of affordable housing in Garden City (D), and (3) the likely number of minorities that would have lived in affordable housing at the site, concluded that Garden City (D) officials' abrupt change of course was a capitulation to citizen fears of affordable housing, which reflected race-based animus. The district court did not err in reaching this conclusion, since it could have reasonably concluded that the citizens' opposition, while not overtly race-based, was directed at a potential influx of poor, minority residents, and that the various citizen comments were code words for racial animus. Empirical evidence supports the reasonableness of the district court's conclusion. Indeed, research suggests that people believe that the majority of public housing residents are people of color, specifically, African American. Garden City (D) residents expressed concerns about their community becoming like communities with majority-minority populations. Moreover, a series of studies have shown that when Whites are asked why they would not want to live near African Americans (no income level is indicated in the question), common responses relate to the fear of property value decline, increasing crime, decreasing community quality (e.g., physical decay of housing, trash in neighborhoods, and unkempt lawns) and increasing violence. Repeatedly expressing concerns that R-M zoning would lead to a decline in their property values as well as reduced quality of life in their community, Garden City (D) residents urged the Board of Trustees to "keep Garden City what it is" and to "think of the people who live here." Considering these statements in context, the district court's conclusion that citizen opposition to R-M zoning utilized code words to communicate their race-based animus to Garden City (D) officials was not clearly erroneous. Once a plaintiff presents a prima facie case of discrimination, the burden shifts to the defendant to proffer a legitimate, non-discriminatory reason for its actions, and here the district court found that Garden City (D) met its minimal burden of production on this issue, as Garden City (D) contended that R-T zoning was adopted instead of R-M zoning because of concerns regarding traffic and school crowding, and because R-T zoning would facilitate the development of townhouses as a residential form. Where, as here, a defendant meets its burden of production, the plaintiff must show that the defendant's actions were based on a prohibited ground. To determine whether Garden City's (D) actions were motivated by racial animus, the district court analyzed whether it would have taken the same action solely on the basis of its purported legitimate reasons for rezoning. Reviewing these alternative rationales, the district court concluded that even accepting these legitimate reasons, Garden City (D) would not have adopted R-T zoning in the absence of discriminatory animus. For example, as to traffic concerns, the district court noted that traffic concerns became important to Garden City (D) officials only after the increase in public opposition to affordable housing, and that, in any event, record evidence suggested any decrease in traffic between R-M and R-T zoning was de minimis. Therefore, the district court did not err in questioning whether such concerns were sufficiently strong to cancel out any discriminatory animus. [Affirmed.]

(2) Yes. Where the Secretary of Housing and Urban Development (HUD) has issued a burden-shifting disparate impact test under the Fair Housing Act (FHA), a federal court must apply that test where courts in the circuit have not held that the FHA is unambiguous as to disparate impact. Here, the district court concluded that the affordable housing developers (P) had established a prima facie case of disparate impact, finding that Garden City's (D) rejection of R-M zoning in favor of R-T zoning had a significant disparate impact on minorities because it largely eliminated the potential for the type of housing that minorities were disproportionately likely to need—namely, affordable rental units. The district court also found that R-T zoning advanced certain legitimate, bona fide governmental interests, including reduced traffic and the construction of townhouses. However, because the district court applied the circuit's test, rather than the Secretary's test, the court held that Garden City (D) did not establish the absence of a less discriminatory alternative, thus effectively placing the burden on Garden City (D) as to this part

Continued on next page.

of the test. Accordingly, Garden City (D) argued that the district court erred in requiring it to prove the absence of a less discriminatory alternative. Under principles of administrative law, because Congress afforded HUD the authority to implement the FHA, the federal courts must defer to the agency's reasonable interpretation unless they have determined that "the intent of Congress is clear." In other words, the circuit's traditional test may only survive if it was previously held in this circuit that the circuit's construction of the FHA follows from the unambiguous terms of the statute and thus leaves no room for agency discretion. Because this circuit's courts did not hold that the statute was unambiguous, the courts in this circuit are obliged to defer to the more recent HUD regulations. Thus, although it is clear that the district court correctly concluded that the plaintiffs established a prima facie case of discriminatory impact—since the court found that the R-T zone's restriction on the development of multi-family housing perpetuates segregation generally because it decreases the availability of housing to minorities in a municipality where minorities constitute approximately only 4.1 percent of the overall population and only 2.6 percent of the population living in households—the case must be remanded to the district court for consideration of whether the plaintiffs satisfied their burden of proving an available alternative practice that has less disparate impact and serves Garden City's (D) legitimate nondiscriminatory interests or reducing traffic, reducing the strain on public schools, and building townhouses. [Vacated and remanded as to this part of the district court's decision.]

ANALYSIS

Section 804(a) of the Fair Housing Act (FHA), also known as Title VIII of the Civil Rights Act of 1968, makes it unlawful "[t]o refuse to sell or rent . . . or otherwise make unavailable or deny, a dwelling to any person because of race, color, . . . or national origin." 42 U.S.C. § 3604(a). The phrase "otherwise make unavailable" has been interpreted to reach a wide variety of discriminatory housing practices, including discriminatory zoning restrictions, and its results-oriented language has been interpreted as favoring the recognition of disparate-impact liability. Thus, the FHA provides for both discriminatory intent and disparate-impact liability.

The United States Court of Appeals for the Second Circuit rejected the plaintiffs' argument that, as a practical matter, the district court had placed the burden on the plaintiffs to show that R-M zoning was a less discriminatory alternative, since the district court had concluded that "Plaintiffs have established, by a preponderance of the evidence . . . [that] less discriminatory alternatives to the current zoning ordinance existed." The court of appeals instead ruled that it was clear that the district court shifted the burden to Garden City (D) to prove both a legitimate, bona fide governmental interest and "that no alternative would serve . . . with less discriminatory effect." The court of appeals reasoned that although the district court may have found Garden City's (D) reasons unpersuasive, that did not mean that the district court placed the burden of proof on the plaintiffs in accordance with the Secretary's test, found in 24 C.F.R. § 100.500(c)(3). To establish a prima facie case of disparate impact under the FHA, a plaintiff must show (1) the occurrence of certain outwardly neutral practices, and (2) a significantly adverse or disproportionate impact on persons of a particular type produced by the defendant's facially neutral acts or practices.

Quicknotes

ANIMUS Intention, will.

DE MINIMIS Insignificant; trivial; not of sufficient significance to require legal action.

DISCRIMINATORY IMPACT The effect of an action that affects one group of persons more significantly than another; insufficient to prove discriminatory intent on its own.

EMPIRICAL EVIDENCE Evidence based on observation or experimentation.

INTER ALIA Among other things.

PRIMA FACIE CASE An action where the plaintiff introduces sufficient evidence to submit the issue to the judge or jury for determination.

Janush v. Charities Housing Development Corp.

Tenant (P) v. Landlord (D)

169 F. Supp. 2d 1133 (N.D. Cal. 2000)

NATURE OF CASE: Federal district court's consideration of defendant's motion to dismiss plaintiff's claims of housing discrimination.

FACT SUMMARY: Janush (P) kept two birds and two cats in her apartment to help lessen the effects of her severe mental health disability. Her lease with Charities Housing Development Corp. (D) prohibited pets in the apartment.

RULE OF LAW

To establish a prima facie case of housing discrimination based upon a defendant/property owner's failure to provide a disabled person with a reasonable accommodation, the plaintiff must show: (1) the existence of a qualifying handicap; (2) the defendant/property owner was aware of the handicap; (3) the accommodation of the handicap may be necessary to afford the plaintiff the opportunity to use and enjoy the dwelling; and (4) the defendant/property owner refused to make the accommodation.

FACTS: Janush (P) kept two birds and two cats in her apartment to help lessen the effects of her severe mental health disability. Her lease with Charities Housing Development Corp. (D) (CHD) specifically prohibited pets in the apartment. In January of 2000, CHD (D) became aware of Janush's (P) pets and opened a dialogue with her as to whether she could keep the pets. Janush (P) alleges CHD (D) prohibited her from keeping the pets. CHD (D) alleges it offered Janush (P) the opportunity to keep the pets, but that Janush (P) failed to provide them with proof the animals had been vaccinated. CHD (D) eventually commenced the eviction process and Janush (P) moved out shortly thereafter. Janush (P) filed in federal court a housing discrimination claim based on CHD's (D) failure to provide her with a reasonable accommodation. CHD (D) moved to dismiss Janush's (P) claims on the ground that federal and state law only requires landlords to allow service dogs in apartments as reasonable accommodations. This decision is the federal district court's consideration of CHD's (D) motion to dismiss.

ISSUE: To establish a prima facie case of housing discrimination based upon a defendant/property owner's failure to provide a disabled person with a reasonable accommodation, must the plaintiff show: (1) the existence of a qualifying handicap; (2) the defendant/property owner was aware of the handicap; (3) the accommodation of the handicap may be necessary to afford the plaintiff the opportunity to use and enjoy the dwelling; and (4) the defendant/property owner refused to make the accommodation?

HOLDING AND DECISION: (Whyte, J.) Yes. To establish a prima facie case of housing discrimination based upon a defendant/property owner's failure to provide a disabled person with a reasonable accommodation, the plaintiff must show: (1) the existence of a qualifying handicap; (2) the defendant/property owner was aware of the handicap; (3) the accommodation of the handicap may be necessary to afford the plaintiff the opportunity to use and enjoy the dwelling; and (4) the defendant/property owner refused to make the accommodation. CHD (D) argues federal and state laws only require landlords to allow service dogs in apartments as reasonable accommodations. In addition, CHD (D) argues it will be inundated with similar requests if it must allow animals in apartments based upon vague allegations of reasonable accommodations. Although federal regulations do specifically cite seeing-eye dogs, there is nothing in the regulations or Fair Housing Act stating that accommodations for other animals are per se unreasonable. Under the regulations, "service animal" is given a broad definition. It includes dogs "or other animal" trained to perform tasks for the benefit of a disabled person. In addition, whether an accommodation is reasonable is typically a fact-intensive analysis. While a plaintiff's needs are considered, those needs must be balanced against the administrative and financial burdens placed upon the landlord to comply with the requested accommodations. At this stage of the litigation, CHD (D) has not produced any documents or evidence to support their claims of an unreasonable financial burden. This case requires additional discovery. Accordingly, Janush (P) has pled that she is handicapped and that CHD (D) was aware of the handicap. She has further alleged the accommodation may be necessary and that CHD (D) has refused. CHD's (D) motion to dismiss is denied.

ANALYSIS

When considering a motion to dismiss, a reviewing court takes the allegations in the plaintiff's complaint as true. It then reviews those allegations and makes a ruling of law whether the plaintiff has stated a prima facie legal claim that should proceed into the discovery phase of the litigation. A court only reviews the allegations in the complaint, does not consider any other outside evidence, and takes no notice of any factual

Continued on next page.

disputes. If the plaintiff fails to state a claim, a court may dismiss the action.

Quicknotes

MOTION TO DISMISS Motion to terminate an action based on the adequacy of the pleadings, improper service or venue, etc.

PRIMA FACIE CASE An action where the plaintiff introduces sufficient evidence to submit the issue to the judge or jury for determination.

Familystyle of St. Paul, Inc. v. City of St. Paul

Group home operator (P) v. City (D)

923 F.2d 91 (8th Cir. 1991)

NATURE OF CASE: Appeal from validation of deinstitutionalization ordinance.

FACT SUMMARY: When Familystyle of St. Paul, Inc. (P) was denied a permit to expand its capacity to house mentally ill persons by adding three homes to its existing campus, it challenged the City of St. Paul's (D) requirement that group homes be located at least a quarter mile apart.

RULE OF LAW

Legislation that requires dispersal of group homes is a legitimate means whereby a state may achieve its goal of deinstitutionalization of the mentally ill, and does not violate the Fair Housing Amendments Act of 1988.

FACTS: The State of Minnesota (D) required that all residential services for people with mental illness and retardation be licensed. In an attempt to deinstitutionalize the mentally ill and integrate them back into mainstream society, Minnesota (D) enacted a licensing regulation requiring new group homes to be spaced at least a quarter of a mile apart. The City of St. Paul's (D) zoning code contains the same dispersal requirement. Familystyle of St. Paul, Inc. (Familystyle) (P) operated group homes and provided rehabilitative services for mentally ill persons on its campus located in St. Paul. Familystyle (P) applied for a license to add three new homes to its campus, but the City of St. Paul (D) denied the application because it violated the dispersal requirement. Familystyle (P) filed suit alleging that Minnesota's (D) and the City of St. Paul's (D) dispersal requirements result in a disparate impact on and discriminatory treatment of the mentally ill, in violation of the Fair Housing Amendments Act of 1988. The district court found that the government's interest in deinstitutionalization sufficiently rebutted any discriminatory effect of the laws. Familystyle (P) appealed.

ISSUE: Is legislation that requires dispersal of group homes a legitimate means for a state to achieve its goal of deinstitutionalization of the mentally ill, and not a violation of the Fair Housing Amendments Act of 1988?

HOLDING AND DECISION: (Wollman, J.) Yes. Legislation that requires dispersal of group homes is a legitimate means whereby a state may achieve its goal of deinstitutionalization of the mentally ill and does not violate the Fair Housing Amendments Act of 1988. First of all, in a Title VIII case, the plaintiff has the initial burden of establishing the discriminatory effect of the challenged law. Once such an effect is shown to disparately impact a nonsuspect class like the mentally ill, the burden shifts to the government to demonstrate that its legislation was rationally related to a legitimate government purpose. In this case, although local and state dispersal requirements for group homes on their face limit housing choices for the mentally ill, the government's method of dispersing group homes was rationally related to its goal of integrating the mentally ill into the mainstream of society. Affirmed.

ANALYSIS

The Fair Housing Act (FHA) prohibits discrimination on the basis of race, color, religion, sex, familial status, handicap, or national origin. Most FHA cases involve alleged discrimination on the basis of race, color, or national origin. Very few cases are brought under the FHA based on gender. However, in *Doe v. City of Butler*, 892 F.2d 315 (3d Cir. 1989), a zoning ordinance that limited group homes to six persons was challenged as gender discrimination when applied to a home for abused women. The court validated the ordinance, finding no intention to discriminate against women, since the provision applied equally to group homes for men. On the other hand, the court condemned as discriminatory a landlord's refusal to rent to a group of males because he believed that male tenants were dirtier than female tenants, in *Baumgardner v. HUD*, 960 F.2d 572 (6th Cir. 1992).

Quicknotes

DISCRIMINATORY IMPACT The effect of an action that affects one group of persons more significantly than another; insufficient to prove discriminatory intent on its own.

REBUT A defendant's refuting of evidence that raises a presumption as to his liability.

M & T Mortgage Corp. v. Foy

Mortgage company (P) v. Homeowner (D)

N.Y. Sup. Ct., 20 Misc. 3d 274 (2008)

NATURE OF CASE: Trial court's interim decision regarding applicable burden of proof in foreclosure proceeding.

FACT SUMMARY: M & T Mortgage Corp. (P) brought foreclosure proceedings against Major Jahn K. Foy (D). Foy (D), a reserve army officer on active duty, sought a hearing to reform the mortgage.

RULE OF LAW

A mortgage granted to a minority buyer with an interest rate that exceeds nine percent creates a rebuttable presumption of discriminatory practice.

FACTS: M & T Mortgage Corp. (M & T) (P) brought this foreclosure action against Major Jahn K. Foy (D), a reserve officer who has served several active duty tours in recent years. Foy (D), a minority living in a minority neighborhood of Brooklyn, sought to modify the terms of the mortgage. The mortgage had an interest rate of nine percent. The court granted a hearing on Foy's (D) motion and had previously ordered that Foy (D) prove that she was the victim of discriminatory lending. In this decision, the trial court now modifies that order.

ISSUE: Does a mortgage granted to a minority buyer with an interest rate that exceeds nine percent create a rebuttable presumption of discriminatory practice?

HOLDING AND DECISION: (Kramer, J.) Yes. A mortgage granted to a minority buyer with an interest rate that exceeds nine percent creates a rebuttable presumption of discriminatory practice. First, the court now modifies its previous order regarding burden of proof. It appears from the record that Foy (D) may have been a victim of "reverse redlining," the practice of extending unfair loans to minority communities. After researching the issue, the burden is now on M & T (P) to demonstrate that the loan is not a "higher priced loan" given as a result of discriminatory practices on the part of M & T (P). A higher priced loan has an interest rate that is three percentage points higher than the normal interest rate for 30-year loans. In 2005, the Federal Reserve published findings of interest rate data. From those findings, we learned that under-served minority groups were more likely than other populations to pay higher prices for mortgages. The mortgage in the instant case qualifies as a higher priced loan, due to its interest rate of nine percent. The court holds that loans exceeding nine percent create the rebuttable presumption of discrimination on the part of the lender. The burden is therefore placed on M & T (P) to produce evidence that the mortgage was granted for other, economic reasons.

ANALYSIS

Many times the judiciary, rather than the executive branch of state government, will be the vehicle to protect under-represented minority groups that are the victims of predatory lending. Here, the court, in an action brought by M & T (P), raised the issue of the high interest rate on its own. It then fashioned an equitable remedy to place the burden of proof on the foreclosing lender that the mortgage was not discriminatory.

Quicknotes

BURDEN OF PROOF The duty of a party to introduce evidence to support a fact that is in dispute in an action.

REBUTTABLE PRESUMPTION A rule of law inferred from the existence of a particular set of facts, that is conclusive in the absence of contrary evidence.

CHAPTER 13

Takings Law

Quick Reference Rules of Law

Kelo v. City of New London

Landowner (P) v. Municipality (D)

545 U.S 469 (2005)

NATURE OF CASE: Appeal from a decision of the Supreme Court of Connecticut allowing a municipality to exercise eminent domain.

FACT SUMMARY: Landowners (Kelo) (P) brought suit against the City of New London (D) alleging that the condemnation of their property by use of eminent domain was an illegal "taking" in violation of the Fifth Amendment.

RULE OF LAW

A development plan to revitalize an economically distressed city involving the acquisition of property by the power of eminent domain qualifies as a "public use" within the meaning of the Takings Clause of the Fifth Amendment.

FACTS: After having experienced decades of economic decline, the City of New London (City) (D) approved a development plan to revitalize its downtown and waterfront areas. The City's (D) development agent purchased property toward that aim from willing sellers and utilized eminent domain to acquire additional properties needed in exchange for just compensation. The plan involved Pfizer, Inc., a pharmaceutical company, building a research facility on the property and the City (D) believed this would stimulate the local economy by creating jobs and tax revenue. Nine people (Kelo, et al.) (P) owning 15 properties resisted. Kelo (P), along with the others, brought suit in the circuit court alleging that their property was not blighted but was only condemned because it was located within the development area. Kelo (P) maintained that the "taking" of their property by use of eminent domain violated the "public use" requirement of the Fifth Amendment. The trial court enjoined the "taking" of part of the properties, but the Connecticut Supreme Court held that all of the City's (D) proposed takings were valid. The United State Supreme Court granted certiorari.

ISSUE: Does a development plan to revitalize an economically distressed city involving the acquisition of property by the power of eminent domain qualify as a "public use" within the meaning of the Takings Clause of the Fifth Amendment?

HOLDING AND DECISION: (Stevens, J.) Yes. A development plan to revitalize an economically distressed city involving the acquisition of property by the power of eminent domain qualifies as a "public use" within the meaning of the Takings Clause of the Fifth Amendment. This is not an instance where a municipality is "taking" property for the purpose of transferring it to a private party. Nor is this an instance where the City (D) is planning to open the condemned land to the public. This is a case where the Court must determine if the transfer of condemned property somehow diminishes the public purpose of the taking. The concept of a "public purpose" or the "public welfare" must be painted with a broad and inclusive brush. The City (D) has carefully formulated an economic development plan to provide benefits to the community at large in terms of jobs and increased tax revenue. Promoting economic development has long been recognized as an accepted function of government. The government's pursuit of public purpose will often benefit private parties. This alone is not fatal to the plan because this case does not present the Court with a singular transfer of property from a private citizen to that of a private business enterprise. Nor is there a requirement that there must be reasonable certainty that public benefits will actually flow from the plan. "Because the plan unquestionably serves a public purpose, the 'takings' challenged here satisfy the public use requirement of the Fifth Amendment." This holding does not in any way restrict individual states from imposing additional restrictions to the public use requirement that are much stricter than the federal baseline. The judgment is affirmed.

CONCURRENCE: (Kennedy, J.) The Court holds that a "taking" is upheld if it is rationally related to a conceivable public purpose. The Court should also note that under this rational basis review a "taking" is not appropriate when a transfer of property favors private entities and there is merely an incidental or pretextual public benefit.

DISSENT: (O'Connor, J.) The Court abandons the basic principles in the Bill of Rights and uses the banner of economic development to clothe the illegal transfer of individually owned property to private business entities for any reason the legislature may deem to constitute a public benefit. Nearly any lawful use of private property can be said to generate some incidental benefit to the public, and today's holding expands the use of eminent domain to the point where pretext alone will determine a property's fate. Economic development "takings" are not constitutional.

DISSENT: (Thomas, J.) The proper reading of the public use clause is that it allows the government to take property only if the government owns, or the public has a right to use, the property, as opposed to "taking" it for any

Continued on next page.

purpose whatsoever. Extending the public purpose doctrine to encompass any economic development guarantees that the losses of property will fall disproportionately on poor communities who are the least politically powerful. Urban renewal projects have long been associated with the displacement of minorities and today's holding will further exacerbate these effects.

ANALYSIS

The courts have seesawed over the proper interpretation of the public use doctrine. Some have advocated the position of Justice Kennedy that the benefits of the intended use predominate over the private nature of the use. Others have followed the test that the property cannot be "taken" unless the nature of the property justifies the "taking." Others would restrict the doctrine to that of any property being "taken" must then be publicly owned, such as for use in building highways. This view would deny private parties from being somehow incorporated into a public redevelopment plan. It would appear that the Court's vacillation is over. Economic "takings," if benefiting the public in some imagined tangible way are now deemed constitutional. The Court's holding in this case has been one of the most controversial issued in recent times. It has sparked a backlash of state legislation designed to reign in the use of eminent domain.

Quicknotes

EMINENT DOMAIN The governmental power to take private property for public use so long as just compensation is paid therefor.

FIFTH AMENDMENT Provides that no person shall be compelled to serve as a witness against himself, or be subject to trial for the same offense twice, or be deprived of life, liberty, or property without due process of law.

PUBLIC USE Basis for governmental taking of property pursuant to its power of eminent domain so that property taken may be utilized for the benefit of the public at large.

TAKINGS CLAUSE Provisions of the Fifth Amendment to the United States Constitution prohibiting the government from taking private property for public use without providing just compensation therefor.

Tee-Hit-Ton Indians v. United States

Tribe (P) v. Federal government (D)

348 U.S. 272 (1955)

NATURE OF CASE: Appeal from claim of taking under the Fifth Amendment.

FACT SUMMARY: The Tee-Hit-Ton Indians (P) claimed that the United States government's contract to sell Alaskan timber constituted a taking of their property.

RULE OF LAW

Mere possession does not constitute ownership for the purposes of the Fifth Amendment.

FACTS: The Tee-Hit-Ton Indians (Tee-Hit-Tons) (P) claimed that they had exercised property rights in the Alaskan territories since time immemorial. Before the Russians came to Alaska, the Tee-Hit-Tons (P) communally owned the land, occupied its expanse, and passed ownership rights through the female line. When the Russians came to Alaska, they occupied the same land with the Tee-Hit-Ton's (P) permission. In 1951, the federal government (D) began selling timber in the Alaskan territories to private entities. The Tee-Hit-Tons (P) brought suit under the Takings Clause of the Fifth Amendment of the United States Constitution. The court of claims found no ownership rights. The Tee-Hit Tons (P) appealed, and the United States Supreme Court granted certiorari.

ISSUE: Does mere possession constitute ownership for the purposes of the Fifth Amendment?

HOLDING AND DECISION: (Reed, J.) No. Mere possession does not constitute ownership for the purposes of the Fifth Amendment. The Tee-Hit-Tons (P) claimed that their use of the land differed from other Native Americans because they claimed tribal ownership, and this constitutes ownership requiring compensation. The Alaskan Indians' use of land might be more substantial than that of other North American Indian tribes, but it gives rise only to the level of sovereignty, not ownership. The United States Constitution does not require compensation without a showing of a property right. The Tee-Hit-Tons (P) do not have ownership. Thus their claim must be denied. Affirmed.

DISSENT: (Douglas, J.) The legislative debate surrounding Section 8 of the first Organic Act for Alaska passed in 1884 demonstrates that congressional intent was to prevent any possible invasion into the rights of Indian residents of Alaska except as was necessary to establish title to mining claims in the territory. Congress recognized the claims that the Indians of Alaska had in these lands. That purpose is now totally contradicted by this Court's interpretation that Congress reserved the issue of title to all of these lands for some future day where those rights may be extinguished without compensation.

ANALYSIS

In 1971, Congress passed the Alaska Native Claims Settlement Act, which compensated Alaskan natives for the taking of their lands without recognizing any actual property rights on their part. Congress ultimately reimbursed the tribes $962.5 million in order to extinguish 335 million land claims. It also transferred 40 million acres of federal land as part of the settlement.

Quicknotes

CERTIORARI A discretionary writ issued by a superior court to an inferior court in order to review the lower court's decisions; the Supreme Court's writ ordering such review.

POSSESSION The holding of property with the right of disposition.

PROPRIETARY OWNERSHIP Exclusive ownership or dominion over property held by a particular person in his own right.

Penn Central Transportation Co. v. New York City

Railroad company (P) v. City (D)

438 U.S.104 (1978)

NATURE OF CASE: Appeal from action claiming that a statute affected a "taking" of property without just compensation in violation of the Fifth and Fourteenth Amendments of the United States Constitution.

FACT SUMMARY: Because Penn Central Transportation Co.'s (P) terminal was declared a "landmark" under New York's Landmark Preservation Law, restrictions were placed on the use and alteration of the terminal site.

RULE OF LAW

A landmark preservation statute that restricts the exploitation of sites determined to be "landmarks" does not affect a "taking" of the property so designated for a public use within the meaning of the Fifth Amendment.

FACTS: New York City's Landmark Preservation Law provided for a commission to designate a building as a "landmark" and allowed the property owner to seek judicial review of the decision. Although it opposed designation of its Grand Central Terminal as a "landmark," Penn Central Transportation Co. (Penn Central) (P) did not seek such judicial review of the designation decision nor of the subsequent decision disallowing construction of a multi-story office building over the terminal. The building project was part of a lease agreement with Union General Properties (UGP) under which UGP was to construct the office building and lease it for $3,000,000 a year, also paying $1,000,000 during construction thereof. Claiming that failure to permit construction of the building called for in this 50-year lease agreement had severely restricted the use of its property, Penn Central (P) brought suit in state court. They argued that the application of the Landmark Law had "taken" their property without just compensation in violation of the Fifth and Fourteenth Amendments and arbitrarily deprived them of property without due process of law. Although the trial court granted relief, the court of appeals reversed, finding that there had been no "taking" because the property was not transferred to the control of the City of New York (D), but was simply subject to restrictions on its exploitation. It was also held that no denial of due process had occurred because the same use of the terminal that was presently going on could continue, there had been no showing that a reasonable return on the investment in the terminal could not be realized by continuing such use, and the fact that development rights above the terminal were specifically made transferable, by the Landmark Law, to other property in the vicinity owned by Penn Central (P) provided significant compensation for any loss of use of the air rights above the terminal itself. From that decision, Penn Central (P) appealed.

ISSUE: If an owner is restricted in the exploitation of his property because it had been designated as a "landmark" under a landmark preservation statute, has there been a "taking" of his property for a public use within the meaning of the Fifth Amendment?

HOLDING AND DECISION: (Brennan, J.) No. The fact that an owner's use or exploitation of his property has been restricted by a landmark preservation statute because it has been designated a "landmark" does not mean that there has been a "taking" of his property for a public use within the meaning of the Fifth Amendment. It is untenable to suggest that a "taking" is established by simply showing that Penn Central (P) has been denied the ability to exploit a property interest that they heretofore had believed was available for development. Nor can diminution in property value, standing alone, establish a "taking." If that were the case, zoning laws could never be upheld. The argument that landmark laws, per se, constitute something akin to discriminatory or "reverse spot" zoning, arbitrarily singling out particular parcels for different and less favorable treatment than neighboring ones, is not compelling. In this case, the landmark legislation involves a comprehensive plan to preserve structures of historic or aesthetic interest wherever they might be found. The decision to designate property as a "landmark" might be somewhat subjective, but it is not arbitrary or unprincipled. Like zoning laws, the Landmark Law may impact more severely on some property owners than others in attempting to promote the general welfare, but that does not in and of itself mean that it "effects" a "taking." In any event, it is not true that Penn Central (P) is solely burdened and unbenefited, the preservation of landmarks being of benefit to all the citizens of New York City both economically and in improving the quality of life in the city as a whole. Nor is this a case where the government has appropriated part of Penn Central's (P) property for its own use, the restrictions on use of the air space above the terminal being akin to the constitutionally valid zoning law that prohibits, for "aesthetic" reasons, two or more adult theatres within a specified area. Here, the basic inquiry is whether or not there has been interference of such magnitude with Penn Central's (P) property as to require an exercise of eminent domain and compensation

Continued on next page.

to sustain it. In that it does not prevent Penn Central (P) from continuing to make reasonable beneficial use of the terminal, the law does not interfere with what must be regarded as Penn Central's (P) primary expectation concerning the use of the parcel. Furthermore, Penn Central's (P) right to the air space above the terminal has not been totally denied. Other plans to build above the terminal might be approved if they harmonized with its character. Most importantly, however, right to exploit the air space above the terminal is transferable to other local parcels on which the desired office building could be constructed. This scheme lessens the severity of impact of the law on the property in question and thereby prevents it from affecting a "taking" under the Fifth Amendment. Affirmed.

DISSENT: (Rehnquist, J.) In this case, only a few property owners must bear the expense associated with the City's (D) desire to preserve a limited number of landmarks. Thus, any analogy to zoning is inappropriate. Zoning places all property owners in an area under similar restrictions for their common benefit as well as for the benefit of the municipality, but such "average reciprocity of advantage" is absent in this case. A few buildings are singled out, all separated from one another, and treated differently from surrounding buildings. In essence, substantial property rights were taken from Penn Central (P). The two exceptions in which such will not constitute a "taking," where the forbidden use constitutes a nuisance or where the prohibition arises from proper zoning laws. Finally, the Landmark Law imposes on a few the cost of preserving landmarks instead of spreading it among everyone. This is precisely the sort of discrimination the Fifth Amendment prohibits, and so the action taken by New York City (D) constituted a "taking" of Penn Central's (P) property. As such, Penn Central (P) is entitled to just compensation, which requires that it receive "a full and perfect equivalent for the property taken" and not simply an approximate compensation. The case should be remanded to determine if the transfer rights afforded by the Landmark Law met this standard of compensation.

ANALYSIS

Many jurisdictions now have what is called "historic zoning" legislation, which obligates owners of historic buildings to preserve and maintain the exterior appearance. Although this imposes a direct financial burden instead of simply limiting use of the property, such laws have consistently been upheld.

Quicknotes

NUISANCE An unlawful use of property that interferes with the lawful use of another's property.

TAKING A governmental action that substantially deprives an owner of the use and enjoyment of his or her property, requiring compensation.

Lucas v. South Carolina Coastal Council

Land developer (P) v. State (D)

505 U.S. 1003 (1992)

NATURE OF CASE: Appeal of the denial of a "taking" claim in action for compensation of property value.

FACT SUMMARY: South Carolina's (D) Beachfront Management Act barred Lucas (P) from erecting homes on two parcels of land near the ocean.

RULE OF LAW

The state must compensate a landowner when a regulatory action denies the owner economically viable use of the land, unless the prohibited use constitutes a nuisance.

FACTS: In 1986, Lucas (P) bought two residential lots near the ocean for $975,000. In 1988, South Carolina (D) enacted the Beachfront Management Act, which sought to counteract coastal erosion. The law restricted new development of beachfront areas and barred Lucas (P) from building homes on his lots as he intended. Lucas (P) brought suit contending that the Act was an unconstitutional "taking" of his property. The trial court ruled that the Act deprived Lucas (P) of any reasonable economic use of the land and was an uncompensated "taking." The South Carolina Supreme Court reversed, holding that the regulation was designed to prevent serious public harm and did not constitute a "taking." Lucas (P) appealed, and the United States Supreme Court granted review.

ISSUE: Must the state compensate a landowner when a regulatory action denies an owner economically viable use of the land, unless the prohibited use constitutes a nuisance?

HOLDING AND DECISION: (Scalia, J.) Yes. The state must compensate a landowner when a regulatory action denies an owner economically viable use of his land, unless the prohibited use constitutes a nuisance. Physical intrusions on property must always be compensated. A regulation that denies all economically beneficial and productive uses of land is the equivalent of physical appropriation and must also be compensated under the Takings Clause. The Court has previously acknowledged that regulations that restrict nuisance-like uses of land may provide an exception to the general rule on takings. The court of appeals attempted to distinguish laws that prevented harmful use from those regulations that confer benefits on the public. This distinction should not provide the basis for our determinations because it is impossible to objectively distinguish the two rationales. The better rule is that the government may only restrict uses that are already unlawful under existing nuisance and property laws. South Carolina's (D) Beachfront Management Act deprived Lucas's (P) land of all economically beneficial use and restricted uses that were previously permissible. Therefore, it was an unconstitutional "taking." Reversed and remanded.

CONCURRENCE: (Kennedy, J.) The trial court's finding that Lucas's (P) land had been deprived of all beneficial use is highly questionable. Furthermore, the nuisance exception should not be the sole justification for severe restrictions when the state's unique concerns for fragile land systems are involved.

DISSENT: (Blackmun, J.) Lucas (P) may continue to use his land for recreation and camping and retains the right to alienate the land. Therefore, the trial court's ruling that the property had lost all economic value is certainly erroneous. The majority opinion today creates regulatory takings in all instances with the limited exception for common-law nuisances. In addition, our prior case law has upheld prohibitions without compensation on uses of property that are injurious to the health, morals, and safety of the community.

DISSENT: (Stevens, J.) The majority's categorical approach, which attempts to reduce "takings" to a set formula, does not take into account the complex problems involved in environmental regulation. The determination is properly made by balancing the private and public interests involved.

DISSENT: (Souter, J.) [Justice Souter wrote separately to indicate that he felt the writ of certiorari was improvidently granted because the state supreme court did not review the trial court's factual conclusion that Lucas (P) had been deprived of all viable use of his property. Without such a review by the state supreme court, the Court should have demurred.]

ANALYSIS

This case established the Supreme Court's "total takings" rule, meaning that one must be compensated only where the regulatory taking removes all economically viable options for the land. Partial but permanent restrictions of the uses of land were not discussed in the majority opinion.

Continued on next page.

Quicknotes

FIFTH AMENDMENT Provides that no person shall be compelled to serve as a witness against himself, or be subject to trial for the same offense twice, or be deprived of life, liberty, or property without due process of law.

POLICE POWERS Power of a state or local government to regulate private conduct for the health, safety, and welfare of the general public.

PUBLIC NUISANCE An activity that unreasonably interferes with a right common to the overall public.

REGULATORY TAKING A governmental action that substantially deprives an owner of the use and enjoyment of his property, whereby the application of a law or regulation deprives the owner of economically viable use of his property, requiring compensation.

PruneYard Shopping Center v. Robins

Shopping center owner (D) v. Students distributing pamphlets requesting signatures on petitions (P)

447 U.S. 74 (1980)

NATURE OF CASE: Appeal from decision permitting politically oriented solicitation on private property.

FACT SUMMARY: PruneYard Shopping Center (D) contended that a California decision mandating that it permit political activity on its property violated the Fifth Amendment.

RULE OF LAW

A state may constitutionally mandate that a private property owner allow political activity on its property.

FACTS: Robins and others (Robins) (P)—high school students—handed out political materials on retail property owned by PruneYard Shopping Center, Inc. (PruneYard) (D). They also asked passersby to sign petitions, which were to be sent to the President and members of Congress. They were peaceful and orderly. PruneYard (D) has a policy not to permit any visitor or tenant to engage in any publicly expressive activity, including the circulating of petitions. After Robins (P) began soliciting signatures, a PruneYard (D) security guard told them they would have to leave because their activity violated PruneYard's (D) policy. The guard suggested they move to the public sidewalk on the perimeter of PruneYard's property. Robins (P) immediately left the premises and later filed suit, contending they had a constitutional right to distribute literature and circulate petitions on the PruneYard premises. The California Supreme Court ruled that, under the California constitution, such a right existed. PruneYard (D) appealed, contending that this ruling deprived it of its property rights, in contravention of the Fifth and Fourteenth Amendments.

ISSUE: May a state constitutionally mandate that a private property owner allow political activity on its property?

HOLDING AND DECISION: (Rehnquist, J.) Yes. A state may mandate that a private property owner allow political activity on its property without violating the Fifth and Fourteenth Amendments. It is true that the right to exclude others is one of the inherent elements of property rights, so long as the property's value is not so diminished that the owner has suffered a "taking." Here, there is no evidence that PruneYard (D) has suffered any diminution in property value, so no taking has occurred. Affirmed.

CONCURRENCE AND DISSENT: (Blackmun, J.) The federal government may be possessed of authority to define what is property.

CONCURRENCE: (Marshall, J.) This Court should adopt the rule adopted by the California Supreme Court. PruneYard's (D) argument that the state is without power to revise the common law of trespass is without merit. That would return the law to the era of *Lochner v. New York*, 198 U.S. 45 (1905), where common-law rights were paramount to the detriment of state regulation. On the other hand, there are limits to the extent the state may step in to revise those common-law rights.

CONCURRENCE: (Powell, Jr., J.) The state may not compel a person to affirm a belief he does not hold. A property owner may be faced with speakers who wish to use his premises as a platform for views that he finds morally repugnant. The strong emotions evoked by speech in such situations may virtually compel the proprietor to respond. However, the record gives no indication that the customers of this vast center would be likely to assume that Robins's (P) limited speech activity expressed the views of the PruneYard (D) or of its owner.

ANALYSIS

The federal Constitution creates a certain floor, in terms of rights, that states may not go below. States are free to exceed the federal Constitution in terms of rights, if they so choose. The underlying California Supreme Court case here is an example. That Court created a freedom-of-expression right the United States Supreme Court does not recognize.

Quicknotes

DUE PROCESS The constitutional mandate requiring the courts to protect and enforce individuals' rights and liberties consistent with prevailing principles of fairness and justice and prohibiting the federal and state governments from such activities that deprive its citizens of a life, liberty, or property interest.

TAKING A governmental action that substantially deprives an owner of the use and enjoyment of his or her property, requiring compensation.

Cedar Point Nursery v. Hassid

Agricultural employer (P) v. State official (D)

141 S. Ct. 2063 (2021)

NATURE OF CASE: Appeal from affirmance of denial of declaratory and injunctive relief in action challenging as an unconstitutional, per se uncompensated taking, a state regulation permitting union organizers to enter onto the property of agricultural employers for the purpose of organizing workers under limited circumstances.

FACT SUMMARY: Two agricultural employers (P), Cedar Point Nursery (P) and Fowler Packing Co. (P), contended that a regulation promulgated by the California Agricultural Labor Relations Board (D) permitting union organizers onto their properties under limited circumstances effected an unconstitutional per se physical taking. They sought declaratory and injunctive relief prohibiting the enforcement of the regulation against them.

RULE OF LAW

A state regulation that grants labor organizations a right to access an agricultural employer's property to solicit support for unionization under specified, limited conditions constitutes a per se uncompensated taking under the Fifth and Fourteenth Amendments.

FACTS: A California regulation promulgated by the California Agricultural Labor Relations Board (D), granted labor organizations a "right to take access" to an agricultural employer's property to solicit support for unionization. The regulation mandated that agricultural employers had to allow union organizers onto their property for up to three hours per day, 120 days per year. Organizers from the United Farm Workers sought to take access to property owned by two agricultural employers (P)— Cedar Point Nursery (P) and Fowler Packing Co. (P). The agricultural employers (P) filed suit in federal district court seeking to enjoin enforcement of the access regulation on the grounds that it appropriated without compensation an easement for union organizers to enter their property and therefore constituted an unconstitutional per se physical taking under the Fifth and Fourteenth Amendments. The district court denied the agricultural employers' (P) motion for a preliminary injunction and dismissed the complaint, holding that the access regulation did not constitute a per se physical taking because it did not allow the public to access the agricultural employers' (P) property in a permanent and continuous manner. The court of appeals affirmed, and the United States Supreme Court granted certiorari.

ISSUE: Does a state regulation that grants labor organizations a right to access an agricultural employer's property to solicit support for unionization under specified, limited conditions constitute a per se uncompensated taking under the Fifth and Fourteenth Amendments?

HOLDING AND DECISION: (Roberts, C.J.) Yes. A state regulation that grants labor organizations a right to access an agricultural employer's property to solicit support for unionization under specified, limited conditions constitutes a per se uncompensated taking under the Fifth and Fourteenth Amendments. The Takings Clause of the Fifth Amendment, applicable to the states through the Fourteenth Amendment, provides: "[N]or shall private property be taken for public use, without just compensation." When the government physically acquires private property for a public use, the Takings Clause obligates the government to provide the owner with just compensation. The Court assesses such physical takings using a per se rule: The government must pay for what it takes. A different standard applies when the government, rather than appropriating private property for itself or a third party, instead imposes regulations restricting an owner's ability to use his own property. To determine whether such a use restriction amounts to a taking, the Court has generally applied the flexible approach set forth in *Penn Central Transportation Co. v. New York City*, 438 U.S. 104 (1978), considering factors such as the economic impact of the regulation, its interference with reasonable investment-backed expectations, and the character of the government action. However, when the government physically appropriates property, *Penn Central* has no place in the analysis—regardless whether the government action takes the form of a regulation, statute, ordinance, or decree. Here, the access regulation appropriates a right to invade the agricultural employers' (P) property and therefore constitutes a per se physical taking. Rather than restraining the agricultural employers" (P) use of their own property, the regulation appropriates for the enjoyment of third parties (here union organizers) the owners' right to exclude. The right to exclude is a "fundamental element of the property right," *Kaiser Aetna v. United States*, 444 U.S. 164, 180 (1979), and the Court's precedents have accordingly treated government-authorized physical invasions as takings requiring just compensation regardless whether they cause only trivial economic loss. The Court has often described the property interest taken as a servitude or easement. As in those previous cases,

Continued on next page.

the government here has appropriated a right of access to private property. Because the regulation appropriates a right to physically invade the agricultural employers' (P) property—to literally "take access"—it constitutes a per se physical taking under the Court's precedents. The view that the access regulation cannot qualify as a per se taking because it does not allow for permanent and continuous access 24 hours a day, 365 days a year is insupportable. The Court has held that a physical appropriation is a taking whether it is permanent or temporary; the duration of the appropriation bears only on the amount of compensation due. The regulation here is not transformed from a physical taking into a use restriction just because the access granted is restricted to union organizers, for a narrow purpose, and for a limited time, as it is undisputed that absent the regulation, the agricultural employers (P) would have the right to exclude the union organizers from their property. The Court has recognized that the government can commit a physical taking either by appropriating property through a condemnation proceeding or by simply entering into physical possession of property without authority of a court order. Any other result would allow the government to appropriate private property without just compensation so long as it avoids formal condemnation, a result that has never been tolerated. The Court's decision in *PruneYard Shopping Center v. Robins,* 447 U.S. 74 (1980), does not cut against the conclusion that the access regulation here constitutes a per se taking. In *PruneYard* the California Supreme Court recognized a right to engage in leafleting at the *PruneYard*, a privately owned shopping center, and the Court applied the *Penn Central* factors to hold that no compensable taking had occurred. *PruneYard* does not establish that limited rights of access to private property should be evaluated as regulatory rather than per se takings. Restrictions on how a business generally open to the public such as the *PruneYard* may treat individuals on the premises are readily distinguishable from regulations granting a right to invade property closed to the public. The California Agricultural Labor Relations Board's (D) fear that treating the access regulation as a per se physical taking will endanger a host of state and federal government activities involving entry onto private property is unfounded. First, the Court's holding does nothing to efface the distinction between trespass and takings. The Court's precedents make clear that isolated physical invasions, not undertaken pursuant to a granted right of access, are properly assessed as individual torts rather than appropriations of a property right. Second, many government-authorized physical invasions will not amount to takings because they are consistent with longstanding background restrictions on property rights, including traditional common-law privileges to access private property. Third, the government may require property owners to cede a right of access as a condition of receiving certain benefits, without causing a taking. Under this framework, government health and safety inspection regimes will generally not constitute takings. In this case, however, none of these considerations undermine the Court's determination that the access regulation gives rise to a per se physical taking. Reversed and remanded.

DISSENT: (Breyer, J.) The majority holds that the regulation at issue amounts to a physical appropriation of property and that nearly every government-authorized invasion is such an appropriation. However, the regulation appropriates nothing, but instead regulates an employer's right to exclude others. It is a temporary invasion, which precedent holds is not a taking unless it goes "too far." See, e.g., *Loretto v. Teleprompter Manhattan CATV Corp.*, 458 U.S. 419, 434 (1982). Such precedent holds that temporary takings are not per se takings, and that they are not takings if they do not unreasonably impair the value or use of the property as it is currently used. The regulation at bar grants a small group of people the right to enter private property for a limited time to speak about a specific subject—a much lesser invasion than similar, less circumscribed invasions that the Court previously held were not per se takings. Accordingly, the majority is wrong to characterize the regulation at bar, or similar regulations, as a per se taking. Recognizing that the categorical, per se rule it announces likely will lead to adverse results, given the large numbers of ordinary regulations in a host of different fields that, for a variety of purposes, permit temporary entry onto a property owner's land, e.g., inspections of all sorts, the majority attempts to create exceptions to this per se rule. It says: (1) "Isolated physical invasions, not undertaken pursuant to a granted right of access, are properly assessed as individual torts rather than appropriations of a property right." It also would except from its per se rule (2) government access that is "consistent with longstanding background restrictions on property rights," including "traditional common-law privileges to access private property." Third, it adds that (3) "the government may require property owners to cede a right of access as a condition of receiving certain benefits, without causing a taking." These exceptions raise numerous questions. As to the first exception, what will count as "isolated"? How is an "isolated physical invasion" different from a "temporary" invasion, and where should one draw the line between trespass and takings? As to the second exception, a court must focus on "traditional common-law privileges to access private property." Just what are they? Do only those exceptions that existed in, say, 1789 count? Should courts apply those privileges as they existed at that time, when there were no union organizers? Or do we bring some exceptions (but not others) up to date, e.g., a necessity exception for preserving animal habitats? And, as to the third, what is the scope of the

Continued on next page.

phrase "certain benefits"? Does it include, for example, the benefit of being able to sell meat labeled "inspected" in interstate commerce? What about the benefit of having electricity? Of sewage collection? Of internet accessibility? Myriad regulatory schemes based on just these sorts of benefits depend upon intermittent, temporary government entry onto private property. In the instant case, labor peace brought about through union organizing is one such benefit, at least in the view of elected representatives, who may well have believed that union organizing brings with it "benefits," including community health and educational benefits, higher standards of living, and labor peace. A landowner, of course, may deny the existence of these benefits, but a landowner might do the same were a regulatory statute to permit brief access to verify proper preservation of wetlands or the habitat enjoyed by an endangered species or, for that matter, the safety of inspected meat. So, if a regulation authorizing temporary access for purposes of organizing agricultural workers falls outside of the Court's exceptions and is a per se taking, then to what other forms of regulation does the Court's per se conclusion also apply? Lastly, the majority did not address what the relief should be for invasions authorized by government regulation. The Constitution uses the phrase "just compensation." However, here, the agricultural employers (P) only seek injunctive and declaratory relief, and do not allege any damages. On remand, California should have the choice of foreclosing injunctive relief by providing compensation.

ANALYSIS

In terms of property rights, the access regulation at issue does not amount to the taking of any traditional property interest in land. It does not, for example, take from the agricultural employers (P), or provide to the labor organizers, any freehold estate (e.g., a fee simple, fee tail, or life estate), any concurrent estate (e.g., a joint tenancy, tenancy in common, or tenancy by the entirety), or any leasehold estate (e.g., a term of years, periodic tenancy, or tenancy at will). Nor does it provide the organizers with a formal easement or access resembling an easement, since it does not burden any particular parcel of property—the burden of an easement in gross is appurtenant to the real property of another, and the burden of an easement or profit is always appurtenant. The Court concludes nevertheless that the regulation amounts to a physical taking of property because it is like cases in which the Court held that appropriation of property rights amounts to a physical per se taking. The dissent, however, argues that the regulation appropriates nothing and merely regulates (but does not appropriate) the landowners' right to exclude. For the dissent, the issue therefore is whether a regulation that temporarily limits an owner's right to exclude others from property automatically amounts to a Fifth Amendment taking, and the dissent concludes it does not. The majority responds by saying that the right to exclude is not an empty formality subject to modification at the government's pleasure, but, on the contrary, is a fundamental element of the property right that cannot be balanced away.

Quicknotes

INJUNCTIVE RELIEF A court order issued as a remedy, requiring a person to do, or prohibiting that person from doing, a specific act.

PER SE By itself; without more; taken alone; not requiring additional evidence for proof; as a matter of law.

TAKING A governmental action that substantially deprives an owner of the use and enjoyment of his property, requiring compensation.

TAKINGS CLAUSE Provision of the Fifth Amendment to the United States Constitution prohibiting the government from taking private property for public use without providing just compensation therefor.

TEMPORARY TAKING A governmental action that deprives an owner of the use and enjoyment of his property for a finite period of time; may entitle owner to compensation or damages.

Dolan v. City of Tigard

Businessowner (P) v. City (D)

512 U.S. 374 (1994)

NATURE OF CASE: Review of appeal upholding the denial of a variance to local zoning provisions.

FACT SUMMARY: The City of Tigard (D) required an easement for a public bike path and flood control area as a condition to issuing a permit to Dolan (P) for property redevelopment.

RULE OF LAW

For a conditioned grant of a building permit to be constitutional, a reasonable relationship must exist between the exactions demanded by the city's permit and a legitimate state interest.

FACTS: Dolan (P) owned a business near a creek, and she wanted to expand the business on her property. The City of Tigard (City) (D) required that 15% of land on each parcel be left as open space, and that any development in or near the 100-year creek floodplain be accompanied by a land dedication sufficient to develop a vegetation greenway in the floodplain to minimize flood damage. The City (D) also required that new developments dedicate a pedestrian/bike path to promote alternative transportation. The City (D) made certain findings that the bike path might reduce traffic congestion. Dolan (P) sought a variance to the required dedications of a greenway and bike path along the creek and was denied. She appealed to the Land Use Board of Appeals, which upheld the Commission findings. The court of appeals affirmed; the United States Supreme Court granted certiorari.

ISSUE: For a conditioned grant of a building permit to be constitutional, must a reasonable relationship exist between the exactions demanded by the city's permit and a legitimate state interest?

HOLDING AND DECISION: (Rehnquist, C.J.) Yes. For a conditioned grant of a building permit to be constitutional, a reasonable relationship must exist between the exactions demanded by the city's permit and a legitimate state interest. If a city is going to exact dedications of property as a condition to issuing a building permit for a development, then the exaction must show the required relationship to the impact of the development. Here, it is hard to see how recreational visitors using a floodplain easement are sufficiently related to the City's (D) legitimate interest in reducing flooding problems. Furthermore, the City (D) has not offered or explored less invasive alternatives to minimize flood damage. And as to the bicycle path, the City (D) has made no showing of how much traffic will be reduced by the required exaction of such a path; no math is necessary, but the City (D) made no effort at all to form a basis for the exaction. To Dolan (P), the loss is the ability to control access to her property. Reversed and remanded.

DISSENT: (Stevens, J.) The Court has added a new hurdle to land-use conditions. In addition to showing that the conditions have some rational nexus to the public purpose, now the City (D) must also show that the harm caused by the new land use is in "rough proportionality" to the benefit obtained by the condition.

DISSENT: (Souter, J.) In *Nollan v. California Coastal Commision*, 483 U.S. 825 (1987), this Court declared the need for a nexus between an exaction of a land interest and the nature of the government interest. Here, the Court adds another question: the degree of connection between an exaction and the adverse effects of development. The easement will help with flood control, and any other use is inconsequential.

ANALYSIS

Many cities require "impact" fees to be paid for new developments. After *Dolan*, the United States Supreme Court remanded a case in which the California Supreme Court had upheld fees that were arguably no more closely related to the governmental purpose than the exactions in *Dolan*. On remand, the California Supreme Court concluded that exactions of physical interest in private property were the most invasive, thus requiring "heightened scrutiny," but that monetary exactions required only a "rational relationship" standard of review. See *Ehrlich v. Culver City*, 512 U.S. 1231 (1994).

Quicknotes

TAKING A governmental action that substantially deprives an owner of the use and enjoyment of his or her property, requiring compensation.

ZONING VARIANCE Exemption from the application of zoning laws.

Glossary

Common Latin Words and Phrases Encountered in the Law

A FORTIORI: Because one fact exists or has been proven, therefore a second fact that is related to the first fact must also exist.

A PRIORI: From the cause to the effect. A term of logic used to denote that when one generally accepted truth is shown to be a cause, another particular effect must necessarily follow.

AB INITIO: From the beginning; a condition that has existed throughout, as in a marriage that was void ab initio.

ACTUS REUS: The wrongful act; in criminal law, such action sufficient to trigger criminal liability.

AD VALOREM: According to value; an ad valorem tax is imposed upon an item located within the taxing jurisdiction calculated by the value of such item.

AMICUS CURIAE: Friend of the court. Its most common usage takes the form of an amicus curiae brief, filed by a person who is not a party to an action but is nonetheless allowed to offer an argument supporting his legal interests.

ARGUENDO: In arguing. A statement, possibly hypothetical, made for the purpose of argument is one made arguendo.

BILL QUIA TIMET: A bill to quiet title (establish ownership) to real property.

BONA FIDE: True, honest, or genuine. May refer to a person's legal position based on good faith or lacking notice of fraud (such as a bona fide purchaser for value) or to the authenticity of a particular document (such as a bona fide last will and testament).

CAUSA MORTIS: With approaching death in mind. A gift causa mortis is a gift given by a party who feels certain that death is imminent.

CAVEAT EMPTOR: Let the buyer beware. This maxim is reflected in the rule of law that a buyer purchases at his own risk because it is his responsibility to examine, judge, test, and otherwise inspect what he is buying.

CERTIORARI: A writ of review. Petitions for review of a case by the United States Supreme Court are most often done by means of a writ of certiorari.

CONTRA: On the other hand. Opposite. Contrary to.

CORAM NOBIS: Before us; writs of error directed to the court that originally rendered the judgment.

CORAM VOBIS: Before you; writs of error directed by an appellate court to a lower court to correct a factual error.

CORPUS DELICTI: The body of the crime; the requisite elements of a crime amounting to objective proof that a crime has been committed.

CUM TESTAMENTO ANNEXO, ADMINISTRATOR (ADMINISTRATOR C.T.A.): With will annexed; an administrator c.t.a. settles an estate pursuant to a will in which he or she is not appointed.

DE BONIS NON, ADMINISTRATOR (ADMINISTRATOR D.B.N.): Of goods not administered; an administrator d.b.n. settles a partially settled estate.

DE FACTO: In fact; in reality; actually. Existing in fact butnot officially approved or engendered.

DE JURE: By right; lawful. Describes a condition that is legitimate "as a matter of law," in contrast to the term "de facto," which connotes something existing in fact but not legally sanctioned or authorized. For example, de facto segregation refers to segregation brought about by housing patterns, etc., whereas de jure segregation refers to segregation created by law.

DE MINIMUS: Of minimal importance; insignificant; a trifle; not worth bothering about.

DE NOVO: Anew; a second time; afresh. A trial de novo is a new trial held at the appellate level as if the case originated there and the trial at a lower level had not taken place.

DICTA: Generally used as an abbreviated form of obiter dicta, a term describing those portions of a judicial opinion incidental or not necessary to resolution of the specific question before the court. Such nonessential statements and remarks are not considered to be binding precedent.

DUCES TECUM: Refers to a particular type of writ or subpoena requesting a party or organization to produce certain documents in their possession.

EN BANC: Full bench. Where a court sits with all justices present rather than the usual quorum.

EX PARTE: For one side or one party only. An ex parte proceeding is one undertaken for the benefit of only one party, without notice to, or an appearance by, an adverse party.

EX POST FACTO: After the fact. An ex post facto law is a law that retroactively changes the consequences of a prior act.

EX REL.: Abbreviated form of the term "ex relatione," meaning upon relation or information. When the state brings an action in which it has no interest against an individual at the instigation of one who has a private interest in the matter.

FORUM NON CONVENIENS: Inconvenient forum. Although a court may have jurisdiction over the case, the action should be tried in a more conveniently located court, one to which parties and witnesses may more easily travel, for example.

GUARDIAN AD LITEM: A guardian appointed by the court to represent a minor or incompetent person in a legal action.

HABEAS CORPUS: You have the body. The modern writ of habeas corpus is a writ directing that a person (body) being detained (such as a prisoner) be brought before the court so that the legality of his detention can be judicially ascertained.

IN CAMERA: In private, in chambers. When a hearing is held before a judge in his or her chambers or when all spectators are excluded from the courtroom.

IN FORMA PAUPERIS: In the manner of a pauper. A party who proceeds in forma pauperis because of his poverty is one who is allowed to bring suit without liability for costs.

INFRA: Below, under. A word referring the reader to a later part of a book. (The opposite of supra.)

IN LOCO PARENTIS: In the place of a parent.

IN PARI DELICTO: Equally wrong; a court of equity will not grant requested relief to an applicant who is in pari delicto, or as much at fault in the transactions giving rise to the controversy as is the opponent of the applicant.

IN PARI MATERIA: On like subject matter or upon the same matter. Statutes relating to the same person or things are said to be in pari materia. It is a general rule of statutory construction that such statutes should be construed together, i.e., looked at as if they together constituted one law.

IN PERSONAM: Against the person. Jurisdiction over the person of an individual.

IN RE: In the matter of. Used to designate a proceeding involving an estate or other property.

IN REM: A term that signifies an action against the res, or thing. An action in rem is basically one that is taken directly against property, as distinguished from an action in personam, i.e., against the person.

INTER ALIA: Among other things. Used to show that the whole of a statement, pleading, list, statute, etc., has not been set forth in its entirety.

INTER PARTES: Between the parties. May refer to contracts, conveyances, or other transactions having legal significance.

INTER VIVOS: Between the living. An inter vivos gift is a gift made by a living grantor, as distinguished from bequests contained in a will, which pass upon the death of the testator.

IPSO FACTO: By the mere fact itself.

JUS: Law or the entire body of law.

LEX LOCI: The law of the place; the notion that the rights of parties to a legal proceeding are governed by the law of the place where those rights arose.

MALUM IN SE: Evil or wrong in and of itself; inherently wrong. This term describes an act that is wrong by its very nature, as opposed to one which would not be wrong but for the fact that there is a specific legal prohibition against it (malum prohibitum).

MALUM PROHIBITUM: Wrong because prohibited, but not inherently evil. Used to describe something that is wrong because it is expressly forbidden by law but that is not in and of itself evil, e.g., speeding.

MANDAMUS: We command. A writ directing an official to take a certain action.

MENS REA: A guilty mind; a criminal intent. A term used to signify the mental state that accompanies a crime or other prohibited act. Some crimes require only a general mens rea (general intent to do the prohibited act), but others, like assault with intent to murder, require the existence of a specific mens rea.

MODUS OPERANDI: Method of operating; generally refers to the manner or style of a criminal in committing crimes, admissible in appropriate cases as evidence of the identity of a defendant.

NEXUS: A connection to.

NISI PRIUS: A court of first impression. A nisi prius court is one where issues of fact are tried before a judge or jury.

N.O.V. (NON OBSTANTE VEREDICTO): Notwithstanding the verdict. A judgment n.o.v. is a judgment given in favor of one party despite the fact that a verdict was returned in favor of the other party, the justification being that the verdict either had no reasonable support in fact or was contrary to law.

NUNC PRO TUNC: Now for then. This phrase refers to actions that may be taken and will then have full retroactive effect.

PENDENTE LITE: Pending the suit; pending litigation underway.

PER CAPITA: By head; beneficiaries of an estate, if they take in equal shares, take per capita.

PER CURIAM: By the court; signifies an opinion ostensibly written "by the whole court" and with no identified author.

PER SE: By itself, in itself; inherently.

PER STIRPES: By representation. Used primarily in the law of wills to describe the method of distribution where a person, generally because of death, is unable to take that which is left to him by the will of another, and therefore his heirs divide such property between them rather than take under the will individually.

PRIMA FACIE: On its face, at first sight. A prima facie case is one that is sufficient on its face, meaning that the evidence supporting it is adequate to establish the case until contradicted or overcome by other evidence.

PRO TANTO: For so much; as far as it goes. Often used in eminent domain cases when a property owner receives partial payment for his land without prejudice to his right to bring suit for the full amount he claims his land to be worth.

QUANTUM MERUIT: As much as he deserves. Refers to recovery based on the doctrine of unjust enrichment in those cases in which a party has rendered valuable services or furnished materials that were accepted and enjoyed by another under circumstances that would reasonably notify the recipient that the rendering party expected to be paid. In essence, the law implies a contract to pay the reasonable value of the services or materials furnished.

QUASI: Almost like; as if; nearly. This term is essentially used to signify that one subject or thing is almost analogous to another but that material differences between them do exist. For example, a quasi-criminal proceeding is one that is not strictly criminal but shares enough of the same characteristics to require some of the same safeguards (e.g., procedural due process must be followed in a parole hearing).

QUID PRO QUO: Something for something. In contract law, the consideration, something of value, passed between the parties to render the contract binding.

RES GESTAE: Things done. In evidence law, this principle justifies the admission of a statement that would otherwise be hearsay when it is made so closely to the event in question as to be said to be a part of it, or with such spontaneity as not to have the possibility of falsehood.

RES IPSA LOQUITUR: The thing speaks for itself. This doctrine gives rise to a rebuttable presumption of negligence when the instrumentality causing the injury was within the exclusive control of the defendant, and the injury was one that does not normally occur unless a person has been negligent.

RES JUDICATA: A matter adjudged. Doctrine which provides that once a court of competent jurisdiction has rendered a final judgment or decree on the merits, that judgment or decree is conclusive upon the parties to the case and prevents them from engaging in any other litigation on the points and issues determined therein.

RESPONDEAT SUPERIOR: Let the master reply. This doctrine holds the master liable for the wrongful acts of his servant (or the principal for his agent) in those cases in which the servant (or agent) was acting within the scope of his authority at the time of the injury.

STARE DECISIS: To stand by or adhere to that which has been decided. The common law doctrine of stare decisis attempts to give security and certainty to the law by following the policy that once a principle of law as applicable to a certain set of facts has been set forth in a decision, it forms a precedent that will subsequently be followed, even though a different decision might be made were it the first time the question had arisen. Of course, stare decisis is not an inviolable principle and is departed from in instances where there is good cause (e.g., considerations of public policy led the Supreme Court to disregard prior decisions sanctioning segregation).

SUPRA: Above. A word referring a reader to an earlier part of a book. (The opposite of infra.)

ULTRA VIRES: Beyond the power. This phrase is most commonly used to refer to actions taken by a corporation that are beyond the power or legal authority of the corporation.

Addendum of French Derivatives

CHATTEL: Tangible personal property.

CY PRES: Doctrine permitting courts to apply trust funds to purposes not expressed in the trust but necessary to carry out the settlor's intent.

IN PAIS: Not pursuant to legal proceedings.

PER AUTRE VIE: For another's life; during another's life. In property law, an estate may be granted that will terminate upon the death of someone other than the grantee.

PROFIT A PRENDRE: A license to remove minerals or other produce from land.

VOIR DIRE: Process of questioning jurors as to their predispositions about the case or parties to a proceeding in order to identify those jurors displaying bias or prejudice.